OFFICIAL PAPERS BY ALFRED MARSHALL

OFFICIAL PAPERS

BY

ALFRED MARSHALL

Formerly Professor of Political Economy
in the University of Cambridge

PUBLISHED FOR THE ROYAL ECONOMIC SOCIETY

BY

MACMILLAN AND CO., LIMITED
ST. MARTIN'S STREET, LONDON

1926

COPYRIGHT

EDITOR'S PREFACE

THIS volume comprises the written Memoranda and Oral Evidence prepared by Alfred Marshall at different times for Government Departments and official enquiries. The Controller of H.M. Stationery Office has accorded permission for the reprint of the passages in question from the various Parliamentary Papers, to which more particular reference is made at the commencement of each extract.

Generally speaking, the Memoranda and Minutes of Evidence have been printed *in extenso* and without modification. A few misprints have been corrected, some passages from the Memoranda repeated in the Minutes of Evidence have been omitted, and a verbal change has been made in accordance with Marshall's known wishes.

This volume contains the whole of Alfred Marshall's contributions to official enquiries on economic questions with the exception of his work on the Labour Commission. Since he was a member of this Commission, and not a witness, it has been impossible in this case to identify or separate his contributions from those of the Commissioners as a whole.

J. M. KEYNES.

CAMBRIDGE,
July 1926.

CONTENTS

ROYAL COMMISSION

ON

THE DEPRESSION OF TRADE AND INDUSTRY

(1886)

ANSWERS FROM PROFESSOR ALFRED MARSHALL TO QUESTIONS
ON THE SUBJECT OF CURRENCY AND PRICES CIRCULATED
BY THE COMMISSION

[Third Report, Appendix C, pp. 31–34, O. 22035—App. 2.]

Questions on the Subject of Currency and Prices, circulated by the Royal Commission on the Depression of Trade and Industry.

1. Has there been, within a period which can be distinctly defined, a fall (i) in the gold prices, or (ii) in the silver prices, of commodities in countries where those metals are respectively the standards of value ?

2. If so, has the fall extended uniformly to all commodities, or has it been confined to some particular class or classes of commodities ?

3. Apart from any circumstances which have tended to lower the price of particular commodities, or of commodities generally, are there any circumstances which have enhanced the value of the metal used as the standard ?

4. Have similar circumstances ever occurred before, and what results did they produce ?

5. To what causes do you assign the fluctuations which have occurred in recent years in the ratio of the precious metals to one another ?

6. Are there any indications that the development of the credit system, or other similar means of economising the use of the precious metals, has tended to counteract or retard the fall of prices ?

7. What circumstances, apart from an appreciation of the metal used as the standard, have tended to bring about a fall of prices generally ?

8. How is trade affected by alterations (i) in the value of the metal used as the standard, and (ii) in the value of the precious metals *inter se*, especially in the case of trade between gold-using and silver-using countries ?

9. What is the effect of the present relations of gold and silver upon the internal and external trade of India, and upon prices in that country ?

3

Reply from Professor Alfred Marshall.

Cambridge,
May 27, 1886.

My Lord,

I beg leave to submit to you a few remarks in answer to some of the questions in your circular of April 20th which was forwarded to me by Professor Price. I have avoided going over the ground covered by the memorandum submitted to you by Mr. Palgrave, the first draft of which I have been permitted to see, and with which I am in general agreement.

QUESTIONS 3, 4, AND 7.

It is interesting to note the causes which Tooke gave (*History of Prices*, Vol. II. pp. 348–9) for " the decline and comparatively low range of prices from 1814 to 1837."

It will be remembered that he had to explain a much greater fall in gold prices (*i.e.* even after allowing for the depreciation of paper) than that with which we are now concerned. Jevons' " actual " (as opposed to " logarithmic ") gold standard index-number for the average of forty leading commodities was 133·5 for the average for the thirteen years 1799–1811; for the ten years 1821–1830 it was 88·7. Turning to the *Economist's* index-number for the years 1850–1886, we find that here also a period of about thirteen years stand out as of exceptionally high prices, viz. those from 1855 to 1867, for which the average (reduced to the same basis of 100) is 138·5, while the lowest ten years' average that we can get is 109·9 for the years 1876–1885—a much less sharp contrast.

Of Tooke's six causes, the first was a series of good harvests following on a series of bad harvests; we have to look in a different direction for the cause of the recent fall in the prices of agricultural produce. And his fourth cause, relating to a rise of the foreign exchanges, is inapplicable to present circumstances. But the remaining four causes are worth quoting in detail.

They are—

" (2) The removal of obstacles from the several sources

of foreign supply; a great extension of some of them; and the discovery of new ones.

" (3) A great reduction of the charges of importation, by the low freights and insurances incidental to a state of peace; and the improved, and cheaper, and more rapid internal communications.

" (5) Improvements in machinery, in chemistry, and in the arts and sciences generally, all tending to reduce the cost of production of numerous articles, or to provide cheaper substitutes.

" (6) A reduction of the general rate of interest, and a more extensive application of individual accumulations to reproductions at a diminished cost."

If to these we add the setting free of middlemen's stocks by the telegraph etc., and if we refer the fall of freights, etc. to the development of steam traffic rather than to the cessation of war risks, we have, I think, a very fair account of those causes of the recent fall of prices which have not their origin in changes in the supply of money. Under the last head I include not only the recent changes in the supply and methods of use of the precious metals, but also disappointment of the hopes that were entertained some years ago as to the extension of the English system of payment by cheques in other countries. No doubt also there has been a check to the increase of bills of exchange; but against that must be set the growth of telegraphic transfers.

I think, however, that there is an objection to Tooke's mode of wording, which applies also to many recent writings on the subject. He has not made it clear that diminution of the cost of production of commodities must not be counted as an additional cause of a fall of prices, when its effects in increasing the supply of commodities relatively to gold have already been allowed for separately. This is a point of some difficulty, and its interest is theoretical rather than practical.

As to the facts of the present available gold supply, I wish only to say that I attach great importance to the influence of hoarding in various forms (see Question 5), about which we cannot from the nature of the case get any statistics. In consequence I look with some scepticism on any attempt to divide the recent fall of prices into that part which is due to changes in the supply of commodities and that which is due to the available gold supply.

[This is the distinction which I take to be intended by the opposition between a " fall of prices generally " and an " appreciation of the standard " in Question 7. Perhaps I may be excused for saying that I think that this use of the term " appreciation of gold " may possibly cause some confusion. I myself prefer to use it as synonymous with " a fall of general gold prices," and again, " a rise in the purchasing power of gold."]

QUESTION 5.

On this question I will confine myself to some remarks as to what may be called the law of hoarding, viz. that the demand for a metal for the purposes of hoarding is increased by a continued rise in its value and diminished by a continued fall, because those people who hoard believe that what has been rising in value for some time is likely to go on rising and *vice versâ*. Thus the law of demand for a metal for the purpose of hoarding is the opposite of the law of demand for a commodity for the purpose of using it.

In consequence of this law the increase in the supply of silver has probably contributed directly to the rise in the purchasing power of gold, by causing people in India and elsewhere to hoard gold instead of silver. Under the head of hoarding I reckon the buying of simple gold and silver ornaments, the value of which consists almost solely of the metal contained in them.

I do not regard this tendency to hoarding of a metal rising in value as likely to come into action until the rise is so palpable and notorious as to be clearly apprehended by the comparatively ignorant people who are likely to hoard. Its force is always greatest after a collapse, such as took place in France in 1882, of commercial undertakings in which the country people have been lured on to invest their savings.

It is noteworthy that the net importation of silver into India was nearly twice as great as that of gold in the fifteen years preceding 1870, and that the two were not very far from equal in the succeeding fifteen years. (See also my answer to Question 9).

QUESTION 8 (i).

I will ask you to excuse my making use of some passages from my own writings in answering this question. First I would quote from the *Economics of Industry*, Book III. chap. i. secs. 5, 6.

" The connection between a fall of prices and a suspension of industry requires to be worked out.

" There is no reason why a depression of trade and a fall of prices should stop the work of those who can produce without having to pay money on account of any expenses of production. For instance, a man who pays no wages, who works with his own hands, and produces what raw material he requires cannot lose anything by continuing to work. It does not matter to him how low prices have fallen, provided that the prices of his goods have not fallen more in proportion than those of others. When prices are low he will get few coins for his goods, but if he can buy as many things with them as he could with the greater number of coins he got when prices were high he will not be injured by the fall of prices. He would be a little discouraged if he thought that the price of his goods would fall more than the prices of the goods of others, but even then he would not be very likely to stop work.

" And in the same way a manufacturer, though he has to pay for raw material and wages, would not check his production on account of a fall in prices, if the fall affected all things equally and were not likely to go further. If the price which he got for his goods had fallen by a quarter, and the prices which he had to pay for labour and raw material had also fallen by a quarter, the trade would be as profitable to him as before the fall. Three sovereigns would now do the work of four, he would use fewer counters in measuring off his receipts against his outgoings, but his receipts would stand in the same relation to his outgoings as before. His net profits would be the same percentage of his total business. The counters by which they are reckoned would be less by one quarter, but they would purchase as much of the necessaries, comforts, and luxuries of life as they did before.

" It, however, very seldom happens in fact that the expenses which a manufacturer has to pay out fall as much in proportion as the price which he gets for his goods. For when prices are rising, the rise in the price of the finished commodity is generally more rapid than that in the price of the raw material, always more rapid than that in the price of labour, and when prices are falling, the fall in the price of the finished commodity is generally more rapid than that in the price of the raw material, always more rapid than that in the price of labour.   And therefore when prices are falling the manufacturer's receipts are sometimes scarcely sufficient even to repay him for his outlay on raw material, wages, and other forms of circulating capital; they seldom give him in addition enough to pay interest on his fixed capital and earnings of management for himself.

" Even if the prices of labour and raw material fall as rapidly as those of finished goods, the manufacturer may lose by continuing production if the fall has not come to an end. He may pay for raw material and labour at a time when prices generally have fallen by one-sixth; but if by the time he comes to sell prices have fallen by another sixth, his receipts may be less than is sufficient to cover his outlay.

" We conclude, then, that manufacturing cannot be carried on, except at a low rate of profit or at a loss, when the prices of finished goods are low relatively to those of labour and raw material, or when prices are falling, even if the prices of all things are falling equally.

" Thus a fall in prices lowers profits and impoverishes the manufacturer, while it increases the purchasing power of those who have fixed incomes. So, again, it enriches creditors at the expense of debtors; for if the money that is owing to them is repaid, this money gives them a great purchasing power, and if they have lent it at a fixed rate of interest, each payment is worth more to them than it would be if prices were high. But for the same reasons that it enriches creditors and those who receive fixed incomes, it impoverishes those men of business who have borrowed capital, and it impoverishes those who have to make, as most business men have, considerable fixed money payments for rents, salaries, and other matters. When prices are ascending the improvement is thought to be greater than it really is, because general opinion with regard to the prosperity of the country is much influenced by the authority of manufacturers and merchants. These judge by their own experience, and in time of ascending prices their fortunes are rapidly increased; in a time of descending prices their fortunes are stationary or dwindle. But statistics prove that the real income of the country is not very much less in the present time of low prices than it was in the period of high prices that went before it. The total amount of the necessaries, comforts, and luxuries which are enjoyed by Englishmen per head was but little less in 1879 than it was in 1872."

I should say very much the same now in 1886 as I said in 1879.

I agree with the general opinion that a steady upward tendency in general prices conduces a little more to the general well-being than does a tendency downwards, because it keeps industry somewhat better employed. But, on the other hand, people of all classes, and especially of the working classes, spend their incomes more wisely when prices and money-wages are falling, and they think themselves worse off than they are, than when a rise of prices and money-wages leads them to exaggerate their real incomes and to be careless about their expenditure. So that, on the whole, I think there is much less difference than is generally supposed between the net benefits of periods of rising and falling prices. It is doubtful whether the last ten years, which are re-garded as years of depression, but in which there have been few violent movements of prices, have not, on the whole, conduced more to solid progress and true happiness than the alternations of feverish activity and painful retrogression which have charac-terised every preceding decade of this century. In fact, I regard violent fluctuations of prices as a much greater evil than a gradual fall of prices. I will venture to quote a passage from a paper on remedies for the discontinuity of industry, which I read last year at the " Industrial Remuneration Conference " :—

" A great cause of the discontinuity of industry is the want of certain knowledge as to what a pound is going to be worth a short time hence. With every expansion and contraction of credit prices rise and fall. This change of prices presses heavily even on those who kept themselves as far as possible from the uncertainties of trade, and increases in many ways the intensity of commercial fluctuations. For just when private traders and public companies are most inclined to reckless ventures, the interest which they have to pay on borrowed capital represents an exceptionally small purchasing power, because prices are high. And in the opposite phase, when their resources are crippled by the stagnation of business the lowness of prices compels them to sacrifice a much greater amount of real wealth in order to pay their interest. When traders are rejoicing in high prices debenture and mortgage holders and other creditors are depressed; and when the pendulum swings the other way traders, already depressed, are kept under water by having to pay an exceptionally heavy toll to their creditors. This serious evil can be much diminished by a plan which economists have long advocated. In proposing this remedy I want Government to help business, though not to do business. It should publish tables showing as closely as may be the changes in the purchasing power of gold, and should facilitate contracts for payments to be made in terms of units of fixed purchasing power.

" Government already does work of the kind desired in regard to the tithe commutation tables. But instead of dealing with wheat, barley, and oats, it would deal with all important commodities. It would publish their prices once a month or once a year; it would reckon the importance of each commodity as proportioned to the total sum spent on it, and then by simple arithmetic deduce the change in the purchasing power of gold. Borrowings could then, at the option of the contracting parties, be reckoned in Government units. On this plan, if A lends B 1,000*l.* at 4½ per cent. interest, and after some years the purchasing power of money had risen by an eighth, B would have to pay as interest, not 45*l.*, but a sum that had the same purchasing power as 45*l.* had at the time of borrowing, *i.e.* 40*l.*, and so on. The plan would have to win its way into general use, but when once it had become familiar none but gamblers would lend or borrow on any other terms, at all events for long periods. The scheme has no claims to theoretic perfection, but only to being a great improvement on our present methods, and obtained with little trouble. A perfectly exact measure of purchasing power is not only unattainable, but even unthinkable. The same change of prices affects the purchasing power of money to different persons in different ways. For to him who can seldom afford to have meat, a fall of one-fourth in the price of meat accompanied by a rise of one-fourth in that of bread means a fall in the purchasing power of money; his wages will not go so far as before. While to his richer neighbour, who spends twice as much on meat as on bread, the change acts the other way. The Government would, of course, take account only of the total consumption of the whole nation; but even so it would be troubled by constant changes in the way in which the nation spent its income. The estimate of the importance of different commodities would have to be recast from time to time. The only room for differences of opinion would be as to what commodities should be taken account of. It would probably be best to follow the ordinary method of taking very little account of any but raw commodities. Manufactured commodities and personal services are always changing their character, and are not easily priced. Manufactured tend to fall in value relatively to raw commodities, and at present, at all events, personal services tend to rise, so that the errors made by omitting both probably nearly neutralise one another. Simplicity and definiteness are in this case far more important than theoretic accuracy. Those who make the returns should work in the open day, so that they could not, if they would, be subject to many influences. This plan, though strange at first sight, would really be much simpler than bimetallism, while its influence in steadying industry would be incomparably greater."

The task of publishing from time to time the currency value of a unit of constant purchasing power cannot, I think, be performed properly except by a permanent Government department. So far as the exports and imports go, the materials for this have been provided by the Board of Trade. Their work is a perfect model of method, which cannot fail to be of use to us; but it is not directly applicable to our present purpose. In Mr. Palgrave's memorandum a most interesting example is shown of the kind of index-number that is wanted. But Government alone can command the machinery requisite to secure properly tested figures for the purpose.

The unit of constant general purchasing power would be applicable, at the free choice of both parties concerned, for nearly

all contracts for the payment of interest, and for the repayment
of loans; and for many contracts for rent, and for wages and
salaries. But as people became more familiar with the plan,
certain modifications might gradually be made, again by the
consent of those concerned, for special cases. For instance, there
might be an agricultural unit, either suggested directly by the
Government or adapted by private persons from the figures supplied
by the Government. This unit would be got from the general
unit by increasing the weight of the prices of agricultural produce.
It might be agreed that while the total amounts spent on other
things should be taken as they are, every 1,000,000*l.* spent on
agricultural produce should be treated for this special purpose as
though it were (say) 4,000,000*l.* This plan would, I think, be
fairer, and, when once thoroughly understood, more popular,
than the plan which has been proposed of fixing agricultural rents
at the price of a certain amount of farm produce. Again, by a
similar modification, a mining unit might be got which would
supersede the useful but not quite satisfactory sliding scales that
are adopted at present; and so for other trades.

I wish to emphasise the fact that this proposal is independent
of the form of our currency, and does not ask for any change in
it. I admit that the plan would seldom be available for the purposes of international trade. But its importance as a steadying
influence to our home trade would be so great, and its introduction
would be so easy and so free from the evils which generally
surround the interference of Government in business, that I
venture to urge strongly its claims on your immediate attention.

To pass to another point. Whatever opinion we may hold as
to the extent to which the recent fall of prices is caused by a check
to the available supply of gold, it is beyond question that changes
in this supply are not accountable for more than a very small part
of the total fluctuations in the general purchasing power of money.
The aggregate of the annual fluctuations of the *Economist's*
index-number (on a basis of 2,200) has been considerably more
than 6,000 since the year 1850, and of these not more than 2,000
at the outside can be attributed to the influence, direct and speculative, of changes in the supply of gold. And, therefore, even
neglecting the practical difficulties in the way of altering the

metallic basis of our currency, I should expect much less benefit from it than from the general adoption of a unit of fixed purchasing power for all important contracts. But I wish to argue briefly that the so-called bimetallic scheme, of which much has been said lately, has no proper title to that name ; and that if it be desirable to disturb our currency with the purpose of basing it on two metals instead of one, there is another plan which ought to be considered, a plan which I believe to have a juster claim to the title of bimetallism, and which, though perhaps somewhat stranger at first sight, is really simpler because it requires no treaties with other Governments.

The ordinary bimetallic scheme proposes that the leading Governments should agree to give free mintage to gold and silver at a fixed ratio. I regard the plan as not impracticable ; I admit the general validity of the arguments adduced in support of it by its abler advocates. I believe it would tend to have the beneficial action which they claim for it, but to a much smaller extent than they claim. Without, however, discussing these points in detail, I wish to point out that much of their argument proceeds on the assumption that the cost of mining silver is likely to fall relatively to that of mining gold. If this should turn out to be the case, the result of fixing the ratio of the values between the two metals will be to stop gold mining, though, of course, some gold would still be found with the silver. What gold there was would then be absorbed almost entirely for war chests, which may be regarded as a kind of public hoarding, for private hoarding, and for the purposes of art and ornament. Nothing would induce English and other civilised people to carry about much more silver than they do now. Not being able to get gold, they would insist on having (convertible) notes ; and there being very little gold in store this would be chiefly on a silver basis. Thus so-called bimetallism would, in my opinion, be very likely to degenerate practically into silver monometallism, silver coins being used for small change, and silver paper for the chief work of business. The value of the currency would then fluctuate with every variation in the value of silver. Without the special advantages of our present currency we should have its disadvantage of being practically dependent on one metal only for the steadying of prices.

I submit that, if we are to have a great disturbance of our currency for the sake of bimetallism, we ought to be sure that we get it. The alternative scheme for which I ask attention is based on Ricardo's *Proposals for an Economical and Secure Currency.* He suggested that we should go at once to that paper currency— except for small change—which would, I think, be likely to result ere long from the general adoption of a fixed ratio for gold and silver. He proposed to base it directly on gold; not on gold coins, but on stamped gold bars of considerable weight. He supposed an ample reserve of these to be kept, and that the bars should be held always ready to be bought and sold for a fixed amount of the currency. Thus the value of the currency would be absolutely fixed at the value of the gold which it professed to represent, while the gold bars would form the best means of settling the balance of international indebtedness that the genius of man has ever devised.

My alternative scheme is got from his simply by wedding a bar of silver of, say, 2,000 grammes to a bar of gold of, say, 100 grammes; the Government undertaking to be always ready to buy or sell a wedded pair of bars for a fixed amount of currency. (It would be somewhere about 29*l*.) This would be true bimetallism. The value of the currency would be fixed absolutely by the means of the values of a gramme of gold and, say, 20 grammes of silver. It would have no chance of deteriorating into a silver monometallism.

Moreover, this plan could be started by any nation without waiting for the concurrence of others. It would require no international contract, but, if adopted by several nations, would constitute by itself a working international currency for large transactions. It would soon lead to the adoption of a currency of uniform denominations in all these countries, by which business would be further facilitated. It would not attempt to exercise any influence on the relative values of the metals.

I wish it to be understood that while I think that Government ought at once to proceed to publish a unit of fixed purchasing power, I do not urge this second proposal of mine for immediate adoption. On the contrary, I think the time has not yet come for changing our currency. I regard both the immediate effects of such a change and its indirect and distant effects as likely to involve very serious evils. I am not convinced that it would be worth while to go through those evils even for the sake of a true bimetallism. My contention is only that if it is understood that we are embarked on the search for a better and more stable currency than our present, we ought to look well around us to see whether there is not, as I believe there is, a plan which would do at once more good and less harm than the so-called bimetallic scheme for fixing the relative values of gold and silver.

QUESTIONS 8 (ii) and 9.

Admitting that the ratios of exchange between a gold and a silver using country are more variable than they would be if the currencies of both countries were based on the same metal, I think that the difference between the two cases is less than is generally supposed. For, firstly, omitting the years of the Indian Mutiny, I find that the changes in the Indian exchanges were on the whole about as great before 1870, when the gold price of silver was nearly constant, as in the later years, during which the gold price of silver has changed much.

Secondly, I think that the disturbance of Indian finances is made to appear much greater than it is by the unnecessary and, if I may venture to say so, perhaps not quite generous, practice of keeping the accounts in pounds sterling instead of in rupees. If they were kept in rupees it would be at once obvious that the change in the gold price of silver affects the Indian Government only in so far as it is under obligations, direct or indirect, to pay away specified sums of gold. I maintain that it is a mistake to say, as is often done, that the rise in the value of gold injures the Indian Government in so far as it is a purchaser of stores, railway plant, etc. in England, for the real purchasing power in English commodities of a draft for Rs. 1,000 is as great now as it ever has been. As regards India's foreign trade, I do not question that a fall in the gold value of silver tends to benefit the Indian exporters and to increase India's exports of goods relatively to her imports; but there are many causes which may hold this tendency in check and prevent it from making great alteration in trade. And, in fact, I think there is conclusive statistical evidence that the fall has not so acted as to give a very large premium to the Indian exporters; for if it had, Indian commodities would have been exported on so large a scale as to give a greatly increased surplus of trade bills on other countries, and these bills would have been converted into silver and gold for importation into India, the gold being taken in consequence of the growing desire to hoard gold in India.   But the net imports of gold and silver in the fifteen years 1860–1884 have been smaller than they were in the fifteen years 1844–59, before the great fall in the gold value of silver, having been 223 millions in the earlier period and only 147 millions in the later.

I have, etc.,

(Signed)   ALFRED MARSHALL.

To the Right Hon. the EARL OF IDDESLEIGH,
    Chairman of the Royal Commission on
      the Depression of Trade and Industry.

ROYAL COMMISSION

ON

THE VALUES OF GOLD AND SILVER

(1887, 1888)

MEMORANDA AND EVIDENCE OFFERED TO THE
COMMISSIONERS BY PROFESSOR ALFRED MARSHALL

(i) PRELIMINARY MEMORANDUM.
(ii) MINUTES OF EVIDENCE.
(iii) MEMORANDUM AS TO THE EFFECTS WHICH DIFFERENCES BETWEEN
THE CURRENCIES OF DIFFERENT NATIONS HAVE ON INTERNATIONAL
TRADE.
(iv) MEMORANDUM ON THE RELATION BETWEEN A FALL OF THE EXCHANGE
AND TRADE WITH COUNTRIES WHICH HAVE NOT A GOLD CURRENCY.

[O. 24358—*App.* 77.]

C

(i) PRELIMINARY MEMORANDUM.

To the Chairman of the Royal Commission on the Values of
Gold and Silver.

MY LORD,

I beg leave to enclose some answers to the circular letter
of questions issued by the Royal Commission on Gold and Silver
in August. I have thought it best to confine my remarks to a few
of the many important issues raised in it.

I am,

Your Lordship's obedient servant,

ALFRED MARSHALL.

Cambridge, November 9, 1887.

V. Has the fall resulted in any material prejudice to the
commercial or general interests of the world?

I think that the general interests of the country are best
promoted by stationary prices; but that the benefits resulting
from a rise in prices and the evils resulting from a fall of prices are
commonly over-rated; and in fact I think it is not clearly established that a rise of prices is on the whole to be preferred to a fall.

Recent changes in the methods of industry have cut off the
careers to which many had looked forward; and have thus caused
some irregularities of employment, which are frequently attributed
to the discouragement of enterprise caused by a fall of prices.
But I doubt whether the influence exerted in this direction by a
slow and gradual fall is very great. On the other hand, during such
a fall a powerful friction tends to prevent money wages in most
trades from falling as fast as prices; and this tends almost
imperceptibly to establish a higher standard of living among the
working classes, and to diminish the inequalities of wealth. These
benefits are often ignored; but in my opinion they are often

nearly as important as the evils which result from that gradual fall of prices which is sometimes called a depression of trade.

Violent fluctuations of prices are less distasteful to the heads of business enterprises than a gradual fall of prices. But I believe they are far more injurious both physically and morally to the community at large. It seems, therefore, important to observe that fluctuations of prices were more violent before 1873 than afterwards; the fixedness of the ratio between the values of gold and silver before 1873 was not able to prevent them; they have died away since 1873 in spite of the changes in that ratio.

The diagram published in the First Report of the Commission has a note calling attention to the fact that since 1873 the gold price of silver has varied with the gold prices of commodities in general. This may suggest the inference that if prices were measured partly in silver and partly in gold they would oscillate much less than if measured in gold alone. I submit that the history of the century regarded as a whole gives no support to this inference, but rather suggests that the parallelism between the movements of the gold price of silver and those of the gold prices of commodities in general since 1873 has been due to a fortuitous coincidence, and this appears to have been actually the case. For recent changes in the volume and the methods of business have tended to raise the values of both the precious metals; but an entirely independent set of changes, which have happened to come into operation just at the same time, have tended further to raise the value of gold, but to check the rise in the value of silver.

To begin with the first set of causes :—During the two decades which followed the discoveries of gold in California and Australia, exhaustive wars in America and Europe had held in check the tendency of modern invention and modern habits of saving to increase the production of commodities. The wars had taken men away from the workshops, had killed some and unfitted others for their work; they had diverted industries to supply the materials of warfare, and had destroyed vast quantities of commodities of all kinds. Since then invention has gone on faster than ever; the habits of saving are stronger than ever, and commodities have increased by leaps and bounds. Meanwhile the use of bank notes and of bills of exchange had not kept pace with the growth of business, and the confident expectations that were cherished before 1873 of the extension of the English cheque system in Austria and elsewhere have been disappointed. These and minor causes have tended to raise the value of both gold and silver.

But, by a strange accident, there happened at the same time another group of causes which tended further to raise the value of gold, but to lower the value of silver. The production of gold diminished, and that of silver increased. Nations ran a race to see which could most quickly substitute gold for silver as the staple of their currency; and partly as a consequence of these changes, War Ministers, Indian peasants, and American negroes began to hoard gold, and showed an indifference to silver. The recent comparative steadiness of the value of silver is due to the coincidence of these two sets of causes, of about equal force and acting in opposite directions. The diagram shows that no such coincidence is hinted at by the statistics of the past : reason forbids us to expect it in the future.

In connection with this question I may state that I dissent from the doctrine which has recently received the support of the Central Chamber of Agriculture, that " the great depreciation of silver acts as a bounty of 25 per cent. upon the import of corn into this country from certain other countries." I believe that it has never given a great bounty, and that it will not give any permanent bounty to the Indian exporter whether of corn or any other produce.

VII. To what extent and in what way are prices affected by the quantity of the metal or metals used as standards of value ?

If, looking at the enclosed diagram, we compare the curves which show the annual production of gold with that showing the movements of general prices, we find that there is no intimate connection between them. While accepting the doctrine that, " *other things being equal*, prices rise or fall proportionately to every increase or diminution in the metal or metals which are used as the standard of value," I consider that the conditioning clause, " other things being equal," is of overwhelming importance and requires careful attention.

Firstly, with regard to a change in the cost of production. The older economists assumed that it could not have a very quick influence on prices, because it could act only through its influence on quantity; and this would be a slow process. The assumption may have been justifiable some time ago, but I do not consider it justifiable under modern conditions. It is true that if gold were never stored or hoarded, a change in the cost of mining would not act considerably on prices till it had had time to alter considerably the total quantity of gold above ground; just as a fall in the cost of building does not act much on house rents till it has had time to increase considerably the supply of houses. But, under existing conditions, a change in the cost of production of gold is canvassed far and wide, and exerts an almost immediate influence on hoarding by Governments, by banks, and by private persons. And since every increase of hoarding diminishes the gold in circulation, changes in the cost of mining are able to act on prices after the much shorter interval required for them to affect considerably the quantities of gold and silver which are put away in stores and hoards of different kinds.

Next, it must be remembered that any change in the use of token coins would affect prices; and that the clause " other things being equal " must be taken to exclude this. The silver coins in circulation in England affect prices just as much as if they were legal tender; and, therefore, the admission of silver money to be legal tender in England would not affect prices unless it were either accompanied by the issue of paper money based wholly or partially on silver, or people consented to use as cash more silver than they do now.

Next, the condition " other things being equal " implies that separate account must be taken of changes in the volume of business and the methods of payment. I doubt whether there is a sufficient statistical basis for an attempt to estimate the allowance that must be made for recent changes of this kind in different countries; all that can be safely said is that they are of importance commensurate with changes in the supply of the precious metals and in the currency regulations of different countries.

In conclusion, I should like to observe that one of the influences that have been most discussed is an improvement in the methods of production of many commodities, leading to a fall in their real cost. This is, no doubt, a true cause. But when we regard the average level of prices as dependent, other things being equal, upon the ratio of the volume of the standard metals to that of commodities, we count in the action of this cause through its influence in increasing the amount of commodities. There is some danger that its direct influence in reducing cost may be counted in as an additional cause of low prices; and this would, I submit, be to count the same thing twice.

VIII. What is the relation, if any, between the supply or quantity of the precious metals and the fluctuations of credit?

While accepting the common doctrine that, *other things being equal*, an increase in the supply of the precious metals inflates credit, because it goes in great measure into the hands of the dealers in credit, I think it important to insist that the supply of the precious metals is only one of many causes that affect the expansion of credit. As the diagram shows, there have been violent inflations of credit while the annual production from the mines has been very small, and violent contractions of credit in 1857-8 and 1866-7 in spite of the plentiful supply of the precious metals which were then coming from the mines.

X. Do you consider that an international agreement could be made for the free coinage of gold and silver as legal tender money at a fixed ratio?

XI. Is it in the power of Governments to maintain such a ratio if agreed upon; and would the practice of the commercial world follow the law?

I shall presently argue that the plan of opening the mints to gold and silver at a fixed ratio has no right to be called bimetallic, and therefore I shall speak of it as FIXED-RATIO-MINTAGE in order to avoid ambiguity.

The phrase "the power of Governments" appears to me ambiguous. If the Governments of the chief commercial countries were to agree to fixed-ratio-mintage, and if they were to subordinate every other end to maintaining this ratio, I have no doubt that they could maintain it, at all events for a very long time. In this sense it would be in their " power " to do it. But hitherto they have not done what is in their power to promote stability of prices : each Government has thought first of the interests of the nation which it represents, and has endeavoured to secure for it a good supply of gold with but little reference to international interests. Our own Government has not, indeed, tried to collect a large hoard of gold ; but it is jealous of the issue of £1 notes, partly because they would drive abroad a part of our gold coinage.

The real question is, then, not what Governments *could* do, but what they *would* do if the inducement to scramble for gold were much increased ? And I submit that the adoption of fixed-ratio-mintage would be not unlikely to increase those inducements very much.

Governments, as well as private persons, hoard gold rather than silver, partly because it is more convenient, but partly also because they think that the value of gold relatively to silver is, on the whole, more likely to rise than to fall.

I venture to think that the arguments by which advocates of fixed-ratio-mintage have endeavoured to establish its stability are vitiated by their paying too little attention to the influence which the adoption of that scheme might have on the one hand in checking the production of gold, and on the other in increasing the inducements to hoard it.

My contention is this :—If fixed-ratio-mintage tied the value of gold at 15½ of silver, then, in the event of a continued fall in the cost of mining silver relatively to that of gold, the following results would take place :—

Firstly : Many gold mines would be closed ; the profits of silver mining would be abnormally high ; and the supply of silver would be much increased. *Secondly :* Whereas at present out of the 20,000,000*l.* of gold produced annually, about 12,000,000*l.* are (according to Dr. Soetbeer and M. Ottoman Haupt) consumed in the arts, while about 3,000,000*l.* are sent to the East ; and whereas this consumption of gold in the arts is to a great extent modern, is the result of the growth and diffusion of wealth, and is likely to increase even in countries in which gold ornaments are not, as in India, valued partly as means of hoarding ; therefore before long the consumption of gold in the arts would probably exceed its total production by many millions annually. *Thirdly :* The stock of gold thus rapidly diminishing, while the stock of silver was rapidly increasing, people would begin to discuss what would happen if anything should cause the fixed-ratio-mintage convention to break down; they would speculate as to whether the value of an ounce of gold would then rise to that of 20 or 30 ozs. of silver, or, perhaps, even higher. *Fourthly :* Discussions of this kind would greatly increase private hoarding. The rate of interest on secure loans of capital is falling and seems likely to fall, and every such fall increases the inducements to hoard a precious metal that is likly to rise in value. If an ounce of gold can be got for the price of 15½ ozs. of silver, if there is reason to believe that it is tied down to that value only by a convention which is in some danger of being snapped, then many people, especially country folk, may come to think that, after balancing risks on both sides, they have as good a chance of getting good interest on their capital by turning it into gold and hoarding as by lending it out. Meanwhile, those countries which were outside the fixed-ratio-mintage convention, but yet used gold coins, whether as legal tender or not, would absorb a great and probably increasing amount of gold for currency purposes. They would think it wise to take advantage of a cheapness which might not last.

Lastly comes the question, what *would* be done by the Governments which had adopted fixed-ratio-mintage ? I will admit that if they chose to reverse their present policy, and instead of scrambling for gold were to give it freely out of their treasuries, they might so disappoint the hopes of those who looked to a rise in its value as to check private hoarding; and then the stock of gold would be left to be attenuated by the comparatively slow process of a consumption for the arts in excess of the production from the mines. But I see no reason for believing they would do this. They would be unwilling to give an ounce of gold for 15½ ozs. of silver, when there was a considerable chance that before long it might be worth 20 or 30 ozs. Each Government would probably prefer national interests to those of an international currency in the future as they have done in the past, and would scramble for gold even harder than now. If so, a very few years would suffice to sweep all gold coin out of circulation in the countries that had adopted the convention. There would be stores of gold at the great banks, but the expansion of the volume of the currency would depend almost exclusively on the supplies of silver. Not that much more silver could be forced into circulation, probably no one believes that it would be easy to get ten millions more of silver into circulation in England. In England and in other countries, where "Western" habits of business prevail, silver coins would be confined, as now, to a subsidiary use, and the main body of the circulation would consist of paper. This paper would, so long as the convention lasted, be based nominally on gold and silver; but, for all practical purposes, it would be based on silver alone; for any gold that came from the mines would at once be absorbed by the arts and by the demands of countries outside the monetary convention, and the fluctuations of the basis of the new currency would depend exclusively on the yield of the silver mines.

The advocates of fixed-ratio-mintage have assumed for it the title of bimetallism. But, in my opinion, bimetallism means that the payment of every debt shall be effected by the delivery of certain amounts of *both* metals (or of paper which represents them). Fixed-ratio-mintage would begin as *alternate* metallism; that is, it would allow a debt to be discharged by the payment of a certain amount of *either* metal; and, on the not improbable contingency of a continued fall in the cost of mining silver relatively to that of gold, it would rapidly degenerate into a system of paper currency on a monometallic silver basis.

Nevertheless, I think that an international currency is badly wanted and must ultimately be adopted, and I should therefore regard the disturbances caused by the introduction of fixed-ratio-mintage as not without some compensation. It would familiarise people with the advantages of an international currency and with a use of paper money. If the cost of mining silver should rise relatively to that of gold, the scheme might be stable, and in this contingency it would be thoroughly satisfactory and a great benefit to the world. And even if the scheme collapsed quickly, we should perhaps be helped on our way to a better and more scientific plan. But I do not myself consider that the experiment ought to be ventured on until more time has been allowed for considering the problem of international currency from many points of view. Very little energy has yet been spent in the search for methods of solving the problem other than that offered by fixed-ratio-mintage, to which a number of causes have combined to give a practical monopoly of public attention.

XII. What would be the effect of such an agreement, if carried out, upon (a) prices, and (b) the production of the precious metals ?

The belief that prices will rise often makes prices rise, because it expands credit; and I should expect a perceptible rise of prices to follow the announcement that silver was to be legal tender at the ratio of 15½. But after a little while prices might perhaps settle down very nearly as before, unless and except in so far as silver were used as the basis of paper money.

As regards the future, I hold (with Mr. Giffen) that when prices have once been adjusted on a bimetallic basis, the gradual growth of wealth and trade is just as likely to cause a fall of prices as it would be if the currency were on a gold basis, except in so far as there is reason to believe that the cost of mining silver will fall relatively to that of gold. And in so far as there is reason for believing this, there is, I have already argued, good ground for believing that fixed-ratio-mintage would degenerate into silver monometallism.

The effects on production of fixed-ratio-mintage would be the exact opposite of those caused by true bimetallism. True bimetallism would attract capital and labour to the production of whichever metal was scarce. Fixed-ratio-mintage would attract capital and labour to the production of whichever metal was being most easily mined, and therefore most plentifully supplied.

XIV. Failing an international bimetallic agreement, what measures could be adopted by the commercial nations of the world for giving increased stability to the relation between gold and silver ?

The objects which it is proposed to attain by giving increased stability to the relation between gold and silver are, I believe, firstly, increased facilities for an international currency, and, secondly, increased stability of general prices. I propose therefore to take this question broadly, as though it asked what measures other than the introduction of fixed-ratio-mintage could be adopted by the commercial nations of the world for attaining these two ends.

I regard true bimetallism as the best basis of an international currency, because it causes the value of legal tender money to vary with the mean of the values of both of those metals which are suited better than any other easily portable commodities to afford a standard of value; and because it would be convenient both to those countries which now chiefly use gold and to those which now chiefly use silver.

It has been proposed to attain a true bimetallism by the issue of legal tender coins composed of an amalgam of gold and silver. But it would be difficult to test the composition of such coins, and their weight would render them almost as unsuitable for general use as silver coins. I propose to avoid these disadvantages by a modification of Ricardo's "Proposals for an economical and secure Currency." I am not bold enough to think that my scheme is the best possible. My only excuse for venturing to direct your attention to it is that it offers an illustration of the important fact that we have not yet fairly attempted to fathom the varieties of currency that may offer themselves to our choice if we no longer regard as a fatal objection to any scheme, that it would involve great changes and lead to an extended use of convertible paper money.

[1] Ricardo suggested that we should use a paper currency resting on a basis, not of coin, but of stamped gold bars weighing 20 ozs. each. If, he argued, the currency were in excess and showed signs of falling below its gold value, it would be taken to the Mint and exchanged for gold bars for exportation; if it were deficient, gold bars would be brought to the Mint and currency demanded. Within the country the paper would be a perfect medium of exchange, while for the payment of the balances of foreign trade stamped gold bars are better suited than coins.

The currency scheme which I wish to submit for consideration differs from his only by being bimetallic instead of monometallic. I propose that currency should be exchangeable, at the Mint

---

[1] Cf. *Money, Credit and Commerce*, pp. 65–67.

or Issue Department, not for gold, but for gold and silver, at the rate of not 1*l*. for 113 grains of gold, but 1*l*. for 56½ grains of gold, together with, say, 20 times as many grains of silver. I would make up the gold and silver bars in gramme weights, so as to be useful for international trade. A gold bar of 100 grammes, together with a silver bar, say, 20 times as heavy, would be exchangeable at the Issue Department for an amount of the currency which would be calculated and fixed once for all when the scheme was introduced. (This number 20, or whatever it might be, would be fixed on arbitrarily once for all. If we wished the value of the currency to be regulated chiefly by gold we should have only a small bar of silver; if chiefly by silver we should have, perhaps, 50 or 100 times as heavy a bar of silver as that of gold. But if we wished the two metals to have about equal influence we should, taking account of the existing stocks of the two metals, probably choose our silver bar about 20 times as heavy as that of gold.)

Anyone who wanted to buy or sell gold or silver alone in exchange for currency could get what he wanted by exchanging gold for silver, or silver for gold, at the market rate. Government fixing its own rates from day to day, so as to keep its reserves of the two metals in about the right proportion, might safely undertake this exchange itself, and then anyone could buy or sell either gold or silver for currency in one operation.

To ensure convertibility the currency would not be allowed to exceed, say, three times the bullion reserve in the Issue Department, except in times of emergency, when the minimum rate of discount was, say, 10 per cent.; and then the rule might be broken, either as now, by the authority of the Government, or, which I think would be better, by a self-acting rule. The country would save so much on the cost of its currency that it could well afford to keep, as a normal reserve, bullion worth, say, 30,000,000*l*. in excess of this limit, and thus prevent the sudden stringencies which we now suffer whenever there is even a small foreign drain of bullion. There would be, as now, token coins of silver and bronze; but since even a small percentage on the value of a gold coin is sufficient to pay the illicit coiner, it is doubtful whether it would be worth while to have token coins of gold.

Ricardo's proposal was made at a time when the mismanagement of paper issues at home and abroad had made the notion of a paper currency repugnant to all prudent people. But now there is a greater tendency to discriminate between paper money which has no sound basis, and which may fairly be called soft money, and paper whose convertibility into hard metal is properly secured. The strangeness of the scheme will make many refuse to examine it closely; but those who can overcome their natural repugnance to the use of paper money will, I think, find that it has the following advantages :—(1) It would be economical and secure; (2) though economical, the largeness of its reserve would obviate the sharp twinges there now frequently occur in the money market; (3) it would vary in value with the mean of the values of gold and silver; (4) as it would in no way attempt to control the relative values of gold and silver, and would not be affected, even if an ounce of gold became worth 50 ozs. of silver, it could be begun at once and without risk by any one nation, and it would be specially suitable to the circumstances of the Anglo-Indian Empire; (5) if adopted by several nations it would constitute at once a perfect international basis of currency and prices. France could, if it chose, still reckon in francs, England in pounds, and America in dollars; but every 20 franc note would state on its face how many francs were exchangeable for a standard pair of bars of 100 grammes of gold and 200 grammes of silver; and therefore the equivalent in £ s. d. of 100 francs would be settled once for all. There would be nothing to be allowed as now for seigniorage or for wear and tear of coins. Francs, pounds, or dollars would alike give a definite command over bars of gold and silver, which would form a perfect medium for international payments.

Without burdening the Commission with more details, I will briefly state that in an article published in the *Contemporary Review* for March 1887 (from which I have already made some extracts, and of which I enclose a copy), I have further argued that :

(i) Even a true bimetallism would afford only a little better standard of value than monometallism. Monometallism may be compared to a standard of length got from the measure of the senior judge's foot at the assizes; while bimetallism corresponds to that got by taking the mean of the lengths of the feet of both judges (pp. 359–362).

(ii) Since prices vary much from place to place, a standard of value which makes any approach to accuracy must be national and not international, and therefore M. Walras' ingenious scheme for steadying the value of gold seems impracticable (footnote on p. 371).

(iii) While a true bimetallic currency is the best basis for international trade and for all the current business of banking and of buying and selling, whether wholesale or retail, the time has arrived for inquiring whether we cannot adopt the suggestion made early in this century, that Government should publish a tabular standard of value for optional use within the United Kingdom in all transactions which extend over a long period of time. It could be used, for instance, in long leases, in mortgages, and all other borrowings of capital for long periods, and even in such contracts formal or informal for the hire of labour and personal services as are of long duration. A theoretically perfect standard of purchasing power is unattainable; and it would probably be best, for the sake of simplicity, to begin with a comparatively rough standard. But the index-numbers with which we are already familiar would give a ten times better standard of value for optional use within the country in long-standing contracts than even a true bimetallic currency. There are great difficulties to be overcome, political, statistical, and scientific. But failure would do very little harm, because it would disturb nothing. Success would diminish much the anxieties of business and the irregularity of employment. And I think the attempt ought to be made (pp. 363–5 and 371–5).

(ii) ORAL EVIDENCE.

December 19, 1887.

THE RIGHT HON. LORD HERSCHELL, the Chairman, presiding.

MR. D. H. BARBOUR, C.S.I.
MR. J. W. BIRCH.
MR. HENRY CHAPLIN, M.P.
SIR T. H. FARRER, Bart.
MR. C. W. FREMANTLE, C.B.
MR. S. MONTAGU, M.P., and
MR. GEO. H. MURRAY, *Secretary.*

Mr. ALFRED MARSHALL examined.

9623. (*Chairman.*) You are Professor of Political Economy in the University of Cambridge ?—Yes.

9624. And you have given some consideration to the questions with which this Commission has to deal ?—Yes.

9625. I believe you wish first to make an observation as to the term, appreciation of gold ?—Yes. I want to explain how I use the term myself, rather than raise controversial questions on a matter on which controversies are very long indeed. I myself should prefer to adhere to the old usage, which is, I think, almost universal amongst academic economists, in which the appreciation of gold simply means a fall of general prices ; I prefer not to make any distinction between the two terms. But there is no doubt that the two are used in different senses among the public, and I have tried to ascertain what it was that was meant when the appreciation of gold was contrasted with a fall in general prices. In reading the evidence that has been given before this Commission, I have found myself often unable to follow what was said, because I could not make out how the word was used, when an appreciation of gold was contrasted with a fall of general (gold) prices. Therefore, in order to make my own position clear, I

32

would like to say that when it is so contrasted, and used as denoting a rise in the real value of gold, I then regard it as measured by the increase in the power which gold has of purchasing labour of all kinds—that is, not only manual labour, but the labour of business men and all others engaged in industry of any kind. To give definiteness to this explanation I will take an example. Suppose that the rise in the purchasing power of gold, as measured by the general prices of commodities, is 30 per cent.; suppose the rise in the power which gold has of purchasing work, or, in other words, the fall in average gold earnings, is 12 per cent.; then, in my use of the term, the fall of prices is due to the extent of 18 per cent. to improvements in production, and to the extent of 12 per cent., to a rise in real value or to an appreciation of gold, in that use of the term in which it is contrasted with a fall of general prices. As regards the depreciation of silver, I am rather puzzled by the statement in the Warrant appointing the Commission, that it is to inquire into the depreciation of silver. I do not admit that silver has depreciated in the sense of having less general purchasing power. I think that it has appreciated, and has now a higher purchasing power as regards commodities than it had before. I think that the fall in the gold price of silver is greater than the fall in the gold price of labour, and that therefore there is a depreciation of silver, in the sense in which it means a fall in the power which silver has of purchasing work, but not in the sense in which the depreciation of silver means a fall in its general purchasing power.

9626. Depreciation of silver, I think, has been generally used in the evidence before this Commission as equivalent to a depreciation in its gold value or price. Of course you do not dispute that there has been a depreciation of silver in that sense?—No, only I cannot see how we are to get on if we do use it in that sense, because then the depreciation of silver, I think, ought to correspond with the appreciation of gold, and it has seemed to me that there has been occasionally some talking at cross purposes, because in one part of an argument depreciation of silver has been taken to mean merely a fall in its value relatively to gold, and in another has been taken to mean either a fall in its power of purchasing commodities, or a fall in its real value.

D

9627. Supposing that any commodity, other than silver, doubled its supply, the demand being in no way increased, and the price was consequently lowered, would not you say that there was a depreciation in the value of that article ?—That would depend on the context, and if the context was such as to introduce the phrase, the appreciation of gold, I should object to using the term depreciation in a sense which had no logical connection with the adjoining use of the term appreciation.

9628. In that case you would not say there was an appreciation of gold. If it was the case, only of one single commodity, the price of which was halved by reason of increased supply, without increased demand, then would not the proper phrase be that there was a depreciation in the value or price of the article, without any appreciation in the value of gold, meaning, in the value of gold generally ?—I should prefer to state a simple fact, that its price had fallen. I would rather do that than say that it had depreciated, if anywhere in the neighbourhood there was the phrase, the appreciation of gold, in an altogether different sense.

9629. To pass now to the question which has been raised of the dependence of the prices upon the quantity of the currency, what observations have you to make ?—I accept the common doctrine that prices generally rise, other things being equal, in proportion to the volume of the metals which are used as currency. I think that changes in the other things which are taken as equal are very often, perhaps generally, more important than the changes in the volumes of the precious metals. A question was asked by the Commission some time ago as to the dependence of prices upon the amount of the precious metal which was used as the standard of value. I object to make any such distinction. I believe that the shillings and half-crowns in circulation have just the same effect upon prices as they would have if they were legal tender; I believe that four half-crowns affect prices exactly in the same way as a half-sovereign does. But putting that aside, I think that we have not the statistics, and that we shall not, in this generation, be able to get the statistics which would enable us to trace any statistical connection between the amount of the precious metals, or, as I would prefer to say, between the amount of currency and the average level of prices ; because, supposing that the volume of the currency remains the same, the height of average prices may yet vary in consequence of several causes. The first of these is a change in the volume of things on sale, and with regard to that no doubt we have fairly good statistics. The second is an increase or diminution in the average number of times each of these things changes hands during the year, and with regard to that we have no statistics whatever; indeed, there has never been any attempt to obtain statistics on the subject. The third cause is the average number of times that each coin or each element of the currency changes hands during the year; on that subject also there are no statistics. The last cause is the proportion which purchases otherwise than by currency bear to purchases by means of currency; on that subject I think we have no statistics which are in the least trustworthy, although, of course, a great many people have given guesses of more or less value. It seems to me that it is an insufficient account to say that average prices depend on the amount of the currency combined with the amount of credit. For without any change in the amount of currency the average level of prices might be altered, not only by a change in the proportion of credit to other means of purchasing, but also by any other change in the methods of business, as for instance the growth of intermediaries.

9630. In what sense do you use the word currency when you speak of dependence of prices on the quantity of the currency?— I do not think that that doctrine depends very much on the question where the line is drawn. I believe that you can make the theory valid with almost any definition of currency, provided, when you have once adopted it, you adhere to it throughout; but I, myself, use the term currency to include everything which passes from hand to hand as a means of purchasing, without requiring any special or trade knowledge on the part of those who handle it.

9631. Then you do not limit it to either gold or silver, or gold and silver?—No, I include paper money.

9632. And not only bank notes, but cheques?—No, because a cheque requires the receiver to have formed some opinion for himself as to the individual from whom he receives it. If a stranger offers me a 5l. note, I am willing to give him five sovereigns for it, if I feel sure it is a genuine note; but if he offers me a cheque, I will not give him anything for that, because I have no special knowledge of him.

9633. Supposing that without any change in the amount of credit which people had at their bankers, the amount of gold and silver which existed in the country were diminished to-morrow, why should prices be lower or higher?—Because, in my opinion, if a change were made suddenly and in the ordinary way, it would then affect at once Lombard Street.

9634. Assume that it so takes place, as not to affect or shake credit in any way; that people believe that they can as safely draw their cheques, and as safely leave their money at their bankers' as they could before. In that case, why should a diminution of the reserve kept by the bankers, if it does not suffice to shake credit, affect prices?—I do not think it would affect prices instantaneously. If you could suppose a diminution in the number of coins in every purse and in every shopkeeper's till and counting-house, that would act on prices directly; but even that might not act suddenly, although the whole structure of our business is based upon retail transactions. I think that the amount of coins which a person cares to keep in his pocket is determined by the amount of business he has to do, and by the proportion which that part of his payments which he finds it most convenient to make in currency bears to the whole.

9635. But is not the greater part of the metal which we possess, gold, in the form of bullion at the Bank of England, and not of coins in people's pockets at all?—In England, surely not. In England, surely the amount of gold in people's pockets is very much larger.

9636. True. Perhaps I should have said, the variation is rather in the amount in the reserve of the Bank of England and other banking reserves, than the amount of coin?—Yes; and therefore, when you ask me what would be the effect of the diminution of the amount of coin, I think of it as affecting the Bank of England reserve and the rate of discount.

9637. But did you include bullion reserves as well as money coined and in the hands of the public?—When I spoke of its effect on Lombard Street I certainly had in view its effect upon bullion as well as upon gold coined and in the hands of the people. When I spoke of the effect of a decrease in the supply of gold on prices as acting through Lombard Street, I then had in view bullion as well as coin.

9638. Do you think that the amount which people have at their credit at their bankers' is an important factor in determining prices ?—Very; but I think that the treatment of the problem from that point of view raises a different set of questions. The relation which the amount of bankers' money bears to the amount of currency has to be discussed as a part of a larger inquiry as to the influence which is exerted on prices by the methods of business ; and, as I have already said, I do not think we are yet ready to deal with that statistically. It has not yet been thoroughly investigated by economists in any country. The most pregnant hints on it are, I think, those given by Mr. Giffen in his *Stock Exchange Securities*. I do not think that his solution is complete, but he seems to have pointed towards the right solution. I am afraid of getting lost in a great maze of reasoning of a very abstract character if I go into the matter; and I would desire at present to confine myself to indicating in a very general way the manner in which I should approach it. I should consider what part of its deposits a bank could lend, and then I should consider what part of its loans would be redeposited with it and with other banks and, *vice versâ*, what part of the loans made by other banks would be received by it as deposits. Thus I should get a geometrical progression; the effect being that if each bank could lend two-thirds of its deposits, the total amount of loaning power got by the banks would amount to three times what it otherwise would be. If it could lend four-fifths, it will then be five times; and so on. The question how large a part of its deposits a bank can lend depends in a great measure on the extent on which the different banks directly or indirectly pool their reserves. But this reasoning, I think, has never been worked out in public, and it is very complex, and I should not wish to tender evidence upon the subject.

9639. But I want to understand why an alteration in the amount of gold in this country, whether in coin or in bullion reserve, should have a considerable effect upon prices. In considering what affects prices, I should be disposed to accept what you put, that the amount of balance which men have at their bankers' must have a very potent effect. What I do not quite understand is, why that effect should be less or greater because of the amount of reserve which the banker holds to support the credit of his establishment. If the credit is fully established, why should it add to prices if he doubled the amount of gold that he kept, or why should it diminish prices if he halved it?—Oh, certainly; I do not think that prices are affected by any accumulation of reserves, such as the Bank of France, for instance, may hold; that is, in excess of what is really wanted for the purpose of establishing its credit.

9640. Supposing that this country had more gold to-morrow than it has to-day, would not that increase show itself only in bankers' reserves or in the reserve of the Bank of England, and not in the pockets or hands of the people?—How does the gold come? Does it come in the ordinary way through the bullion dealers?

9641. Yes; suppose any assumption you please.—Then I should say it would act at once upon Lombard Street, and make people inclined to lend more; it would swell deposits and book credits, and so enable people to increase their speculation with borrowed capital; it would, therefore, increase the demand for commodities and so raise prices.

9642. That is to say, by making money cheap, and so fostering speculation, and by facilitating speculation, increasing prices?— Yes, supposing gold to come in the ordinary way through Lombard Street.

9643. But that would not be because it added very much to the volume of the currency, but it would be the indirect effect of making loanable money cheap?—That would be only its immediate effect, but it would have the ultimate effect of adding to the volume of the currency required for circulation, as I think; because, prices having risen, a person who had found it answer his purpose to have on the average 17*l*. in currency in his pocket, would now require 18*l*. or 19*l*.; and so on for others.

9644. But do you think it would alter in the least the amount of currency which people had in their pockets? Is not the tendency more and more to leave all the money at the bankers' and merely to keep what you want for small change in your pocket—on the part of tradespeople ?—Oh, undoubtedly; that is the reason why we have been able to sustain prices, although business has increased at such an enormous rate; changes in the methods of business are certainly diminishing the amount of currency we require to do a given amount of business. But except in so far as the methods of business change, a rise of prices requires people to use more currency for retail transactions, and, other things being equal, an increase in the amount of the precious metals seems to me to raise proportionately the uses of them for all purposes.

9645. One more question to illustrate what I want to get from you. Supposing that the balance which people had at their bankers' was doubled, would not that be likely to have a greater effect upon prices than adding merely a large amount, which would be by no means anything like as large, to the metal in the country ?—I do not see how the balance could be increased, the amount of precious metals remaining stationary, unless there was a change in the methods of business; and a sufficient change in the methods of business would enable prices to be ten times as high as they are with the same amount of gold and silver.

9646. But why do you say that ? Have you any information which would lead to the conclusion that the state of things to-day is not that of very large increase in credits at the banks of the country, with no increase at all practically in the amount of coin in circulation or bullion reserves in the banks and in the Bank of England ?—I think what you say is quite correct, but I submit that that is due to a gradual change in the methods of business, and my belief is that it has been this gradual change in the methods of business which has enabled us to do some twenty or thirty times as much business as we did before with a volume of gold and silver only two or three times as large as we had before, and if that change should go on fast I believe that prices would rise.

9647. You mean without any addition to the currency ?— Without any addition. I believe—and in this I think I am supported by the Austrian economist Dr. Wirth, who wrote a very important book on crises—that the rise of prices before 1873 was to some extent in consequence of the tendency to the use of bank credits in Austria. There is no doubt that at that time Austria did go rather bank-mad, and after 1873 it became clear that the hopes that people had of the speedy adoption of the English banking system in Austria were destined to be disappointed. The movement was premature, and I have always thought that to be one of the important causes of the fall in prices which happened in 1873.

9648. Then I gather that your expression, all other things being equal, covers so much ground, is so extensive a qualification of the statement of your general rule that prices depend on the quantity of the currency, that you would agree that there might be a sensible increase or diminution of the quantity of the currency without a sensible increase or diminution necessarily following in prices ?—Yes. As Voltaire said, an incantation will destroy a flock of sheep if it is accompanied by a sufficient dose of arsenic. So a great rise of prices is possible without a change in the supplies of gold and silver, provided there is a sufficient change in the methods of business. And, as I have already said, we have no statistics of changes as to the methods of business; a great number of statistics which we ought to have in order to get near a statistical treatment have not even yet begun to be sought for, and therefore I myself despair of arriving by the direct statistical method at any decision of the question whether there is a scarcity of gold. The only direct statistical method or semi-direct statistical method that I can think of is to find out what is the change in the purchasing power of gold in terms of labour of all kinds.

9649. You gave one illustration of the method in which you thought the addition to the metallic currency might affect prices, namely, the indirect effect produced by its increase of loanable capital by lowering the rate of discount, and so enabling men to borrow more cheaply and readily, and so stimulating speculation. Have you any other suggestion to make as to the mode in which the increase or diminution of the supply of the metal affects prices ?—I take the question to refer to a country such as England now ?

9650. Yes.—I think that if there was more gold in circulation than people wanted to do that part of their business which they prefer to do with currency, they would simply send it to the banks. From the banks it would go into the reserve; from the reserve it would go back on to the general market, inflating credit, increasing speculation, enabling people to borrow who could not borrow before, raising prices. When prices had once been raised, say, 10 per cent. all round, then supposing there to be no dose of arsenic with the incantation, and the habits of business to be exactly the same as before; then people would require 10 per cent. more cash in their pockets than they did before.

9651. The evidence that has been put by some witnesses before us has been intended to show that so far from any connection being traceable between plentiful money and a low rate of discount and a plentiful supply of the precious metals, the evidence was just the other way?—Oh yes, that is certainly true as regards permanent results; the supply of gold exercises no permanent influence over the rate of discount. The average rate of discount permanently is determined by the profitableness of business. All that the influx of gold does is to make a sort of ripple on the surface of the water. The average rate of discount is determined by the average level of interest in my opinion, and that is determined exclusively by the profitableness of business, gold and silver merely acting as counters with regard to it.

9652. The next point to which you propose to direct our attention is the conditions under which bimetallism would raise prices?—I do not think that there is any evidence that bimetallism —that is, the use of the two metals instead of one—in every country in the world would raise prices all the world over directly; that is, not in gold countries and silver prices taken together. Indirectly it might, but directly I do not think it would, because I think that all the gold and silver in the world that is not wanted for the arts or production or hoarding is already acting as currency, and I do not think its efficiency would be increased by the adoption of bimetallism. If bimetallism caused larger supplies to be raised from the mines, that would affect prices; if it caused less to be hoarded, that would affect prices; if it led to a silver paper being issued upon a thin reserve of silver, that would inflate prices; but by itself I do not see that it would affect the average of prices all the world over. If, however, bimetallism took the

particular form of fixing the value of silver, say 20 per cent.
higher than its market value now, I should then expect it to raise
prices some 10 per cent. or perhaps a little less in gold countries,
and to lower them some 10 per cent. or perhaps a little more in
silver countries, leaving the average all the world over very much
as it was before. As regards the future I do not think that it
would in the least tend to diminish the difficulties of increasing our
supply of the precious metals. Mr. Giffen has put this pro-
minently forward, and it has not, I think, been answered. Except
in so far as it is likely that silver would be more easily mined
than gold in the future, bimetallism would not make it easier to
increase our currency in proportion to our increase of business
than it is now. It would be just as hard to add 10 per cent.
to each of the two metals as to add 10 per cent. to gold alone.

9653. I should like to ask one question upon your statement
as to the effect of bimetallism if the gold value of silver were
raised 20 per cent. higher than it is at present. You say that it
would raise prices something like 10 per cent. in gold-using
countries; do you mean all prices?—Yes; I see no reason for
one price being affected more than another.

9654. You do not make any distinction between the price of
articles that are the produce of silver-using countries and other
articles which have no special connection with them?—Well, of
course, the immediate effect of the fall might be to cause a flow
of silver from one country to another, and the flow of silver from
one country to another will, of course, affect the exchanges between
that country and others; but I do not think that effect would be
very great.

9655. Why do you think that to fix the ratio between gold and
silver 20 per cent. higher as regards the value of silver than it is
at present would raise gold prices in this country 10 per cent.;
how, I mean, would it operate to have that effect?—I think that
we should certainly use more silver. It is difficult to answer the
question without some assumption as regards silver paper. I
believe that Englishmen would strike against any law that compelled them to carry about a pound's weight of silver, and unless
silver paper of some form were allowed, I believe that the Government would not have the power of carrying out a bimetallic law;

I believe that a law making 15½ ozs. of silver legal tender as an alternative for an ounce of gold, involves as a necessary consequence (in the present condition of our gold and silver supplies) an issue of paper based upon silver in some form or another. On this assumption I think there would be an addition to our currency, and that would raise prices.

9656. But how would that come about? Of course the Government would not issue the paper against the silver or the bank, or anybody, except some demand were made. You mean people would bring silver to be minted and then issue paper against it?—Yes.

9657. Well then, supposing that that were so—supposing 10,000,000*l.* of silver were brought to be minted, and silver certificates or notes were issued against this 10,000,000*l.* of silver or 20,000,000*l.* of silver, why should that raise all prices 10 per cent.?—I think we should contemplate one change at a time. Assuming the habits of business to remain unchanged, the amount of coin which a person finds it convenient to carry about, taking one with another, depends upon his general wealth. A shop-keeper with an income of 1,000*l.* a year would be likely to use a great deal more gold than an architect with the same income, but if prices rose generally so that the money income of each increased 10 per cent., and the expenditure of each in every direction increased also 10 per cent., then (their habits of business remaining unchanged) each of them would, I believe, keep 10 per cent. more money in his purse. In the first place, this bullion would probably go through the money market; it would enable people, as I have said before, to borrow who otherwise could not have borrowed. There would be, therefore, a flutter of prices upwards and that flutter would be sustained; because of there being this larger amount of silver to be had people would have the means of keeping a larger quantity in their purses.

9658. This is what puzzles me; why does anybody want to keep more currency in his purse; why should not people be without any currency in their purses? Will you let me put a further question in order to point out my difficulty? The silver that came here would not come here without something going in return. The silver that finds its way here must be here in the shape of a credit that somebody obtains as against something that he has given for it ?—Yes.

9659. Well then, upon the basis of that he gets, we will say, notes. So far as he, by reason of that, has more money to spend, or that the people who bring it here have more money to spend than before, they will be people coming into the market as purchasers, and therefore tending to raise prices. That I understand, but apart from that fact, I do not quite understand why adding to the volume of the currency—why, because it is represented by notes rather than by simply a credit against which people may draw—it should have any effect upon prices.—I do not say that I think the amount of currency one wants depends entirely upon the level of prices. It depends chiefly on one's habits. But the habits remaining the same, it depends on the level of prices. I have watched that with regard to myself when travelling in different countries. I used to spend something like 15l. a month when travelling in the cheaper parts of Germany. When I went to America I calculated to spend, and I did spend, exactly four times that amount. No doubt I travelled over larger distances then, but I wanted to carry three times as much money in my pocket to pay my way at American hotels as at German country inns. I admit that the tendency is for all well-to-do people to keep less cash about them, and in fact when a person is living at home he very likely may hardly handle any money at all; but when he travels he has to calculate what his expenses will be, and he generally calculates it very closely, so as not to burden himself with superfluous cash. Well, the common people have no bank accounts, and we must recollect that with regard to numbers, it is common people that count and not the well-to-do people. The working and lower middle classes are getting wealthier, and they are able to have more money in their pockets. I have noticed a good deal of evidence to the effect that " the people " do not carry about with them as much coin as they used to. Those who do not are the upper million, or perhaps the upper three million, but the remainder make almost all their purchases with gold and silver.

9660. But then how would people get more of this currency, notes, or whatever it is, in their pockets, unless prices had first gone up and they were richer and could have more in their pockets, because I do not know that anybody has experienced a want of getting money who has anything to give in return for it?—No, but my view is that if the extra silver goes to the banks in the ordinary way, its first effect will be to cause a flutter of speculation and that will raise prices, and prices being higher people will find that they have to keep more about them in order to pay their way.

9661. Ah, that I understand. Then you come to the greater volume of currency as the result arising from the increase, owing to prices having previously become higher; but the higher prices do not result from the greater volume of the currency?—The ultimate cause is, in my opinion, the increase of currency. I think that, the habits of business being unchanged, a rise of prices requires an increase of the coin in people's pockets to sustain it. But I have been pressed to explain the process by which I think that an influx of silver coming in, in the way in which in our modern civilisation it would come in, through the banks, would find its way into people's pockets. And what I say with regard to the rate of discount is intended to account, not for the permanent rise of prices, but for those larger supplies of currency in the pockets of the people who sustain the prices permanently. If a postman could go round and distribute to everybody the increased currency straight off, then I think that would in a primitive state of society act upon prices directly.

9662. Then that comes really back to the point that you put before, that the way in which the prices are affected is that increased bullion lowers the rate of discount, promotes speculation, and so raises prices, and then the result of that is that prices being raised people will need more currency to carry on their transactions. Does that properly represent your view?—Yes, when I say lowering the rate of discount, I do not mean anything more than a flutter downwards. I conceive the average rate of discount during the last ten years has had nothing to do with the supply of precious metals, except in so far as the fear of a further fall of prices has deterred people from new enterprises. If the supply of the precious metals had been twice larger, then the average rate of discount would not have been affected considerably.

9663. (*Mr. Barbour.*) You think the average rate of discount would not have been lowered if the supply had been twice as great as it actually has been ?—No, would not have been lowered.

9664. Do you think it might have been higher in the case supposed ?—I do not think it would have been affected either way considerably.

9665. (*Chairman.*) When you say bimetallism at that ratio would have that effect upon prices, it is merely a temporary effect of any addition to the bullion in the bank causing a flutter of the discount rate and so a flutter by speculation ?—No, my view is that the flutter would affect the speculation, but the prices once having been raised, and there being a larger volume of currency to sustain higher prices, higher prices would be sustained.

9666. But is not the general effect of lowering the rate of discount in that way owing to an increase of the bullion—to send bullion out of the country ?—Oh, I thought we were discussing the effects of adding a good deal of silver coin, or silver paper, to the currency of all gold-using countries.

9667. You mean there would be an increase in all countries in bullion ?—In all gold countries.

9668. (*Mr. Birch.*) That is, supposing that the production from the mines increases ?—No. I am supposing that silver is made legal tender at 15½, and in consequence we get a good deal of silver from silver countries.

9669. (*Chairman.*) Yes, but in France it is still 15½, the ratio at which it is legal tender ?—Nominally.

9670. Then it would become so, if you please, really; but why should that silver come from them to us ?—I do not say it would come to us from them.

9671. Why should it come from America to us? I do not see where it would come from other than from growing production of the mines ?—I think it would come from India.

9672. (*Mr. Barbour.*) India might import less ?—I think India might import less, we should stop it on the way from the mines.

9673. (*Mr. Birch.*) Surely the silver that came would only replace the gold; silver would replace gold, that is all; the amount of metal in the country would be the same ?—I think that the silver would be added to the gold. I think that some silver would come to England. The fundamental or original cause of the change of prices would be our using a different counter. Whereas now we use a counter of a sovereign we should then use a counter of a half a sovereign and a half of four-fifths of a sovereign. On this supposition it would have just the same effect in my view as if we were to decide to cut off a tenth part from all our sovereigns, and, indeed, I must say that many of the arguments in favour of a change of our currency seem to me to point to that. That is a much simpler and more efficient way of doing what is wanted by those advocates of bimetallism, who desire it chiefly because they believe it would raise prices. Their real purpose would be made more clear if they would openly propose that since a smaller sovereign would now be worth as much as a larger sovereign used to be, we ought to have a smaller sovereign. I do not say that this criticism applies to all arguments in favour of bimetallism, but it does apply to some.

9674. (*Chairman.*) That would not touch the arguments arising from the inconvenience of the altering relation of the value of gold and silver as between gold-using countries ?—No, of course not, but I would like to take this opportunity of pointing out the immense difficulty of predicting anything as to the future use of gold and silver respectively in different countries. It is commonly said that poor districts would not be likely to use much gold. That may be so, but there is no certainty about it. The use of gold seems to depend on habits which are not easily traced and measured statistically, but which are, perhaps, closely connected in some parts of the world with the hoarding of gold. For instance, more than 80 per cent. of the value of the coins in circulation in some of the poorest parts of France consists of gold, while in some of the richer districts the value of the gold in circulation is less than that of the silver. Here is a map which shows the proportionate value of land in different departments of France; that which is shaded most darkly being that which is most valuable. (See *La France Économique* by A. de Foville, p. 311.) Here (p. 68) is another map which shows the use of silver; that which is shaded most darkly is that in which there is the largest proportion of silver, and there is no connection between those two maps. Of course, some departments in which the value of agricultural land is low have a rich urban or manufacturing population. But the case is not altered much when allowance is made for this.

9675. Reverting to the question of the effect of a quantity of silver coming in the way you have suggested, from the banks, and so affecting the rate of discount, do you think it necessarily follows that that would promote an amount of speculation, owing to cheapness of money, that would affect prices? Would not that depend a great deal upon other considerations, such as whether trade was likely to be profitable, or whether the supply was outstripping the demand in most branches of trade?—Oh, certainly I think that the supply of the precious metals is only one of the many causes which govern prices; and if any other changes should take place at the same time, I think it is likely that they would throw into the shade the effect of the change in the supply of the precious metals; but, other things being equal, I can see no reason for doubting that the proportion of business in general to the business done with gold and silver in any country would be affected by an increase in the supply of the precious metals.

9676. But what I was rather thinking of was this. During the last year or two we have had times when money has come down very low indeed, as low as it would be likely to do, perhaps, from the present rate, if there were a considerable addition to the metal by making silver a part of the currency of the country in the way suggested. I am not sure that it is at all shown that that fall in the rate of discount has tended to stimulate speculation and raise prices. Prices seem, in spite of that, to have been falling, and I am not sure that I can tell why, because the rate at which people can get money is produced by some different kind of change— monetary change—if the effect produced is the same, namely, a fall in the rate of discount; why that should any more stimulate speculation and raise prices?—I do not myself put the rate of discount into the first place; my own way of looking at it was rather to lay stress upon the actual amount of money in the market to be loaned.[1]

---

[1] This refers to short-period events, as the context shows; but it might do harm if quoted alone. 9678 completes it. I expect I was interrupted here before I had finished.—A. M.

9677. Yes. Well, I put it in that way; but the amount of money in the market to be loaned has a good deal of connection with the rate at which it is loaned. If there is much to be loaned, the price at which you can get it is cheaper ?—Yes; but I think that the direct effect is that of the amount of money itself. If there is an extra supply of bullion, bankers and others are able to offer easy terms to people in business, including the bill brokers, and consequently there is more money on loan, and consequently people enter into the market as buyers of things, as starting new businesses, new factories, new railways, and so on.

9678. Yes, but what I was putting to you was that there seems to have been that abundance of loanable capital in the money market—such an amount as people are hardly able to get rid of at any price, if I may say so—for two years, and we have no evidence that that has stimulated speculation and raised prices, but we have evidence of a fall of prices in spite of that ?—Yes, but that is what I should have expected. It seems to me that the great economic feature of this age, more important than every other fact put together, is that the amount of capital is increasing many times as fast as that of population. It is increasing faster than ever in England, and, what is much more important, there is a very rapid increase in America, where everybody almost is saving. The " extravagant " American is saving more than any other person. In spite of all the inventions which are continually making new uses for capital in the form of machinery and in other ways, this vast increase forces down the interest that can be got in business. The rate of discount, in my opinion, is merely the ripple of a wave on the surface, the average level is the rate of interest which can be got for the investment of capital, and this is being lowered by the rapid and steady growth of capital—I do not mean the growth of credit, I mean the growth of things, the actual excess of production over consumption. I do not see any necessity at all why interest should be more than 2 per cent. a century hence. I should not be at all surprised if a railway company could borrow on debentures at 2, or even less than 2, per cent. in the next century.

9679. Yes, but why, if the ripple produced by increase of loanable capital, or whatever it may be, during the last two years,

E

has been as great a ripple as would be likely to be produced by a considerable addition of silver to our stock of metallic currency, why should the latter stimulate speculation where the former did not ? What I mean is, let us assume that the introduction of this metallic currency would bring into the market 20,000,000*l.* to be loaned, and that the effect of that would be that bankers would be willing to lend at 1½ per cent., instead of 2½, at which the rate stood before, why should that drop of 1 per cent. necessarily stimulate speculation and raise prices when we have had experience of several years that an abundance of loanable capital in the money market has not stimulated speculation and raised prices ?—Because of the cause by which it has been produced. It would be produced by a large excess of loanable capital. This 20,000,000*l.* of extra bullion would be multiplied, I think, in the loan market, and become the basis of credit which supplied the power of purchasing real capital, that is bricks, iron, wool, etc., to the extent of much more than 20,000,000*l.* This would have a considerable effect in fluttering prices upwards, and when once fluttered upwards they would be held up by the fact that there was currency to sustain the higher prices.

9680. (*Mr. Birch.*) Are you conversant with the rate of discount during the last two years in Lombard Street and the available capital seeking employment in discount ?—I know there has been a great plethora of capital. I believe that the plethora of capital is likely, in all ordinary times, to increase; and of course there is a special reason why people should be unwilling to borrow now, because they have lost so much by borrowing and investing in things of which the prices have fallen.

9681. And the rate of discount, are you aware what it is ?—I am aware it is extremely low.

9682. I understand you to say that the low rate of discount and the large amount of available money to discount bills, and so give activity to commerce, was likely to raise prices ?—I cannot accept the substitution of a change in the rate of discount for a change in the amount of capital in the hands of speculative investors. I must go back to the cause of the fall in the rate of discount. If a fall in the rate of discount is produced by the overcrowding of the field for investment it might not have that

effect; but if it arises from an increase in the amount of capital
which is in the possession of those who supply loans I think it
will make it easier to float new companies.

9683. (*Chairman.*) But I thought you said that there had
been nothing so remarkable of late years as the increase of this
loanable capital which has been going on from year to year?—
Yes.

9684. And yet it seems to have been attended with the very
reverse of what you anticipate, namely, limited speculation and
a low rate of prices?—That is because, in my opinion, the permanent rate of discount has no connection with the amount of
currency. The centre about which discount fluctuates in my
opinion is determined by the profitableness of business.

9685. My question had no relation to the rate of discount at
all, but what you were suggesting was that the regulating consideration was the amount of loanable capital?—Yes.

9686. And if the amount of loanable capital has been increasing year by year why should not that, inasmuch as each year's
addition was added to what went before, why should not that
have stimulated speculation and raised prices instead of, as we
have seen, prices languishing?—My position is that the mean
rate of discount is governed by the mean rate of interest for long
loans; that again is determined by the extent and the richness
of the field for the investment of capital on the one hand, and on
the other by the amount of capital seeking investment. The
amount of capital has been increasing so fast that, in spite of a
great widening of the field of investment, it has forced down the
rate of discount. The fall in the rate of discount so caused failed
to stimulate speculation, because it was itself caused by the
difficulty of finding good openings for speculative investment;
this difficulty being in part due to the fear that prices would go
on falling. Equilibrium is found at that rate of interest for long
loans (and the corresponding rate of discount for short loans)
which equates supply and demand. But next, this equilibrium
being established, we set ourselves to inquire what will be the
result of a new disturbance, viz. the influx of a good deal of bullion
into the City. This does not increase the amount of capital, in
the strictest sense of the word; it does not increase the amount

of building materials, machinery, etc., but it does increase the amount of command over capital which is in the hands of those whose business it is to lend to speculative enterprise. Having this extra supply, lenders lower still more the rate which they charge for loans, and they keep on lowering it till a point is reached at which the demand will carry off the larger supply. When this has been done there is more capital in the hands of speculative investors, who come on the markets for goods as buyers, and so raise prices. Further, it must be remembered that the influx of bullion would have caused people meanwhile to expect a rise of prices, and, therefore, to be more inclined to borrow for speculative investments. Thus it might not be necessary to lower the rate of discount very much. The increased demand would meet the increased supply half-way, and, after a time, might outrun it, causing a rise in the rate of discount. But as this rise would be merely an incident in a series of changes which put more command over capital in the hands of speculative investors, it would go with an increased demand for goods and a continued rise of prices. This then is my account of the way in which this extra supply of the precious metals would bring prices up. Having been raised they would be sustained because the methods of business remaining stationary, if a man with an income of 1,000*l*. keeps on the average 12*l*. in his pocket, and if there is more currency in the country so that his share is increased from 12*l*. to 14*l*.; then what was bought by 12*l*. would in future be bought by 14*l*.; the higher prices are sustained by the fact that the amount of cash which a person cares to keep depends upon the habits of business in his particular rank of life, together with his individual peculiarities; if they are not changed any increase in the amount of currency which falls to his share will raise proportionately prices so far as he is concerned.[1]

9687. You have suggested that it would be erroneous to consider that the volume of currency was chiefly in the hands of people who would have banking accounts, and that one ought to regard more the mass of the people, who would have no banking account?—I think that the demand for coin is chiefly the demand from the lower 70 or 80 per cent. of the population.

[1] Cf. *Money, Credit and Commerce*, pp. 255, 256.

9688. Yes, but do not those classes very soon after they get the money pay it away to people who generally have a banking account, so that all that would happen would be that they may possess it for a day or two, or three days, but that within the course of a week it will have found its way to someone having a banking account, and they may have the same money given up to them the next week ?—That is true, no doubt, of a very large part of the population. Were it not so I think we should require two or three times as much gold as we do.

9689. (*Sir T. Farrer.*) And is not that a process which is developing ?—I am not sure whether it is going on very fast just now. I spoke just now about our want of statistics. Of course the co-operative movement and the habit of paying cash, even when dealing with shopkeepers, does tend to cause the working man to keep cash by him a little longer, though I admit he has still a habit of emptying his pockets in a very short time after he receives the money.

9690. (*Mr. Barbour.*) I suppose you would admit that there must be a certain relation between prices in England and prices in the other countries with which England is in commercial connection ?—Certainly.

9691. So that if prices were raised in England there must be, other things being equal, a rise in the prices in other countries too ? —Unless there is a change in the countries in which they are estimated. I mean that if 15½ ozs. of silver were made legal tender in payment of a debt of 1 oz. of gold, prices might rise in what had been gold-using countries, while falling in what had been silver-using countries.

9692. Assuming England is in commercial relation with another country having a gold standard, and prices rise in England, say from speculation, or credit, or a change in the mode of business, and that there is no increase in the precious metals, even in that case prices must rise in the other country too ?—Yes.

9693. Now if that other country was one which depended very much on gold, prices could not rise there without an increase of gold, though they might rise in England from an increase in speculation and credit. England, we will say, uses credit largely ; the other country simply uses gold, but the prices in the two countries must bear a certain relation to each other, because they have commercial intercourse; and though prices in England could rise owing to an extension of credit, they could not rise in the other country without an increase in gold?—I am not sure whether this is a new question or a development.

9694. It is a development of what went before; you said prices could not rise in this country unless there was an additional supply of gold, or an increase of credit, or a change in the mode of doing business; and I want to bring in a further point that if there is another country in commercial relationship with England which uses gold, it is the want of gold in that country which may check the rise of gold prices in England, and not the want of gold in England?—Yes, I quite admit that the level of prices in terms of gold must be determined all the world over; that is, with regard to all gold-using countries.

9695. And that the pressure of the want of gold might come in in any one or more of those countries?—Certainly.

9696. (*The Chairman.*) I pass now to the question with which you are also prepared to deal, how far bimetallism would steady prices?—What I said before as to the importance of watching changes in the methods of business at least as carefully as changes in the supplies of the precious metals, had for its object to lead up to this, that I do not consider that the main causes of fluctuations of prices have been fluctuations in the supplies of the precious metals. I believe that changes in the methods of business and the amounts of the commodities, or, as we may say, changes in the commercial environment, have much greater effects in disturbing prices than changes in these supplies of the precious metals. With that in view I have prepared a diagram showing the fluctuations in gold prices from the year 1782. Now, when we look at the changes in prices in recent years, we see that, great as they are, they are very much less than those in the early part of the century. Prices were almost halved between 1809 and 1816. That then is my first point, that during all this period when the supply of the precious metals was approximately constant, there were violent fluctuations of prices. Since 1848 the supplies of the precious metals have fluctuated violently, but the fluctuations in prices have been less violent and not more violent. My second point relates to bimetallism. I want to consider whether it is true that the substitution of two precious metals for one as the basis of our currency would have had any great effect on steadying prices. Much light is thrown on this question by the fact that these violent fluctuations took place at a time at which the gold prices of silver were approximately stationary, when the prices were approximately bimetallic. It is not, however, true that the gold price of silver was exactly stationary. I have found no means of ascertaining what the gold price of silver was in England in early times. The only set of statistics that I have found is one given by Mr. Del Mar for the United States, and I think it is very likely that one change in particular, the great fall in 1816, may not have extended to the same extent to England. But on the supposition that Mr. Del Mar's figures are trustworthy, what I find is, that in so far as the silver price itself differed from the gold price, it was not more steady but less steady than the gold price. In 1809, when prices are so high in terms of gold, the prices in terms of silver are higher still, and in 1816, when they fall so violently, they fall in terms of silver even more than they do in terms of gold. Hence I conclude that, violent as were the fluctuations of prices when the gold price of silver was approximately stationary, they would have been still more violent if we had had universal rigid bimetallism.

9697. How do you ascertain that; what is the basis for that statement ?—The way in which I ascertain what would have been the level of prices measured in silver is this : I take the gold index-number, I then take Mr. Del Mar's statement of the gold price of an ounce of silver, and then I divide the one by the other.

9698. (*Mr. Barbour.*) For what place does he give the gold price of silver ?—For America. He quotes from a document published by the 21st Congress of the United States.

9699. But those being gold prices for England, the price of silver in England would be more closely connected with them ?—I have admitted that it is quite likely that some of the changes, and, in particular, those early in the century, were not exactly the same in England as in America, but after a long search I have found no other tables than Mr. Del Mar's.

9700. (*Chairman.*) But do you suppose that at that time

there would be any very substantial difference in the price of silver
in America and in this country ?—The American currency at that
time was in a very disorganised state, and I would wish to allow
any qualification that is to be made on that account. I do not
stand sponsor at all to the trustworthiness of Mr. Del Mar's figures
as applied to England. I now will approach an argument which
is implied in the diagram published in the first volume of your
Report, that the variations of the gold price of silver have been
parallel to those of the gold price of commodities since 1870;
from which I understand it to be inferred that a bimetallic price
would be a good deal more stable than a gold price. When I
examine closely the figures from the year 1873 to the present, I
find no such parallelism as is at first sight suggested. I admit
that there has been since 1873 a set of causes tending to lower the
value of silver relatively to gold, and another set of causes tending
to raise the value of gold relatively to commodities, and I admit
that these two causes have in the main balanced one another, so
that the value of silver relatively to commodities has not changed
very much. But this fact that they have about balanced one
another is, I consider, an accident, and after all the balancing is
not very exact. The diagram which I submit to you differs from
the diagram that is printed in the first report of the Commission
in these respects, that I have taken Mr. Sauerbeck's index-number
instead of the *Economist's*, and that I have traced the history of
the gold prices of silver from Mr. Pixley's figures instead of the
Economist's. I get a considerable rise in the curve representing
the movements of the index-number for the year 1875 to 1876,
while the curve representing the changes in the gold price of
silver is going downward. That is, I think, due to the fact that
the diagram in the Report takes the prices for the year 1876 at
the beginning of the year. It happened that in the middle of
the year there was an enormous fall which was not corresponded
to by commodities, and that if you take the prices for the average
of the year, and, moreover, if you take Mr. Sauerbeck's index-
number instead of the *Economist's*, you get a very considerable
divergence between the two curves. I now pass to another
point. If there is any necessary connection between the price of
silver and the price of commodities, it ought to show itself not

in England only, but also in all countries which have a gold standard. I have therefore thought it interesting to compare the movements of the gold price of silver with these diagrams which represent the movements of index-numbers in France, Germany, America, and India respectively. Now, when you compare any of these with the diagram which shows the changes in the gold price of silver, you find that there is no correspondence in detail, nothing beyond the general fact that the gold price of silver has fallen, and that the gold prices of commodities have fallen. There is no close correspondence. I admit that in the year 1881 there was a tendency to a rise in the gold price of silver and the gold price of commodities, but I contend that that does not go far towards establishing a necessary connection between the two.

9701. I suppose you would say that at a period when speculation was rife, especially in metals, there might be a reflex action upon silver, and that might tend to rise in price also as the other metals rose ?—I quite think so.

9702. And therefore that you might find silver and a great many prices going up at the same time, the rise in the price of silver being rather the effect than the cause ?—Yes, I think that the rise in the price of silver is sometimes an effect and sometimes also partly a cause. I think that in 1881 there was a notion that there was a good chance of bimetallism being adopted with the ratio of 15½; and therefore there was a rise in prices, and that sent prices up. I think in 1881 there was a distinct parallelism between the movement of the gold price of commodities and the gold price of silver, but taking the period as a whole I see no minute correspondence between them. The case seems to me to be exactly parallel to the history of the gold price of wheat. For about fifty years from 1820 the mean price of wheat in terms of gold remained almost stationary; and if we applied the method of concomitant variations hastily, we might say that that showed that there was a connection between the two. But the real explanation of the stationariness of the gold price of wheat is that until 1850 there was a continually growing scarcity of wheat accompanied by a growing scarcity of gold. By an accidental coincidence we stumbled on rich mines of gold, just at the time that England opened her ports to corn. Consequently, after 1850 there was a growing abundance of corn accompanied by a growing abundance of gold. This continued till 1873; after that corn became even more abundant, but gold became scarce. The accidental coincidence was over, and the result was a fall in the gold price of wheat. It so happens that free trade came in with the new supplies of gold, and in my opinion the attention which is now given to currency questions is due chiefly to this, that the effects which are caused by the introduction of free trade have been ascribed to the gold mines. I believe that the growth of prosperity which began in England in 1850 increased more or less until it had obtained its full force, and is now going on, though not so fast as it was; that increase, I believe, is due chiefly to the impulse given by free trade. I believe that the influx of the precious metals did not cause the increase of prosperity, but on the contrary has had the effect of making the movement spasmodic and unhealthy instead of gradual and healthy.

9703. (*Mr. Barbour.*) But do you think that the rise of prices which took place from 1848 or 1850 up to 1873 was due to free trade ?—I think that was due chiefly to the influx of gold and to the development of the banking system. It was the increase of prosperity that I ascribed to free trade.

9704. And if that increase in gold had not taken place prices would have fallen very much, probably ?—That is my opinion.

9705. (*Chairman.*) Do you think that a fixed ratio between the two metals with free mintage would be a permanent system ? —I have nothing of importance to add to what I have said in my printed letter. It is really my answer to Questions 10 and 11.

To that I should add that since this answer was written, the rumours of gold mines at the Cape, and what is probably of much less importance, in Wales, have become stronger, and I quite admit that in case we should during the next fifteen years have an increased production of gold on a large scale, that would, so long as its effect lasted, enable a fixed-ratio-mintage to sustain itself. The main arguments which I have adduced for doubting whether a fixed-ratio-mintage would be stable if the silver mines continue to give a richer yield than the gold mines, are, that it would cause the production of gold to decrease, and that it would cause hoarding in different forms to increase. I think that if the ratio were fixed at 15½ many gold mines would be closed; but of course some gold would be still extracted from some of the silver ores. Next, the consumption for the arts is great. Its great increase during our own generation is due to causes which seem likely to go on. I believe, therefore, that the excess of consumption over production of gold would amount to many millions a year. I believe that would increase the tendency to hoard on the part of private persons and of Governments. As to the former, I do not admit what many people say, that anybody who hoards must be foolish, and that there are not likely to be many people foolish enough to hoard who can afford to do it. We must recollect that the numbers of the population are large, and the amount of gold is small. If 50,000,000 of people put by an average of ten sovereigns against a rainy day, that would absorb nearly all the gold we have. It seems to me that, if it once came to be generally thought that the value of gold was artificial, that it depended on a convention which might be broken, and that the breaking of that convention would raise the value of gold very much, people would hoard, as they did in a parallel case in the years 1800 to 1815 in England. Tooke tells us that when cash payments were about to be resumed, a surprising amount came from the hoards of the people. (Tooke and Newmarch's *History of Prices*, Vol. I., p. 133.) Next I may refer to Mr. Barbour for the authority that there are probably something like 130,000,000*l*. of gold hoarded in India since 1835. Next, as to the amount of gold which is in the principal banks, I think that there is a great deal of it that is practically hoarded—that is to say, there is more gold than is wanted for the purposes of the banks. No doubt as the French peasants become educated, and as the habits of investing small sums in the Government loans extends among the people, they are likely to hoard less, though I do not think that Frenchmen are at all clear that French peasants have given up the habit of hoarding. But as they grow out of hoarding other nations grow into it. It is a stage, I think, through which nations pass when they become rich enough and settled enough to have gold to hoard, when their security from the taxgatherer is sufficient to enable them to save, and when they have not arrived at that extremely elaborate system which there is in England and France enabling the poor, if they wish, to buy small sums of Consols and Rentes.

9706. Then I understand your view to be that the course of a system of bimetallism, by inducing possible doubt as to the future of gold, might intensify hoarding and so actually diminish the amount of the precious metals that would be in use as currency ?—Yes ; the amount of gold.

9707. (*Mr. Barbour.*) Assuming that there is not bimetallism, and that the idea becomes prevalent that silver is likely to be more and more discarded as currency and gold substituted for it, would not the value of gold be raised in that way too ; might not the same tendency to hoard gold be called into existence ?— Certainly I think that is a danger that we have to look forward to.   At the same time, if gold is left to seek its own market, then any person who thinks that gold is likely to rise in value is, so to speak, setting his judgment against the judgment of the market ; whereas if the price of gold is tied to that of silver, not by the judgment of the market but by a law which, according to the judgment of the market, is very likely not to be sustained, then the case would be like that of the suspension of cash payments in England when a law put the gold guinea at a value at which the market did not believe that it would have.

9708. (*Sir T. Farrer.*) And then the danger of breaking down the convention would be intensified ?—Yes. Supposing that the gold mines continue to become poorer, while the silver mines continue to become richer, I believe that in a very few years there would not be a sovereign seen anywhere in circulation. We should have a great deal of gold in the banks and a great deal of gold hoarded.   But the currency would be exclusively a paper currency (supplemented, of course, by silver and bronze token coins) on a basis nominally of gold and silver.   But the gold remaining stationary or rather diminishing, the increase of the currency would depend entirely on the silver.   When that result had been reached we should have got all the effects and all the evils of, firstly, a paper currency, if there are evils of that system, and secondly a silver monometallic currency.

9709. (*Mr. Barbour.*) I think the chief uses for the precious metals at the present day are for the arts, for ornament, for hoarding and for currency, and to keep up the bank reserves ?— Yes.

9710. And I believe that at the present day, as far as the estimates go, a larger proportion of the new gold that is produced every year is used in the arts and for ornament, and for hoarding, than is used for currency or banking reserves. Dr. Soetbeer puts it at about 16,000,000*l.* for hoarding and arts ?—I think he gives a very small balance for currency.

9711. Yes, but he gives about 16,000,000*l.* for other purposes ? —Oh, yes, certainly.

9712. So that at the present day the yearly production of gold is more largely used for those purposes than it is for currency ? —Certainly, that is true of the new gold.

9713. Well, even if gold ceased to be in active circulation, it would still be used for the arts and for ornament and for hoarding ?—Yes.

9714. So that it would still continue to discharge what I may call one of the functions of the precious metals ?—Yes; I do not say that that function is of the same order as its function in money, but I accept your statement.

9715. It would discharge that function to which the great bulk of it goes at present ?—To which the great bulk of the new gold goes at present, yes.

9716. And if the market ratio differed from the Mint ratio and gold rose in relative value above the Mint value, that would stimulate its production again ?—It could not rise in value while people had the power of demanding it from the Mints.

9717. Might not gold rise in value if it became scarce, as you say it might; so that it was no longer in circulation ?—You would then contemplate the fixed-ratio-mintage to take the form that though a person brought gold to the Mints to be coined he could not demand gold in return for the silver.

9718. He could not demand gold in return for the silver ?— Yes, on your supposition that would be true, but that is a limitation of the fixed-ratio-mintage which I had not understood to be made.

9719. So that even under the circumstances that you have

put forward, that is to say, of gold ceasing to be in circulation, gold and silver taken together would still be discharging those duties which fall on the precious metals at the present time, with this difference, that gold instead of being used both for hoarding, and the arts, and for currency and reserves, would be entirely used for hoarding and the arts?—Yes, that is so; it would perform no functions as money.

9720. No direct functions as money, but of course if there was no gold in the world more silver would be wanted for hoarding and ornament, and this demand would indirectly affect the value of money?—I would not say that gold would not affect the value of money, but I would say that it would not perform any functions as money.

9721. (*Chairman.*) Would not the fact that three-fourths of the gold would be still wanted for a purpose independent of the currency diminish the extent very largely to which the production of gold would be likely to be affected by the change to a bimetallic system?—Well, I did not base my answer on an interpretation of the law establishing the fixed-ratio-mintage, which, if I understand rightly, it has just been suggested that I ought to have.

9722. But my question is quite apart from that. Taking your own view as to the proposed bimetallism, would it not be true that the fact that there would still be a demand for a purpose entirely apart from the currency, for three-fourths of the gold that is produced, diminish the effect which the bimetallic system would have in causing the production of gold to be lessened?—It seems to me that everything turns on this, whether under the fixed-ratio-mintage plan a person can demand gold in exchange for silver at the Mint. If he can, which is what I had assumed, then I think that the scheme would, so long as it lasted, fix the value of gold at $15\frac{1}{2}$, and if it could not be mined at that rate it would not be mined at all; in fact if the mines go as they have done, at all events recently, I do not think any gold would be mined, except it were found in silver mines. If, on the other hand, the scheme of fixed-ratio-mintage were so framed as not to give people the power to demand gold for silver then I think it would cease almost at once to have an influence over the gold value of silver; the ratio of 15½ would be a legal fiction. The real ratio in the market would be something very different; the banks would keep stores of gold, but nobody would come to them with any more.

9723. But would not the fact that everybody might pay their debts either in a piece of gold or in 15½ pieces of silver as equivalent to gold—would not that tend to keep the ratio up?—No, because nobody would be able to get the gold to pay his debts with. The gold would be at once absorbed by the banks and by the arts and production. Of course anybody would be at liberty then to pay in gold, but nobody would pay in gold because he would be allowed to discharge a debt of 15½ ozs. of silver with only one full ounce of gold; whereas the gold piece would be worth perhaps 20 ozs., so that nobody would use gold.

9724. (*Mr. Barbour.*) But do you think the banks could safely hoard the gold, the gold having become more valuable in the market than it was at the Mint; might there not be a run on the banks to get gold?—I understood you to say that they could not get the money out of the banks.

9725. They could not get gold from the Mints in exchange for silver; no bank could pay all its liabilities at once. If the market ratio differed from the legal ratio, and the banks had the greater part of their reserves in gold, would not there be a rush on the banks to get the gold, and would not that danger prevent banks from hoarding gold very largely?—I had thought that you had used the word Mint as practically covering the large banks. I am afraid I do not exactly understand your supposition. My position was : as soon as it was clear that the gold mines were giving up little and the silver mines were giving up much, people would hoard gold and the banks would try to increase their supplies of gold, and that consequently gold would cease to discharge the functions of money, the minting having ceased in consequence of the value given to it being less than the value at which it could be mined.

9726. (*Chairman.*) But is not the gold, or whatever metal it may be which is what you call hoarded with the banks, really in use as money by keeping up the credit of the bank, upon which basis the transactions take place by means of cheques upon it?—

Yes, I believe it has an effect in that way, but since its amount would be rather diminishing than increasing, and the fluctuations of the currency would depend upon the fluctuations in silver, consequently the gold would have no steadying influence on prices at all; but every change in the productiveness of the silver mines would exert its full effect in producing changes in the currency just as though there were no gold in existence at all.

9727. (*Sir T. Farrer.*) Have you speculated upon what would be the probable action of the Governments in such a case with respect to gold, if gold came to bear a larger real market value than silver?—Well, I think that is for the people who advocate fixed-ratio-mintage to decide; I think it is for them to propose a scheme of Government action. I myself do not think that fixed-ratio-mintage is advisable except as a means of transition to a true bimetallism.

9728. Do you think that if an arrangement were made, one could trust Governments not to hoard or keep gold, and to allow it to come into the market freely?—I believe Governments would hoard gold.

9729. (*Mr. Montagu.*) With what object?—With the same objects as they hoard gold now intensified—that is, they believe that they could get for 15½ ozs. of silver an amount of gold which after a little while would be worth a great deal more.

9730. (*Mr. Chaplin.*) Did they pursue that practice when bimetallism prevailed before?—I do not think that any particular attention had been paid to the subject, and so far as bimetallism in the past goes, one must recollect that the bimetallic scheme was extremely fortunate in having new supplies alternately of gold and silver; and I quite admit that the fixed-ratio-mintage can be sustained permanently if the mines will only obligingly yield us gold and silver alternately.

9731. Then hoarding did not take place, I understand, by Governments, as long as bimetallism did prevail?—France had a large reserve towards the end of the bimetallic period, but I have no special statistics on the subject.

9732. There is no reason to suppose that they would hoard in the future more than they did before, under a similar system?—Oh, circumstances have changed since then, I think. The reasons which I have given for believing that they would hoard, are based on conditions of demand for and supply of the precious metals which exist now, but did not exist then. For one thing, I think that the experience of the Continental wars has altered the views of Governments very much on the subject of gold.

9733. Since when?—I think that part of Germany's fondness for gold arose after the war with Austria.

9734. (*Mr. Montagu.*) That was in bimetallic times?—What I mean is that the desire for a stock of gold for the purposes of war is due, I consider, to changes in the methods of war, and not in the circumstances of the metal.

9735. (*Chairman.*) Pass now to a different subject. It has been suggested that the fall in the gold price of silver gives a bounty to exporters of produce from silver-using countries. What have you to say upon that point?—My own view is that *a priori* it is impossible. I will first endeavour to prove this by general reasoning, though I am aware that such a method of argument is not convincing to all minds. I submit that if Spain is sending oranges to England in exchange for cutlery, the question whether more oranges will go to England—whether the English market will be flooded with oranges—depends solely upon the relative values of oranges and cutlery in England and in Spain. That doctrine was established by Ricardo, and I do not know that any person has shaken it in the least; in fact, I do not myself believe that it has ever been seriously attacked by anyone who has taken the trouble to understand it. If cutlery should rise relatively to oranges in Spain, then there will be a larger trade done, or if oranges should rise relatively to cutlery in England there would be a larger trade done. I do not think that any change in the counters which are used will have any effect whatever upon the general course of trade. I admit that silver is something more than a counter. I admit that it is a very large commodity counting for a great deal in India's imports, and in so far as it is a commodity, I allow it every effect which I should to a commodity of equal volume, copper, or iron, or cutlery, but no more. Well, although that argument seems to me conclusive, I know that there are many who are not convinced by it and I will therefore interpret the substance of the argument into the language of the

F

money market, and go into the matter in detail. In answer then
to the question, does a fall in the Indian exchanges give a bounty
to the Indian exporter, I submit that there is no answer to be
given to that question at all, unless it is known what is the cause of
that fall in the Indian exchanges. And it appears to me very
strange that general attention has not yet been directed to the fact
that a fall in the Indian exchanges may be so caused as to have
exactly the opposite effects to those that are commonly attributed
to it, and give a bounty to the Indian importer, and to impose a
penalty on the Indian exporter. Let us then take one by one
the causes which may produce a fall in the rate of the Indian
exchanges. We shall find that the effect of that fall depends on
the nature of those causes, and that it acts sometimes in one
direction and sometimes in the other. Firstly, let the cause be a
superfluity of silver in Europe, then there will be a fall in the purchasing power of silver there; the purchasing power of gold so
far being unchanged, the result will be a fall of the Indian exchange.
The gold price of a silver bill on India falls; the sending of goods
other than silver to India is *pro tanto* unprofitable because prices
have not risen there. For the same reason the sending of goods
from India is profitable; consequently silver goes to India.
How long silver keeps on flowing to India depends chiefly on what
is done with it when it gets there. In so far as it goes into the
hoards it will not affect prices; in so far as it does not go into the
hoards it will gradually raise prices. It will gradually raise the
exchanges, and the benefit to the Indian exporter will be so far
over. Therefore on the supposition that the fall in silver prices
takes place in Europe before it takes place in India, there is an
interval in which the Indian exporter gets a bounty equal to this
difference. The extent of that difference I will consider afterwards; but to the extent of this difference, and so long as it
lasts, I admit that a bounty to the Indian exporter does accompany a fall in the Indian exchanges. But, secondly, let us take
the opposite cause of a fall in the Indian exchanges. If the silver
mines had been discovered in India instead of in America, and
silver prices had risen in India before they rose in Europe, then
the exact opposite results would have arisen. There would then
have been a tendency for silver to flow from India to England

in lieu of other commodities, and there would then have been a tax on the Indian exporter equal to the difference between silver prices in India and in Europe. I contend, therefore, that the bounty which is caused one way or the other by a fall in Indian exchanges depends merely on the question whether the change in the price of silver takes place first in Europe or first in India. If it happens that silver falls in value in Europe before it falls in India, I admit that in proportion to the differences between prices measured in silver in Europe and prices measured in silver in India, to that extent there will be a bounty to the Indian exporter; but that this bounty is due not to the fall in the exchange itself, but to the particular cause which produces that fall, is shown by the fact that if the silver had been discovered in India, and if silver prices had risen in India before they had risen in Europe, then the difference between them would have been a penalty on the Indian exporter and a bounty on the Indian importer.

9736. (*Chairman.*) When you say the value of silver falls in Europe before it falls in India, you judge of the value having fallen in Europe by the gold price of silver?—Yes, I take account of that.

9737. How do you judge of its having fallen in India?—But I desire to explain further : I judge of it in England in this way; I find the purchasing power of gold in England in terms of commodities; then I find the price of silver in terms of gold; then I divide the one by the other, and so find the purchasing power of silver in England. I find the purchasing power of silver by the ratio of its value to gold, as compared with the ratio of gold to other commodities. The purchasing power, the value of silver in India, I measure by an index-number such as Mr. Palgrave submitted to the Commission on the Depression of Trade and Industry.

9738. By prices in India?—I get the prices of commodities directly in India; I get the gold prices in England, and divide out by the gold price of silver.

9739. Is not the evidence rather this, that whilst the price of silver or value of silver has fallen largely in England, it has not fallen at all in India?—My belief is that silver has greater purchasing power, both in England and India, than it had before. I take Mr. O'Conor's figures as representing roughly the truth, that gold prices are 30 per cent. lower, and silver prices 10 per cent. lower, than they were.

9740. (*Mr. Birch.*) How do you take your silver prices in England ?—I think that the gold price of silver has fallen about 20 per cent. and the gold price of goods has fallen about 30 per cent., and therefore the silver price of goods has fallen about 10 per cent. I do not mean to insist on this 10 per cent. as being at all exact. There are reasons, of course, why the index-numbers should vary as between the different countries; indeed one of my reasons for comparing the index-numbers of America, France, and Germany was to show that you cannot expect an exactly parallel movement in the index-numbers in different countries, whether having the same currency or not.

9741. (*Chairman.*) But, on the other hand, considering the view you were putting before us, this is just an illustration of the case where the gold value or price of silver has fallen in England prior to its having fallen in India ?—If it falls in England before it falls in India there will be a small bounty on the Indian exporter equal to the difference between its fall in the two places.

9742. In the present case it has fallen in England first ?—Yes.

9743. Then in your view has there been a bounty to the Indian exporter for some years past ?—So long as their imports of precious metals were above the average there was a very trifling bounty, a bounty exactly similar to that which would have arisen if they had wanted any other of our commodities. Supposing, for instance, that we had discovered the way of making Indian ploughs of such a character that the Indians would really buy them and use them, that would give a bounty to the Indian exporter of all things in so far as India has an increased demand for any commodity, whether it is silver or ploughs which England has. Then so far there is a bounty, but a very small bounty, to the Indian exporter.

9744. Will you let me put to you a case which has been suggested as showing a bounty, or I think it is very much the view which has been put forward, although I do not know that it has been put exactly in this way before. Supposing the gold price of wheat to have fallen from 40s. to 30s.; when the gold price of wheat was at 40s. and the rupee was at its old value, the grower in India got precisely the same number of rupees and no more than he gets now with the lower value of silver. When wheat is at 30s. he would get, with the fall of 25 per cent. in the value of silver, precisely the same number of rupees with wheat at 30s. as he did with wheat at 40s. Well now, supposing that the rupee will pay the wages of the people employed in the production of his wheat, and purchase as much of everything as it did before in India, the Indian producer is in precisely the same position with wheat at 30s., but with the lower value of silver, as he was with wheat at 40s. I am putting that assumption to you. Then it is said that that is substantially in accordance with the fact that there may be some slight change of silver prices in a few articles, but that as regards wages and matters that go to the cost of production it is true, and therefore the Indian producer with wheat at 30s. is in as good a position as he was at 40s. Now it is said that the English producer with wheat at 30s., although he might be in the same position as the Indian producer if wages and everything else had gone down 25 per cent., is now in a worse position than the Indian producer, because wages, more particularly, and other matters which go to the cost of production, have not gone down to the same extent; therefore it is said that the more favoured position of the Indian producer may be regarded as a bounty. Could you question the reasoning or the effect?—I should say that there was a *petitio principii* in the argument, and that the conclusion arrived at had unconsciously glided into the argument. The fact that industry is now capitalistic alters, in my opinion, the substance of the problem very little, but makes a considerable change in its form; therefore I will ask to be allowed to pay no attention to the fact that industries are capitalistic for the present, and to take account of it afterwards. It is, of course, true that India can export wheat or tea more profitably when exchange is 1s. 4d. than when it is 1s. 6d., if we suppose that the fall in exchange has not been accompanied by any changes in prices; but then it is of the nature of the case that it will be so accompanied, and to suppose that it is not, is to assume unconsciously the conclusion against which I am arguing. It is a

petitio principii. The argument is like this :—If a man is in the
cabin of a ship only ten feet high, and the ship sinks down twelve
feet into a trough, his head will be broken against the roof of the
cabin. This argument implicitly assumes that when the ship
falls he will not fall. But really the law of gravitation acts on
him and on the ship together. He does not break his head against
the roof of the cabin, because there is a natural law which makes
him move together with the ship. In just the same way the
change in the exchange is itself a part of a more sweeping change.
If wheat is selling at 36*s*., and a scarcity of gold lowers exchanges
from 1*s*. 6*d*. to 1*s*. 4*d*., it will also lower wheat from 36*s*. to 32*s*.;
and the Indian exporter will be where he was. Of course, silver
might fall a little faster than wheat, owing to a panic in the bullion
market; that would give a bounty to the Indian exporter equal to
the small difference between the two falls. There is no reason
why the gold price of silver should fall at a different rate from the
gold price of wheat, unless there should be a panic in the bullion
market, and, after all, such a fall would be temporary, and if it
led to silver going to India when it was not wanted there, there
would be a reaction. The argument that the fall in the gold
price of silver gives a great bounty to Indian exporters assumes
that there is great difference between silver prices in India and
Europe (after allowing for carriage). That is impossible. To
assume that it is possible is the *petitio principii* of which I complain. There can only be a small difference, and the fact that
Indian importation of silver is not large shows that the difference
is only (as it was before 1873) just enough to pay the freight of
the silver. It is a fundamental law of commerce that the silver
price of things must be the same in two countries which have free
trade with one another, after allowing for differences in the cost
of transport. If there had been for a short time any considerable
premium of this kind on exportation from India, if there had been
even for a short time a large fall in the gold price of silver in
England without a large fall in the gold price of commodities,
there would have been an enormous export of silver from Europe
to India, on a scale such as has never been approached, though
some faint indication of it was given about the year 1866, when
the French bimetallic law prevented silver from rising in Europe

relatively to the newly-imported gold, and in consequence India imported 20,000,000*l.* of silver in one year.

9745. (*Mr. Chaplin.*) What silver is there in England to go to India ? Is there a great reserve of silver in England that could go ? Where is it, I mean ?—I am not arguing that such a thing could happen. On the contrary, what I say is, that unless there were some 100,000,000*l.* of silver or so that we did not know what to do with, there could not be a great fall in the price of commodities measured in silver in England without a parallel fall in the price of commodities measured in silver in India. The assumption that there is such a bounty assumes that an event of this kind has occurred. It never has occurred and never can occur.

9746. (*Chairman.*) Still I do not think that you have quite touched the point that I have put to you, because you are accepting in your statement that the Indian producer, if the fall in silver corresponded, as you say it necessarily would, with the fall in the price of wheat, or the exported article, would be where he was before. That is just the suggestion made, that he is where he was before, but that the English producer with the same fall is not where he was before, but in a somewhat worse position ?—In that argument I understand you to refer to the special circumstances of a capitalistic producer. So I will next submit my views as to the extent to which the problem is affected by the fact that most English industries are capitalistic. It is urged that when gold rises in value relatively to silver and cotton, the Indian capitalist cotton manufacturer is not struck in the same way as the English. That is true and important. But it does not prove that there is a bounty on exportation from India. The loss to the English manufacturer is due to the fall of gold prices, and would exist whether he had an Indian competitor or not. It may be answered that is true only in the first instance ; if he had no Indian competition there would be a check to the supply of cotton manufactures, their price would gradually rise and the English manufacturer would be set on his legs again. The Indian manufacturers' competition in India and China prevents this rise, and so injures him. That is, I think, the point at issue. I contend that no such effect is possible, at least on any considerable scale. As a matter of fact the Englishman does not discontinue his business. It is

quite true that if combinations among the producers in England
were common and on a large scale, then when the supply of the
precious metals diminished by 20 per cent. they could diminish
production until the supply of goods was diminished, say 20 per
cent., and keep prices up.   That would, of course, be a great
national calamity.   Fortunately we are saved from it by the fact
that producers cannot combine in that way with one another.
We do not require the Indian producer to save us from that.
The English manufacturer, after finding that he has not made good
profits, is inclined, so to speak, to strike for a time.   If he is the
right man in the right place, he goes on after a while, but if he
is not the right man in the right place, he gives place to somebody
else who does go on.   If it had been possible for India to go on
exporting cottons and other things to England, or supplanting
English manufacturers all around and on a large scale in the Indian
market, there would have been a large number of commodities
sent from India to England without anything in return.   That is
the fundamental difficulty;   it brings us back to the broad statement with which I began, that since our imports have to be paid
for by our exports, unless the change lowers the value of Indian
cottons relatively to something else, it cannot increase the exportation of Indian cottons;   it cannot anyhow increase Indian expor-
tations altogether.   This is the main issue.   But it is worth while
to notice in passing the remarkable fact that the chief fall in
prices which is ascribed to Indian competition is not in cottons,
which are capitalistic, but in wheat, which is not capitalistic in
its production, at all events in the great wheat countries.   In
America and in Russia, wheat is not capitalistic.   Cotton is
capitalistic;   and when inquiring how far the fall of prices puts a
special penalty on capitalistic industries, we should remember
that it is Indian wheat which produces the chief disturbance, and
that competes with things which are not produced, at any rate
except in England, on the capitalistic plan.

9747. Would you let me again put the case in a concrete form,
because I am not quite sure that your observations meet the point
which I put ?   Is this suggested bounty a bounty only in this sense,
that the English producer is in a worse position than the Indian
producer by reason of the fall in the value of silver, supposing

a fall in prices which is equivalent to the fall in the value of silver ? I am not saying whether one is the effect or cause of the other, or whether they are simply coincident, a fall of 25 per cent. in the price of wheat, a fall of 25 per cent. in the gold value of silver. Now, what is put is this : supposing when wheat is at 40s., that the English producer pays one-half of that in wages and other fixed payments, and in the result he is left with 20s. Wheat goes down to 30s., he still has to make—it will simplify the case if I say there has been no drop in wages or any of the fixed payments—he still has to make a payment of 20s. in wages and fixed charges, and all that remains to him is 10s., consequently his profit is exactly 50 per cent. of what it was before. Well, you would not dispute on the hypothesis that that was a correct calculation ?—No ; but I should still say that the solution was implied in the hypothesis.

9748. Why, I am dealing only with the English producer now ; I have not come to my problem yet. My case is simply that the English producer in that case is only getting 50 per cent. of what he got before ?—On your hypothesis the results would be as you say, so far.

9749. Whether the results are as great as the hypothesis or not, if it is a fact that the wages and fixed charges have not gone down as fast as the price of wheat *pro tanto*, the English producer is in a worse position than before ?—Certainly ; on the understanding that the English producer is a capitalist farmer.

9750. I merely put it at this fixed amount in order to make my question clear. Now, suppose that the gold value of silver having gone down, the number of rupees which the Indian producer gets is the same as he got before, namely, 20 as it was before, and he pays exactly the same proportion of it away in wages and fixed charges as he did before, because they have not altered, and he gets the same residue as he did before, unless that residue will purchase for him only 50 per cent. of what it did before, is not he in a better position than the English producer ?—That I admit, and indeed I started by giving exactly that case.

9751. That is what I put to you as the suggested advantage which the Indian producer gets. I understood you to say that he got no such advantage, and that the whole thing was assumed in the form of the question ?—What I admit is, that in so far as the industry of England is capitalistic there is a great difficulty put upon the whole of it by the rise in the value of gold. What I deny is, that even when we take account of the influence of the capitalistic form of English industries, the value of silver has anything whatever to do with the fact that we import wheat from India in exchange for goods which were produced by us on the capitalistic system; the only exception which I admit being the case of our having a large quantity of silver which we do not want and India does. I hold that exactly the same argument that you have put with regard to wheat applies with regard to cutlery, which India does not produce. I hold that if the producer of cutlery has been selling a certain amount of cutlery for 40s., and in consequence of the scarcity of gold he can only sell it for 30s., and if his fixed charges have not diminished in proportion, he is so far at a loss. I admit that prices do fall faster than wages, and that the fall of prices, which I believe, on the whole, to have been no great disadvantage to the country, has put increased purchasing power into the pockets of the wage receivers. My position is that, in fact, the change has been exclusively a change in the value of gold, and that silver has had scarcely anything to do with it.

9752. Why a change in the value of gold and not silver, when you are looking at it as between a silver and a gold using country ?—The argument that the fall in gold prices injures the capitalistic producer would have applied to cutlery exactly as it applies to wheat; and the only answer that could be given from the other side is this, if cutlery manufacturers could only sell their cutlery for 40s., and they were not able to reduce their fixed charges, they would then combine and diminish the supply of cutlery, and by diminishing the supply force up its price. They cannot do that with regard to wheat, and in so far as they cannot I admit that the producers of wheat are in a worse position than the producers of cutlery.

9753. But supposing you had a case of a manufacturer of cutlery, whose fixed charges had gone down precisely in corre-spondence with the fall in the price; would not he have an advan-tage in competition with the man who had to take an equally lower price without the fixed charges going down in the same ratio ?—He would be putting more money into his pockets than the other man; I do not deny that while the Indian capitalistic producer is making money, the English capitalistic producer is losing money. But that does not enable the Indian producer to undersell the English in one class of goods more than in another. And the Indian exporters cannot undersell the English exporters all round, for if they did we should get a great number of commodities presented to us for nothing.

9754. (*Mr. Chaplin.*) When you speak of the cutlery being produced, are you assuming that it is produced in India as well as in England ?—No. My position is that the difficulty which the employer finds in getting wages to follow prices—a difficulty at which I rejoice, on the whole—that that difficulty has nothing to do with silver; that it exists in the cutlery trade every bit as much as in those trades which are in competition with silver countries.

9755. What I mean is this : if the cutlery is not produced in India as well as in England, it is not an analogous case to the wheat question where it is in both countries ?—That is why I bring it forward; I submit that the difficulty exists without any reference to silver, and would be the same if India had a gold currency.

9756. (*Chairman.*) But let me put this : You admit that the producer in India may be making a larger profit; that the Indian producer can be making a profit when the English producer can be making no profit ?—Certainly.

9757. Well, if that is the case, wil not the tendency be that the cultivation should cease in the place where the producer cannot make a profit, and go on in the place where the producer can make a profit ?—There might be such a tendency; the fall of profits resulting from low prices might throw production in England out of gear, our factories might stand idle; we might bring back our capital from abroad and import Indian goods without sending back English goods to pay for them. But the export statistics prove that there has been no such tendency.

9758. Still there may be goods to go back as against wheat, because if the production of wheat ceased to-morrow all over England, there would be goods to go back ?—That appears to me to assume that the change in the price of wheat is due to a change in the value of wheat relatively to other commodities.

9759. I am expressing no opinion upon it at all; what was suggested was that the effect of this change in the relation of silver to gold might be that the Indian producer could make a profit at a price at which the English producer could not make a profit, and the result might be to throw land out of cultivation in this country—in wheat I mean—whilst it would still remain profitable for wheat-growing in India, and that was what was called giving a bounty to the Indian producer, giving him an advantage in competition ?—The whole point turns on your first sentence. You say there would be English commodities to go back. Everything turns on that. If I admitted that I should admit everything. My whole point is that the change in the relative values of gold and silver does not lower the value of wheat relatively to other commodities, and that therefore there is no reason why we should accept wheat and send cutlery in exchange, unless there has been some independent cause tending to lower the value of wheat relatively to cutlery in India, or the value of cutlery relatively to wheat in England.

9760. Yes; but supposing we accept wheat, why should we not in return for that wheat send Manchester goods ?—Because the change which we have so far considered, that is, the change in the gold value of silver, has not altered the value of wheat relatively to Manchester goods. Of course wheat is a very awkward thing to take, because there are so many things that disturb its value; it is affected by harvests and by many other causes special to it. I would prefer to take cottons or anything of that kind. There is no reason why cottons should be sent here, or why there should be a falling off in the sending of cottons from here to India, and the place of those goods taken by some other goods. The question whether cutlery goes in place of cottons depends on the relative values of the two. If the value of gold has risen relatively to cottons and cutlery equally, then there is no reason why cutlery should go instead of cottons.

9761. Take the great staple commodity which does go from this country to India—cotton goods; supposing that India cannot get more for her produce than she could get before in rupees, not a larger number of rupees, which means a lower gold price; if she cannot get more rupees for her produce she cannot pay more rupees for produce that she wants to buy in return for it, and get back in exchange for it, but she can give the same number of rupees, which means a lower gold price, would not that be calculated to lower the price of the commodities which are sent from this country to India, inasmuch as she could only give the same number of rupees, which means a lower gold price? This country would have, if possible, to supply them at a lower gold price, so that might not the prices react in that way, the one on the other? —I cannot see how a fall in the gold prices, all round, accompanied by, I will say, stationary silver prices, all round, should enable India to increase her exportation of anything unless by diminishing her exportation of something else, or by her increasing her importation of something else, including silver.

9762. (*Sir T. Farrer.*) May I go back to your cutlery illustration? You say that the English manufacturer of cutlery would be just as badly off in the case of a fall of the gold price as the manufacturer of something in which India competes with him; but supposing a manufactory of cutlery were started in India which made exactly the same things that the English manufacturer made in cutlery, and that the Indian manufacturer pays only the same wages that he did before, would the competition of the Indian manufacturer of cutlery be an additional item as against the English manufacturer?—My position, you see is, that when gold prices fall, wages tend to fall. In so far as they do not fall, the employer has to suffer, and I pity him as an individual. What I do not see is, that a change in the distribution of wealth between employer and employed, which is common to all industries, affects the relative values of different commodities. I cannot see how India can send us more goods unless we send her more goods in return. If she has been sending us more of one thing, and we send more of something else in return, that can be only because the amount of money at which the things she sends us can be sold in England will buy in England a larger amount of things, so that she will get these new things at a cheaper rate than she could get them at before, and consequently is willing to buy things which before she had not cared to take. But that means that there has been a fall in the relative expense of production of those two things.

9763. (*Chairman.*) But why necessarily in the relative expense of production ? Why may it not be the things that were previously sent at a considerable profit may now be sent at a bare margin of profit ?—Because there is no reason why there should be a larger rate of profit in the cutlery trade than the cotton trade. You must assume, of course, that both trades are in the same condition.

9764. A man who wants to get rid of his article, if he cannot get a high price for it, will take the lowest price at which it is profitable for him to make it, and if India, having the same number of rupees as before, can only exchange these rupees for a smaller amount of gold than before, must not that tend to bring down the gold price ? India cannot give more rupees ; she wants the goods ; must not that tend to bring down the price to such a point as may leave a bare margin of profit, but be still profitable to the English manufacturer ?—May I put the case definitely in this way ? I will take the case in which India is selling cottons in China as against the English producer.

9765. That is entirely outside my question, which relates to trade between England and India, I am not on that Bombay case at all. The question is whether there is or is not a tendency, owing to the fall of silver, to reduce the gold price of the articles which we export to India ?—My opinion is that the gold prices of all commodities fall together in consequence of the scarcity of gold, and that if it were possible for India to send us cotton and take back cutlery, that would be only because cutlery could be produced in England at a lower rate relatively to cotton than before.

9766. But may it not be as much from the abundance of silver as from the scarcity of gold ; why always the scarcity of gold ?— Because there has not been an abundance of silver ; silver prices have not fallen, and therefore I prefer to take the cases as they are. If you take the other case you would then have to go away from actual facts, but even then you would arrive at the same result by another route.

9767. But is it perfectly clear that all gold prices have fallen ? —That the average of gold prices has fallen, that is all that I want.

9768. But is it all that you want ? You would not say because one commodity had fallen largely that there has been an appreciation of gold. How many must fall before you would say there is an appreciation of gold ?—That is what I wanted to guard myself about in my first answers. I quite admit that it would be possible for there to be a general fall of prices without anything that you could call a rise in the real value of gold. But on further consideration I see I need not pursue that point further. I can alter my wording so as to avoid the necessity for recalling the distinction I then made between the different uses of the term "appreciation of gold." I may drop the phrase "a scarcity of gold," and say there is a fall of gold prices. That is all I want, I do not want the scarcity of gold. It is enough for my present purpose that there is, as matter of fact, a fall of gold prices.

9769. But one of the things we have to consider is what has produced that fall of gold prices, because there are those who assert that the fall of gold prices has been produced by the fall in the relation of silver to gold, and that that is the very thing which has brought about a fall in gold prices, so that to solve that question one can hardly solve it by starting simply with the proposition that there has been a fall in gold prices. One suggestion made to us is this : the demonetisation of silver, and the throwing of a large quantity on the market, changed the relation of silver to gold and brought down the value of silver, and, consequently, made the ratio of silver to gold different to what it was before. Then it is suggested that the effect of that is to tend to bring down the gold price of those articles which are produced in the silver-using country, and to bring down the gold price of those articles which are exchanged with the produce of the silver-using country; that that is the primary effect upon prices, but that reacts upon other prices, and so tends to bring down prices generally. That is one theory which has been put before us. That, you will admit, is hardly solved by saying that there has been a general fall in prices ?—No, I do not admit that the suggestion you have just quoted has any reasonableness, but I need not enter on that question just now. All I meant was that I did not want, for the purpose of this particular argument, to assume anything as to the cause of the fall of prices. I only require to assume that the relation of gold to commodities, and the methods of business, is such that there has been a fall in the prices of most commodities. I argue that the producer of cutlery is under just the same advantage as the producer of cottons, and that therefore the fall in the gold price of silver cannot enable the Indian producer to send us cottons and to take back cutlery, or to send us anything else that is not affected by some special cause and take back cutlery. The argument that the producer of wheat is hampered by having a fall of price, and having great difficulty in reducing his fixed charges, applies to the producer of cutlery equally. It applies to the producers of those things which are sent to India in exchange for her goods, as well as to the producers of those English goods which compete, here or elsewhere, with Indian goods.

9770. (*Mr. Montagu.*) Lord Herschell put a question with regard to the facilities afforded to the producer of wheat in India. Well now, if he has those facilities, and the cultivation of wheat is extended in India, surely those cultivators who reap the advantage of the extended cultivation might be enabled to take Manchester goods in exchange for a greater amount of wheat sent her, and consequently, although the manufacturer of Manchester goods might be in a good position, it would not affect the agriculturist ?— Quite so, in so far as the facilities which the producer of wheat has are peculiar to wheat, and do not extend to jute and silk and cotton and other things. I quite admit that the fall in the price of wheat has been very great. I say it is due exclusively, or almost exclusively, to the fall in the price of iron; that silver has had no effect upon it whatever; but that the fall in the price of iron and steel has affected it.

9771. But does that affect the relative positions between the cultivator of wheat in India and the cultivator of wheat in England ?—Yes, certainly, because if you look at the map of India contained in the statistical atlas published by the Government, you will see that it is not, like rice and jute, grown on the bottom lands; it is grown inland, and therefore the development of railways has lowered the value of wheat relatively to other things at the seaboard. And if we may now turn aside from general reasoning to the statistical aspects of the problem, we find, I think, that the increased importation of Indian wheat is due to causes which have changed its value relatively to other Indian products, and not to changes in the gold value of silver which affect all Indian products alike. For one thing, I have analysed the exports of India, and I admit that her exports to silver countries have positively fallen off. While her exports to gold countries have increased enormously her exports to silver countries have fallen off.

9772. (*Chairman.*) Raw products as well as manufactured articles ?—Yes. Of course opium is an important element in the list of Indian exports to China.

9773. (*Mr. Barbour.*) What are the silver-using countries the exports to which have fallen off ?—China and the Straits Settlements.

9774. Have her exports to China fallen off ?—Yes, to China and the Straits Settlements.

9775. I can only think of two exports of importance to China, one is opium and the other is cotton goods ?—The exports are in the *Statistical Abstract for India.* She has gained in tea as against China, she has lost in silk as against gold countries. If we are to look at it as a matter of statistical evidence, everything points to the fact that there is no gain whatever to India in selling in a gold country. Her production of silk has fallen off very much under the competition of gold countries. Her production of tea has increased though she has had to compete with a silver country. And again you see my contention is that the importation of Indian wheat here is due exclusively to the development of railways and the lowering of freights. To those two causes perhaps I should add, as a temporary cause which is likely very soon to pass away, a series of very favourable harvests. Should India have a famine the exportation of large quantities of wheat would, of course, all be stopped. If the cause of that large exportation had been the rate of exchanges, then we should have found Indian wheat coming a long time ago. In 1876 the price of silver was low, but she exported then only 1,000,000*l.* of wheat as against 8,000,000*l.*, and only 300,000*l.* worth of cotton twist as against 2,800,000*l.* now.

9776. (*Mr. Chaplin.*) But surely that was very shortly after the depreciation of silver, or at all events the exchange between

G

gold and silver, occurred?—That is what I say; the exchange between gold and silver has nothing to do with it. The facilities for bringing the wheat to the seaboard have been the cause of it. If it were owing to the exchange it would have begun a long time ago.

9777. (*Mr. Montagu.*) Was it not quite temporary in 1876? Did it not recover immediately after to higher than the present price?—Yes; but my position is that if the low rate of exchange did give a large bounty to the Indian exporter we should have had Indian goods coming in long ago.

9778. (*Mr. Chaplin.*) The Indian wheat?—So far as it was grown; but it could not be carried to the seaboard because there were few railways.

9779. You would admit that that would develop a great trade in wheat in two years?—It might have developed a great deal, but they could not carry the wheat to the seaboard because there were few railways.

9780. (*Mr. Montagu.*) That lasted only two or three months. How would you expect that to have any effect at all?—There was a considerable fall which continued for some time.

9781. (*Mr. Barbour.*) There was a panic in the middle of 1876; it ceased towards the end of the year?—But the average price of silver was low about that time.

9782. (*Mr. Chaplin.*) Do I understand you then to deny that the exchange does give a bounty at all to the exporter of Indian wheat?—Absolutely.

9783. But I think you said in the earlier part of your evidence that it did give a bounty during a certain interval?—During the interval in which she was importing silver in exceptionally large quantities, but that is a thing which she is not doing now. If she were to take an increased amount of silver, that would give a small bounty to her exporters, so long as she was taking it; and for several years she did take a great deal.

9784. That interval, you contend, now has expired?—Practically, as is shown by the statistics of the imports of silver into India.

9785. I think you said silver has appreciated in relation to commodities?—I take that statement chiefly from Mr. O'Conor.

9786. But you agreed with the statement ?—I have no direct knowledge.

9787. Would that mean everywhere ?—His statement was with regard to India. The statement that it has appreciated with regard to England, I got from the statistics which have been submitted to you by Mr. Sauerbeck.

9788. At all events you would not dispute that the rupee in India, for instance, buys as much or more commodities at present as it ever did ?—I admit that it does.

9789. But it has depreciated in relation to gold ?—Yes, it has a lower value relatively to gold.

9790. The rupee used to be worth nearly 2s., I think ?—Yes.

9791. And it is now worth about 1s. 5d. ?—Yes.

9792. Then 2l. in gold formerly, with the rupee at 2s., would buy 20 rupees ?—Yes.

9793. 1l. 10s. in gold at the present price of the rupee would buy nearly the same ?—Yes.

9794. Then, as a matter of fact, the Indian grower of wheat who now gets 1l. 10s. for his quarter of wheat is as well off as when he got 2l. ?—Yes.

9795. The position of the English grower meanwhile is that he is losing 10s. on every quarter, and to that extent he is worse off ?—On the supposition that the prices of other things have not fallen in the same proportion, and in so far as he has to hire labour ; for I am happy to say that he has to pay higher real wages.

9796. But it is the case, is it not, that, but for this difference in the exchange between gold and silver, they would both equally be losers ?—I think that if we had had a bimetallic currency throughout there would probably have been very great losses to wheat farmers in England and in America in consequence of the great increase in the areas of the wheat farms of the world. Indian farmers need not have lost, because the railways and low freights would have enabled them to get as good a price as ever on the farm, even while the price in English ports fell.

9797. But still, if the rupee were now worth 2s. instead of 1s. 4d., the Indian grower would not get so many rupees for his wheat now at 1l. 10s. a quarter as he did when it made 2l. ?—No.

9798. Then to that extent he would be a loser ?—The question would be what would have happened to the prices of other things. I think you are taking a particular supposition as to them.

9799. No; but I am urging on the supposition that the rupee at present does buy, as you have told us, as much as it bought before?—But what I contend is that if there had been no change in the exchange silver, prices in India would have fallen as fast as gold prices in England.

9800. I am asking you questions about what happened at the present moment?—I think that you slip your conclusion into your question by assuming that a person will knock his head against the ceiling of a cabin if a person is in the cabin of a ship the roof of which is ten feet high, and the ship sinks fifteen feet. I say, no. In order to get at your conclusion, you have to assume that he remains stationary when the ship sinks, and that is the whole question.

9801. I do not want to ask you questions as to what he would do or what would happen to him, but I am trying to arrive at facts as to what does happen at the present moment. You have admitted then that the position of the English grower is worse by 10s. a quarter than it was when his wheat was 2l. a quarter?— No, I have not admitted that.

9802. But is that capable of dispute?—Yes; because that assumes that the prices of other things are the same. Supposing that the wages and rents had fallen in proportion to the fall of other commodities, he would not be affected at all, he would simply use fewer counters; he would get fewer counters, and he would pay away proportionately fewer counters.

9803. But I gathered from you that the position of the Indian grower at all events was this, that the rupees that he got were as valuable to him as ever they were inasmuch as they would buy as much as they did at any other period?—Certainly.

9804. Very well, to that extent he must be a gainer, must he not, as compared with the English producer; in so far as he is receiving the same price for his wheat as compared with the English grower, who is losing 10s. a quarter?—I deny that the English grower is losing 10s. a quarter.

9805. But in price I mean?—But price does not matter. Supposing the price of everything were doubled, nobody would be any richer; it is simply a question of using more counters. Of course, in so far as the English farmer is not able to reduce his fixed charges, in so far he is suffering. He has to go without income which, by a better distribution of wealth, tends more and more in the favour of the working classes; this fall of prices causes the wealth of the country in my opinion to be more equally distributed than it would be if the high prices of 1873 had been maintained.

9806. You hold that the working classes have been gainers ?— Yes.

The witness withdrew.
Adjourned till Monday, January 16, 1888.

January 16, 1888.

THE RIGHT HON. LORD HERSCHELL, the Chairman, presiding.

MR. D. M. BARBOUR, C.S.I.
MR. J. W. BIRCH.
MR. HENRY CHAPLIN, M.P.
MR. L. COURTNEY, M.P.
MR. C. W. FREMANTLE, C.B.
MR. S. MONTAGU, M.P., and
MR. GEO. H. MURRAY, *Secretary.*

Mr. ALFRED MARSHALL re-called and examined.

9807. (*Chairman.*) You have considered the question as to
the effect upon the Indian Government of the lowered value of
silver?—Yes. There is a belief among the general public that
the Indian Government loses a very great deal more than really
it does. I am aware that that view is not shared by the leading
Indian officials; in fact, I have noticed evidence to that effect,
and I therefore do not propose to offer any remarks on that part
of the subject. But I thought that in some evidence, with which
in other respects I entirely agree, it was implied that the prospects
of a future fall in the gold price of silver afforded a strong reason
against private investments in Indian railways. I submit that
the value of silver has scarcely anything to do with the question,
whether it is worth while for private people to start new railways
in India. I admit that if the Government has to draw its income
in rupees, and the number of rupees is inelastic, then, in so far
as it gives a guarantee for the payment of a certain number of
pounds to English investors, in so far the Government is incurring
a greater risk if the gold value of silver is likely to fall than if it
is not. But if we look at a railway, started entirely by private
enterprise, without any Government guarantee, it seems to me
that the question whether it is worth while to borrow a million

pounds, at say 4 per cent., depends entirely upon the future value of gold, and that the value of silver has nothing to do with it in the long run. Of course, I admit that if the fares, which they were at liberty to charge, were fixed by the Government in such a way that when they wanted to raise their rupee charges they could not, then a further fall in the gold price of the rupee might injure the investors. But in general a railway is practically free to fix its fares at that level which will give it the greatest net return, and it seems to me that the position, therefore, of an Indian railway is substantially the same as that of an Australian railway. If an annual payment for interest on debentures of 40,000*l*. will have a greater real value twenty years hence than now, that is, so far, a reason against starting new railways in India or in Australia. What I wish to submit is, that the two cases are parallel. That the Indian railway being free to so fix its fares and rates as to give it the greatest net returns, if the gold price of the rupee falls, and therefore more counters are used in India, they will simply have accounts kept in a larger amount of counters; they will not have to pay a greater real value to their debenture holders than the Australian railway.

9808. Yes, but what has been suggested is, that the uncertainty of the return keeps people from investing. For example, supposing railway fares to remain the same, and expenses the same, and consequently the net earnings the same, in two succeeding years, with the rupee in the one case at 1*s*. 6*d*., and in the other at 1*s*. 3*d*., the dividend which the English investor would get would be very different; because, although he would get the same rupee dividend, he would get a gold dividend differing very much in amount ?—Yes, but that does not seem to me to be conclusive. It seems to me that supposing the rupee fare remains unchanged, and the gold price of the rupee falls—I will take now that the value of gold remains stationary—that would mean that the real value of the rupee has fallen, and therefore that the railways have lowered their real charges. Now everybody knows that it is a great question whether many of our railways could not improve their dividends by a further lowering of their fares; and I think that considering that the railway companies have practically the power of raising their charge, if they find that the number of the rupees that they charge for a certain distance gives them a less total net return than they would get from making a higher charge; a change in the value of the rupee will not alter the real profitableness of the railway, so long as the real value of the gold which has to be paid to the debenture holders has not changed, and if the value of gold should rise, the extra burden arising from the payment of fixed gold charges would fall with equal weight on the shareholders of an Indian and an Australian railway.

9809. But supposing that nobody gets higher wages in India or higher prices for his produce, by reason of the fall, or coincident with the fall in the gold price of silver, people would not be able to afford to pay more rupees for their travelling, would they? —If the fall in the gold price of silver is brought about by a stationary value of gold and a fall in the value of silver, then I think that the evidence that we have, that, in spite of popular opinion to the contrary, prices in India fluctuate as much as they do in England, would lead us to believe that prices and wages would follow the movement.

9810. But I rather thought the evidence was that although the gold price of silver had fallen 25 per cent., wages and other things in India had not risen to anything like the same extent? —As matter of fact I believe they have fallen. I accept Mr. O'Conor's result, that the gold price of silver has fallen about 30 per cent., that the gold price of commodities has fallen 20 per cent., and that the silver price of commodities has fallen 10 per cent. Since the fall of the gold price of commodities has been greater than the fall of the gold price of silver, there has been no reason at all why silver prices should rise. Silver prices naturally fall because the gold price of silver has fallen only 20 per cent., while the gold price of commodities has fallen 30 per cent.

9811. I do not quite understand. Do you dispute that there would be the uncertainty, which has been suggested, as to the return for the investment; an uncertainty not depending upon the mode in which the business was carried on, or the circumstances that affect it, but arising from changes in the value of silver; do you deny that that uncertainty would exist, or do you say that people would not be affected by it?—I deny that it would exist as an important element. Of course when a railway makes a decision to charge any particular fare for a journey, it has to make a rough shot at what is likely to be the future of prices. Probably a good many prices charged, particularly in the South of England, are higher than the true economical rate, that is, than the rate which would give the greatest net return to the company; there is always a certain risk in fixing any rate. You may misjudge the nature of the future traffic, and find afterwards that you would have got a greater net return by choosing a rate either a little higher or a little lower than that which you have fixed on. One cause of this risk is the chance of changes in the value of gold; and this exists quite independently of the silver question, and in countries in which fares, dividends, and interest are all paid in gold. In fixing the charges of an English railway, for instance, if you thought that gold prices were going to rise you would naturally fix your rate a little higher than if you thought gold prices were going to fall. On the average, railway companies do manage so to fix their rates as to give them something near the maximum net dividend. That maximum net dividend is a maximum net income of real purchasing power; and it makes very little difference in the long run whether it comes from the first in the form of gold, which gives a certain real purchasing power, or whether it comes in the first instance in rupees, which give the same real purchasing power. But of course the shareholders do not get all this net income; they have to pay out of it interest on debentures, probably in gold, and here the value of gold is of real importance, it is not a mere counter. If there should be any rise in the value of gold, that would, I admit, put an extra burden on a private railway company in India; but it would put exactly the same extra burden on a private railway in Australia.

9812. (*Mr. Barbour.*) I should like to give an example of what might actually occur. In the first six months of 1876 the price of silver fell about 20 per cent., I think?—Yes.

9813. And recovered again. A railway company having to remit home its dividend in the middle of the year would have lost 20 per cent. by the exchange alone. It could not have raised its fares or lowered them, as the silver fell first and rose afterwards ?—Yes, I quite admit that so far as temporary fluctuations go there would be a very considerable difficulty. But I am looking at the value of the property in the long run.

9814. (*Mr. Montagu.*) Is it not a fact that the last issue of stock of a private railway company in India has occasioned loss to the public ? The Bengal and North-Western, for instance, pays 4 per cent. gained without a guarantee, but it is at a considerable discount, whereas stocks with a gold guarantee of 4 per cent. are all at a premium. Would not that show that in the public estimation the difficulty connected with silver would prevent their investing ?—Of course the fact that a railway has paid more than 4 per cent. for a given number of years is not a guarantee that it will go on paying as much as 4 per cent. A person who understands the circumstances of the railway minutely may have special reasons for believing that it will continue to pay 4 per cent., or even that after a time it will pay 6 per cent., and then he will give a high price for it. But *primâ facie* it is not worth so much as a guaranteed debenture of 4 per cent.

9815. (*Chairman.*) But is it altogether unreasonable, this apprehension of the public ? Although property may in the long run, as you say, be worth as much, people do not like, owing to a change which has no relation to the enterprise in which they have invested, their income to be varying from year to year ?—I do not deny that. I admitted that to Mr. Barbour completely.

9816. Passing from that to the question of the effect of the fall of prices, which has taken place as regards most articles, what have you to say ?—What I have to say is more negative than positive. Looking at the periods in England in which there has been the greatest distress, I find that they are periods of rising prices. There has never been, I think, anything like as much distress in England as under the later Tudors and at the beginning of this century; and in each of these periods prices were rising very fast. I quite admit that when prices are falling everybody who undertakes a business risk is likely to have his risks turn out worse than if prices were rising, and I admit that when a fall of prices sets in, many business men strike. That is, they say, "We will not keep our mills running full time," or "We will go out of business." But after they have struck for a little while it occurs to them that there is no great use in striking, that although they may lose money by working their mills, they would lose more money by not working them. Of course if they can manage to get a combination to check production of one particular article, and so artificially raise its price, then, no doubt, they may gain at the expense of the community by so doing. But such schemes have never lasted on a large scale for any long time, and after a little while the undertaker of the business generally finds that running half time loses him more money than running full time, and therefore if he can see his way to going on with full work he does. Of course there are a few men who positively refuse to go on with their business. Some great works have been completely closed, and never reopened; but these are exceptional cases, due to exceptional causes. As a rule when closed they are sold to new men, who, purchasing them at a comparatively low rate, have all the benefit of the past fall of prices, and are able to go on, and make profits. Therefore I think that one wants very much stronger statistical evidence than one yet has to prove that a fall of prices diminishes perceptibly and in the long run the total productiveness of industry. Supposing that it does not diminish considerably the total productiveness of industry, then its effect is, I think, on the whole good; because it certainly tends to cause a distribution of wealth better than that which we should otherwise have. No doubt some rich lenders of money in the form of debentures and other ways get their incomes increased at the expense of the public, which I regret; but the greater part of the redistribution is in the direction of giving higher real wages and real salaries to the employés, and that, I think, is a gain. If then a fall of prices has the effect of not much altering the total amount of production, but putting more real value into the hands of the poorer classes, I regard it so far, not as a loss to the country, but as a gain. I was very much struck by observing that in some of the evidence given to show that the fall of prices was doing great harm, it was argued that we were suffering from general over-production, a malady which I contend we cannot suffer from, and that that was partly due to the fact that improvements were going on now much faster than at any other time;

and the reason given for this was that when prices are falling, manufacturers are put on their mettle and exert themselves to the utmost to invent improved methods and to avail themselves of the improvements made by others, and I know, from my own observation, that this is true. But when prices are rising manufacturers are well contented to let things go on as they are. Of course the effect of these improvements in production is very often temporarily disastrous to the particular trade which makes them. It results in an excessive supply of that particular commodity, which therefore falls in value relatively to others, and those in it really lose by the improvements by which the community gains. But I have not seen any reason to doubt that those changes are for the benefit of the community. Again, those who have control of our loan fund are much more careful about their loans when prices are falling than when prices are rising; and this works, I think, two ways. No doubt sometimes they refuse loans to young men who might have turned the loans to good account, but in quite as many cases, I believe, they are saved from lending to people who had the capacity for riding upon the surface of the rising tide, but who had not the capacity for contending against the stream; and I think it is best in the interests of the community that people of this sort should not be able to borrow very easily; it is best that their weakness should show itself soon, and that they should make way for stronger men, that these loans should not be made. I see that a good deal of evidence has been given with regard to the unsteadiness of employment now.

I have now to approach a matter on which I must speak with diffidence, for I have very little to go by except general impressions, and general impressions on a matter of this sort are not worth much; but, on the other hand, I do not know that anybody else has anything else but general impressions, and I have been studying for many years the question whether the tendency of our modern forms of industry is not to increase irregularity of employment. I believe that it is not, and I believe that the statistical evidence brought forward to prove that it is, is invalid. I [1] spent a winter some years ago at Palermo; the mediæval

---

[1] Cf. *Money, Credit and Commerce*, p. 242-3.

traditions of industry go on there; and everything that one reads about with regard to the *clientèle* of the well-to-do houses among the working-men in the Middle Ages one finds in Palermo now. If you had tried to collect statistics of want of employment you would probably have found next to none. Scarcely anybody was thrown out of regular employment because scarcely anybody ever was in it; there were none of those interruptions of employment which arise from modern forms of industry, and about which sensational articles are written in the newspapers. But I doubt whether the average employment of the handicraftsman in Palermo is more than half as great as in the East End of London in depressed times; and the average annual earnings are probably not a quarter as high. I know that there are certain cases in which hirings were made for the year and in which the employer was practically bound to give some sort of sustenance to the employé for the year, but I believe that in those parts of the Middle Ages in which that system prevailed, the employé in return often gave up so much of his freedom that it might be questioned whether he was completely a free man. I have been struck by the objections which were brought forward at a recent meeting to discuss the existing distress, objections raised to the sufficiency of the official returns of unemployment. It was said that when people worked at their own homes, you could not prove that they were thrown out of employment because the irregularity of their employment was the rule and not the exception. If they had no work to-day they might have it to-morrow, if they were in work to-day they had no reason for supposing that they would to-morrow. Now those people were in the same conditions as the majority of people in the mediæval times— they took a job when it came to them. They consequently never were " out of employment "; there was nothing to get into the newspapers as it were. When now a factory with 5,000 hands works half time or closes its doors the fact is telegraphed all over England; but if 5,000 people, each working in their own homes, get a little less steady employment than before there is nothing to attract attention, at all events outside of their immediate neighbourhood. I do not know whether the Commission are inclined to attach any weight to the evidence that has been drawn

in newspapers and elsewhere as to the want of employment from
the returns published by Mr. Burnett in his excellent report on
Trade Unions. I think I should perhaps like to give my reasons
for believing that those returns do not show exactly what they
appear to do. Mr. Burnett gave, firstly, a list of the growth of
a number of the leading trades unions, and secondly a statement
of the payment for unemployed benefit in each successive year,
and although the present time is not nearly the worst, yet there
is no doubt that on the average there has been a movement to
the bad, and it is said, if this is true of unionists the state of want
of employment of non-unionists must be even worse. That
seems to me not valid. In the first place, the growth in the
number of the unionists shown by the first table is enormous.
Now I have been told that there are some working men who
believe that the proportion of skilled labourers to unskilled has
increased as fast as the number of unionists. If we admitted
that we should admit a great deal more than I want to prove.
It would imply that the proportion of skilled to unskilled labourers
has been multiplied something like fourfold since 1850, and that
would mean that the average rate of wages in different occupations
throughout the country would have very much increased. I
think it is important in this connection to point out that the
tendency, in a country which is growing into the use of skilled
industry, is for the rate of wages to fall in many employments at
the same time that the average rate of wages of all the wage
receivers taken together tends to rise. The statistical paradox
that average wages may rise while the wages in every single trade
are falling, has long been familiar to statisticians; but as I do
not think it has been brought before the Commission, and is a
matter of very great importance in interpreting these statistics,
I think I should like to give you an instance. Suppose that
some time ago skilled labour had 40s. and unskilled labour 16s.,
but at that time the unskilled labourers were twice as numerous
as the skilled; suppose that after a time there is a fall in the
wages of every trade; that the skilled wages fall to 36s., and
the unskilled wages to 15s.; but that at the same time the number
of skilled increases till it is twice as great as that of the unskilled;
the result would have been a fall of wages, as shown by almost

every statistical method that is used not by the very, very few statisticians who are really careful, but by certainly 90 per cent. of people who write about statistics. But the real result would be that the wages which were on the average 24s. in the former period would have risen to 29s. in the latter. If, therefore, it is true that the ranks of skilled industry have increased in nearly as great a proportion as the ranks of trade-unionists, we may be quite sure that the extremest estimates that have been given of the rise of the average wages in the working classes are below the real truth.

9817. You mean owing to the increase in the proportion of skilled to unskilled ?—Yes. I myself think that the proportion of skilled to unskilled workers, though it may have doubled since 1850, has not increased nearly fourfold. It is most unfortunate that our industrial statistics are in so deplorable a condition that one cannot verify this statement exactly. But without pretending to minute accuracy, we may safely conclude that the unionists, though still consisting chiefly of picked workers, have so far extended their numbers that their average efficiency is not so much above the average efficiency of all the members of their respective trades as it used to be; and that is a reason for believing that the unions would have a larger share of unemployed than they used to have. But next it is urged by those who lay stress on Mr. Burnett's tables that the unionists, being on the average the best men in their trade, would be likely to be employed when the non-unionists were not employed; and this, both on general grounds and in particular, because every unionist regards it as his duty to tell every other unionist of a good opening, before he tells a non-unionist of it; and of course this is specially important in the case of a unionist foreman. On the other hand, it must be remembered that many employers object to having a unionist as foreman. I do not wish to lay very great stress on this, because it is said, and I am quite convinced that it is true, that in a great many works in which the employer says confidently that he has no unionists at all he has many, and in particular his foremen are often unionists when he thinks they are not. I admit that; I think that an important argument on the side of those who regard these figures as significant. But, on the other hand, these arguments, based on the tendency of unionists to help one another to find work, told in favour of unionists in the earlier times as much as they do now. My next point is that unionists are often prevented by their rules from accepting employment which non-unionists are very glad to take. Almost every union is discussing from time to time the question whether it does not lose more by those rules that keep out competent non-unionists than by altering those rules so as to admit them. There is one trade, the statistics of which have been made more use of in popular discussions than any other, the founders' trade. I have studied that trade very carefully by inquiries among the employed, as well as among the employers in the trade, and I believe there are many places in which a very large percentage of unionists are out of employment, and scarcely any non-unionists. It is a trade in which mechanical appliances are displacing manual skill faster than almost any other, and in which the displaced manual skill finds it difficult to get any other occupation. It is quite different from the engineers' trade in that respect, and a great many of the most progressive works are works that do business in a way which the union will not allow. My next point is, that there is a perpetual change in the character of the work which goes under any particular name. In agriculture probably the real demand for skill is increased. It is probable that the variety of implements which the farm labourer has to use really causes him to require greater intelligence now than he did some time ago. The same is true of a few other trades. But some of those trades which had from the first to do with machinery require now not more than half or even one-fourth of the skill which they did twenty or thirty years ago. The improvement of the machines has made them so far automatic that the person who minds them, and goes by the old name, is now a man of altogether different class from the man who was entered by that name before. The men who would have managed the machine when it was a difficult thing to manage have now passed on to some other trade, probably some of those new trades which are now being developed, as, for instance, those concerned with electricity, and which take picked men from other trades. My next point is the difficulty about old men. Everybody knows that an insurance society's budget looks very much better when it is young, and has none but young men in it, than after it has been in existence some time. Now a trades union is to a very great extent an insurance society. The average age of the unionists in 1886 is greater than that of the unionists twenty years ago, because nobody is admitted to join a union when he is approaching to the age at which he would become a burden on the funds. And this brings me to my last point, which is, that the unions having a fixed minimum wage for each locality, perhaps it is to the interest of the employer to dismiss a man as soon as he begins to show grey hairs, when if he were a non-unionist he might take a lower wage. Complaints on this ground against the employer are very bitter, as bitter perhaps as any which are made. I do not myself acquit the unions of blame. It is true that within the last few years they are very slowly opening their minds to the fact that it would be better policy to allow a man when he gets old to work for a little less than the standard wage, and many unions have moved in that direction, and I believe there will be further movements in that direction; but meanwhile, the difficulty which grey-haired men find in getting work, if they may not take less than full wages, is, I believe, one of the chief causes why the number of unemployed unionists increases. All these considerations support the belief that if the average steadiness of employment throughout the country had remained stationary, changing neither for better nor for worse, the unemployed benefit of the trades unions would have increased faster than it has done.

9818. (*Mr. Chaplin.*) I think you expressed the opinion that the greatest distress prevailed, generally speaking, during a period of high or rising prices?—No, I do not say that. I think I stated that the two periods of greatest distress that I knew were two periods of rapidly rising prices. I do not mean that in every period of rising prices there has been distress.

9819. You mean to say then that there have been periods of rising prices when there has been great prosperity?—Yes, but I think that the prosperity has been caused by other things, and I think the real prosperity has not been greater than it would have been if prices had not risen so fast. I think the rise of

H

prices has caused the apparent prosperity to be much greater than the real; has caused an immense number of incompetent persons to get into the control of a business which they cannot manage except when prices are rising. As soon as prices fall, and sooner or later they must fall, these people fail, and their failure reacts on others and causes widespread distress. That is what I regard as the chief evil of a sudden rise of prices, the premium it gives to incompetent business men, enabling them to retain the control of concerns which they do not manage well, and which collapse as soon as the artificial support of rising prices is taken away.

9820. What are the two periods to which you specially refer? —The influx of silver which bore its full fruits in the time of the later Tudors, and the early years of this century.

9821. Coming to quite later years, do you remember the celebrated speech which was made by Mr. Gladstone about the year 1872, and in which he spoke of the prosperity of the country as being so great that it was increasing " by leaps and bounds " ? —Yes, I remember that.

9822. That was at a period of, I think, exceptionally high prices, was it not?—Yes, but I think in the first place what prosperity there was then was due chiefly to the increased intercourse among the nations owing to a great number of causes, and that in the main it was a mistake that the prosperity of the country was increasing at an enormous rate : the counters by which the wealth of the country was counted were growing very rapidly in number; but the real prosperity was not increasing at anything like the rate at which it appeared to be if one neglected the fact that prices were rising, and that property which had not changed in real value had its money value reckoned by more counters than before.

9823. Do you share the general opinion that during the last few years we have been passing through a period of severe depression ?—Yes, of severe depression of profits.

9824. And that has been during a period of abnormally low prices ?—A severe depression of profits and of prices. I have read nearly all the evidence that was given before the Depression of Trade and Industry Commission, and I really could not see that there was any very serious attempt to prove anything else than a depression of prices, a depression of interest, and a depression of profits; there is that undoubtedly. I cannot see any reason for believing that there is any considerable depression in any other respect. There is, of course, great misery among the poor; but I do not believe it is greater than it used to be. I do not mean that we should idly acquiesce in the existence of this misery, and regard it as inevitable. I hold rather extreme opinions in the opposite direction.

9825. (*Chairman.*) Then I understand you to think that the depression in those three respects is consistent with a condition of prosperity?—Certainly.

9826. (*Mr. Chaplin.*) The depression of profits, does not that more or less affect all classes?—No, I believe that a chief cause of the depression of profits is that the employer gets less and the employé more.

9827. You think that during a period of depression the employed working classes have been getting more than they did before?—More than they did before, on the average. I do not deny that during the years of spasmodic inflation everybody was working very hard; everybody got exceptionally high returns, employers and employed together. But, as I have already said, I think that history shows that those times have always sown the seeds of coming disasters.

9828. Can you speak as to the fact whether there has been a larger number of the working classes than usual unemployed altogether during this period of depression?—My belief is that there have not been a larger number of people unemployed during the last ten years than during any other consecutive ten years. Of course there are many more unemployed now than there were in 1872–73.

9829. Do you speak with knowledge of the thing and of the working classes?—I speak from personal observation ranging over many years, and a study of almost everything of importance that has been written on the subject.

9830. Are you aware that we have had evidence given by gentlemen speaking with definite knowledge of a directly opposite nature to what you are stating now?—I am aware that some persons actively engaged in business have given evidence that they believe there is an increasing unsteadiness of employment. But the facts which they bring forward are, in my opinion, out-weighed by the statistical and other evidence in the opposite direction. I have given reasons for believing that the statistics showing unsteadiness of employment require to be carefully interpreted; because the more people are employed in factories the more every interruption of employment shows itself in statistics. I have, however, omitted one thing of very great importance. I think that whatever had been the condition of prices there would have been a special reason causing irregularity of employment now; that is the transitional stage in which a great number of industries are. When an improvement is brought into an industry it benefits the public at once, and in the long run it is pretty sure to benefit even the trade into which it is introduced; but in many cases an improvement in the methods of the industry injures that industry, and throws people tem-porarily out of employment. Now, I do not think there has been any period in which there have been so many great changes. That has been put before you by Mr. Fowler, and it has been argued at great length in Mr. Wells' articles that this has been a period of great changes in the methods of industry, changes of such a kind as to tend to throw people out of employment. But in spite of that, I do not believe that the want of employment is, on the average, greater than it has been.

9831. But you mean to say that these changes, as you have described them, in the methods of industry have not been continuing now for a great number of years ?—I think there have been exceptionally great changes within the last few years. Many of them are to be traced to America, and before about 1868 or so, the Americans had other things to do; they had not settled down after the great war sufficiently to exert their full influence in changing the methods of industry. The changes are, I think, chiefly due to the great fall, the unparalleled fall, in the cost of transport, which renders it worth while to do a great many things that it was not worth while to do before; but besides this there are an immense number of changes in all industries, chemical and mechanical. I think Mr. Wells' evidence points very strongly in that direction.

9832. I suppose this very depression of profits, of which you speak, would in itself tend to lower the cost of transport ?—Yes; unless it were accompanied by an equal rise of wages; it would not then lower the real cost of transport.

9833. (*Mr. Barbour.*) You said that in so far as the fall of prices had tended to give the wage-earning classes more for their labour, it was a distinct gain ?—That is my opinion.

9834. And I think you said in your former evidence that if the bimetallic par had not been broken, silver prices would have fallen somewhat in India, and gold prices been somewhat higher in this country ?—I think so.

9835. So that in so far as the breaking of the bimetallic par has kept up prices in the silver countries, and given the wage-earners less for their labour, they have suffered just as the wage-earners in this country may have gained ?—They have not bene-fited as much as they would have done : I prefer this phrase, because of course the value of silver has not risen but fallen in India.

9836. That is to say, the breaking of the bimetallic par operates on the wage-earning classes in different directions in the two countries ?—Yes.

9837. (*Chairman.*) I believe you have formed an opinion as to what would be the best practicable method of dealing with the difficulty which has been put before this Commission, owing to the altering values of the precious metals ?—The main con-clusion that I have come to is that any step taken at present ought to be very small and very tentative. I have a bimetallic hobby of my own, about which I should not venture to feel any confidence if I had not submitted it already to a good deal of criticism. I have had it by me now for more than ten years, and I have not found anybody to show any flaw in it beyond the mere remark that its strangeness will prevent it from being adopted. But when I read the discussions on the bimetallic controversy, I find it is said that the older economists regarded bimetallism as altogether unworthy of discussion, and that there has been a great change in their attitude. But what the older economists chiefly said was, " There is no good in discussing a change in our monetary system, because the people would not have it." They do not say that the fixed-ratio-mintage is altogether absurd in itself; they say, it is absurd to spend valuable time in discussing a practical proposal which is utterly impracticable. But now people are willing to listen patiently to a proposal not merely for abandoning the sovereign as our standard of value, but even for binding ourselves by international agreement with regard to it. And I think that as public opinion has changed so far, it may change a little further, and be ready in time to consider patiently my own favourite scheme among others. I do not claim for it any exclusive favour. I believe that there is an immense number of possible schemes which we ought to discuss. This one scheme of the fixed-ratio-mintage has had the monopoly of discussion, partly because it had historical prestige, partly because it was capable of being explained easily, and partly because it got the unfair advantage of calling itself by a name to which it had no title, calling itself bimetallic when it is really alternative metallism. I believe that if we wait, if we adopt for the present merely palliatives, we shall gradually see the reason for thinking that what now passes for bimetallism is only one among a great number of schemes; and the scheme which may ultimately be adopted—for I do most seriously think that we shall have an international currency—may be something entirely different from anything yet proposed. I gave last time my reasons for believing that if the future history of the development of gold and silver monies should be similar to that of recent years, fixed-ratio-mintage would be likely to land us in silver monometallism, that is a paper currency on a silver basis. I think that if we do want bimetallism we should have to make sure that we get it, that is to say, we should make a rule that every debt should be discharged by the payment of a certain amount of gold and silver instead of a certain amount of gold or silver. What I have to say on this subject is really contained in an answer which I drew up to Question XIV. of the circular issued to the commission.

9838. (*Mr. Barbour.*) But did not Ricardo recommend silver as the standard of England?—I am not aware that he did.

9839. The principle is the same, but I think he recommended the silver standard in 1816?—His proposal was a bar; gold bars in 20 ounces is what he proposed for safe international currency.

I know that he proposed that; I do not know that he proposed the other.

9840. No doubt his system could be adapted to either gold or silver. The principle is the same, but this is what he said, " The only objection to the use of silver as the standard is its bulk, which renders it unfit for the large payments required in a wealthy country; but this objection is entirely removed by the substituting of paper money as the general circulating medium of the country. Silver, too, is much more steady in its value, in consequence of its demand and supply being more regular, and as all foreign countries regulate the value of their money by the value of silver, there can be no doubt that, on the whole, silver is preferable to gold as a standard, and should be permanently adopted for that purpose "?—I had not noticed that passage. He does not, I think, make any distinct proposal for silver bars; his proposal is, I think, for 20-ounce gold bars, is it not?

9841. In the early portion of his proposal for a safe and economical currency he recommended silver and not gold as the English standard?—It seems to me, in fact, that to use gold for domestic purposes is an anachronism. It would be just as reasonable, I think, to propose that a judge should be like the chief of an early tribe, strong enough to enforce his decisions. In modern times the judge is not required to be a strong man; all that is necessary is that he should represent force. And so, if paper currency is thoroughly well based upon gold or upon gold and silver, it seems to me that it has all the advantages which coin would have for the purposes of the internal trade of a country. I think there is no clearer proof that fixed-ratio-mintage has no right to call itself bimetallism than that, while true bimetallism would cause us to replenish the supply of that metal, which was becoming scarce, and so to keep a good supply of both, fixed-ratio-mintage, or alternative metallism, would draw all the mining away from those mines which were yielding their produce with difficulty towards those which are already yielding it with great abundance. Mr. Montagu, I think, threw out a suggestion that we might perhaps have universal bimetallism with seigniorage of one per cent. on silver. I understand the coins to be internationally current in both cases.

9842. (*Mr. Montagu.*) No, that was not my suggestion. It was that you would find that one per cent. seigniorage would prevent silver coins being preferentially used by the different countries for international payments; they would only be convertible in other countries at their intrinsic value, that would be less the loss of the seigniorage?—In that case it is in some measure similar to another proposal which has occurred to me recently. I have not kept it by me long enough to feel at all confident of it, but it seems to me that it deserves discussion. It is simply a universal " limping " double standard, or, as M. Cernuschi has called it, " humpbacked mono-metallism," like that in France now. I mean that there should be an international gold currency, combined with unlimited legal tender of silver in every country, each country being at liberty to put as much or as little silver into its coins as it likes. Of course the value of silver coins can exceed that of the metal in them by a much larger percentage than is possible in the case of gold coins, without encouraging illicit coining.

9843. (*Chairman.*) You mean without free mintage, to anybody who chose to bring it in?—Well, I would leave the silver currency to every country to be regulated by the country itself, with the understanding that there should be a very considerable silver currency. I think there might be some stipulation as to the minimum amount of silver that each country should have.

9844. (*Mr. Birch.*) That it should coin, or should have current?—That it should be a currency in the broad sense in which coin or bullion against which silver certificates are issued is counted as currency.

9845. (*Mr. Fremantle.*) Would you propose a seigniorage or a Mint charge?—This proposal is much newer to me than my favourite proposal for what I regard as a true bimetallism; and I do not profess to have thought it out in all details. But at present I am inclined to let each country do what it likes, merely to stipulate that it should have a great deal of silver, and that it should allow that silver to be unlimited legal tender. That would, of course, imply that it issued silver certificates, or that it authorised some scheme of silver certificates.

9846. In that case, silver would be the standard, and therefore would not be subject to a seigniorage but only to a Mint charge. The imposition of a seigniorage would immediately make the coin a token, and not a standard coin, would it not?—I am not sure whether I understand that. I mean to make it a token coin of unlimited tender, just as the five-franc pieces are now; it would then be useful for banks, and the basis of the issue of bank notes.

9847. (*Mr. Barbour.*) But there is to be unlimited coinage? —I would leave each Government to do what it liked, subject to the conditions, firstly, that they did not coin less than a certain amount of silver, and, secondly, that their silver coins had no value outside of their own country.

9848. That would give a universal gold standard, with silver as a token coin in limited quantities?—With silver as a token coin; that is why I call it " a limping double standard." Silver is to be legal tender. Of course unless silver is unlimited legal tender, and that practically means unless it is the basis for silver certificates or something of that sort, you cannot get more silver into circulation in England than there is now.

9849. (*Chairman.*) You would say if silver is unlimited legal tender, even though it be only a token, you might have a very large amount of it in use without gold being at a premium in relation to it?—In use and the basis of silver paper.

9850. (*Mr. Montagu.*) Surely if you allow each country to fix its own charge for seigniorage, that country where the largest charge was made would get no silver at all, and that country where the smallest charge for seigniorage was made would attract the silver from all the neighbouring countries?—Well, I think that might be likely to settle itself. I do not quite like the phrase seigniorage. I would propose that the Government should buy the silver in the open market, and coin it into pieces of such size as it chose, subject to the practical condition that if it coined its silver small its coins would be imitated fraudulently.

9851. But would it not be a greater advantage to come to an international agreement as regards the seigniorage?—I have not a very strong opinion on that matter; I would prefer myself that it should be elastic; I think that the values of gold and silver should be allowed to change their values as much as they liked.

I think that the changing circumstances of gold and silver would require perhaps modifications, and I would rather each country followed its own device, because I do not think it is wise to use silver token coins as international currency.

9852. (*Chairman.*) When you say they should be allowed to change their value in any particular country, they would have a fixed relative value, would they not, so long as you allow either of them to be unlimited legal tender?—Unlimited legal tender, but not unlimited mintage. Their being unlimited legal tender would not tie their value to one another. Each Government would buy the silver at the market price, and coin it into as many coins as it liked.

9853. No; but take the United States. The Government there purchases the silver, and coins so much of it, and issues the certificates, but still they have got now issued about 35,000,000*l.* sterling, which is really only worth 75 per cent. of what it goes current for?—That is exactly what I mean by a limping double standard, or humpbacked mono-metallism. I think that is the essence of the difference between fixed-ratio-mintage according to which, as in France some time ago, there was free coinage of both metals, and the humpbacked mono-metallism existing in America and France now, where there is no free coinage of silver.

9854. (*Mr. Birch.*) And these coins, as I understand you, are not to be international in any shape?—Not the silver coins.

9855. (*Mr. Barbour.*) That scheme would not prevent fluctuations in the relative value of gold and silver?—I do not want to do that. That is why I like the scheme, because it would not be necessary to attempt to prevent fluctuations in the relative value of gold and silver.

9856. So that it would not remedy the difficulties of a country with a purely silver standard?—The proposal would be that it should be at once adopted, at all events by India. That is the great charm of it for us as Englishmen.

9857. (*Chairman.*) But supposing it were adopted by all countries, and there was a large amount of this silver coinage in all countries, would not that tend to steady the value of silver in relation to gold?—It would not depend for its existence on there being no fluctuations in that value. But I think it would tend to steady the relative values of gold and silver, and that I regard as an advantage.

9858. (*Mr. Courtney.*) Could you give any hint as to the principles which would govern the Government in buying silver? I mean the extent to which they would go?—Well, I think myself that no Government would coin more silver than it was bound by treaty to; I think there would be a certain risk in it, and I think that the minimum would be also the maximum. I should think it would be best to agree on the amount to be kept in circulation if it is possible to get statistics of what is in circulation, and that no doubt could be done, because there would be no advantage to be gained by boiling the silver down.

9859. (*Mr. Montagu.*) Would there be any advantage in coining at all, if circulation were not required? Would it not be an advantage to store bar silver as bar gold is stored till required for circulation?—Well, that is so to a great extent as regards such a country as England. I think we should use only about as many silver coins as now, our silver certificates being based on bullion rather than on coins. I think that if greater facilities for the issue of bank notes for small amounts were given, together with certain conditions about silver being used as the basis of those—I think that the main benefit of the change would be got so far as England goes. But that would not touch India, and I think there is a great deal to be said for the scheme of keeping the rupee just as it is, of making no change in the rupee that the ryot would know anything about, keeping it as the domestic coin for India, but at the same time fixing the exchanges by making the rupee a token with unlimited legal tender and subordinate to a gold coin which had international currency. I should, perhaps, add that although I think that any change in the direction of an international currency that we make ought to be inspired by our desire to do the best we can in the spirit of fraternity; yet we should remember that our position is due to a very great extent to the excellence of our coinage, and if we have an international system, other people must have as good a coinage as we have. I think it is right to promote the well-being of the world, even at the expense of our own country. But while it is very likely true that we ought to be ready, when the time

comes, to subordinate the private and "selfish" interests of
England to those of the world at large, we ought to ascertain
what is the private interest of England. And I do not think it
is to her interest to put any pressure upon other countries to
follow our example of enabling anybody to draw a cheque for
100,000 gold coins, and get them.

9860. (*Chairman.*) Is there any advantage which your last
scheme would have over what is commonly called bimetallism,
which you call alternative metallism, except that it would not
tend to diminish the production of gold and stimulate the production of silver, so as to incur the danger of gold disappearing,
and our finding ourselves on a silver mono-metallism?—I understand you to refer not to the scheme which we have just been
discussing, but to my favourite scheme. It would have the further
advantage that, as it would not be interfered with by a change
in the gold value of silver, one of the chief dangers of its breaking
down would be removed.

9861. (*Mr. Montagu.*) Would not a ratio of, say, 20 to 1
give all the advantages and prevent any rise in the price of silver?
—Well, I myself regard fixed-ratio-mintage with the ratio of
20 to 1 as not a very great evil, but you see the arguments
published in favour of fixed-ratio-mintage are, certainly nine-
tenths of them, in favour of the $15\frac{1}{2}$ ratio. What I regard as
the chief dangers of fixed-ratio-mintage would be very much
diminished for the next twenty or thirty years at least if it were
not combined with the ratio of $15\frac{1}{2}$ to 1, which so far as we can
see would require a good deal of pressure to keep it up.

9862. But supposing that the Great Powers were to consent
to fixing the ratio at 20 to 1, you would have no objection yourself?—I would rather that no international agreement were
formed until the matter has been threshed out. I feel that the
whole question of international currency is only two years old,
because until about two years ago it was assumed that the English
people would not enter into an international currency. I regard
all the discussions that went before as not really solid. The
old-fashioned economists said, "There is no good in proposing
to the English public to give up its sovereign," and the consequence is, fixed-ratio-mintage has been discussed at great length

and no other proposal for an international currency in which both gold and silver are turned to account has yet received any considerable attention. I do not think that we ought to enter upon an undertaking of such enormous magnitude as an international currency until we have spent a great many more years in deciding what would be the best plan.

9863. But the great object in having a fixed ratio is to have steadiness of trade with silver-using countries, therefore if you want to enter into a treaty surely that would be the chief object to be aimed at?—You see the plan that I have proposed for a true bimetallism would not require a fixed ratio between gold and silver; it would avoid all the difficulties connected with that ratio at the same time that it attained all the practical advantages of an international basis for currency, which the advocates of fixed-ratio-mintage claim for their scheme.

9864. (*Mr. Barbour.*) Would you see any objection to adopting the ratio of 20 to 1 as a preliminary measure to keep gold and silver steady for the present and then considering whether any further steps could be taken towards establishing an international currency, and if so in what direction?—No strong objection; but I do not think that the matter has been threshed out enough. That is a reason for not being in a hurry. Another reason, which affects England only and to which I do not attach very much importance, is that any good international currency would tend to diminish the importance that London has in the banking of the world, because it would give other countries as good a currency as we have, and I do not think, therefore, that we ought to be in a hurry to rush forward to make a change which would benefit other countries so much more than it would benefit us, and even more or less at our expense.

9865. But there is the practical difficulty that if we do nothing in the meantime things may get worse as regards the value of gold and silver. Would it not be better to adopt the market ratio or something close to it as a preliminary step, to hold things in their present position, and see whether you could take any further steps or not?—If it were understood as a temporary and tentative step, I should have no great objections to it; but as a transitional step I should prefer an agreement to issue small notes. I think that is a much simpler agreement. I think that we as a nation are losing many of the commercial and industrial advantages which our situation gave us; not that we are losing ground, but that other countries are gaining ground, and freeing themselves from the artificial disadvantages that they had. I am therefore not anxious to give up our banking supremacy until the time has come for doing it, and I believe that we might make our banking supremacy for some time, at least, very much stronger than it is. While admirable in every respect, our banking system undoubtedly does suffer from its extreme sensitiveness. There is no country which works on so slender a basis of reserve as we, and that is partly because we use so expensive a system of coinage for domestic purposes. My own desire would be to retain the main body of our system entirely unchanged, but to issue one-pound notes, and to increase very much the average reserve of the Bank of England.

9866. (*Chairman.*) Would you issue the one-pound notes only against so much bullion in the bank as the Americans do with their gold, or would you increase the fiduciary issue ?—I would increase the fiduciary issue. I would make the reserve so strong that the bank could afford to lose 5,000,000*l.* or 6,000,000*l.* or more gold without feeling bound to act at all violently on the money market.

9867. (*Mr. Birch.*) But with regard to the reserve, is it to be in the issue department or how would you arrange that ?—Of course with the Act of 1844 there is an algebraical connection between the issue of notes, the stock of coin and bullion, and the reserve in the banking department. The new law would be different in form from the old. What I want is that there should be about 20,000,000*l.* of bullion and coins in the banking reserve above what was wanted for current business in ordinary times; in order to prevent a small exportation of bullion from causing a stringency in the discount market.

9868. You want 20,000,000*l.* more gold kept ?—20,000,000*l.* gold, or gold and silver, kept specially for this purpose.

9869. And what is your idea as to who is to keep that gold ? —That would depend upon who keeps the ultimate reserve. There is, of course, a growing feeling in the country that we have not sufficient banks; that we should be much better off if we had as many banks as Scotland, and that a plan of issue of one-pound notes might be devised which would induce the starting of a great many more banks. I myself do not go very far in that direction, but I do not think it would be possible to consider how the law should be framed until it was settled what was to be the position of private banks with regard to the issue of notes and to the ultimate reserve. The details of the law would be left until it was decided whether the persons who were ultimately responsible for the management of the basis of notes should be, as at present, the Bank of England, or a committee of Lombard Street.

9870. But the idea of keeping such a large amount of gold would be for international purposes?—Yes, I am basing myself upon the arguments at the end of Bagehot's *Lombard Street*, and pushing them rather further than it does.

9871. (*Mr. Courtney.*) I am afraid I do not quite follow your plan. Supposing we take the position of things now, with the Bank divided into two departments, one of which issues a certain amount of notes upon a certain fixed fiduciary limit, 16,000,000*l*., or whatever it is, and the rest upon gold only; and the other the banking department. Starting with that as the actual basis, now you propose, as I understand, that one-pound notes should be issued upon a deposit of gold of the same amount?—Not exactly so. To simplify the matter I will now suppose that the private issue of bank notes is not to be allowed; that all the notes are to be issued by the Bank of England. There would then have to be a new treaty by the Government with the Bank of England, by which, in return for certain privileges, it would have certain new duties. I have never seen any advantage in limiting the fiduciary issue to 16,000,000*l*. as a fixed sum. That plan seems to me to have had a curious historical origin, and to be one which nobody would have dreamed of deliberately adopting, and I would propose in lieu of it that the Bank should keep in the form of gold coin and bullion (or perhaps gold and silver coin and bullion) 1,000,000*l*. for every 2,000,000*l*. notes of whatever denomination is issued. I would lump one-pound notes and larger sums together. But the directors should have the right to neglect that restriction in times of great pressure : they might, for instance, be empowered to issue notes in excess of twice the value of their metallic stores when the minimum rate of discount had risen to 10 per cent. In ordinary times, however, when there had been no special demand for bullion for exportation, they should be under an obligation to keep the normal reserve of gold at about 20,000,000*l.* more than this minimum. Supposing they had 120,000,000*l.* of notes in circulation they would have, say, 60,000,000*l.* as their minimum reserve, and in addition it should be obligatory on them to keep 20,000,000*l.* more, that is, in all 80,000,000*l.* in ordinary times, it being understood that when the reserve was below 80,000,000*l.* they would begin to think about raising their rate of discount : but not being so near the end of their tether as now, the flow of some 5,000,000*l.* or 6,000,000*l.* of gold out of the country would not cause them to act so rapidly or so violently on the rate of discount. When I speak of them as being under an obligation to think about raising the rate of discount, when this first line of defence, this 20,000,000*l.*, was being trenched on, I have in my mind not so much an obligation defined in set legal phrase, as a moral obligation, in which much would be left to their discretion, they acting on their knowledge of the special circumstances of each case.

9872. Then what I understand is this, that these two departments would be fused together and would be reconstituted one; that the law would enable the one bank to perform all the functions of banking, of issuing notes to any extent, provided that it kept in the form of cash reserve half plus 20,000,000*l.* ?—Yes.

9873. That, however, would be a counsel of perfection ?—Yes : perhaps you may put it so.

9874. The 20,000,000*l.* might be trenched upon up to a certain limit, below which it should not be trenched upon, unless the bank rate went above a certain rate; is that what you mean ? —Yes, only I do not altogether like the phrase, a counsel of perfection. I would have the understanding that 20,000,000*l.* should be their average reserve, that they should keep their reserve in ordinary times as near as they conveniently could to 20,000,000*l.*

9875. Still there would be no law ?—There would be no law

any more than there is now.   There is a fixed law now, as regards the issue department, but when the Bank raises its rate of discount it does it from a desire, partly to protect its own notes, but partly too from the point of view of the general interests of the country.

9876. You fix no hard-and-fast line with regard to the minimum; it is merely general views ?—No; I merely give the figure of one-half of the notes issued for the sake of definiteness of ideas.   I do not profess to determine that that is exactly the right proportion : perhaps two-fifths, or three-fifths, might be better.

9877. Did you explain fully, with respect to this tentative and temporary arrangement that you talked about, what was to be done in India ?—I understand you now to refer, not to the proposal which I have just been discussing, and which I am ready to advocate for immediate adoption, not to my own favourite scheme of a " true bimetallism," but to a plan which I suggested for consideration.   In the scheme for a universal " limping " double standard, or, to call it by its other name, universal hump-backed mono-metallism, the rupee would hold exactly the same position as the five-franc piece does in France.

9878. (*Mr. Fremantle.*) Then you propose that gold should be the standard ?—Yes, on that plan, gold would be the international standard.

9879. (*Mr. Courtney.*) Extending to India ?—Extending to India.

9880. And a limited coinage of the rupee ?—Yes.

9881. (*Mr. Montagu.*) Would there not be danger of India attracting gold to the great disadvantage of Europe ?—I do not know that it would be to the great disadvantage of Europe, provided that we should be prepared to issue, as we should be on that plan, silver certificates; we should then be willing to take some of their silver, and issue notes on the back of it.   I admit that a universal limping double standard would send a good deal of gold to India, unless, as Mr. Daniell would suggest, such a change brought gold out of the India hoards.   But I think that if we had made provision for getting more currency by the silver certificates, we could afford a little gold to go to India.

I

9882. (*Mr. Barbour.*) What objection do you see to adopting formally a silver legal standard everywhere, and making gold legal tender at a fixed ratio; what is the evil that would arise from that?—I think there are several reasons against it; in the first place, I do not agree that history shows that silver is more stable than gold. There has been a very great rise in prices measured in silver since the Middle Ages; and meanwhile a considerable rise in the value of gold measured in terms of silver; and therefore if the prices had been measured throughout in gold, the rise would not have been as great as it has been.

9883. I did not mean to raise the question of stability. I was merely asking what objection you see to that plan. We have to use gold and silver as money somehow, and we formerly used them in this way, that silver was the legal standard, and gold was legal tender at a fixed ratio. What is the objection to that system?—Without going into details, I think it is to the point to say that gold is a better metal, on the whole, than silver.

9884. As a standard?—Yes.

9885. But you are no doubt aware that gold has never been really tried as the legal standard, unconnected with silver, before 1873, so far as I am aware?—Yes, I admit that.

9886. Is it not premature to say that it is the better standard till we have had longer experience of it?—I think it is difficult to say anything decidedly, but as far as statistical history goes, my own inclination is to think, though not without doubt, that gold is, on the whole, a better standard than silver. Another reason is, that if we had silver as the secondary coinage, we should have silver certificates based on it, and the English tradition of liking to handle its sovereigns, of which we have heard a good deal at different times, need not to be so violently broken into. But my chief reason is that a gold token coinage would require to be constantly changed, because if its nominal value were allowed to rise even a small percentage above its real value, it would be produced largely by illicit coiners. At the same time I wish frankly to say that I do not see any overwhelming objection to that plan. I think it would be nearly equally good, but the very fact that it is possible to propose a plan so entirely different from anything else that has been proposed, shows that it is premature to enter upon any sweeping international currency scheme.

9887. But do you think that the plan to which I have alluded is a new scheme? Is it not the old scheme that existed all over Europe until England altered the silver standard in 1816?—Not as an international scheme, I think.

9888. Not internationally, but that was what every nation did; every nation had a standard of silver, with gold as legal tender at a fixed ratio?—That is just the point. The question is whether we know enough about the way in which an international currency will work to be ready to decide which would be the best kind of international currency.

9889. The international currency is a different question. I did not mean to raise it; I was merely asking whether you saw any objection to every nation making silver the standard with gold as legal tender at a fixed ratio; all nations adopting the same ratio, say the market ratio of the day?—Well, I should prefer it the other way about for the reasons I have given; that is all I would say.

9890. But you do not see any very great objection to that system?—Not any very great objection.

9891. You said in your former evidence that you considered that the fall in the gold price of silver did not give any material bounty on exports from silver-using countries?—Yes.

9892. That, in fact, trade is carried on between different countries with respect to comparative cost of production of commodities?—Yes.

9893. I do not know whether you go so far as some of the older economists, who say that all trade tends to be conducted as a system of barter, and that money is only a mechanism by which that gigantic system of barter is carried out?—So far as permanent effects go I accept the doctrine without any qualification.

9894. That was laid down by Ricardo, who, I think, is a very strong supporter of the principle?—Yes.

9895. Money, whether made of gold or silver, as well as credit, is merely the mechanism by which the system of barter is carried out?—Yes, of course gold and silver are very important commodities of trade, but they are merely the mechanism by which the system of barter is carried out. I am speaking only of permanent, not of the temporary effects.

9896. A good or bad monetary system, or a good or bad organisation of credit, may in a greater or less degree facilitate or impede the working of the system, but they do not alter its real nature ?—No.

9897. When the price of a commodity rises, other prices remaining the same, does not that really mean that a less quantity of that commodity will exchange for the same quantity of other commodities than was previously the case ?—Yes.

9898. What is really meant by one article being worth 10*l.* a ton, and another article 5*l.* a ton, is that one ton of the former will exchange for two tons of the latter ?—Yes.

9899. And taking the case of an article which very largely enters into the international trade, you would say that the price of that article is determined from time to time with reference to the demand and supply in all countries, and not with reference to the demand and supply in any particular country ?—Yes.

9900. And would the rise or fall in price mean that the article exchanges for a greater or less quantity of other commodities ?—Yes.

9901. And the price determined in that way, what may be called the international price, would regulate the price in different countries from time to time ?—Yes, allowing for cost of carriage.

9902. You would say that the price is regulated in such a way as that the demand shall take off the supply ?—Yes.

9903. You recollect what Professor Cairnes says on the subject ?—Yes.

9904. He deals at some length with it, and holds that the price from time to time is so regulated that the demand shall take off the supply, that there shall be nothing wasted, nor that there shall be too little ?—Yes.

9905. To come back to the question of international trade. You know that India imports articles from this country such as piece goods, iron, copper, and other things, and looking to the real nature of the trade, would you say that India really obtains them by bartering jute, and tea, and seeds, and her other products for them, gold and silver being only the mechanism?—Yes, in the long run.

9906. You are aware that India also imports gold?—Yes.

9907. And that gold is not a legal tender in India, nor coined to any considerable extent, it merely comes as a commodity? —Yes.

9908. In your opinion, does India obtain that commodity gold simply by bartering her products for it or does she get it in any other way?—Simply by bartering her products as she would get any other commodity, yes.

9909. That is the only way she could get it unless she borrowed it or somebody gave it to her for nothing?—Yes.

9910. I should now like to consider the case of such a country as France. France does not produce gold, but there is a demand for gold there to be made into watches and chains and ornaments of various sorts. Do you think that France gets that gold in the same way that India gets her gold, by bartering her products for it?—In the long run.

9911. Then taking the case of the gold that France uses as money, do you think she gets that by bartering her products for it in the same way?—Yes, in the long run.

9912. There is no other way she could get it in the long run? —No.

9913. Do you think we may extend that to all countries, and say that, in the international trade, at any rate, gold is simply bartered against other commodities just as these commodities are bartered against one another?—Gold and silver.

9914. Gold, and silver too, but my question referred to gold? —Yes.

9915. Simply a commodity?—Yes. I think Ricardo lays that down very strongly. I will read you what he says and ask you if you agree. "It is particularly worthy of observation that, so deep-rooted is the prejudice which considers coin and bullion as things essentially differing in all their operations from other commodities, that writers greatly enlightened upon the general truths of political economy seldom fail, after having requested their readers to consider money and bullion merely as commodities subject to the same general principles of supply and demand, which are unquestionably the foundation on which the whole superstructure of political economy is built, to forget this recommendation themselves, and to argue upon the subject of money and the laws which regulate its export and import as quite distinct and different from those which regulate the export and import of other commodities." Would you agree generally with that ?—Yes.

9916. (*Chairman.*) Do you limit that to the laws which regulate its import and export, or do you mean that in all respects gold and silver are just the same as any other commodities ? —Well, gold and silver have a medicinal effect upon the money market when the money market is diseased, and I think that is the only correction that is to be made. There is no doubt that in a diseased state of the money market the arrival of 100,000 sovereigns has quite a different effect from the arrival of 100,000*l.* worth of goods of any other kind. Assuming the money market to be in a healthy state, the arrival of gold loses its medicinal effects, and I put gold and silver on exactly the same footing as tin and lead.

9917. But would not the fact that vast superstructures of credit are erected on the basis of gold cause it to differ, at all events, in that important particular from any other metal or commodity ?—Oh, as regards indirect effects, there is, no doubt, a great difference. For instance, if a person produces lead in large quantities, he makes very little difference to anybody except those who have to do with lead, but if people produce gold in large quantities, they may take hundreds of millions away from men who have nothing to do with gold mines, and give them to others who have also nothing to do with gold mines.

9918. Then is it not also the fact that because it is money it will be taken by everybody in exchange for every description of commodity ? Is not that the difference also between it and any other metal or commodity ?—I think that that affects its medicinal effects. When the money market is much disturbed people have not time to take commodities and translate them into money; they want the money straight off, but when trade is in its ordinary state, when there is no panic, I think that the causes that make increased supplies of gold and silver come in are just the same as those which make increased supplies of tin and lead come in.

9919. But is that so? What was passing through my mind was this, that take any other commodity, and I suppose an increased production of it, that increased production without any increased demand would at once lower the price of the commodity, so that although you have produced more you may get no more for the increased production; might not the effect be at all events very much less in proportion in the case of gold which is exchangeable against all commodities, which the owners of all commodities are willing to take in exchange for it as compared with tin, we will say, which will only be bought or taken by people who want to purchase tin, although in the end it may result in the exchange of one commodity for another?—Of course there are great differences between different commodities. A small increase in the supply of copper, for which there is a limited demand, may have a much greater effect on its price than an equal increase in the supply of grains which can be used as cattle food and so on.

9920. That is not what I was referring to. Is there not a difference from the very fact that it is money? Being money it is exchangeable directly against all articles?—Well, I think myself that an increase in the supply of money does act upon its value very quickly, but of course that is a matter on which there is a difference of opinion. In so far as it may be true that an increase in the supply of money does not act on its value quickly, in so far I should merely class it with that kind of commodity, the supply of which could be considerably increased without acting on its price.

9921. I do not know whether Ricardo intends to assert, or that you intend to assert, that it is the fact that a metal or money makes no difference in respect to all the incidents that will attach to it to what would apply if it was any other commodity which has not been made money or does not pass as money?—I kept on, when assenting to Mr. Barbour, repeating " in the long run " in order to guard myself against that particular point, because the temporary incidents might be different.

9922. (*Mr. Montagu.*) In stating that you consider gold a

commodity that cannot apply to the internal arrangements of this country, you mean to say that France pays for gold by giving something in exchange for it ?—It was only with reference to Mr. Barbour's particular question whether gold came to a country, and went from a country, subject to the same laws in the long run as tin.

9923. You would not call gold a commodity in this country ? —No.

9924. (*Chairman.*) What I was thinking was this : that 100*l.* worth of any substance comes to this country, and comes to this country for sale. Well, its price will be affected by a variety of things; the quantity coming forward, the demand for it, and so on, and that particular commodity may be affected and others remain stationary. But supposing a man brought here a ton of gold, he would get it at once converted into so many pounds sterling ?—Yes.

9925. And he would not get it converted into more pounds sterling, or less pounds sterling, because of any demand for gold, or diminished supply of gold ?—No.

9926. The only effect that would be produced would be, if owing to something relating to gold all prices were affected, so that gold would purchase more or less than it did before ?—Yes. Of course the gold price of gold is unity, always, and by the nature of the case; but what I was looking to was that the influx of a certain amount of gold would tend to lower the value of gold, in terms not of sovereigns, which are only one special form of gold, but of commodities in general in the same way as an influx of a certain amount of lead would tend to lower the value of lead, but whether the effects were produced as extensively or rapidly in the one case or the other might be subject to inquiry. The market for gold is much larger than that for lead.

9927. (*Mr. Courtney.*) You defended yourself by the use of the words "in the long run "?—Yes.

9928. Suppose, for example, 100,000 tons of tin were at once introduced into the English market. The purchasers of tin are few in number; they know the demand for tin, they know the annual consumption of tin, they know the supplies of tin that are coming forward, and their offers for the tin so introduced are confined to that limited number acting upon that knowledge possessed by them?—Yes.

9929. If, on the contrary, 100 ounces of gold are brought into the country, they may be taken to the Mint, and the owners of them at once obtain, at a certain fixed rate, a certain amount of coined gold in exchange for them; and they may ultimately affect, and possibly will ultimately affect, prices, and in that respect gold is a commodity; but that may take a much longer time to produce than the immediate effect which would be produced by the introduction of a large quantity of tin?—Yes, because the market for gold is so much larger. With 100,000 tons of tin one ought to compare a very large quantity of gold—several million ounces of it.

9930. And it does not immediately operate upon the users of gold. The first effect is the lodging of the gold really at the Bank of England or some other bank where it is coined into sovereigns in a short time and it is added to the currency of the country?—Yes.

9931. (*Chairman.*) It operates in a different way and shows itself by different effects. You may say that in the long run it is subject to the same loss, but at all events those losses do not act as directly and do not exhibit themselves by the same phenomena?—Well, I think the particular point that Ricardo had in view was this, that a person who had to bring home the returns of any sales in a country had to elect what commodity he would bring, and the question whether he should bring lead or tin was governed in his mind by exactly the same conditions as whether he should bring lead or gold. If after allowing for expenses of carriage you get a little more by bringing home the lead and selling it than by bringing home the tin, he would choose the lead; if he would get a little more by bringing home the gold and selling it, he would bring home the gold. It was that idea that I had specially in view when I said that in the long run the action would be exactly the same.

9932. (*Mr. Barbour.*) And in the international trade a ton of gold passing from America to this country would be paid for by English produce?—Yes.

9933. In that international trade one commodity is bartered against another and gold is simply a commodity?—Yes.

9934. You said that in the case of an article which entered very largely into the international trade, such as wheat, the price was formed with reference to the demand and supply in all countries ?—Yes.

9935. The commodity gold enters into the international trade more widely than any other. It is in use in every country, and I suppose you would say that the ratio which gold bears to commodities is determined with reference to the demand and supply in every country and not with reference to any particular country ?—Yes.

9936. And that the value determined in that way would regulate the value in each particular country ?—Yes.

9937. And if at that value, at the value given to gold, there happened to be more gold in any country than it wanted, the excess would be exported just as wheat would be exported under similar circumstances ?—Yes.

9938. It has been said that there cannot have been any appreciation of gold, in the sense of any rise of price which could not be explained by cheaper production, because the rate of discount has been low in recent years. I do not think you agree with the principle of that argument ?—No.

9939. If there was a short crop of wheat, what you would find would be that the price of bread would rise say 20 per cent. in London. At that higher price you could always get bread ?—Yes.

9940. What would happen would be that you would have to pay a higher price for it, that is, to give more of everything in exchange for bread ?—Yes.

9941. Do you think that that principle applies to gold, and that what happens with relation to gold is that if there is a scarcity of gold sufficient to affect prices, the way in which a scarcity would show itself would be by the fall of prices, and not by any permanent obvious deficiency in the circulating medium ? —I cannot answer that because I do not quite know what deficiency of the circulating medium means.

9942. At any rate you would say that a scarcity of gold will exhibit itself in the form of a fall of prices ?—Yes.

9943. You might infer scarcity from reduced production or

increased demand. With that exception would scarcity show itself in any other way ?—There I have to repeat somewhat. I think that depends on the way in which it comes into the country. If it comes into the country a little here and a little there I think the direct effect would be a rise of prices; but in this modern world it does not come in that way. In this modern world it comes into Lombard Street, and as soon as it comes into Lombard Street it can be drawn against directly; but whether it is or not, it generally has the effect of putting into the hands of lenders a greater command over capital, and therefore lowering the rate of discount, that is, making it lower than it would have otherwise been.

9944. The scarcity of gold would show itself by a fall of prices, and might or might not show itself by a temporary fluctuation in the rate of discount ?—In the modern world it would show itself in the discount market as well as in prices, because in the modern world it generally comes in viâ the money market.

9945. Let us suppose that the scarcity of gold shows itself by a temporary rise in the rate of discount in America, which had the effect of lowering prices, and that before the rise affected the bank reserves in this country the lower American prices have lowered prices in this country also, so that so much gold is not required in this country. Do you think that in such a case a deficiency of gold might not appear in the reserves of the Bank of England at all ?—I would not like to go so far as to say that no such event could ever happen under any conditions; but it does not seem to me to be a probable event, because the international market for discount distributes the effect of a change much more quickly than the international market for goods; and if the scarcity of gold should bring about a rise in the market rate of discount, I think that that would affect our rate of discount before the fall in prices in America effected a fall in prices here; therefore, although I would not be prepared to say that such an event could never happen under any circumstances, I should not regard it as a likely event.

9946. The rate of discount in this country might be affected for the time being, but if subsequently English prices were affected by the change of American prices, the pressure for gold in this country would be relieved, that is to say, if prices fell so much gold would not be required ?—Yes; my view is that if there was a scarcity of gold in America not accompanied by a scarcity of gold in England, the tendency would be for gold to go from England to America, and that the same result as has been traced in other cases would arise.

9947. And the fall of prices that would ultimately take place in England would enable so much gold to be exported without interfering with business ?—Yes, that is conceivable though a very improbable thing.

9948. But if that was not the case, where would the gold come from ?—Oh, I mean that the order of events is I think improbable.

9949. But if a demand for gold in any other country leads to gold being taken from this country, and there is no change in the mode of business, how can that gold be supplied from this country unless there be some fall in prices ?—Well, I think the first thing is for the gold to go, the second thing would be a slight check to speculation, the third, a fall of prices, and the fourth, prices now being low, a new equilibrium between the diminished demand for gold and the diminished supply.

9950. (*Chairman.*) Supposing all the gold that went was simply a diminution of the reserves of the Bank and did not diminish the amount that was in use in the shape of coin amongst the people, why should that produce any effect upon prices at all ?—I have already said, and I think it is a very important thing to bear always in mind, that when a bank has more gold than it really wants as the basis of its currency, which, of course, the Bank of France is supposed often to have had, that that gold is to all intents and purposes hoarded. If gold comes out of the hoards of a country it does not act on prices at all. It seems to me that that is very important to bear in mind with regard to Indian prices.

9951. It would only act on prices if it came out of coin in circulation ?—Only if it came out of coin or bullion which was acting as the basis of currency, or if it affected credit.

9952. If it affected credit no doubt; but supposing it does not arrive at the point of affecting credit, could it affect prices except

so far as it was coin going out of circulation?—My view is that a
bank requires to keep such reserve as is necessary to sustain its
credit; that if it keeps more than that, it is hoarding; that if
it only keeps that it cannot give up money without acting on
credit. In so far as it hoards, I put its hoards on the same footing
as other hoards.

9953. Yes, but has it not, in order to keep itself really safe, to
keep something beyond what even the average demands on it
are likely to be?—Oh, yes; I call that part of what is necessary
for the stability of its credit, and I do not think that any of the
reserve which it keeps for that purpose could go without affecting
credit, unless it happens to be known that there is some special
explanation of it.

9954. But why not? A great deal of that may go without any
human being knowing that it is gone; why should it affect credit
except by producing in people's minds a fear, owing to their
knowledge that the money is gone?—If it is not known that it is
gone I admit that it does not affect prices; but then I should
have thought it always was known.

9955. I asked you because I have not found anybody yet who
can explain to me how this effect is produced upon prices by gold;
we will say, going from this country to another, how it comes to
affect prices. The rate of discount rises and falls and more goes
out or more comes in; the people go on with their daily work in
the same way. I want to know how you suggest that the effect is
produced upon prices by, we will suppose, a certain amount of
bullion flowing to America?—Well, I think that it goes from
Lombard Street, and I think that its departure is known at once.

9956. Yes, but supposing a certain amount of money goes to
America for the purpose of investment from British people who
want to invest their savings as profitably as they can; how does
that affect prices; where does it come in to touch them? Who
gives less for anything on account of it?—Supposing a given
number of people are going over to America and each takes 20
sovereigns in his pocket of which nothing was known, it would
have no effect upon prices in England for a considerable time.
Ultimately bankers would find that they did not have so much,
they would find that their customers in the place from which these

people went had not enough to carry on ordinary transactions to buy their groceries, etc. with gold. The consequence would be that those people who had the power to draw money from the banks, would draw money from the banks; and the local banks would find it necessary to get more gold from London.

9957. Can you trace any operation of that kind at all during recent years?—No, because the case we are supposing is a fictitious case.

9958. We are supposing that there is a scarcity of gold, and prices have fallen by reason of scarcity of gold?—I want to try and trace that if I can and see how it comes in to affect prices, which puzzles me down to this moment.

9959. (*Mr. Courtney.*) Would this be an explanation of what you hold to be the case? Banking in England is always conducted on business principles we will suppose. The banker in the country keeps at hand just as much cash as he finds necessary to defend himself against daily and weekly demands. If he finds a surplus of cash accruing in his country safes he sends it up to London?—Yes.

9960. And in that way all the surplus money above what is wanted to defend the country banker against these country demands gravitates to London?—Yes.

9961. And being in London the London bankers in the same way send it to the Bank of England?—Yes.

9962. So that the Bank of England is ultimately the focus to which the surplus money of England is directed?—Yes.

9963. The Bank of England again conducts its business on the same principles as the private banker?—Do we require that the Bank of England conducts its business more or less on the same principles as a private banker?

9964. Its rate goes up?—Yes.

9965. The banking department of the Bank of England conducts its business on the same principle, at all events so far as this, that it recognises, within certain limits, the necessity of keeping a certain balance against possible demands, and if that sum increases, its rate of interest goes down, and if it decreases, its rate of interest goes up?—Yes; I quite agree to that.

9966. If that is a picture of the mechanism, if there is a demand

for money to pass from England to America in consequence of a
rise of the rate of discount in America, the first place to which
the demand is directed in England is the Bank of England ?—Yes.

9967. The Bank of England, if the pressure bears there so as to
reduce perceptibly its resources, sends up its rate of discount ?—
Yes.

9968. That rate of discount being sent up produces possibly—
this is the suggestion at all events—a desire on the part of holders
of stock, who want anything to sell ?—Yes.

9969. And hence produces a decline of prices ?—Yes, that is
my view.

9970. (*Chairman.*) Yes, but is there the slightest evidence
that in that way the rising of the rate of discount does bring
about forced sales of all commodities, and so bring down all
prices ?—It brings about forced sales, or diminishes purchases.

9971. Yes, but it is admitted that during all this recent time
people could discount their bills at a lower rate than they ever
could before.   If it depends at all upon a pressure which diminishes
the terms upon which people can discount bills, then all the
evidence is against the existence of that during the last ten
years ?—That I cannot admit.   The *Economist*, on the 6th June,
1885, published a very able article endeavouring to prove that
position.   But its arguments were not convincing to my mind.
It based these on the following figures, that the average annual
range of bank rate estimated as the difference between the highest
and the lowest was 3·4 for the years 1860 to 1871, and 3·8 for the
years 1872 to 1883; while the average rate of discount was 4·12
in the former period, and 3·46 in the latter.   The number of
changes was positively smaller in the latter than in the former.
These figures would no doubt tend to show that the pressure of a
scarcity of gold has not been felt in the money market, if it were
true that the general condition of the money market had remained
mean, while unchanged in other respects.   But this is not true;
the latter twelve years have seen many progressive changes, all
tending to lower the rate of discount and to diminish its fluctuations.   In the first place, the growing tendency of intercommuni-
cation has shown itself in the discount market more than in any
other; fluctuations in the price of wheat are being held in check

by the growing internationality of the wheat market; but the discount market is becoming international more rapidly even than the wheat market; the tendency, therefore, for a stable rate of discount is growing more fast than the tendency for a stable rate of wheat. My next point relates to the management of the Bank reserve. I know that the causes which determine the Bank directors to raise the rate of discount are such as a person like myself cannot understand in every instance. I am aware that there are many facts of which they have knowledge of which not only I but even a person living in the midst of the City is quite ignorant; but even I know enough to be sure that the Bank management has been of a higher order within the last few years than it was. It is a matter of public knowledge that the attention that has been paid to the principles on which the reserves should be managed has been much greater. Mr. Bagehot himself and other economists after his date, writing both in books and in newspapers, have been continually urging the Bank to avoid the necessity for moving the rate of discount about so much. My next point is that the earlier period of twelve years was a period, not of threatenings of war as the last period has been, but of actual wars. The whole of the basis of international business was much less violently disturbed in the latter period than in the former. And lastly, the great diminution which there has been in the rate of interest to be obtained by the investment of capital in business enterprises might by itself have been expected to lower the average rate of discount very much. If we bear in mind all these four independent causes, we must conclude that if there had been no scarcity of gold, the mean range of the rate of discount in the years 1872 to 1883 would have been much less than in the preceding twelve years, whereas, in fact, it was somewhat greater; and the mean rate of discount would probably have been much lower than it has been; it seems to me, therefore, that the statistics of the Bank rate of discount so far as they show anything at all, do rather show that the scanty supplies of gold have made themselves felt a little in the Bank parlour.

9972. (*Mr. Barbour.*) You said that the price of wheat was determined in such a way as just to take off the supply, from time to time, to make the demand equal the supply?—Yes.

9973. Do you think the same principle applies to gold, and that the ratio of gold to commodities is, indirectly no doubt, determined from time to time in such a way as to make the supply just equal to the demand upon it ?—Yes.

9974. I want to know whether you think that the influence of the supply of gold upon prices is exerted, speaking generally, in this way; the price of every commodity is continually rising or falling from influences which are almost entirely connected with that commodity and nothing else ?—Yes.

9975. The rises and falls in price due to increased or reduced demand for that commodity, or to increased or reduced supply, are very much greater and more frequent than the rises and falls that come from the gold side of the balance ?—Yes, so far as individual commodities go.

9976. The prices of individual commodities are continually either going up or going down, from what we may call trade causes, and they are not moving always in the same direction; in fact, they are certain to be moving in different directions ?—Yes.

9977. Then do you think that the increase of gold acts in this way, that it rather strengthens the influences which are at work to raise the prices of particular commodities, and that, on the other hand, a reduced supply of gold rather strengthens the influences which are at work to reduce prices ?—That is my opinion.

9978. So that, in the long run, although only trade influences appear to affect prices, really the reduced or increased supply of gold tends to bring about a lower or higher average level of prices ?—Yes.

9979. I should like to ask you a question about the influence of a temporary rise in the rate of discount on prices; you said that if a supply of gold came into this country the rate of discount would temporarily be lower than it otherwise would have been, and that there would be a little speculation and a rise in prices. Then you were asked whether or not the rate of discount had not been sufficiently low of recent years to produce any amount of speculation. Now I want to know if there is not this difference in the two cases, that if the rate of discount is low because credit and capital are in abundant supply, and if, at the same time, the reserves are low from want of gold, if a little speculation arises

K

the rate of discount has to be raised immediately, owing to want of gold, and checks that speculation. That is to say, the influences which tend to raise prices generally are killed off at once by a rise in the rate of discount or killed off very quickly?—I should hesitate a little before accepting that last part.

9980. I should like to get your explanation of what takes place?—That is not the exact way I should put it myself. I do not quite see that an increase of speculation would necessarily act upon the rate of discount. I think it would be very likely to do so in many cases; but I should not like to lay down a general rule about it. For in many cases I should rather regard the rate of discount as acting on speculation than the other way.

9981. Let us put aside speculation and say that there is a tendency to a rise in prices; would not that act upon the bank reserve, and the bank reserve being low there would very quickly be a rise in the rate of discount?—I think we agree in substance, but perhaps I might put it in my own way. In my view the rate of discount is determined by the average profitableness of different business; that is, determined partly by the amount of capital that is seeking investment as compared with the openings for new docks, new machinery, and so on; and the extent of these openings is itself practically determined to a great extent by the belief that people have that prices will rise or fall, other things being equal, for people are unwilling to borrow if they think that prices will fall. The supply of loans on the one hand and the desire of people to obtain loans on the other, having fixed the rates of discount at anything, 8, 6, 5, or 2 per cent., then the influx of a little extra gold, going as it does into the hands of those who deal in credit, causes the supply to rise relatively to the demand; the rate of discount falls below its equilibrium level, however low that was, and therefore stimulates speculation. This is, I think, the answer to the question Lord Herschell put. A fall which had been produced by the thinning out of the field for the investment of capital relatively to the supply of capital could not increase speculation, because it had itself been caused by the difficulty of finding a profitable opening for speculation. But when discount has already fallen sufficiently low to absorb the capital even in spite of the thinning out of the field for profitable employment of speculative capital, so that a new equilibrium at the lower rate of discount has been arrived at, then an even lower rate is required to again establish equilibrium between the demand for loans and the supply of them; this new rate effects the equilibrium by causing capital to go into the hands of speculators who would not take capital at the old rate, but do take it at the new; and whatever form their speculation may take, it is almost sure, directly or indirectly, to raise prices. This is the main issue. There is, however, a side issue which should not be overlooked and may be in some cases more important than the main issue. It is this : when the gold comes to the country it is known and people expect that prices will rise. Now if a person doubting whether to borrow for speculative purposes has reason to believe that prices will rise, he is willing to take a loan at 3 per cent., which before he would not have taken at $2\frac{1}{2}$ per cent., and consequently the influx of gold into the country by making people believe that prices will rise increases the demand for capital and raises therefore, in my opinion, the rate of discount.[1]

9982. (*Chairman.*) Is there evidence that an influx of gold into the country leads people to think that prices will rise?—I think so.

9983. Prices of stocks and shares and matters of that kind may rise because money is easy, but do prices of all commodities rise because there is an influx of gold into the Bank of England?—I think if the influx is considerable. Of course 100,000*l*. is a very small sum. 100,000*l*. would hardly exercise any influence, but 2,000,000*l*. or 3,000,000*l*. would exercise a perceptible though not a great influence.

9984. Surely not all prices. Things fluctuate much more than that, and they have no effect upon prices. It does not send them up or down when it comes in or goes out?—I agree with Mr. Barbour that the increased supply of gold has the effect of making prices that would have risen anyhow, rise a little faster, and of making prices that would otherwise have fallen, fall a little slower, or perhaps even not fall at all. It would not cause all prices to rise; it would merely raise the average.

9985. (*Mr. Barbour.*) I wish to ask you a few questions with

[1] Cf. *Money, Credit and Commerce*, pp. 75, 76.

regard to your comments on the diagram published in the first report of the Commission. You thought on looking into the matter that no parallel could be traced between the fall of gold prices generally and the fall of the gold price of silver, and that the parallelism which exists, no doubt, in the case of the *Economist's* index-numbers was merely an accident, or mainly the result of accident?—I think that it is unquestionable that various causes have tended to lower the value of silver relatively to gold at the same time that they have tended to raise the value of gold relatively to commodities, with the net result of leaving the silver value to commodities without any very great change. I do not think that the coincidence is one to be wondered at. I do not think that it shows itself in minute detail. I think that if you take the *Economist's* numbers you get in several small details a coincidence which you do not get if you take Mr. Sauerbeck's or Mr. Pixley's, and I think if you take the index-numbers of foreign countries you would find that they have had much less tendency to accompany the gold price of silver than the English numbers.

9986. Assuming that there was any such parallelism, would you not expect to find it shown most clearly by the curves representing the average price of the articles which enter into the international trade, and especially the articles interchanged between gold and silver countries?—I should have, *a priori*, expected what you have said to be true. I should have expected that the coincidence would show itself more clearly in the case of those commodities which are either sold to silver-using countries, or bought by silver-using countries, than with regard to any others; but I should not have expected there to be any very great difference, and as matter of fact it appears to me that the statistics rather go the other way. I have here traced the movements of the prices, both by Mr. Sauerbeck and Dr. Soetbeer, for several groups of commodities, for vegetable food, for animal food, for sugar, coffee, tea, and for minerals : and what I find is, that the greatest fall of all has been in minerals, and that, with the exception of animal food, minerals are those commodities which have least to do with Oriental countries. They are not exported in large quantities there; they are not bought in large quantities there; so while I should have expected minerals, therefore, to fall with silver less than other things, I find that so far they fall more, and the statistical evidence there seems to indicate that this cause which you have brought forward and which I admit to be a true cause, is one very feeble in its operation.

9987. But do you find that the fluctuations in the prices of the minerals correspond with the fluctuations in the gold price of silver very closely?—Yes, I think quite as closely as the fluctuations of other things.

9988. But not more closely?—No, but the great point is, that the fall in minerals has been much greater than the fall in other things.

9989. Can you say what the minerals are that you have taken? —Yes, Mr. Sauerbeck's are iron—two kinds of iron, two kinds of coal, copper, tin, and lead. I do not recollect what Dr. Soetbeer's are.

9990. Well, most of these articles are exported in considerable quantities to the silver countries. Copper, for instance, is largely exported to India, and iron and manufactures of iron?—I speak subject to correction, but I should have thought that the Indian market for iron and steel was not a very large part of the whole market for iron and steel.

9991. I daresay iron and manufactures of iron come to 3,000,000*l.* a year. Copper possibly 1,500,000*l.* a year. Metals would probably amount in all to 6,000,000*l.* yearly, which no doubt is not of any great importance. But it seems to me that in the case of Mr. Sauerbeck's index-numbers there is a considerable parallelism?—A considerable parallelism; and I am prepared to admit that when it was thought that we should have silver fixed at the ratio of 15½, the probability of that action being taken increased the price of silver and also increased the price of goods, because it was thought, justly in my opinion, that the fixed ratio of mintage at the ratio of 15½ would raise prices in England.

9992. And there is a certain amount of parallelism too in Dr. Soetbeer's figures?—I cannot trace any considerable parallelism.

9993. Dr. Soetbeer's figures agree to a certain extent with Mr. Sauerbeck's?—The agreement is in my opinion not very close, and the difference between Mr. Sauerbeck and Dr. Soetbeer is sufficient, I think, to wipe out almost every element of correspondence that there was in the case of Mr. Sauerbeck. I do not myself trace any close parallelism between the movements of Mr. Soetbeer's index-number representing general prices, the curve for which I have drawn here, and Mr. Pixley's figures for the gold price of silver which I have here drawn in an adjacent curve.

9994. The only strong divergence I find is between the years 1880 and 1883 when silver was falling and prices according to Dr. Soetbeer were rising, apart from the divergence in the case of 1876 which is common to both?—Well, between 1871 and 1872 Mr. Soetbeer's index-number is rising fast.

9995. I only take it from 1873, the time at which the bimetallic system ceased in France?—But Mr. Pixley's figure shows a very considerable fall in the gold price of silver between 1871 and 1872.

9996. Yes, but I was only referring to what has occurred since the coinage of gold at a fixed ratio ceased?—Yes. I do not think that we can cut out what happened in the year 1871 to 1872, however, I even find that in the year 1872 to 1873 there was a very great fall, almost the largest of all the falls in Dr. Soetbeer's index-number, and a comparatively small fall in Mr. Pixley's index-number.

9997. That is still before the fixed ratio was adopted?—I ought to have said, from 1874 to 1875.

9998. There was a fall in both, between 1873 and 1874?—A fall in both, but a very great fall in the index-number, and only a moderate fall in the gold price of silver.

9999. As regards the American prices, the New York prices, given by the Director of the United States Mint, I do not know whether you are aware that they were calculated gold prices, that the prices at that time were for inconvertible paper, and that the paper price and the gold price only came together some time in 1878, or say the 1st January, 1879; that, of course, would be a disturbing element?—I should admit that that would be a disturbing element to a slight extent, but only to a slight extent.

10,000. You do admit that there are certain difficulties connected with the state of the currencies of the different countries at the present time?—Certainly.

10,001. Do you think that these questions can finally be solved without some sort of international agreement or an international understanding or consultation?—I am very anxious that economists in all countries should devote their minds to consider what is the best form of international currency. The point which I desire to urge, more than any other, is that no action in the direction of international currency ought to be taken until they have the time to do what has not yet been done—consider the merits of different schemes for an international currency.

10,002. Do you hold the opinion that gold used alone would give as stable a standard as gold and silver used at a fixed ratio, supposing it were possible to do so?—No, not quite. I think the difference would be perceptible, but not very great.

10,003. It has been said that the supply of gold relatively to the total stock of gold is likely to be as steady as the supply of gold and silver, relatively to the total stock of gold and silver, but is there not this, on the other hand—that the demand for gold may increase at a very different rate to the demand for silver for the purpose of hoarding and ornament?—That is so.

10,004. That is a difficulty that has to be taken into consideration?—That is a difficulty. I think it should be bracketed with this, that the tendency to use cheques and other forms of banking credit liberates gold more directly than it liberates silver.

10,005. On the other hand, is there not this difficulty: how are you to ensure that a nation may not change from the silver to the gold standard? That is a disturbing element unless you have some sort of an agreement. It might again give rise to such a disturbance as we have had in recent years?—I think that there is a real, though very slow-moving, tendency for national interests to overrule provincial interests, and international interests to overrule national, and I think the time will come at which it will be thought as unreasonable for any country to regulate its currency without reference to other countries as it will be to have signalling codes at sea which took no account of the signalling codes at sea of other countries. I am only arguing for delay before entering on so vast an undertaking as an international currency convention.

10,006. There is also this, a theory which you have no doubt heard, that wealthy nations, no matter what you do, will take to a single gold standard as they get wealthier on account of the

greater convenience of gold for making large payments. Do you
think that is a sound theory?—I think it is sound, provided we
go on using coins as the chief element of our currency, but I very
much prefer myself using paper money to using gold for the
purposes of internal trade.

10,007. But if there be this irresistible tendency—Lord Liverpool described it as almost universal—there is no help for us
except to adopt a universal gold standard?—Lord Liverpool
lived at a time when the use of paper money had made every
cautious person regard it with horror. I think paper money is
a very delicate and difficult matter, not fit to be dealt with in the
earlier stages of civilisation. The management of a paper
currency in the future will, I think, depend very much on the
extent of information which we get by means of the telegraph
and the printing press. I think that we will have a paper currency
in the future organised and secured in a way that Lord Liverpool
could not have contemplated.

10,008. But Lord Liverpool says that the English people
attached a higher value to gold than the Mint regulations gave it,
simply for the sake of having a gold currency, and rejected silver.
Do you think that this is correct?—I think that that was the
product of the circumstances of the time. I do not think that
there is anything in the nature of the case to prevent a civilised
country with our modern organisation of the printing press, and
the telegraph, from having a thoroughly good paper currency
resting on an ample basis of one or both of the precious metals.

10,009. I do not know that you have given any special attention to inquiring as to whether Lord Liverpool was right in that
account of the matter or not?—No; I have not.

10,010. I will read you what Ricardo says upon the point.
He evidently does not agree with Lord Liverpool on the subject :
—" Lord Liverpool supposed that when gold became the standard
measure of value in this country, it arose from some capricious
preference of the people to gold; but it can, I think, be clearly
proved, that it was caused entirely from the circumstances of the
market value of silver relatively to gold having become greater
than the mint proportions." That shows that Ricardo did not
accept that account of Lord Liverpool?—Yes, I think so.

10,011. And there is another passage too which I should like to read you. The matter is of some importance, because if there is this tendency towards the gold standard in spite of law, which Lord Liverpool says there is, it is useless to resist it : "It was proposed by Mr. Locke that silver coin should be the only fixed legal standard of currency, and that guineas should pass current in all payments at their bullion value. Under such a system a guinea would have partaken of all the variations in the relative value of gold and silver, it might at one time have been worth 20s., and at another time 25s., but contrary to Mr. Locke's principle the value of the guinea was first fixed at 22s. and afterwards at 21s. 6d., when its value as bullion was considerably below it. At the same time the silver coin, for the very reason that gold was rated too high, passed in currency at a value less than its bullion value. It was to be expected, therefore, that the gold coin would be retained, and that the silver coin would disappear from circulation. If the value of the guinea as currency had been lowered to its true market value in silver, the exportation of the silver coin would then directly have ceased, and, in fact, this was the remedy which was at last adopted." Ricardo says it was due to the rate at which the relative value of gold and silver coins were fixed, that silver was exported and gold retained, whereas Lord Liverpool says that it was due to the preference of the people for gold ?— I should think that Ricardo would not have denied that the people had a great preference for gold ; and I myself hold that in the earlier part of the century, when paper currencies in England and still more elsewhere had been badly managed, it was a very reasonable thing to do to prefer a gold currency to a silver currency; because gold could be used as the means of large payment, and silver could not, and it was not safe then to do what I think it is safe to do now—that is, to issue small notes.

10,012. I do not think it was a question at that time of paper convenience in making payments, because in 1700 payments were not of such very great magnitude. Certainly payments in England could not have been so great as they were in France in 1840, when France used silver ?—No ; but of course even at that time England was very much more a country of the large commerce than France was.

10,013. Than France was in 1840?—No.

10,014. What Ricardo says is that gold was over-valued and silver undervalued, and, therefore, silver was exported. What Lord Liverpool says is that the people preferred gold simply on account of its convenience as a currency, and chose it on that ground, and not because it was the cheaper metal with which to pay debts?—I have not specially studied the facts of the case, but I should be inclined to think that Ricardo was right in his main contention; at the same time I should think that there was a strong desire, a strong sentimental liking as some persons have called it, among the English people for a gold currency.

The witness withdrew.

Adjourned till January 23.

January 23, 1888

THE RIGHT HON. LORD HERSCHELL, the Chairman,
presiding.

MR. D. M. BARBOUR, C.S.I.
MR. J. W. BIRCH.
MR. HENRY CHAPLIN, M.P.
SIR T. H. FARRER, BART.
SIR JOHN LUBBOCK, BART., M.P.
MR. S. MONTAGU, M.P.
MR. GEO. H. MURRAY, *The Secretary.*

Mr. ALFRED MARSHALL recalled and examined.

10,121. (*Mr. Barbour.*) You said in your former evidence that
if a bank accumulated more gold than was necessary fully and
completely to maintain credit, you looked upon that excess of
accumulation very much as a hoard which had no effect upon
prices ?—I regard it as a hoard.

10,122. So that if foreign banks or foreign Governments in
recent years have from various causes been accumulating more
gold than is necessary to fully and thoroughly maintain credit,
such excess of accumulation would tend to lower the general
average of prices instead of raising it ?—Yes, given the total
supply of metals, the larger the part of that supply which is
locked up in hoards, the lower will prices be.

10,123. Therefore, I suppose you would say that to take the
totals of the reserves of foreign Governments and foreign banks
in, we will say, 1870, and again in 1887, and to say they were
twice as great in 1887 as they were in 1870, and that therefore
the scarcity of gold could not have affected prices, would not be
a sound argument ?—I do not consider that argument valid at all.

10,124. (*Mr. Birch.*) In reply to a question by Lord Herschell,
you said that prices generally rise, other things being equal, in

proportion to the volume of metals which are used as currency; but this you qualified later on by saying that you included paper money. From this, I understand that you admit that all instruments of credit circulating freely as perfectly secure, have the same influence on prices as the precious metals with which they are admitted side by side in all payments ?—A similar influence. Of course the precious metals circulate many times during the year, while a cheque only circulates once as a rule; and again the precious metals are used as a basis of credit while bank notes are themselves a product of credit. I hold substantially the old-fashioned opinion that was expressed by Mill. I think that there was some evidence given before the Commission with which I do not at all agree, to the effect that Mill overlooked the influence of credit in helping currency to support prices. I think it is relevant to point out that in the chapter on the subject by which the opinions of the greater part of those who are now fairly well-advanced in years were in some measure formed, credit is stated distinctly to be " a purchasing power similar to money." That is the heading of one of his sections; and then he goes on to discuss the limitations of this doctrine due to the difference in the rapidity of circulation of different forms of credit, bills, cheques, and so on.

10,125. Then you said, with reference to an increase in the imports of gold, " Prices having risen, a person who had found it answered his purpose to have on the average 17*l.* in currency in his pocket would then require 18*l.* or 19*l.*" Now, as you repeated this on several occasions, and my experience is at variance with this opinion of yours, I am anxious to know if you have any absolute data to go upon, or is it merely a matter of opinion ?—I think that it would be quite possible for changes in the methods of business to diminish the total amount of purchasing power that people require to keep with them; that, for instance, the growth of the use of small cheques, the extension of banking accounts generally, might diminish the amount of currency. This is what I think you have in view. You certainly have far better means than I have of knowing how far the use of small cheques is diminishing the amounts of coin used by those who have banking accounts. And I should not venture to set my opinion against yours even on the question whether the growth of cash payments has not increased the amount of coin which is kept in the pockets of those who have no banking accounts. But in the passage to which you are referring, I was not intending to express any opinion on this debatable question, I regard what I meant to say as an identical proposition. It is only this, that given that the habits of business are the same, and that the amount of purchasing power that the people care to keep with them remained constant, then if 18*l.* are required to give the same purchasing power as 17*l.*, they will keep 18*l.* instead of 17*l.* I do not regard it as the result of experience, but as simply stating the same thing in two different ways.

10,126. But the inference I drew from your answers to questions put by Lord Herschell was that it was gold that was carried in the pocket, not instruments of credit; and then you said that gold was distributed in the pockets of the people more ?—Currency; I did not mean to say gold more than bank notes or silver.

10,127. I quite agree with your statement that if a postman could go round and distribute to everybody an increased amount of currency straight off, then this increase would act directly on prices, as a sudden demand would spring up for all sorts of commodities; but when gold comes in simply as a remittance from abroad to pay for debts contracted and for which other commodities are not forthcoming, I cannot see how this gold can affect prices ?—I hold that it does not always act on prices directly and immediately; that its first action is on Lombard Street, and that it affects prices afterwards through its action on Lombard Street, though of course the holder of the gold may in some cases draw against it, and purchase commodities, and thus act on prices immediately to some extent.

10,128. Then Lord Herschell asked you if there is any evidence that an influx of gold into the country causes a rise in prices, and you stated in reply that although 100,000*l.* would hardly exercise any influence, 2,000,000*l.* or 3,000,000*l.* would. Now I do not know whether you are aware that whereas the average amount of gold held in the Bank of England in 1878 was 23,000,000*l.*, in 1879 it was 32,000,000*l.* The index-number fell from 87 to 83, which is entirely opposed to your idea that gold

coming in would raise prices ?—It is not opposed to my ideas as
I understand it. I think it is quite possible that the stores in
the banks may increase during the next fifty years very much
indeed, and that prices may go down continually, the average
rate of discount going down also. I think that the effect of a
scarcity of gold is not necessarily to raise the rate of discount,
but simply to make it a little higher than it otherwise would
have been, and somewhat to check speculation.

10,129. Do you not think that if commodities came in, such
as wheat, tea, coffee, etc., which might have to come if the gold
did not, that would cause a fall in prices of such commodities
rather than the import of gold which might, as constantly does
happen, come in excess of our currency requirements ? These
commodities accumulating in stocks here would rather tend to
lower prices ?—Certainly.

10,130. Because gold must come for something; it must come
instead of commodities. It comes to pay off a debt or it is sent
to purchase commodities; but it is not sent here simply for the
fun of sending it ?—No ; of course the causes that govern the
flow of gold are complex, but as a rule it comes in the place of
commodities. We must, however, bear in mind that the net
trade in gold, that is the excess of imports over exports, is really
a very small element in our total trade. I mean that if 2,000,000*l.*
of gold were to displace other imports, the effect in producing a
scarcity of imports would be very slight in proportion to the
effect that that extra 2,000,000*l.* would have on Lombard Street.

10,131. I do not exactly understand your reference to Lombard Street. You know gold, although it ultimately comes to
the Bank of England, comes to be distributed. It is sent here
for employment in some way ?—Yes, but though it may come
in in a great number of different ways it all flows into one reservoir,
and is all seen in the Bank returns.

10,132. In reply to questions by Mr. Barbour, you stated
that while you would have expected minerals to fall with silver
less than other commodities, you found that so far they fell
more. Of course you are aware that a great portion of this
copper, tin, and lead are minerals largely imported from silver-
using countries ?—I said that while I should have expected

minerals, and especially iron, to fall less than other commodities, they had fallen more.

10,133. Have you any particular reason for this opinion?—I do not think that the total proportion of the metals as a whole that comes from silver-using countries is very great indeed. Since Mr. Barbour called attention to this point, I have referred to statistics on the subject; and I have come to the conclusion that my original statement was, roughly speaking, true. Of course coal and iron are very much the most important of the so-called metals, and they are almost exclusively of home origin. And a very considerable part even of those comparatively unimportant metals lead, tin, and copper comes from gold countries.

10,134. Then you are aware, I suppose, that copper within the last six months has risen enormously?—Yes.

10,135. That tin has gone up also?—Yes.

10,136. And that lead which was 12*l.* in July 1887 was 16*l.* in 1888?—I have not followed the change in lead.

10,137. The price of tin on the 1st July, 1887, was 102*l.* 10*s.*, and on the 1st January, 1888, 162*l.* Silver was the same price. Copper on the 1st July was 40*l.* 2*s.* 6*d.*, and on the 1st January 85*l.* Lead, which was 12*l.* in July 1887, is now 16*l.*; that would be a curious statement to compare by the side of yours?—It seems to me to support my general view that the gold price of silver has very little influence upon the gold price of other commodities.

10,138. (*Mr. Barbour.*) But do you not think it unsafe to found that general statement upon merely the price of three metals subject to special influences at a particular time?—I merely say it is consistent with my general opinion, formed on other grounds.

10,139. (*Mr. Birch.*) Yes; but a special reference was made to metals, and to those particular metals that I referred to. Mr. Barbour also asked you if Ricardo had not recommended silver as a safe and economical currency, and quoted an extract from his writings in favour of this metal. Doubtless you are aware that the same writer, in an article on " Currency and Banks," third edition, page 432, says : " A currency is in its most perfect state when it consists wholly of paper money, but of paper money

of an equal value with the gold which it professes to represent."
Then again, with regard to a double standard—gold and silver
—Ricardo says in the same article : " It appears that whilst each
of the two metals were equally a legal tender for debts of any
amount, we were subject to a constant change in the principal
standard measure of value. It would sometimes be gold, sometimes silver, depending entirely on the variations in the relative
value of the two metals. And at such times the metal which
was not the standard would be melted and withdrawn from
circulation, as its value would be greater in bullion than coin."
That I had always understood was the opinion of Mr. Ricardo ?
—Yes, I think that does represent his opinion, he having in view,
of course, a national scheme for fixed-ratio-mintage, and not an
international. As regards the particular point raised by Mr.
Barbour, I think that the quotation which Mr. Barbour gave did
not exceed, but fell rather short of Ricardo's true opinion. For
I have since found a footnote to Section IV. of his *Proposals for
an Economical and Secure Currency*, in which he expresses even
more strongly and in a less qualified way his personal preference
for silver. He did not seem to regard it as a proposal that was
likely to meet with general favour, but he himself would certainly
have preferred a paper currency based upon silver bars to one
based on gold bars.

10,140. Now, in your remarks upon the export and import
of commodities with reference to India, and the effect on the
exchanges, I think that little or no mention was made of the
drafts of the Secretary of State for India, paid in India in silver,
and the equivalent received here in gold. What effect, in your
opinion, have these drafts on the export and import trade of
India ?—I think that they differ from trade bills in this way,
that, whereas trade bills are likely to vary in nominal amount
with the prices of the commodities which enter into the trade,
the council bills for the greater part represent payments fixed
in gold; and I consider that this is a disturbing element in the
trade of India, but not more than, nor in substance different from,
that which is found in the trade of Australia and New Zealand.
In fact, I think it is very likely that an increase in that purchasing
power of gold of 1 per cent. causes a greater real extra burden to

New Zealand in proportion to its resources than it does to India. New Zealand has to make very heavy gold remittances; India has to make very heavy gold remittances. If an ounce of gold will purchase more commodities than it would, then the burdens on both countries are raised in proportion, and I think it is doubtful whether the fixed payments which New Zealand has to make are not a greater portion of her whole income than in the case of India; I think it is likely that the increased purchasing power of gold has pressed more heavily upon New Zealand than it has upon India.

10,141. That means to say, that if it cost New Zealand 1 per cent. to put money here to pay the interest on her debt, which is the reason why she sends it, and it costs India 25 per cent., India does not feel it so much as New Zealand feels 1 per cent. ? —No; that is not at all what I mean. I mean that if India and New Zealand both have to pay 1,000,000*l.* in interest in England, and if in consequence of the increased purchasing power of gold both India and New Zealand find that 1,000,000*l.* is worth as much as 1,100,000*l.* used to be when the contract was made, then I think that force presses equally heavily upon New Zealand and on India. I think that the fact that India has a silver currency does not cause the burden upon her—I am not talking now of the Government, but of the nation—which is caused by a rise in the real value of the interest on gold debentures, etc. that she has to pay to other countries, to be greater than it would be if she had a gold currency.

10,142. (*Sir T. Farrer.*) The fact that the Government of India has to buy its commodities with silver in order to pay its debt makes no real difference in the ultimate payment to England ?—No. But I prefer to separate the Government of India from the people.

10,143. (*Mr. Birch.*) But there is a balance against India of 15,000,000*l.* sterling, which she has to remit in commodities ? —Yes.

10,144. If she was a gold country and her commodities did not suffice, she could send gold ?—Yes. Though of course she might send gold now if she chose. But I should now like to analyse roughly that 15,000,000*l.* For I do not regard all parts

L

of it as acting in the same way on Indian trade. First then are two very large items of interest on the State debt and the railway debt, amounting together to five and a half millions. With regard to that part I admit that every fall in the value of silver enters as an extra burden to the Government to its full extent, excepting so far as the Government is able to raise a higher silver revenue in consequence of an ounce of silver being now a less burden to levy than it would be if silver had risen in value as fast as gold. But this is almost the only part of the expenditure with regard to which I am prepared to admit that there is an increased burden to the full extent of the fall in the gold price of silver. All the other important items in the expenditure of the Indian Government in England come under the two heads—payments for services and payments for goods. Now in so far as the Indian Government has to import railway material, provided the rupees, which she gets in taxation, will buy as much railway material as they would before (and of course they will buy a little more than they would before), in so far I can see no extra burden at all. Of course if she had the same amount of rupees, and those rupees had risen in value as fast as sovereigns had, the Indian Government would be doing what our Government is doing—raising income from taxation, 30 per cent. larger than it pretends to raise. As a matter of fact, it is raising, I think, about 10 per cent. larger than it would be if the rupee had its old value.

10,145. (*The Chairman.*) What is the amount of the purchase of material?—Well, it is rather hard to say, but I think that, speaking roughly, something like one-third of the payments, which are not payments on interest, are payments for stores, and two-thirds are payments for services. We are now getting to the fringe of a very large question, which, I think, Governments will have to consider in case gold should continue to rise in value. If we look at the process which determines the payment by Government of their officials, we find that, generally speaking, it is in this way. When gold is depreciated, it is said that 100*l.* does not purchase nearly as much as it did, and therefore their nominal salaries ought to be raised in order that their real incomes may not be diminished. In the course of time gold is appreciated, the purchasing power of money rises and prices fall, but the officials do not come forward and request that their salaries should be lowered; their salaries stay where they were. Well, now, I think that the natural tendency in all countries, our own certainly included, is to think that it is better to somewhat diminish the number of highly paid officials, and to increase their real payments. I think the question of the gold value of silver had very little to do with the payments that are made to the Indian officials. I mean that while the English taxpayer is paying to English officials and officers in the army salaries 20 or 30 per cent. higher in real value than they would have been if the value of gold had not risen, the Indian taxpayer was not likely to escape some extra burden. The Government of India may perhaps be too expensive in some respects. But it is more important that we should have able officials than that we should increase their number, and while English officials are getting higher salaries, the Indian Government cannot expect to get as able men as it wants without paying higher real salaries also.

10,146. But are not these payments, many of them, pensions? —In so far as they are pensions, then we must simply regard it as a contract entered into a long time ago, and if it is true that the Indian Government is legally bound to pay those pensions in gold (which is, with regard to some of them, I believe, more or less, a matter of dispute), then the Government has presumably already got the benefit of that certainty, in getting a better man for the post than they would have done if they had not guaranteed him his pension. In so far as the Indian official spends his money in India, he gets 10 per cent. more for it than he would if all prices had been where they were twenty or thirty years ago.

10,147. Do you suppose that at that time it would have made any difference as to the people who were engaged, whether it had been agreed that they were to get the equivalent of so many rupees in England, or so many pounds sterling?—I admit that it did not then make any very great difference. But I think we have to take this simply as a case in which, if the Government were to act on the rupee with the object of lowering its value, that would be, in substance, quite as great a breach of faith as it would be to pay in silver, things that they had contracted to pay in gold. Putting aside the pensions, which I admit stand on a rather different footing from engagements with officers that have entered the service since the gold value of silver had begun to show signs of falling, I do not see any reason for believing that the extra payments which the Government makes its servants are wasted. It is to be hoped, that paying them, as they do, 10 per cent. higher so long as they are in India, and 30 per cent. higher while they are in England, the Government gets better services in proportion to the higher payments.

10,148. (*Mr. Birch.*) The Government of India are largely interested in railways, and so far as they are thus interested, they derive benefit from the increased revenue which has arisen from the developing of these railways?—Yes; the Government gains by the traffic in two ways : firstly, there is a less deficit on it for the railways to make up; and, secondly, the traffic of the railways increases the taxpaying power of the native.

10,149. What do you suppose would be the effect of any action on the part of the Government with regard to raising the value of the rupee? Suppose it was got back again to 1*s*. 10*d*., what effect would that have upon India?—If they did that while gold retains its present purchasing power, it would be an indirect —its opponents, no doubt, would call it an underhand—way of raising rents 20 per cent.

10,150. What rents?—The rents of the Indian peasant.

10,151. (*The Chairman.*) But when you say that it would have that effect, do you assume that such an alteration would have any effect or no effect on gold prices or silver prices?—I purposely guarded myself by saying, that supposing they brought the value of silver up to that of gold, and that the value of gold did not change, the effect would be to raise the real burden 20 per cent.

10,152. Are you supposing silver prices to change or not? —That was Mr. Birch's suggestion, that the gold prices were not changed. One way of doing this would be to withdraw free coinage, and make the rupee scarce till it rises to the value of one-tenth part of a sovereign, the sovereign remaining unchanged in value.

10,153. Yes, but supposing silver prices in India remained the same, with the rupee back again at 1*s*. 10*d*., should you say then that there was any alteration or benefit?—Yes; that would be taking a supposition the very opposite of that on which I answered. That supposition would be that the value of gold was brought down to the value of silver. Then, I think that the Indian Government would be in very nearly the same position as now; it would gain in the matter of paying interest on loans, but not much in any other respect.

10,154. I am only supposing gold to fall in relation to silver; I am not supposing the prices of commodities are affected. I am supposing that, as suggested, by a bimetallic arrangement, you rehabilitated silver. Supposing that is the direct, immediate primary change; now I want to know whether you say that in that case a benefit would be conferred upon the peasant in India, or whether his position would be the same, or what?—I cannot understand the question, because I cannot conceive as possible a change in the gold price of silver, unless there is a change either in the gold price of commodities or in the silver price of commodities. But I can suppose a rise in the gold price of silver accompanied by stationary gold prices and a fall of silver prices, or else accompanied by stationary silver prices and a rise in gold prices.

10,155. Why do you say that, because silver prices have not risen in spite of the fall in the exchange, though the rupee has gone down from 1s. 10d. to 1s. 5d., silver prices have not risen? Why should silver prices necessarily fall if the rupee went up again by the reversal of that process from 1s. 5d. to 1s. 10d.? —I do not think that there need be any change in silver prices, provided gold prices changed backwards. Gold prices have fallen. The gold price of silver has fallen *pari passu*. It will be conceivable that that change should be reversed, and that we should still have the silver prices approximately stationary.

10,156. Then does your view involve this: that the gold prices have fallen because the relation of silver to gold has altered? —No, of the two I would rather say that the relation of silver to gold has altered because the relation of gold prices to silver prices has altered.

10,157. Do you think that that is really the cause of the change; that it has nothing to do with the monetary changes of

1873 ?—No, I do not ignore the effect of those monetary changes; they have, of course, determined the distribution of the precious metals and made that different from what it otherwise would have been, as I have explained more fully in my *Memorandum* as to the effects which differences between the currencies of different nations have on international trade. The gold price of silver is normally determined by the relation of gold prices to silver prices; in other words, the silver prices in any two countries are kept equal by forces which control the gold price of silver; but when there are abnormal changes in the supply of one of the precious metals, through changes at the mines, or in the demand for one of the precious metals, through changes in currency or hoarding, then those abnormal changes cause a redistribution of the supplies of the precious metals between the two countries. While that redistribution is going on, while there is a large flow of silver one way or the other, there is a disturbance of trade, a bounty on one set of exporters and so on; but as soon as the silver has found its equilibrium, we have again silver prices equal in both countries.

10,158. I do not understand what you mean by silver prices in a country which has only gold as a standard ?—I regard silver prices as found by dividing gold prices by the gold price of silver.

10,159. (*Mr. Barbour.*) It is the price estimated in silver at the market rate of the day ?—Yes.

10,160. (*The Chairman.*) Well, that cannot remain for any length of time; whatever elements enter into the proposition, you cannot have for any length of time between two countries with rapid communication a different silver price for the same article ? —That is the substance of my whole contention; that silver prices must remain the same, so that the gold price of silver can never have any very large effect upon trade, but must itself inevitably be adjusted by the flow of precious metals from one country to another, till silver prices are equal in all countries, allowance being made for carriage.

10,161. Yes, but a variety of things may have an effect on the silver price of commodities in the country which uses silver, and the gold price of the silver in the country which uses gold? —Yes, my view is, that given the amount of gold in a gold country, and the amount of silver in a silver country, given the extent of business, given the extent to which cheques and other substitutes for money displace currency, then the level of gold prices in the one, and of silver prices in the other, is determined; if this gives a gold price of silver different from that which is sustained by the general circumstances of demand and supply for gold and silver, there is instantly a flow of one of the precious metals from that country in which it has a lower purchasing power.

10,162. It was stated to us by a gentleman of great experience, on the last occasion of our sitting, that in the wheat trade, if there is a fall in exchange, that immediately affects the price at which Indian wheat is sold here. It is sold at a lower price; it is not that there is a change in the distribution of gold or silver, or the amount of gold and silver in the two countries, but the fact of a change in the rate of exchange; a fall in the price of silver here causes people to sell at a lower gold price, because they know that they can buy at the same silver price in India ?—I should think that this may happen, exactly as he has put it, with regard to market fluctuations; but in most cases I should think that the fall in the exchanges would have been influenced by changes in the relations between importers' and exporters' bills; and that, so far as permanent effects go, a fall in the gold price of silver would have been itself caused by a rise of silver prices relatively to gold prices.

10,163. But his evidence is exactly to the contrary of that. He said it invariably happens, and he was speaking, not only from watching the market, but as being directly engaged in it to a large extent for very many years past.—But would it be true that he had watched the right things ? My supposition is that this change in the wheat market was probably affected by the supply of bills in other trades, and unless he had a thorough knowledge of the bills and other trades, I should regard his evidence as not bearing on the point. The whole point is whether the fall in the gold price of silver or the fall in the exchange was not partially caused at any particular time by an excess of bills (including, of course, council bills) held in England on India. If he had watched that, his evidence would be to the point : but if he has only watched the corn trade he appears to me to give no evidence at all bearing on that particular opinion which I had just submitted to you.   Of course it is obvious that whether the country with which we are trading has a gold or a silver currency, anything that makes the exchanges favourable to us (and in the case of India this is called a fall of the exchanges) gives a temporary premium on importation of goods from that country, and tends to lower temporarily their price in this market.   And when we are trading with a silver country a wave of distrust coming over the silver market may have this effect.   But in that case there will be an increased purchase on English account not only of Indian wheat, but of all other Indian commodities; and consequently silver will go to India.   If silver does not go, that is a proof that the fall in the Indian exchanges, by which the exporter of wheat from India benefits, was really due to a relation to the exportation of other commodities from India, or to a relative increase of extra-commercial payments from India; that is, to causes which would exist now if India had a gold currency.   My views on this point are given at length in my *Memorandum*.[1]

10,164.   (*Sir T. Farrer.*) Have you thought about what the effect of council bills is in preventing silver from going to India ? —I regard council bills as simply bills drawn by a certain particular large drawer, the Government, in return for personal services, or, as some economists say, for " immaterial goods " as well as material goods.   I do not consider that the council bills have any permanent effect different from that which other bills have.   One way of looking at it is to say that the Indian Government is like an absentee who chooses to spend some of his money here, and I would regard the drawing of council bills very much like the drawing of New Zealanders resident in England.   Taking it that there are a good many New Zealanders who are drawing their means of living from New Zealand and spending them in England, and also that there is a good deal of money lent to New Zealand on which interest has to be paid in gold, it seems to me that India and New Zealand are so far on all fours.

[1] *See* pp. 184-8.

10,165. My question had reference to what has been said, that the council bills operating as remittances to India and being bought by people who have to pay for goods in India operate to prevent them sending silver to India, which they otherwise would send?—There is, in my opinion, nothing peculiar about this mode of action. They operate just in the same way as bills drawn by a New Zealander who lives here and spends his income; by so doing he prevents things being sent to New Zealand which otherwise would go, including silver.

10,166. But if silver falls to a certain extent compared with commodities, silver will still go to India, council bills or no council bills?—Yes.

10,167. (*The Chairman.*) Would not that depend on the amount of remittances that people wanted to make, one way or the other, upon the balance of trade between the two countries?—Yes.

10,168. I think Sir Thomas Farrer was rather pointing to silver going there, because the silver price was lower; but now, in these days of telegraphic communication, does not the gold price here so immediately conform to your silver price that you would not have that flow which you would have had when there was no communication by telegraph and no rapid communication by sea?—The permanent effects would, I think, be very similar in the two cases; but of course the telegraph and the increased rapidity of transport would change very much the temporary effect of drawing an exceptionally large quantity of council bills in any particular week.

10,169. (*Sir T. Farrer.*) Let me explain more precisely what I mean. One of our puzzles has been to know why, if silver has fallen so much in the West, it has not gone to the East in larger quantities? One reason given by some of the witnesses is that council bills operate as remittances and therefore prevent silver going there which otherwise would go there?—I regard council bills as having a permanent effect on trade simply the same as the drawing of bills has against commodities. Of course, the more English civil and military servants India imports, and the higher she pays for them, the more her invisible imports take the place of her visible imports, the more, therefore, silver as well as other things has to stay behind.

10,170. For ordinary purposes a council bill or a telegraphic transfer is a cheaper thing for the merchant to buy who wants to make a payment in India, than silver ?—Yes.

10,171. But supposing that silver falls so much here, that the profit of sending silver to India, of buying goods there, and sending them back here is greater than what he would save by buying a council bill, he will send silver to India, will he not, council bill or no council bill ?—Yes; the council bills act exactly as private bills, and have their origin just as private bills have.

10,172. (*Mr. Montagu.*) Would not the council bills immediately follow a fall in silver ?—Yes.

10,173. Therefore, as the Indian Government must draw, it has always the effect of displacing or substituting the remittance of council bills for silver. It is the debt due by the Indian Government to England that necessitates the smaller amount of silver being sent ?—Well, the way in which I put it is, if the Indian Government draws 16,000,000*l.* of council bills, then that means that we have to send 16,000,000*l.* less of commodities than we otherwise should, and among these commodities silver may enter or not. The question whether silver does enter or not depends merely upon whether its value here relatively to commodities is lower or higher than in India.

10,174. If the council found that they could not sell their bills, then India would have to remit in sterling ?—Yes; but my point is that the Government bill acts exactly in the same way as the private bill in the long run.

10,175. Excepting that you send nothing for it ?—Excepting that you send immaterial commodities for part of it, and another part is drawn, as many private bills on New Zealand are, with the ultimate effect of paying interest on railway debentures, etc.

10,176. (*Sir T. Farrer.*) I have not yet made my point quite clear. You agreed, I think, that if the profit of sending silver to India and buying goods with it is greater than the saving effected by buying a council bill or a telegraphic transfer, the merchant will send silver and will not buy a council bill. Mr. Montagu adds, and I agree with him, that the price of council bills rises or falls with the price of silver, and further that the Government of India must sell their council bills. The point I

wish now to put is, that the price at which the Indian Government must sell their council bills is the price of silver in India,
and not the price of silver in London, and that therefore if silver
is worth so much less in London than in India as to make it
worth while to buy it and send it to India, the merchant will
find it cheaper to buy silver for his remittances than to buy
council bills. Under such circumstances the council bills will
not prevent silver from going to India more than they prevent
other goods going, and we must look for other reasons than the
council bills to show why silver has not gone to India in larger
quantities. It seems probable, as has been stated by some
witnesses, that these reasons are to be found in the fact that
other English things, such as cotton goods and iron wares, have
fallen in price still more than silver, and that therefore it has
been more profitable to send them than silver. Do you agree in
the above statement?—Yes, I agree generally with that statement. I should indeed hesitate to say that the price of council
bills was determined exclusively by the (gold) price of silver in
India. Their value, like that of all other bills, as, for instance,
bills on Melbourne or Berlin, is affected by the general course of
trade; it is, for instance, affected by a change in the price of
lead or iron in London, because that is likely to affect the importation of these wares, and thereupon to alter at once the expectation
that Englishmen form as to the amount of foreign bills which
there will be in their market. I should, therefore, expect a change
in the gold price of silver in London to affect slightly the price
of council bills, even if it were a small change which had not yet
been communicated to India. But this is a minor point, and
really not relevant to the main issue. Substantially, I agree
with you. Only it would come more naturally to me to word
my statement a little differently. I hold generally that the
price which traders will give for a bill on a foreign market has its
upper limit in the expense of delivering in that market goods
which will sell for an amount equal to that of the bill. This
expense consists of the English price of the goods, and the trade
charges, direct and indirect, of sending them; allowance has to
be made for interest on their value during the time they are on
the way, but against this has to be set interest on the bill for the

time it has yet to run.　In ordinary trade discourse the precious metals are separated from other goods; but in an argument of this kind it is not necessary to do so.　They have minor incidents of their own, the chief of which is that less risk, less difficulty, and less special knowledge are required in finding a market for them than in finding a market for other goods.　We say that gold goes from London to Paris when " specie point " is reached, that is, when a bill on Paris sells in London for more than the value on the face of it by the expense of sending gold.　It is equally true that lead goes when " lead point " is reached, that is, when a bill on Paris sells for more than the cost of buying in London and sending to Paris lead that will sell for the value on the face of the bill.　Thus these council bills have to be sold for a price not higher than the cost of buying in England and sending to India iron, or cotton goods, or silver, whichever may happen to be the most profitable business.　If the value of cotton goods is low in England relatively to India they will be going, and the price of council bills for the time will be regulated by them.　If, on the other hand, silver falls in England relatively to India (or, which is the same thing, if silver prices rise in London relatively to India), it will be the turn of silver to go, and then that will regulate the price of council bills.　In the former case the unexpected drawing of extra council bills will just prevent a little cotton from going to India which otherwise would have gone there; in the latter it will stop a little silver which was just on the point of going, but in consequence of the plethora of bills does not go.　The effect is just the same as if a native of India residing in England should buy a house here, and draw a bill on India to pay for it.　If the amount of council bills were permanently increased by, say, Rs. 50,000,000, India would send us a little more of all sorts of goods, and take from us a little less of all sorts of goods.　Suppose she took on the whole 2,000,000*l.* worth less of all kinds of goods; then, seeing that her imports of cotton goods are generally about 40 per cent., and her imports of specie are about 20 per cent. of her total imports, it is reasonable to suppose that she would import about 800,000*l.* less of cotton goods and 400,000*l.* less of specie.　Thus I accept unreservedly the statement that the main reason why more silver has not gone

to India is that the prices (measured in silver) of many kinds of
cotton goods and other things, for which there is a good market
in India, have fallen in England at least as fast as they have in
India; or, as is commonly, though not quite so accurately said,
because the gold prices of calico, etc. have fallen as fast as the
gold price of silver. Of course the lowering of freights always
tends to make heavy goods displace light goods; it helps Indian
wheat more than it helps Indian silk in coming to England, and
it helps calico and railway iron more than silver in going to India.
To complete the case I should remark, though attention has often
been called to this point, that Indian borrowings have somewhat
diminished lately, and that the less she borrows, the less she imports, other things being equal, of all goods and silver among them.

10,177. You spoke of the rate of discount. You said it might
very well happen that we might have low prices and a high rate
of discount, with abundance of gold. Supposing you had a state
of things for a number of years under which in the Bank of
England, which acts upon purely commercial principles, there
was an abundant supply coupled with a low rate of discount,
would not that at all events be evidence that if there were low
prices, and what has been called depression of trade, that was
not due to a scarcity of gold?—It would be difficult to answer
that question directly; for we should have to consider the relation
between bank notes and bullion It might mean only that there
were more bank notes in circulation, and therefore more bullion
in the cellars; and as a matter of fact the gold in the English,
Scotch, and Irish banks of issue was less in 1885 than it was in
1872, according to Dr. Soetbeer's figures, printed in an Appendix
to the First Report of the Commission. Depression of trade I
put on a different footing from a fall of prices. I think that it is
quite possible that banks may choose for various reasons to
increase their reserves, that at the same time the rate of discount
may be low, because the rate of interest on permanent investments is low, and yet all the while there may be a diminution
in the amount of gold relatively to the amount of business it has
to do, which brings about a fall in prices.

10,178. How, in that case, would the diminution in the
quantity of gold bring about a depression of prices?—Let us

suppose that everything else remains unchanged; that the habit of paying small cheques remains unchanged, the habit of using cheques remains unchanged, the proportion of bank notes to gold remains unchanged, the volume of business, the total amount of things manufactured remains unchanged; everything remains unchanged, the only difference being that America and Germany having taken a gold currency, we have less sovereigns in the country. Among the things that are to be unchanged is the total volume of capital, the total profitableness of industries, so that the ordinary rate of interest for given loans remains the same, say 4 per cent. throughout. It is only on such a supposition, it seems to me, that we can get one cause isolated. The result, I believe, would be that gold being a little scarce the Bank directors would find a pressure on the reserve in the banking department, accompanied by a scarcity of gold relatively to notes in the issue department; and they would begin to think about raising the rate of discount, or rather they would have to raise the rate of discount when otherwise they might have kept it stationary; they would have to keep it stationary when otherwise they might have lowered it. The result would be a check to speculative investments, a diminished demand for commodities, and a fall of prices; that is my view of the way in which the gold would act permanently on the fall of prices.

10,179. Then it would operate on prices, not directly, but by causing the Bank directors either slightly to raise the rate of discount, or not to lower it when they otherwise would have lowered it?—Yes. Then the level of prices being lower than it had been, people would not want so much money to do their retail business, on the supposition that they did their business on the same plan as they did before, that is, not altering the ratio of their payments by cheques to their payments by coin, etc. Had the fall in prices been brought about by any temporary distrust in the money market, and had it not been accompanied by a diminution in the supply of gold, the result would have been that with these low prices people would have found that they did not want so much gold about them, there would have been a gradual flow of gold to Lombard Street, and from Lombard Street to the Bank of England.

10,180. (*The Chairman.*) But if you had prices affected in that way by a diminution of speculative activity, brought about by a slight rise in the rate of discount, would not the reverse operation lead to discount coming down, recreate that speculative activity, and send back prices to their old level?—That is what I was guarding against by what I last said. If this action on the money market had been caused by some temporary distrust, say, the failure of some large firms, then people would find that they had more currency than was necessary to do their business at the lower prices. Currency would flow, therefore, through the banks to Lombard Street, and through Lombard Street to the Bank of England; the Bank directors would again find their reserves superabundant, and would again stimulate speculation by lowering the rate of discount.

10,181. Then prices would go up to their old level?—Yes, that is, on the supposition that there had not been a real scarcity of gold. But in the answer I gave to Sir Thomas Farrer, I was considering the case of a scarcity of gold in England caused by the adoption of gold currencies in other countries. I was endeavouring to distinguish that fall of prices which is due to diminution in the supply of gold from that fall of prices which is due to a disturbance of credit such as might be caused by the failure of an important firm.

10,182. Then do you assume that in the one case the people have more gold in their pockets than in the other, and that flows back to Lombard Street and so gets into the reserves; and if so, how have they got that excess in their pockets?—You see, I assume in starting that the only change is a change in the supply of gold. If the only change is a change in the supply of gold; if the real wealth of the country is just the same as it was before, and the habits which people have of paying certain shop bills by cheques and certain shop bills by cash, remain the same as before, then it follows it is an identical proposition, merely saying the same thing in other words, that they get the same purchasing power in their pockets as before, and if prices have fallen 10 per cent. they therefore have 10 per cent. less coin in their pockets. That is not a thing to be proved; it is involved in the supposition on which I started, and is merely saying the same thing in other words.

10,183. If they keep 10 per cent. less coin in their pockets by reason of lower prices there will be 10 per cent. more going into the reserves of the Bank of England?—Yes, 10 per cent. will go to replenish the reserves.

10,184. And why will not that lower the rate of discount again by sending up the reserves and so restoring prices to their old level?—Because the supposition we are taking is that the gold had gone out of the country; if it had not gone out of the country, and the fall of prices had been due to some temporary panic, that result would have followed; but the gold having gone out of the country there is only enough gold to keep the Bank reserve at its old rate, and to keep the same purchasing power represented by fewer sovereigns in the pockets of the people.

10,185. (*Sir T. Farrer.*) When the Bank raise their rate of discount does the gold which they obtain generally come out of the pockets of the people, out of the counters the people are using, or does it come from abroad?—I think that depends not upon whether the rate of discount rises simply, but upon whether it rises relatively to other countries. If it rises relatively to other countries, the tendency is for the gold no doubt to come from abroad, but if there is an equal rise in the rate of discount in other countries, then it is not likely to come from abroad, and it must be got in such a way as to check speculation in this country.

10,186. (*Mr. Barbour.*) The general average of prices rises and falls from time to time. It used to be said that there was a ten years' or an eleven years' fluctuation?—I know that used to be said.

10,187. Well, suppose that at a time when prices were high, something occurred which brought about a scarcity of gold and an additional demand for gold, and at the same time another cause came into operation which lowered prices, you would have simultaneously two sets of causes at work, one causing a scarcity of gold and the other lowering prices. Is it not possible under these circumstances that the scarcity of gold might not for the time being show itself in the reserve at all?—Yes, I should not expect that any one cause when its action was combined with that of others would necessarily bring about the effect which would naturally follow from it if its action were not so disturbed.

10,188. But these two sets of causes might act in the way I have supposed for the time being?—Yes, quite so.

10,189. And prices having fallen in the ordinary course of trade and gold having become scarce for special reasons, when the time came in the ordinary course of trade for a rise in prices, the alteration in the supply of gold would tend to check that fluctuation upwards?—Yes.

10,190. (*Sir John Lubbock.*) Referring to Question 9814, with reference to the Bengal and North-Western Railway, which, it appears, pays 4 per cent., gained without a guarantee, but is at a considerable discount, whereas stocks with a gold guarantee of 4 per cent. are all at a premium. Putting aside the question of the gold, you would expect, would you not, that a railway which paid 4 per cent. on its own merits would hardly stand as well as another railway which, in addition to earning 4 per cent. on its own merits, had a Government guarantee?—Not unless those who knew the railway had reason to believe that its dividend in the future would be considerably above 4 per cent.

10,191. *Ceteris paribus* the additional guarantee would tend to raise stock higher?—Yes, of course.

10,192. Then turning to Question 9869 you said that we should be much better off if we had as many banks as Scotland. I suppose you mean bank offices?—I mean if we had as many banks and branches of banks in proportion to the population. I think I was not expressing my own opinion; I think I was alluding to the opinion that others held, that it would add very much to the well-being of England if it had a great many more branch banks. I, myself, do not attribute so much importance to that as some others do.

10,193. But the point that I want to elicit is whether you mean bank offices or branch banks, because there are very few banks in Scotland, and a great many banks in England?—I mean bank offices in proportion to the population.

10,194. Then you went on to advocate the issue of 1*l.* notes because it would tend to increase the number of bank branches. But that would hardly be the case unless they were issued by the banks themselves. Do you mean allowing the Bank of England to issue 1*l.* notes as against gold would have any tendency

M

to increase the number of banks or bank offices in this country?
—I was throughout alluding to proposals that had been made
by others. I do not know that I would care to give evidence
upon it, because it is not my proposal.

10,195. I merely want your opinion as to whether the issue
of 1*l*. notes would necessarily have any tendency to increase the
number of bank offices?—The proposal which I had in view was
one by which private banks should be allowed to hold a reserve
of Government notes without paying interest for them except in
proportion as they used them, giving Government securities as
against the notes. That proposal has been made, I think, by
Mr. Foxwell. It was to that that I alluded. If we once go into
the question of the issue of 1*l*. notes, and I think that the country
ought to go into the question, we should naturally reopen the
broad issue whether it is worth while for the country to exert
itself to increase the number of branch banks in small towns.

10,196. You would consider, would you not, that one great
reason why there are more branches of banks in small towns in
Scotland than in England is on account of the Scotch banks not
being put to any expense in the matter of till money by having
the right of issuing their own notes?—Yes.

10,197. In your answer to Question 9871, you said, " I would
propose that the bank should keep in the form of gold 1,000
sovereigns for every 2,000*l*. of notes of whatever denomination
is used." You are aware that one reason against that was that
if that were enacted, then at any time of gradually growing
stringency the Bank of England would be obliged to double the
amount of their sovereigns for every pound of notes that came in
for payment, and that the reason for adopting the present system
is that it would not have that effect in times of stringency?—Well,
I know that was held, but it seems to me that the whole business
of banking is one which each generation has solved for itself.
I have myself very little interest in the past controversies on the
Bank Act, because almost all the arguments that were brought
forward on either side seem to me to be based on conditions that
do not exist now, or at all events not exactly in the form in
which they existed then. Of course it is true that in case we
ever should be invaded there might be an almost unlimited

demand for bullion, but unless we should meet with some disaster which was next door to the destruction of the nation, I cannot myself think that with our present appliances of the telegraph any such run would be probable.

10,198. But in times like 1847, 1857, and 1866, as the law at present stands, if the Bank loses 1,000,000 of sovereigns their reserve is reduced by 1,000,000, but under your proposal it would be reduced 2,000,000. I do not think that this question quite falls within the scope of our inquiry; but as you have expressed the opinion, I should like to ask you whether you have considered the point thoroughly, and whether you do not think there is an advantage in the present system?—Well, you see, I think it is essential as part of my system that the average reserve of the Bank should be about 20,000,000 more than this minimum reserve. You will perhaps notice that I proposed that when the rate of discount should rise to 10 per cent., the directors should be able, without waiting for the authority of the Government, to issue notes in excess of twice their bullion reserve. But while admitting that the wonderful efficiency and economy of the English banking system has been a great aid in our progress, I hold very strongly that by far the greatest evil that we have to deal with is the occasional pressure in the money market. I know that that is much less now than it used to be, but to my mind this silver question is not of anything like so great importance to the nation as the question of the right constitution of our banking reserve.

10,199. I am glad to hear your proposal of 10 per cent., because it exactly tallies with the amendment I myself proposed in Mr. Lowe's Bill when he was Chancellor of the Exchequer; but so far as the proportion which the Bank is to hold as against its bullion, the effect upon the banking department of the Bank would simply be that in the one case, for every million of gold which it lost, it would have to call in two million notes, and in the other case it would only have to call in one, and I gather that you really think there would not be any disadvantage in that change? —No, because this would not operate, of course, until 20,000,000 had gone, which is a very large sum to go.

10,200. Then you propose to fuse the banking and the issue departments in that case?—Yes.

10,201. Because, if you do not propose to fuse the banking and the issue departments, then, of course, whatever the amount of the reserve might be, even if it were 50,000,000, still if the Bank lost 5,000,000 your 50,000,000 would be reduced by 5,000,000, and in the other case by 10,000,000 ?—The change which I propose would abrogate the 1844 Act, and the distinction between the banking and the issue departments would therefore go as a part of the change. I wish to say again what I think I did say last time, that I give these numbers only for the sake of definiteness. I should not dream of presuming to give any opinion as to what the numbers should be, as to whether the notes should be twice or three times, or one and a half times as large as the bullion, nor as to whether the ordinary reserve in excess of this should be 20,000,000 or 30,000,000. If there would be any doubt as to whether 20,000,000 would be sufficient to guard us from ever being likely in any ordinary time to have the reserve getting down to its minimum at which the bank had to withdraw two notes for every sovereign withdrawn from it, I should be inclined to raise that 20,000,000 to 30,000,000 or more. Of course we could afford to do that, because we should have diminished in other ways the expense of our currency. Also it must be recollected that in no case would it be necessary to withdraw two notes for every sovereign after the rate of discount had risen to 10 per cent.

10,202. But if you should propose that the Bank should be obliged to withdraw any given proportion of notes as against a loss of sovereigns, then you would be obliged, would you not, to keep the issue department separate from the banking department, because otherwise, practically what you are indicating is merely that they should have a certain minimum of reserve ?—I think the new Act might be so worded as to create a new issue department. But I do not see that it is essential to have a separate department in order to carry out the Act I now propose.

10,203. (*Mr. Montagu.*) In your evidence in answer to Question 9841, you refer to my suggestion with regard to a convention for universal bimetallism, or a fixed mint ratio, as you term it, of about 20 to 1, with a seigniorage of 1 per cent. on silver. You have no objection, on principle, to a seigniorage. I think your evidence shows us that you rather advocate a seigniorage on silver ?—I should have no objection, but I cannot exactly be said to advocate it, because I do not think that a seigniorage of 1 per cent. would be sufficient in amount to prevent there being a great strain on the adopted ratio between gold and silver, though the strain would be somewhat less, perhaps, than under fixed-ratio-mintage pure and simple; yet there would, I think, still be a danger of a strain upon that ratio.

10,204. I also suggested a seigniorage of one quarter per cent. on gold to cover the cost of minting. You advocate in your evidence the use of gold bars for international payments. Would not a small seigniorage on the gold, and, say, a larger seigniorage on silver, tend to bring about that result, that bar gold and bar silver would be preferentially used for international purposes ?— I think it would. At the same time I have myself a great objection to a seigniorage on gold, unless the gold coins are supplemented largely by paper money. If they are supplemented largely by paper money, if the basis of our currency is a very large volume of bars, then I think it is desirable to have a seigniorage on gold coins; but if we have a state of things at all like the present, with our real reserve supposed to be in the pockets of the people, then by levying a seigniorage we cause the exchanges to have, of course, a larger margin of fluctuation than they otherwise would have if there were no seigniorage, and I regard that as a great evil. One of the chief motives which I, as well as Ricardo, had for advocating the use of bars instead of sovereigns was, that as things are at present, in consequence of the wear and tear of coins, and in some cases of the seigniorage, there is a greater fluctuation in the rates of exchange between different gold-using countries than there ought to be.

10,205. Are you aware that in Germany and France, and in most other countries, there is a small charge, about equivalent to one quarter per cent., on coining ?—It was such cases as those that I had in view.

10,206. And that in consequence the bar gold is chosen preferentially; if bar gold exists, say, in the national banks, the coin is not melted up ?—Yes, I was aware of that.

10,207. Therefore to that extent it would be an advantage ?— Yes.

10,208. Would not a seigniorage of 1 per cent., or, say, even 2 per cent., as is charged in India, prevent the settlement of international balances in silver coin if there were an international convention ?—It would tend that way.

10,209. Because gold would have to be at a premium of 2 per cent. before silver could take its place ?—Yes.

10,210. If all mint regulations were identical under conventions, and silver bars were sent to this country, the motive could not be in order to get gold, because silver would be a legal tender equally with gold ; you agree with that ?—Yes.

10,211. Therefore, if silver bars were sent to England because the exchanges were in our favour, when the exchanges turned against us we could export that silver in lieu of gold ?—Yes.

10,212. In answer to Question 9856 you state that you do not wish to prevent fluctuations in the price of silver. Is there not a certain disadvantage in trading with our Indian fellow-subjects, owing to variations in exchange, which frequently varies 1 per cent. in a day ?—That is not what I meant. You are now reverting to an answer which refers to my favourite scheme ; for what I have called a true bimetallism. I meant that under it there would no longer be any necessity for trying to prevent changes in the gold value of silver ; beause those changes would not disturb the course of international trade, as they do now. One chief merit that I claim for the scheme is that it would work on steadily and supply a stable international currency in spite of these changes.

10,213. But do you not see an advantage in having a steady exchange with India and silver-using countries ?—My object in that scheme is to get a steady exchange without its being necessary to fix the gold value of silver.

10,214. But I understood you to suggest, that different countries should agree to coin silver in large quantities, and yet you leave to them the conditions under which they would issue the silver. Consequently the silver would fluctuate perhaps even more in such a case than it does now ?—You are now alluding to a different scheme, that which I have called universal humpbacked monometallism. In that scheme I propose that a seigniorage should be levied on silver in most countries about as heavy as it could bear ; that silver should not be international tender at all ;

that for international purposes we should have nothing whatever but gold; and that therefore the fluctuations in the gold value of silver should not cause any disturbance in the exchanges. I would wish, however, to repeat that this is not my favourite proposal; it is not one that I am prepared to advocate, though I think it is one of many schemes which has as much right to a full and fair discussion as fixed-ratio-mintage has before any action is taken.

10,215. Would it not be disadvantageous to all governments to make frequent changes in their currency ?—Yes.

10,216. Therefore, that proposal which you made, whether your own or of others, would cause frequent changes of necessity— I should say frequent changes in the value of the silver coins ?— I am aware of that disadvantage, and it seems to me to be the greatest disadvantage that the scheme has. It has been that more than anything else that has prevented me from saying that I would like it introduced, though, so far as I can see at present, I would myself prefer it to fixed-ratio-mintage.

10,217. In such a case if you have no international convention, silver might be quite depreciated, and the countries having to coin silver according to that plan would have to change the weight of their silver coins to prevent forgery ?—The difficulty would not be greater than it is in France now.

10,218. With regard to the rise that is mentioned in tin and copper, are you aware that the rise is attributed to a speculative syndicate ?—Yes.

10,219. One more question with regard to the Indian Government; would not the payment of pensions in sterling involve a loss of net exchange in the same way as the loss on the interest on the gold debt ?—Yes, except in so far as it may be supposed that the persons who receive the pensions were induced to enter the service of the Government by the promise that their pensions should not be affected by the fall in the value of silver.

10,220. I forgot to ask you with regard to the market ratio being fixed at 20 to 1, what is your principal objection, if any, to that proposal ?—My own objection to fixed-ratio-mintage with a fixed ratio of 20 to 1 is not at all strong. I should regard it, however, as very likely only a transitional arrangement.

10,221. Say, under a convention for twenty years ?—Yes.

Well, I would myself rather it was made a convention to last as long as it could last. I would not propose to put a definite limit to it. I then should not regard it as in any way an evil, but I could not exactly advocate it; I should rather be neutral with regard to it. But I should be distinctly opposed to its being adopted in a hurry before other schemes had been fairly discussed.

10,222. (*The Chairman.*) Supposing that the increased supply of money at the Bank of England led to a lowering of the rate of discount and so stimulated speculative activity, would not a great deal of that speculative activity, perhaps the greater part of it, be likely to expend itself in new production, whether it is starting fresh mills, sinking fresh mines, or increasing the production of commodities?—Certainly, in the long run, but then this effect that we are looking at is, from the nature of the case, only a temporary one, and the immediate effect of the starting of new companies is to add to the demand for commodities much more than to the production of commodities.

10,223. Is that so, does it not very speedily arrive at the addition to the quantity of commodities?—I should doubt that.

10,224. Within a year would it not? For example, in the west of America we are told that the greater part of the land there is cultivated by means of capital coming from the east. Well, that capital would result in increased cereal production within probably a year or a couple of years at the outside?—Yes, but a year is a long time when we are talking of the action of a rate of discount upon speculation and prices. I mean that supposing that gold comes into the country to Lombard Street in the first instance, it scatters itself over the country in much less than a year. From that point of view a year is a long time.

10,225. Yes, but supposing that you are right in your view as to the way in which the addition to the store of gold would affect prices or the diminution would affect prices, that effect would only be temporary, because in the long run and within three or four years the effect might be increased production and reduced prices, owing to the very activity that you have stimulated?—I do not think that the stimulated activity due to a cause of that kind would have an effect of very great volume on production. Of course it is possible that the influx of gold from the mines in the last thirty years may have caused production to have been very much greater than it would have been. Opinions differ on this point. My opinion is that it has not in the long run any great effect; that it has caused the movements to be spasmodic; but that the increased production would have been very much the same without the new gold.

10,226. (*Sir T. Farrer.*) You have sent us a paper giving your views concerning the effect of a fall of exchange on trade with silver-using countries. Will you be so good as to put it in as part of your evidence ? And will you be so good as to turn to Mr. Nisbet's evidence, and especially to Questions 10,026–10,033, 10,044, 10,068, 10,077, and 10,113, in which he states specifically that a fall in the exchange value of the rupee at once lowers the gold price of Indian wheat in the English market, and gives instances of it ? And will you be so good—either in answer to this question or in your paper—as to tell us what in your view is the real explanation of the cases Mr. Nisbet mentions : whether the fall in the value of silver has any, and if any what, effect on the English gold price of Indian wheat ; what are the real causes of the fall in exchange and of the fall in the price of the wheat respectively ; and how it is that the two phenomena coincide so as to lead to the common belief that the one is the cause of the other ? I should like to ask you further whether, if there had been no fall in the gold price of silver, other circumstances remaining the same, there would not probably have been a greater fall in the silver price of Indian wheat than there has been ? Will you at the same time be so good as to look at Mr. Barclay's evidence in which he says that the fall in exchange has precisely an opposite effect on the sale of English cotton manufactures in India, and that by increasing the number of rupees which the Indian consumer has to give it either prevents sales or compels the English producer to take a lower gold price ? And will you be kind enough to explain how in your opinion this fall in exchanges, which *primâ facie* seems to have the effect attributed to it by Mr. Barclay, really operates ?—I shall have much pleasure in doing as you request.

(iii) Memorandum as to the Effects which Differences between the Currencies of Different Nations have on International Trade.

It is impossible to discuss adequately in a memorandum the causes which determine the course of the foreign exchanges and the reciprocal influences which they exert on the course of trade. I must, therefore, start by taking for granted the solution of these questions with regard to the trade between two countries, A and B, each of which have a gold currency.

Ricardo's reasoning on this subject has been developed by Mill, Mr. Goschen, Mr. Giffen, Professor Bastable, and others; and it is now clearly established that trade tends so to adjust the supplies of gold relatively to the demands for gold in the two countries as to bring gold prices at the seaboards of the two countries to equality, allowance being made for carriage.

If [1] they are higher in A than in B, there will be a small temporary bounty on exportation from B to A corresponding to this difference, which must always be small. Bills drawn in B on A will multiply, and, specie point being reached, gold will go from A to B till prices in B are as high as in A. If B hoards gold this process may be a long one, otherwise it is sure to be short.

The fluctuations of the exchanges measured in terms of gold bars, that is, of gold regarded as a commodity, are limited under ordinary circumstances to the double cost of carriage of gold. But when measured in terms of the currencies of the two countries the limits of these fluctuations are liable to be extended by the sum of the seigniorages (if any) charged in the two countries, and in extreme cases by the sum of the amounts lost by wear and tear, not indeed from the average coins in circulation, but from those picked coins which are selected for the purposes of export.

[1] Cf. *Money, Credit and Commerce*, pp. 225–7.

170

It may not be an unnecessary caution to remark that even when the exchanges are at par, the trade bills on the one side need not exactly balance those on the other, for those on either side are likely to be supplemented by paper documents or telegrams representing (i) the transfer of newly borrowed capital, (ii) the repayment of business outlays and the payment of interest or profits on previous investments of capital, (iii) the drawings by absentees who live temporarily or permanently in one country and derive their means of support from another, and (iv) the drawings of a government which expends in one country part of the income which it derives from another.   Under the first head come such items as the transfer or telegraphic sale of " international securities," that is, of securities which, whatever be the country of their origin, have a market in both A and B.

When thus it is said that an increase of purchasers abroad makes the exchanges unfavourable to either country, it is always tacitly implied that other things are equal; that is, either that there is meanwhile no such disturbing cause as a transfer of stock exchange securities, etc. from one country to another, or that separate allowance is made for its effects.   For instance, if B should fall into political discredit, and those who had invested capital in B should want to bring it home, that would cause a premium on bills drawn on A by exporters in B.   Under the second head come trade expenses of many different kinds, and especially in connection with the shipping trade.   The wording of the problem is further complicated, but its substance is in no respect whatever changed if we consider A's trade not merely with B, but with all other countries which have gold currencies.

But while referring to the ordinary text-books for the general treatment of this part of the question, I wish to observe that its real nature has been in some measure disguised by the habit, borrowed from the City, of describing the trade in the precious metals in different language from that used in describing the trade in any other commodity.   If on the balance B is indebted to A, and in consequence the exchanges are "favourable" to A, merchants in B will consider what things they can send to A, and sell there at a price higher than they could get by investing the same money in a bill on A, on which they have to pay a premium ;

in every case they have to allow for cost of carriage, etc., and for interest on the time required for realising. If the premium on the bill is just equal to the cost of carriage of gold, so that it is indifferent to a merchant whether he buys a bill or sends the gold, it is said that " gold point " has been reached. But with equal appropriateness it might be said that " lead point " is reached, or that " Egyptian point " is reached, when the difference between the prices of lead or of Egyptian bonds in the two countries is just balanced, after allowing for the charges of transport, by the premium at which bills on A sell in B. The question whether any one thing, such as lead, can exercise any important influence in adjusting the balance of trade, depends partly on its portability and partly on the extent of the market which it finds in either country. The power of gold for this purpose is therefore of primary importance between two countries which have a gold currency, for gold has in each a practically unlimited market. But its influence would be much weaker if one of the countries had a paper currency or a silver currency.

Firstly,[1] let us consider the trade between England and Russia. Gold prices in England and rouble prices in Russia are determined by the work which the currency has to do in either country on the one hand and the volume of that currency on the other. And when trade is in equilibrium, the gold price of the rouble will be fixed just at the ratio which gold prices in England bear to rouble prices in Russia. For, suppose that it were not at this level, but were, say, below it; that is, suppose the number of roubles which exchanged for $1l.$ to be increased above the ratio which the goods that were priced at $1l.$ in England bore to those which were priced at a rouble in Russia, allowance being made for transport. Then exporters from Russia would sell their goods for gold which, when converted into roubles, would give them more than ordinary trade profits; while importers into Russia would lose money if they sold their bills on Russia at the current rate of exchange. The immediate result would be that these importers would refuse to sell at that price, but would prefer to buy Russian goods and bring them back. Exporters' bills in Russia would therefore be without any market at the old rate, and their value, or, in other

---

[1] Cf. *Money, Credit and Commerce*, pp. 315-8.

words, the rouble price of the sovereign, would fall almost instantaneously.   That is, the gold price of the rouble would rise almost
instantaneously until it was equal to the ratio in which gold
prices in England stand to rouble prices in Russia.   In the same
way it can be proved that the gold price of roubles cannot be in
equilibrium above this level; and therefore that in equilibrium
it must be at this level.

Next, suppose that the trade being in equilibrium, there is a
sudden fall in the gold value of the rouble due to some extraneous
cause, as, for instance, political apprehensions.   To put the case
in the strongest way, let us suppose that these apprehensions are
not shared in Russia; and that at first there is no depreciation
of the rouble in Russia, and no rise of rouble prices there.   Russian
exporters will then expect to sell at an unchanged gold price, and
to convert that gold price into a greater number of roubles, and
thus to make abnormally high profits.   All those, therefore, who
were in doubt whether to export or not will do so in order to gain
the anticipated bounty from the exchanges.   There will be a
flutter of increased exportation from Russia.   The excessive
supply of Russian exports in the English market may lower their
price there a little.   But this bounty on exportation from Russia
can last only until Russian exporters try to dispose of their bills;
the moment they do that they will find that since a bill for 100*l.*
will give the means of purchasing only as many English commodities as before, and since by the hypothesis there is no
depreciation of the rouble in Russia, these can be only sold for as
many roubles as before, and no one will continue to pay a premium
for the bill; the gold price of the rouble will adjust itself almost
instantaneously to the ratio which gold prices bear to rouble
prices.

Different suppositions may be made as to the causes of the
fall in the gold value of the rouble, but it will be found that by
similar routes we get in all cases to the same result, namely, that
a fall in the gold price of the rouble cannot give any permanent
stimulus to importation from Russia, because it must almost
instantaneously accommodate itself to the ratio which gold
prices bear to rouble prices.   But of course this does not exclude
disturbances of the Russian exchanges due to fluctuations in the

relative supplies of importers' and exporters' bills and other international obligations. Such disturbances may, as we have seen, occur between two countries with gold currencies. They may give a bounty on exporters' bills in consequence of excessive importation; or through one country lending to others, or, which is more probable in the case of Russia, through other nations withdrawing some of the capital which they have lent to her. It is worth while to remark that this last event is especially likely to happen when political distrust has lowered the price of the rouble; and this fact is perhaps accountable for much of the popular belief that a fall in the value of the rouble gives a permanent bounty to Russian exporters generally.

For people see that a fall of the gold price of the rouble is accompanied by a prolonged bounty on exportation from Russia; and think the first event is the cause of the other. But the real cause in this case is a general distrust of Russia's economic future, which makes investors desire to withdraw their capital from Russia; at the same time that it makes the price of the rouble fall, and so long as they are withdrawing capital, the exchanges must necessarily be such as to give a general bounty on exportation from Russia.

Before quitting this subject we must consider another way in which a Russian exporter may appear to be receiving something more than a temporary bounty from a fall in the value of the rouble, when really this gain is due to causes that are independent of the currency; but whereas, when capital is withdrawn from Russia all her exporters get a bounty, in this case some of them get the bounty at the expense of others. Suppose, for instance, that the Russian wheat grower is able to deliver his wheat at a profit in the English market at a lower price relatively to that which the exporters of other Russian produce require in order to get a fair profit. If Russia had a gold currency, the price at which she could deliver wheat in England would fall a little, and people would see in the change merely the substitution of wheat for other Russian exports. As it is, however, this fact is likely to be disguised. The exporter perhaps sees the gold price which he gets for his wheat go on falling even faster than the rouble price at which he can afford to sell it, but since the gold price of roubles is falling too, he gets enough roubles to pay him.   He and others attribute his successful sales to the fall in the gold price of roubles.   But the fact is that if he had not been able to deliver his wheat at a lower rate relatively to the average exports from Russia than before, he would have got no bounty ; the sustained high profits which he does make are not dependent on the nature of Russia's currency, but would exist equally if Russia had a gold currency.

Next, let us consider the trade between England and a country which has a silver currency, say India ; this case differs from the preceding only in consequence of the fact that silver is an exportable commodity, and roubles are not ; and, therefore, while the gold value of the rouble adapts itself almost instantaneously to the ratio which the gold prices of goods bear to their rouble prices (allowance being made for carriage), the adjustment is liable to be delayed in the case of the rupee.   For whereas Russian exporters could generally make no use of their bills on England except to buy with them (or to sell them to others who want to buy) commodities in the English market whose gold price had not altered, it would be otherwise with the Indian exporters.   If silver has fallen in value in England and not in India, they will make a good business by using those bills to buy silver, and so long as this state of things lasts there will be a steady flow of silver to India.   During the whole of this process there will be a bounty on the exportation of goods from India ; and, therefore, it is interesting to inquire how long it will last.

In the first place it must be admitted that a fall in the gold price of silver may cause Englishmen to distrust Indian securities, public and private.   This will lead them to withdraw capital from India, or at least to check their lendings to India ; and this will diminish the number of bills which India is able to draw on England, and thus give a premium to the bills of exporters from India.   But, as in the parallel case relating to Russia, we may put aside a disturbance arising from this cause as extraneous to our main investigation.   And if this be put aside we shall find that the premium cannot last long.

Those who hold the contrary opinion generally insist that as custom forbids silver prices to change in India, they must be taken as a fixed point, and we must expect any change in the gold price of silver to cause a parallel change in the gold prices of commodities in the Western world. I myself think that the force of custom in India is much less than is generally supposed, but in order that my main argument may not be taken in the flank by an attack on this point, I will for the present assume that their premises are correct. Assuming then that the flow of silver to India will not appreciably affect the purchasing power of silver there, it is clear that the flow of silver will go on until either the gold price of commodities has fallen in the English market or the gold price of silver has risen there, or, lastly, there has been a little of each of these changes, with the effect in each of the three cases of making the gold price of silver again equal to the ratio which the gold prices of goods in England bear to the rupee prices of goods in India (allowance being made for carriage). So much is common ground, but there is a difference of opinion as to the way in which this result will be brought about.

According to the older, and, as I believe the juster view, prices in England are determined by the relation in which the amount of business done in England stands to the volume of the currency, account being taken of the methods of business. Thus those purchases which are made by cheques and other instruments of credit are set on one side, and there are left remaining those purchases which are made with currency. Changes in the habits of business would, of course, alter the proportion which these purchases are of the total business; and the effects which such changes have in raising or lowering prices may at any time be much greater than those due to changes in the volume of the currency. But it is clear that a change in the gold price of silver has no effect on the methods of business, that, for instance, it does not either increase or diminish the proportion of the purchases in which payment is made by cheques. Therefore, if the gold price of silver affects gold prices in England, it must do so either by increasing the amount of goods that are brought into England or by diminishing the volume of her currency. Now it is admitted on all sides that the readiness of the East to absorb large quantities of silver (and indeed of gold also) has caused the volume of the currency throughout the West to be less than it otherwise would;

and that although England's own demand for silver is at present very inelastic, yet the absorption of gold by other countries of the West to take the place of their lost silver has tended to lessen the volume of England's currency, and therefore to lower prices in England.

[1] The precious metals are then so distributed throughout the world, that, independently of the demand for them for the purposes of hoarding and of the arts, each country has just that aggregate amount of the two metals which corresponds in value to the volume of that part of her business which the habits of her people cause her to transact by payments in coin, account being taken of the rapidity of circulation of coin, and of the absorption of some quantity of the precious metals to act as the basis of a paper currency. The question what part of a country's share she takes in gold and what in silver is determined entirely by her own tastes. (If she mints them freely at a fixed ratio, it is then determined for her by Gresham's law; but just now we are not concerned with this case.)

Thus then I regard the volume of the business in each country which requires the use of coin as determined by each country's wealth and habits; the proportion between the gold and silver which it uses, whether for currency, for hoarding, or for the arts, as determined by its tastes; and these conditions all the world over as determining the aggregate demand for silver and the aggregate demand for gold. The aggregate supply of each metal may be taken as a fixed quantity at any time, because its annual increase is in any case but a small part of the total stock existing; but yet this is slowly modified by the annual production, which is governed by the richness of the mines on the one hand, and the value in terms of commodities of an ounce of the metal on the other. The value of each metal is determined by the relation in which the supply of it stands to the demand for it. The ratio between the two values thus determined is the gold price of silver.

According to this old, and I had thought well-established, doctrine, the gold price of silver is determined by the ratio between the prices of commodities in gold and in silver countries. If any

[1] Cf. *Money, Credit and Commerce*, pp. 229, 230.

sudden discoveries of silver mines in the West, or any discarding of silver from Western currencies, should disturb the equilibrium, the silver that was not wanted in the West would go to the East; and even if its influx into the East did not lower its value there, its efflux from the West would raise its value there till it and the ratio which gold prices bear to silver prices were equal to one another. As a matter of fact, partly in consequence of improvements in production, the volume of currency in the West has diminished relatively to the work it has to do, and this has caused gold prices to fall and the value of gold to rise relatively to commodities. This change, together with the (greater or less) fixity of silver prices, has, I contend, raised the value of gold relatively to silver, i.e. has lowered the gold price of silver. It is true that no trustworthy statistics are forthcoming by which to establish independently the statement that the volume of currency in the West has decreased relatively to the work which it has to do. But the account which I have given claims to be consistent with all our economic knowledge, and to ascribe no effects to any cause save those which the cause is known to be likely to produce.

This being the older view, we may next turn to consider the new doctrine which has been put forward in opposition to it by Mr. Barclay and others. I understand it to be that some external cause has produced the fall in the gold price of silver, and that in consequence, (i) Indian exporters being content with the old silver prices, and their silver prices being equivalent to lower gold prices than before, they are willing to accept lower gold prices, and therefore the gold prices of Oriental goods fall in England. (ii) English exporters can sell their wares in India for only as high silver prices as before, and as these are worth less gold than before, English producers of goods that are sent to India get into the habit of accepting lower prices wherever they sell their classes of goods, and (iii) by sympathy there is a fall in the prices of other English goods, this fall being produced not, as the older economists maintain, by a diminution of the volume of the currency in gold countries relatively to the work which it has to do, but by the direct effects of the fall in the gold value of silver.

I will first consider the theoretical side of this argument, and turn to its statistical basis later on. I reject as invalid its first step, because I think that Indian exporters to England are not likely to sell their goods for a less price than they can get. Goods which they have offered for 100*l*. they will still offer for 100*l*., only instead of using their bills to buy English goods in return, they will give their attention to that one commodity, silver, which, according to the hypothesis, has fallen in the English market and not in the Indian. It is true that, finding their trade exceptionally profitable, they will probably increase their exportation to England, and slightly glut the market, and perhaps have to sell temporarily for 99*l*. what they had sold for 100*l*. But neglecting as they necessarily would other goods, and taking back silver almost alone, they would want a very great deal of it. Next, turning to the second step of the argument, I reject that on similar grounds. If the exporters from England find that they cannot sell their goods in India at as good prices as elsewhere, they will look about for other markets, and perhaps stint their production a little. Less being sent to India, there will be a lack of bills on India, and this again will make the flow of silver to India more violent. In this way 5,000,000*l*. a month of silver could easily be absorbed, and such a drain would speedily exhaust the surplus store of silver in Europe, and raise the gold price of silver to its old level. When that was done things would go on as before.

It has been urged in answer to this argument that there is not a large stock of silver in England free to be sent to the East. But in so far as this is the case, my argument is not weakened, but strengthened. For when the fall in the value of silver in the English market has caused Indian merchants to select it in preference to English goods for importation into India, then the scantier the available supplies of silver, the more quickly will the demand for it raise its price to the old level. In practice, however, the English market has, of course, the power of causing by indirect means deliveries of silver in India greatly in excess of the free stock of silver at the time in England.

I contend then that, if the currency in gold countries is large relatively to the business which it has to do, prices then will be high, and if any external cause brings down the gold value of silver, without subtracting anything from the currency of gold countries, there will be a violent and rapid flow of silver to India; this will be not a quiet current, but a deluge like that which occurs when the embankment of a reservoir breaks down and water rushes from its higher level violently over the plain, so that the level in the reservoir sinks to that of the plain almost instantaneously.

The actual course of events appears to have been that an increased production of goods, combined with the adoption of many countries of a gold currency, and a slackening of the growth of many (though not of all) the artificial substitutes for the currency as means of payment, has gradually raised the value of gold in the West.   Whenever the West has had a little more silver than usual to spare, the East has promptly taken it; when its gold value has fallen below the ratio which gold prices bear to silver prices by ever so small a percentage, it has flowed in a largely augmented current.   Its value never has diverged to any considerable extent and for any considerable time from this level.   That it has not done so is proved both by our general knowledge of the trade and by the fact that there never has been a torrent of silver flowing to the East such as would have been immediately caused by such a divergence.   And indeed the fall in the real value of silver in Europe relatively to India seems to have been greater, and to have given a higher premium on the importation of silver into India and the exportation of goods from India before 1873 than after it.   For her importation of silver during the fourteen years ending 1872–73 was 837 lakhs annually, and only 654 lakhs annually during the following fourteen years; while her net exports of commodities were about equal in the two periods, in spite of the fact that she was borrowing foreign capital more freely in the former than in the latter period.   These facts are in accordance with the truth that a fall in the gold value of silver does not by itself cause an exportation of silver from gold to silver countries; it may or may not be accompanied by other events which do cause that exportation.

Thus then, I conclude, that the gold prices of goods in the West cannot be affected to any considerable extent by a change in the gold price of silver independently of a change in the relation between the volumes of the currencies in gold countries and the work which they have to do.   When a fall in the gold price of silver is accompanied by the exportation of silver to India, the question whether that exportation will affect gold prices depends on whether the silver is surplus silver or not. If it takes only surplus silver and does not narrow the basis of Western currencies relatively to the work which they have to do, it will not affect prices. If it does narrow that basis, it will lower the gold prices of goods ; and then people may attribute this fall not to its true cause, the narrowing of the basis of the Western currencies, but to an event which happened to accompany it, the fall in the gold value of silver.

So far I have been content to speak as though silver prices in India were practically fixed by custom.   But rather to relieve my own mind than because it is necessary for my argument, I should like to state that minute inquiries from persons engaged in business in India, and a study of Indian history and statistics, have convinced me that the rule of custom is feebler than is generally supposed, and that it does not extend to many of the most important classes of goods, especially those with which international trade is chiefly concerned. For instance, having drawn side by side curves representing the movements since 1870 of index numbers, representing the course of general prices in England, Germany, France, America, and India respectively, I find that the curve which shows the greatest variations is that of India.   And the case would be even stronger if account be taken of the facts that in India there are at one and the same time greater local variations of prices than in any Western country, and that many of the sharpest of the variations in price destroy one another when added together to find an average price for the whole of India.

I believe that India is changing her economic character very rapidly.   There is a great increase of what mediæval economists call *adœrations*, that is, the substitution of payments by cash for barter, for the exchange of services, for labour dues, and for produce rents. This has caused a greatly extended need for currency, and would have lowered prices very much if silver had not flowed in in large quantities.   In spite of the fact that the hoarding of silver overshadows its use as currency in India, I think we may reasonably suppose that this influx has caused prices there to be higher than they otherwise would have been.

I will now pass to the statistical side of the argument that the gold price of silver influences the course of trade in a way which the reasonings of the older economists fail to explain. I have read, I think, nearly everything that has been written on this subject, and have not found a single instance of well-authenticated facts which do not seem to me in complete harmony with the older doctrines. India has undersold other countries in certain goods in which she has obtained a relative advantage, and no doubt partly in consequence, she has been undersold in others. In some goods she has been undersold by gold countries and in some by silver countries, in some goods she has undersold gold countries and in some silver countries. A fall in the gold price of silver has been coincident sometimes with an increase in her trade with gold countries and a fall in her trade with silver countries, and sometimes *vice versâ*. All these facts are in accordance with the older doctrines and are difficult to be explained by the advocates of the new opinion that changes in the gold price of silver exert a great influence on the course of trade.

Much stress has indeed been laid on the fact that India is now able herself to manufacture some of her own raw cotton. But the prophecy that if England allowed her once to have a good start, she would supply herself with all the coarse goods she wanted was made before much had been heard of a continued fall in the gold value of silver. Colonel Raynsford Jackson, for instance, says (*Fortnightly Review* for June 1876), "Such are the elements of advantage on the side of the Indian manufacturer that he can retain the coarse trade without a duty. . . . This trade is virtually gone from England." As a matter of fact it has left England so much more slowly than was then prophesied that, if we argued *post hoc, ergo propter hoc*, we might conclude that the fall in the gold price of silver had retarded the growth of Indian cotton mills. And though it is not strictly pertinent, I cannot forbear to say that if we so governed India that she had to continue always to send her cotton to England to be manufactured, our rule of India could not be justified at the bar of history.

I will now turn to the wheat trade. It has already been

brought before the Commission that the growth of the Indian importation of wheat has been influenced by a series of good harvests in India, by the making of railways, through wheat districts, by the lowering of freights, and by improvements in the methods of cleansing Indian wheat and fitting it for European consumption.   The good harvests have kept the price of wheat on the inland fields from rising, the railways have in several ways done more in helping the price of wheat at the Indian seaboard to approach near to its price on the field than they have done for any other important Indian product.   The lowering of ocean freights has brought the price at which Indian wheat can be delivered in England very much nearer its price at the Indian seaboard.   The improvements in the arts of cleansing, etc. have raised the price which millers are willing to give for it relatively to other wheats. That, under these circumstances, it should have succeeded to so very small an extent in displacing other Indian produce in European markets is a fact which seems to me to require special explanation.   And this I find in observing that wheat is in many new countries practically a by-product, the main product is often cultivated land; people are willing to grow wheat at a loss, if meanwhile they get a good title to the fertile land which they have been bringing into cultivation.   Whether this is the true explanation or not, the mystery to be solved seems to me not to be the rapidity, but the slowness of the growth of the Indian export trade in wheat.

It is well known that the price of wheat is determined permanently by the cost of producing it, not under the easiest, but under the most difficult conditions, and, to use an old-fashioned and awkward phrase, by its cost of production on the margin of cultivation.   But of course it is true that when supply is already adjusted to demand, the effect of throwing an extra supply for unconditional sale on the market is to lower the price all round. This fact has been elevated into a law, in what I regard as a misleading manner; it is being said that the price of wheat is determined by the price of the cheapest supply.   On general grounds I should expect cases in which this was in any sense true to be rather rare with reference to such a commodity as wheat, which does not perish quickly, and in which a large trade is done in "*futures*." I should have supposed that any small extra importation of Indian wheat would have had but a very small and transient effect in diminishing the price of wheat in English markets generally, that it would have been more likely to induce a few farmers in North and South America to consume a little more of their own wheat on the farm than to cause a plethora of wheat here and keep the price of wheat in general here considerably lower than it otherwise would have been. But it has long been known that some of those engaged in the corn trade do not share this opinion, and now I am asked to direct my attention specially to the evidence recently given on this subject before the Commission by Mr. Nisbet.

I do not imply that he or anyone else has suggested that the price of wheat in a year in which the harvests of the world had been bad would be low merely because the price of silver was low. But I fail to see the drift of his evidence unless he means at least this much, that the minor movements upwards and downwards of the price of wheat, those extending over a few weeks, have been accompanied and in a great measure caused by parallel and, roughly speaking, proportionate changes in the price of silver. On such a matter as this the opinion of experts, infinitely more important as it is than the opinion of those who are not experts, has yet to be received with some caution. For it is the natural tendency of the human mind to be impressed by striking coincidences, and even though they are few in number, to attach to them a greater importance than to many other cases in which there has been no coincidence; and therefore we ought in all such cases to check the results of general impressions by the aid of arithmetic, when that can be brought to bear. And it fortunately happens that we have thoroughly trustworthy statistics of the price of silver and the price of wheat. One sixteenth of a penny is about a seven hundredth part of the price of an ounce of silver, and a halfpenny is just about the same fraction of the present price of wheat; and therefore Mr. Nisbet's evidence would lead me to suppose that, if not as a general rule, yet in the majority of cases a fall of four or five sixteenths in the price of silver would be accompanied by a fall of four or five halfpence in the price of wheat. In order to test his evidence therefore I have gone over the files of the *Economist* for 1886 and 1887, and selected those weeks in which the Gazette average price of wheat arrived at a turning-point, either a *maximum* at which it ceased to move upwards and began to fall, or a *minimum* at which it ceased to fall and began to rise.

I have taken out the prices of fine bar silver for the Friday afternoons of the same weeks (I have thought that no considerable error would be introduced by taking these to represent the prices of corresponding weeks); I have shown the changes of the one in halfpence and of the other in sixteenths of a penny. Then I have shown what parts of their movements were "together," and what movements were "apart." For instance, if each of the different columns showed + 4, or each showed − 5, I regard that as a coincidence confirming Mr. Nisbet's view, and enter four or five, as the case might be, in the column of movements together. If one different column showed + 4 and the other + 7, I regard that as a movement together to the extent of four, so far confirming his views, but a movement apart to the extent of three, tending so far to invalidate his views. The result is as follows. (See table on page 186.)

Thus, so far as these figures show, the movements together of the two prices have amounted to 84, and those apart to 1,053. The latter have been more than twelve times as extensive in the aggregate as the former. I am ready to believe that persons acquainted with the corn trade may be able to point out several minor deductions which ought to be made from the force of these figures : I can even see a few myself. But after ample and liberal allowance has been made for them, there will, I think, be enough force left in the figures to prove conclusively that fluctuations in the price of silver have no considerable influence on the general prices of wheat in the English markets.

Passing away from this point, I find much to agree with, and very little to differ from, in Mr. Nisbet's instructive evidence. I agree with him when he says (Questions 10,054–55) : " I believe very little in bimetallism or monometallism as far as regards the supply of produce. If produce is wanted it will come. . . . Things would be no better for the British farmers were India and Russia placed on the same footing (as regards currency) as the rest of the

Week ending.	Price of silver in pence.	Difference in sixteenths of a penny.	Price of wheat in shillings and pence.	Difference in half-pence.	Movements together.	Movements apart.
	d.		s. d.			
1886 :						
January 2	46 13/16		30 3			
January 30	46 7/8	+ 1	29 7	— 16		17
February 6	46 1/2	— 6	29 9	+ 4		10
March 6	46 3/4	+ 4	29 0	— 18		22
March 27	46 11/16	— 1	30 9	+ 42		43
April 10	46 5/8	— 1	30 4	— 10	1	9
May 29	45 1/2	—18	32 5	+ 50		68
July 10	44 7/16	—17	30 9	— 40	17	23
July 31	43 1/8	—21	32 0	+ 30		51
August 7	42	—18	31 8	— 8	8	10
August 28	42 1/2	+ 8	33 2	+ 36	8	28
October 16	45 1/4	+44	29 8	— 84		128
1887 :						
January 22	47	+28	36 4	+160	28	132
February 26	46 5/16	—11	32 7	— 90	11	79
March 5	46	— 5	32 9	+ 4		9
March 12	No quotation.	0	32 7	— 4		4
April 2	44 5/16	—27	33 3	+ 16		43
April 23	44	— 5	32 6	— 18	5	13
June 11	43 13/16	— 3	35 4	+ 68		71
July 16	44 1/16	+ 4	34 0	— 32		36
July 23	44 1/16	+ 6	34 3	+ 6	6	0
September 17	44 1/2	+ 1	28 8	—134		135
September 24	44 7/16	— 1	28 9	+ 2		3
October 1	44 1/2	+ 1	28 5	— 8		9
November 12	43 7/8	—10	30 6	+ 50		60
November 19	43 7/8	0	30 5	— 2		2
December 3	43 7/8	0	31 3	+ 20		20
December 31	44 3/4	+14	30 9	— 12		28
Totals .					84	1,053

NOTE.—January 2, 1886, and December 31, 1887, are taken as the first and last weeks in the two years, not as weeks showing maxima or minima prices of wheat.

world; because they could produce and really do produce such large crops that they must be exported "; and again (10,065), " I do not for one moment believe that bi- or mono-metallism has any effect on imports of wheat, for this grain each year comes in from all parts of the world, and it is the natural course of affairs that it should do so."

On the other hand, I am perfectly willing to accept from him the statement (10,030) " that when silver went up in the market two per cent. . . . the large houses to whom we looked for the supplies put the wheat up sixpence a quarter " (10,097); " a special variation occurring on any particular day in the exchange from what happened the day before immediately affects the price offered (for wheat).   I can get wheat within six or eight hours at 6*d*. a quarter cheaper sometimes, and I have had to pay 6*d*. a quarter more according as the Indian telegrams come in." The statistics which I have just quoted, taken together with general considerations, lead me to suspect that even in these cases, other and less obtrusive causes may have assisted the Indian exchanges in putting the price of wheat up or down.   But no innovation on the older doctrines of money and the exchanges is required to explain the fact that a fall in the Indian exchanges makes it profitable for an Indian exporter to take a price, which otherwise he would have just refused, for a batch of wheat which he has on hand, and that by so doing he tends to lower for a time prices in the wheat market.   No one denies that a gust of wind will bring down apples that are ready to fall; but we should note that it leaves fewer apples to fall with the next wind.   All this then is not inconsistent with the account which I have submitted, according to which the gold price of silver is itself determined by the ratio which gold prices bear to silver prices; gold prices being determined by the circumstances of demand for a supply of currency in the gold countries, and silver prices being determined by the circumstances of demand for a supply of currency in the silver countries.   When asked to express a direct opinion on the action of the causes which it is the purpose of this paper to discuss, he deliberately declined to do so (see *e.g.* 10,124), and I submit, therefore, that such parts of his evidence as seem to bear indirectly on this question are to be taken as *obiter dicta*.

The study of his and similar evidence has given me no reason to doubt the validity of the older explanation of the facts which he recounts.

I still hold that though, " other things being equal," a fall in the Indian exchange tends to increase temporarily the sales of Indian wheat here and temporarily to lower the price of wheat, the careful interpretation of the clause " other things being equal " deprives this fact of the greater part of its apparent significance, and I will now sum up my conclusions as to the different ways in which a fall in the Indian exchanges may affect Indian trade.

In the first place, the fall might conceivably be caused by a fall in the value of silver in India arising from the discovery of rich mines there, or from a diminution of hoarding there; in that case silver would be a surplus commodity in India, and would flow to Europe, taking the place of other exports from India. The exporter from India would find that though the Indian exchanges had fallen and the gold price of silver had fallen, yet the ratio which gold prices in England bear to silver prices in India had fallen even more, and in this case, therefore, the fall in the exchanges would be accompanied by a penalty and not a bounty on his trade. It is true that in the actual course of events it is the West and not the East which has produced silver from its mines, and has discarded it from its currency. Nevertheless, this case is significant because it has been overlooked by those persons who have maintained that every fall in the Indian exchanges must give a proportional bounty to the Indian exporter.

Next, the fall in the exchange may be due to such a cause as a rumour that the Bland Bill will be repealed. If so the stimulus which it gives to exportation from India will be followed by an exactly equal check as soon as the rumour is contradicted.

Next, it may be due to an excessive drawing of bills on India by traders who have exported goods to India or by the Government which has exported personal services to India; in this case again the premium on exportation will be balanced by an equal penalty as soon as the tide turns the other way, it is a variation of the exchanges which would exist equally if India had a gold currency.

Next, the fall in the exchange may be due to an increased production of silver from Western mines, or to a discarding of it from Western currencies. Then it will give a real bounty to the Indian exporter which will last so long as there is an extraordinary flow of silver to India; and the extent of which will be determined by the volume of that flow. But in this case silver acts as a commodity, and if, instead of extraordinary imports of silver, India were to take from us extraordinary imports to an equal aggregate value of other metals or any other commodities, the Indian exporter would receive a bounty different in form, but exactly equal in substance and in volume. It must, however, be constantly remembered, that if silver is discarded from Western currencies so as to diminish their volume relatively to the business which they have to do, there will result a fall of gold prices.

Lastly, we may consider the case in which the fall in the Indian exchange is caused by an increase in the work which Western currencies have to do relatively to the volume of those currencies. This change might have the collateral effect of causing a flow of silver to India, and if so that would, as we have already seen, give a premium on exportation from India so long as it lasted. This is the only real effect that it would have on trade, though it would alter the nominal amounts of trade bills. Every bill on England would be expressed in terms of fewer counters, but the same amount of Indian goods would sell in England for the means of purchasing as many English goods as before; English goods would sell in India for the means of purchasing as many Indian goods as before; there would be no surplus of importers' or exporters' bills, no premium on exportation or on importation. Oscillations in the number of these counters might cause inconvenience to individuals, especially to those who were doing business with silver countries. But it would cause no great or permanent difference in the nature of the trade or the profit at which it was being carried on.

There is, however, a slight qualification to be introduced on account of those bills, whether drawn by the Indian Council or by private persons, the gold value of which is fixed independently of changes in the purchasing power of gold; for they count for a greater real value in Indian trade when gold prices are low than when they are high. But this result is independent of the fact that India has a silver currency; it would be true equally if her currency were, as that of New Zealand is, convertible with England's. A rise in the value of gold increases the real value of bills drawn to cover the payment of a fixed amount of gold, whether that payment has to be made by a country which uses gold or a country which uses silver.

In conclusion, I admit that the evils of oscillations in the exchanges with silver-using countries are in the aggregate so great as to afford a strong argument for the adoption of an international currency, but I think that action should be delayed until we have accomplished the task, which we have hardly yet fairly begun, of examining the principles on which such a currency should be based. And perhaps I may be pardoned for remarking that a great part, perhaps more than half, of the recent oscillations in the gold value of silver are due to the varying prospects of success or failure on the part of those who are endeavouring to make 15½ ounces of silver exchange for one of gold, and that this evil would at once be much diminished if the advocates of a fixed-ratio-mintage were to adopt the ratio of 20 : 1 as the basis of their scheme.

ALFRED MARSHALL.

(iv) Memorandum on the Relation between a Fall of the Exchange and Trade with Countries which have not a Gold Currency.

I venture to submit to Members of the Commission on the Values of Gold and Silver an abstract of my opinions on the complex question of the relation between a fall of the exchange and our trade with countries which have not a gold currency. It is to the same effect as the evidence which I gave on December 19th, but its more orderly arrangement will, I think, make it a better basis for my examination on Monday next, so far as this point is concerned.

Let two countries A and B trade with one another. Let A have throughout a gold currency.

I.   Let B also have a gold currency. Then trade tends so to adjust the supplies of gold relatively to the demands for gold in the two countries as to bring gold prices at the sea-boards of the two countries to equality (allowance being made for carriage).

If they are higher in A than in B, there will be a small temporary bounty on exportation from B to A corresponding to this difference (which must always be small). Bills drawn in B on A will multiply, and, specie point being reached, gold will go from A to B, till prices in B are as high as in A. (If B hoards gold this process may be a long one, otherwise it is sure to be short.)

II.   Let B have an inconvertible paper-currency (say roubles). In each country prices will be governed by the relation between the volume of the currency and the work it has to do. The gold price of the rouble will be fixed by the course of trade just at the ratio which gold prices in A bear to rouble prices in B (allowing for cost of carriage). If this equilibrium were disturbed by a fall of rouble prices in B without a parallel change in gold prices in A, there would be a small temporary bounty on exportation from B :

191

this would cause a deficiency of bills drawn in A on B, which would therefore rise to a premium. That is, the gold price of the rouble would rise till it was as high as the ratio of prices in A to prices in B. A disturbance so caused would be adjusted almost instantaneously, and may be set aside. When then it is asked whether a fall in the gold price of the rouble gives a bounty on exportation from B, the answer is : Not unless it is caused by excessive importation into B; in that case it may give a small temporary bounty. But as a rule it merely indicates that prices in B have risen faster (or fallen slower) than in A.

But meanwhile B may have gained an advantage in the production of, say, wheat relatively to other things. If B had a gold currency, the price at which B could deliver wheat to A would fall a little, and people would see in the change merely the substitution of wheat for other exports of B. As it is, however, this fact is likely to be disguised. The exporter perhaps sees the gold price which he gets for his wheat go on falling even faster than the rouble price at which he can afford to sell it, but since the gold price of roubles is falling too, he gets enough roubles to pay him. He and others attribute his successful sales to the fall in the gold price of roubles. But the fact is that if he had not been able to deliver his wheat at a lower rate relatively to the average exports from B than before, he would have got no bounty; for the balancing of exporters' and importers' bills compels the gold price of the rouble to equal the ratio which average gold prices in A bear to average gold prices in B, allowance being made for carriage.

III. Let B have a silver currency. This case differs from the preceding only in consequence of the fact that silver is, and roubles are not, an exportable commodity. Trade tends so to adjust the supplies of gold and silver in the two countries relatively to the demands, as to bring gold prices in A to bear to silver prices in B (after allowing for carriage) a ratio equal to the gold price of silver.

If we divide gold prices in A by the gold price of silver, we get what we may call *silver prices* in A. And thus the above proposition becomes similar to I, and we may say that trade tends to make silver prices equal in the two countries. If they are higher in A than in B, there will be a temporary bounty on exportation from B to A. Bills drawn in B on A will multiply, and specie point being reached, silver will go from A to B till prices in B are as high as in A. This temporary bounty cannot be large : because silver prices in A cannot rise by more than a very small percentage above silver prices in B without causing a violent movement of silver from A to B. If there is no such movement, that by itself proves that silver prices in the two countries are nearly equal, and that the bounty on exportation from A is very small, if there is any at all. And though the gold price of silver be falling steadily, there will be no bounty whatever on exportation from B, if silver prices are falling as fast in A as in B. While if they should happen to fall faster in A than in B there will be a bounty on exportation from A.

Thus a permanent fall in the gold price of silver merely indicates that the conditions of supply and demand for the two metals are such that the equality of silver prices in the two countries (allowance being made for carriage) requires as a condition that an ounce of gold should exchange for more ounces of silver than before.

If any change in the mines or the bullion market should lower the value of silver in A, without affecting B, so that it raised silver prices in A, and not in B, then there would be a temporary bounty on exportation from B, causing B's goods to undersell A's, silver being taken back in return. If silver does not, in fact, go in abnormal quantities from A to B, that proves that the apparent rise of silver prices in A relatively to B did not really exist; and that that particular fall in A's exchanges on B did not give even a temporary bounty to the exporters from B.

The case in which the exportation of one commodity, wheat, gains an advantage over others, may lead to exactly the same misunderstanding as in the case of the rouble.

Next, to take account of the fact that many industries, especially those of a capitalistic form, have fixed money charges, the burden of which is increased by a fall of prices. This burden may be so great as to paralyse a great part of the business of the country : less will then be produced both for home consumption and exportation. Diminished exportation will cause diminished importation, unless in the special case in which the country borrows

o

from abroad or diminishes its foreign investments; and the change will probably injure the exporters (taken as a body) from countries with which it trades.

If, however, when prices are falling in A, some industries, as *e.g.* the cutlery industries, are able to reduce their fixed charges more rapidly than, say, the cotton manufacturing industries, then the change will give a real bounty to cotton manufacturers in B. They will be able to undersell A's cotton manufacturers at home or in neutral markets. For, though under other circumstances this would have caused an excess of bills drawn by A over those drawn on A, and have caused a reaction by making the exchanges favourable to B, and thus making the exporters from B sell their bills at a discount, this reaction would be prevented by a new supply of cutlery bills drawn by A.

So far as general reasoning goes, it is possible that the capitalistic form of modern industries might be an important cause of disturbance as regards England's trade with India; but statistics show that it is not. It so happens that American wheat is exceptionally free from fixed charges; and therefore this cause has acted rather against than for Indian wheat.

Next, to consider whether, assuming there to be no change in the relative expenses of production of different commodities, a general fall in gold prices in A will, during the process of the fall, give a temporary bounty to the producers in B, silver prices remaining stationary. If there were no trade between A and B, B's producers would escape an increasing burden of fixed charges to which A's producers would be subject : the former might be making good profits while many of the latter were failing, and as it is, the two countries trading with one another, B's capitalist producers of course retain this good fortune. But do they get any special bounty from the trade ? If silver prices in A rise temporarily above those in B for any cause, of course they get a temporary special bounty; but this is independent of the question whether industry is capitalistic, or such as to be free from the burdens of fixed charges; and so long as silver prices are equal in the two countries, they get no bounty, whether they sell their bills on A, or use them as a means of importing from A. The fixed-charges element, therefore, has no importance except in so far as it falls unequally on different branches of production; pressing, say, more heavily on A's calico than A's cutlery.

It is, however, true that if A's calico producers tried to raise the price of calico by restricting production, they would be likely to be defeated by the fact that B's calico producers were well contented to work full time, and would therefore prevent the value of calico from being raised relatively to other things.

In conclusion, a fall in the Indian exchange will give a bounty to exporters from India if it is caused by a fall in the value of silver (a rise in silver prices) which is felt in other countries before it is felt in India : this will happen if more silver is raised in the West, or less silver is wanted there; or if India has an increased demand for gold or silver (for the purposes of hoarding) or for any other commodity, or if she has to pay higher (silver) pensions, etc. to English officials, or if the remittances which she has to make to Europe for interest, etc. increase while her new loans diminish. But if the fall of exchange should be caused by a fall in the value of silver occurring in India first (through the discovery of silver mines in India or through a disinclination to hoard silver), that would give a bounty to the European exporter to India. These conclusions would remain substantially true if England and India had the same currency; though that would, of course, diminish the minor disturbances arising from fluctuations of the Indian exchange.

ALFRED MARSHALL.

Cambridge, January 13, 1888.

ROYAL COMMISSION

ON

THE AGED POOR

(1893)

MEMORANDUM AND EVIDENCE OFFERED TO THE
COMMISSIONERS BY PROFESSOR ALFRED MARSHALL

(i) PRELIMINARY MEMORANDUM.
(ii) MINUTES OF EVIDENCE.

[86630 W^t 21840.]

(i) PRELIMINARY MEMORANDUM.

A. PRELIMINARY STATEMENT.

THE problem of poverty is changing its character. Pauperism, after several fluctuations, reached its maximum in the first third of this century. There was then a fear that paupers would pull down the working men of England to their own level. That has passed away, and with greater wealth, knowledge and social activity a hope is arising that not only paupers but all the very poor may be improved away. But that needs the active co-operation of the working classes; and for this purpose if for no other we should strive to remove any reasonable objections that are urged by the working classes against the existing administration of poor-relief public and private. I do not think that the ablest and most far-seeing members of the working classes are at all blind to the great benefits which the poor themselves have derived from the firmer administration of the Poor Law since 1834, and the general tendency to replace lax and undiscriminating out-relief by discriminating private charity with the workhouse open to all in the background. I myself hope that not only lax out-relief but every kind of relief that is not accompanied by personal care and sympathy will gradually be discontinued.

I am thus generally in accord with the prevailing tendencies of public and private relief. But the most prominent and uncompromising advocates of those tendencies lay great stress on interpretations of history, in which I do not entirely concur; and on certain economic doctrines and ethical principles which appear to me to be too unqualified, and to be less applicable to our own times than to those of the beginning of the century, when they were first formulated. After arguing this, I propose to submit, with great diffidence, a plan of action which I think is adapted to the present time. I lay no stress on its details, but it will serve to make more clear the general aim which I have in view.

B. SOME MODERN INDUSTRIAL CHANGES THAT SPECIALLY AFFECT THE AGED AND INFIRM.

I wish to point out first—though it is not very important for my main purpose—how the growing sense of duty towards the aged and infirm and the general increase in the means of supporting them have been opposed, and are likely still further to be opposed, by the growth of large towns and other industrial changes, which have increased the cost of supporting them, and have diminished their power of contributing to that support :

1. By raising the cost of housing them.

2. By diminishing their power of earning money in their own trades.

3. By lessening their opportunities of making themselves useful in the house and in the garden,

4. Except in certain districts, where there are many young children to be cared for while their mothers are at work.

Such facts may account in some measure for the geographical distribution of old-age-poverty. (See Sir Hugh Owen's answers 57–59.)

5. The same causes have increased the urgency of the problems of sanitation and housing generally, on which the extinction of the residuum much depends.

6. And they have separated the rich from the poor, and thus made necessary the middleman in voluntary charity.

C. EXCEPTIONAL CONDITIONS OF ENGLAND IN 1834.

Reasons for specially distrusting any inferences based on the experiences of England early in this century as to the results which are likely to follow from granting out-relief or any other kind of relief under modern conditions :

1. The frequent insufficiency of wages then to support life.

2. The war policy of the Government with regard to population early in the century.

3. Political instability and timidity of the Government till after 1832.

4. Exceptional follies in administration.

5. The resulting degradation of the labourers must not be ascribed to any one cause.

D. The Report of 1834 how far applicable to our Own Age.

1. The admirable Report of 1834 went very much on earlier lines, but contained marks of the exceptional period in which it was framed.

2. But its conclusions are of two different kinds, true principles valid for all time, and working rules adapted to that particular time.

3. Principles contained in it that are for all time.

That " character is the parent of comfort " : that money gifts are of little avail by themselves : that relief by official routine is less discriminating than personal charity : that certainty and absence of suspicion of favouritism are advantages that outweigh a good deal of hardship ; and above all that the position of the dependent, whether in health or illness, should not be better than that of the independent worker in like case.

4. Working rules contained in it applicable to that time, but to be judged on their merits with regard to any other time.

That relief must be given only to destitution ; and without regard to merit ; and that the workhouse must ultimately be the universal test of destitution.

E. The Relation of Public Relief to Wages.

I pass next to certain exaggerated versions of true economic doctrines which are frequently quoted by advocates of the restriction of all public relief, and especially out-relief.

1. The doctrine that " grants in aid of wages lower wages " is true as a working rule for most practical purposes.

2. But it tacitly assumes certain conditions, and these are not universally present.

3. A tax levied on the well-to-do for the benefit of those whose means are small may be secured from ultimately lowering wages, provided care be taken that the money is spent for the benefit of the rising generation, or if the relief granted by it is accompanied by more stringent sanitary and educational regulations in their interest which might not be otherwise practicable. With these precautions Mr. Charles Booth's scheme would not lower wages, in spite of the heavy tax it would levy on capital.

F. Ethical Aspects of Limitations of Poor-relief.

1. Well-to-do persons who have satisfied themselves that some kinds of limitations of expenditure on poor-relief are in the interests of themselves are apt to find their consciences rather easy about other limitations, which have not that defence, *e.g.* the insufficient supply of relieving officers.

2. The doctrine that it is unjust to levy taxes for the relief of poverty that falls short of indigence is not valid unconditionally.

3. There is no ethical absurdity in the proposal that the taxes levied for the relief of distress should be held returnable, in a manner not specially distasteful, to the payers of those taxes if they fall into distress through no special fault of their own.

4. Too much stress is often laid both from the ethical and from the economical point of view on those forms of thrift which result in material provision for sickness and old age, in comparison with those forms which benefit the coming generation.

This is greatly due to the influence exerted on the administrators of poor-relief and charity by the economic and social philosophy of the early years of this century.

G. Possibilities of Discrimination.

1. I do not propose to discuss the vexed question of the absolute difficulty of discrimination between the worthy and the unworthy; but to argue that such discrimination as is now effected in practice could be put on a basis more beneficial to the nation in general and the poor in particular by more reorganisation and development of the existing public and private agencies, and without the introduction of any important difficulty that is new in kind.

By " worth " I mean, for the present purpose, thrift combined with the absence of notorious ill conduct.

2. Discrimination by a private friend in the administration of relief is fundamentally different from that by a public official.

3. But private charity in the strict sense is becoming very difficult in large towns.

4. The disadvantages of local authorities as compared with so-called private incorporations for poor-relief are, in some measure, the result of accident.

5. Public bodies do, in fact, discriminate more than at first sight appears.

6. It is difficult to overrate the debt that the nation owes to the Charity Organisation Societies.

7. But they have some weaknesses.

Their funds are limited, their action and even their existence is haphazard and their basis is oligarchic. And perhaps they underrate the moral and economic evils of anxiety.

8. More evidence is needed from the persons most concerned as to how far even in places where charity is well organised it covers all the area of distress, except that which may be suitably relieved in ordinary workhouses.

9. Patience in bearing other people's sufferings is as clear a duty as patience in bearing one's own, but it may be carried too far.

10. There are some who think that the present methods of poor-relief and charity will very soon leave very little suffering, which is not needed to educate people to braver and stronger lives; and they are right in calling for patient adhesion to present methods.

11. But such patience appears excessive to persons who, like myself, think that there are still many hardships which cost more pain than they are worth for the purposes of education.

12. We should strive tentatively to apply the modern resources of discrimination so as to mitigate such hardships. The State ought not now to leave the relief of the deserving as contrasted with the vicious poor, without taking some security that private charity will be systematic, effective and free from great errors whether in defect or excess. But all arrangements which have in them the smallest taint of pauperisation should be elastic, and of such a nature as to shrink away of themselves as the causes of poverty dry up.

Such action would enlist the sympathies of the best of the working classes on the side of a wise and firm treatment of pauperism and poverty generally and would render it possible to deal with the problems of the residuum.

H. Conclusion.

1. The strength of public authority should be combined with the versatility, sympathy and delicacy of volunteer agencies.

2. Details, suggested for the purposes of illustration, of a plan applicable to the relief of the aged poor at once, and perhaps to be extended to other classes of impotent poor.

Where suitable Charity Organisation Societies exist, they should be semi-established, have certain public authority and responsibility, but not handle public money themselves. Every case of distress to be examined in the first instance by the C. O. S.; and the guardians acting on the advice of the C. O. S. to have much greater freedom of classification in workhouses and outside according to thrift and past conduct than they have at present. It would remain true then as now that guardians must go more by fixed rule than C. O. S. committees; and cases which seemed likely to establish dangerous precedents would be relieved from C. O. S. funds. Provision to be made for the addition of public representatives, including some working men (by preference experienced members of Friendly Societies), to the C. O. S. committees, and vice versa for the admission of some (other) members of the C. O. S. committees to the Board of Guardians. Some committees or sub-committees to sit in the evening, when working men could attend.

Where such societies do not exist and cannot be formed, the guardians to be charged to call together volunteer visiting committees, and to have some freedom of discrimination; but relief would necessarily be more by fixed rule than if the guardians were aided by independent Charity Organisation Societies.

June 5, 1893.

(ii) MINUTES OF EVIDENCE TAKEN BEFORE THE ROYAL COMMISSION ON THE AGED POOR, JUNE 5, 1893.

THE RIGHT HON. C. T. RITCHIE (in the Chair).

HIS ROYAL HIGHNESS THE PRINCE OF WALES, K.G.
THE RIGHT HON. LORD LINGEN, K.C.B.
THE RIGHT HON. LORD BRASSEY, K.C.B.
THE RIGHT HON. JOSEPH CHAMBERLAIN, M.P.
Mr. J. J. HENLEY, C.B.
Mr. ALBERT PELL.
Mr. JAMES STUART, M.P.
Mr. A. C. HUMPHREYS-OWEN.
Mr. C. S. ROUNDELL, M.P.
Mr. C. S. LOCH.
Mr. JOSEPH ARCH, M.P.
Mr. CHARLES BOOTH.
Mr. HENRY BROADHURST.
Mr. J. J. STOCKALL.

Mr. E. AUSTIN BROWNE, *Secretary.*
VISCOUNT MORPETH, *Assistant Secretary.*

Professor ALFRED MARSHALL called in and examined.

10,187. (*Chairman.*) You are Professor, I think, of Political Economy at Cambridge ?—Yes.

10,188. And you have given a great deal of consideration to what I should call the Poor Law problem ?—Yes. I think I should perhaps say that I have devoted myself for the last twenty-five years to the problem of poverty, and that very little of my work has been devoted to any inquiry which does not bear on that. But I do not regard the problem of pauperism, as distinguished from the problem of poverty, as of so great importance as it seems to other people to be.

10,189. Have you yourself any practical experience of the administration of the Poor Law ?—No, none.

10,190. You are not, I understand, in favour of a lax administration of the outdoor relief even of the aged poor ?—I am opposed to lax administration of relief of every kind.

10,191. At the same time, I understand you do not concur with those who think the abolition of outdoor relief is either possible or desirable ?—I do not think that its sudden abolition is desirable. I agree with people, like Mr. Vallance, who say that it would be a very great mistake to attempt to abolish outdoor relief before private charity is ready to take its place in cases in which relief ought to be given.

10,192. How would you arrive at the conclusion that private charitable relief was sufficient to justify the abolition of outdoor relief by means of the guardians ?—I think that would have to be very much a matter of opinion, and I am not quite sure that my own opinion, and that of Mr. Vallance and people who agree with him, would entirely coincide upon that. But I think that certain conditions might be laid down. In the first place there must be, I think, an organised means of applying charity, whether public or private, by individual, and that practically means by volunteer aid. I am opposed to any sharp shutting off of outdoor relief until we are ready either by the aid of the Charity Organisation Societies, or, where Charity Organisation Societies cannot be called into existence, by the aid of volunteer committees, subsidiary to the guardians, to enter into each individual case; and to take care that private funds, through the Charity Organisation Societies in some cases, direct in other cases, should go to relieve the distress of people for whom the workhouse test would not be applicable.

10,193. Is it not the case that that co-operation exists at the present time in many places ?—In a few places; but I think we have not sufficient evidence that in London, for instance, the Charity Organisation Societies and the Poor Law between them supply all that is necessary. We have indeed abundant evidence to that effect; but unfortunately it comes only from one side, it comes from the side of the administrators; and we know that the working classes as a body believe that the administrators are mistaken. The working classes may be wrong; but we cannot decide that they are wrong until some means has been got of testing their opinion, and that is in my opinion a matter of very great difficulty which has not yet been grappled with at all.

10,194. But you know the case of St. George's-in-the-East?—Yes.

10,195. And you know that there is practically no outdoor relief even to the aged poor there?—Yes.

10,196. And you are aware that there is co-operation between the Charity Organisation Societies and the Poor Law authorities in that parish?—Yes.

10,197. I do not know whether you are aware of the evidence that we have recived here, that there seems to be no indication whatever among the people of St. George's-in-the-East, who are almost altogether of the working classes, that they are antagonistic to the method pursued by the Board of Guardians in St. George's-in-the-East?—I am aware that that statement has been made; but it does not seem to me that the evidence on which it rests is conclusive.

10,198. Is it not the fact that the electors in that parish continually send men of the same type as administrators again and again back again to the Board of Guardians?—I believe that is so; but that does not appear to me to be at all conclusive. It appears to me to go a very little way towards proving the proposition. The test of the proposition, I think, is to be sought in the direct expression of opinions by working men. I have been led to take this line after frequent conversations with them. I always find that they do not believe that the Charity Organisation Societies and the Poor Law between them do all that is needful; and I do not think that it would be at all easy to get a great number of working men to say that they did. Until working men's evidence has been brought forward on this subject, the evidence that has been got by this and previous Commissions seems to me useful in a way, but, so far as this particular question goes, the least important half; until the more important half has been produced, it seems to me that we cannot regard the question as a settled one. I think, however, that there would be the very greatest difficulty in getting working men to come forward and give the evidence needed; and that, if the inquiry were made by a Commission, some departure would have to be made from the ordinary course of procedure of a Commission; otherwise I think they would not come.

10,199. What do you mean by some departure from the ordinary course of procedure of a Commission ?—Well, we have got, I think, to put ourselves into the position of the working men. There are not very many of the working men who are at all ready to submit themselves to the ordeal of examination by a Commission. Of those, a great part are in the higher ranks of the artisans, who, under ordinary circumstances, have no more to do with the Poor Law than any well-to-do citizen. They may have " black sheep " relatives who have come under it, as anybody may; and they may have been brought into contact indirectly, particularly if they have been local officers of trade unions, with hard cases under the present system; but the chief officers of trade unions would not be at all likely to have any personal experience of the Poor Law; and in fact they say they have not.

10,200. Any personal experience ?—Any personal experience of the kind wanted. They lead very busy lives. Those whose opinions I should myself most care for on labour questions in general are probably nearly as busy as a Cabinet Minister; and they have, from their own point of view, work as important to do. They know very little about the gossip as to which of their neighbours has got into this or that misfortune, and how much fault there was in the case; and if they were asked, as they were by the Select Committee of the House of Lords in 1888, to give evidence, they would certainly say that they were not authorised to do it. I have noticed that if a representative of a trades union is asked for information which he is not distinctly authorised by his trades union to give, and he answers the question, it may be taken for granted that the rest of his evidence would be worth very little. All those men whose evidence is worth having are extremely careful to refuse to give any evidence on matters on which they are not distinctly authorised to speak, although occasionally, though not always, if pressed to give information in their capacity of private individuals, they will do so.

10,201. You have told us the evil which you think exists, but I rather want to get at a suggestion as to the remedy. I mean, you have told us that you think that Commissions ought to be differently constituted ?—No, I did not say that.

10,202. I beg your pardon; that there ought to be some change in the procedure; was that it?—Well, if the inquiry is made by a Commission, as distinguished from Assistant Commissioners, I think that probably one thing to do would be to start with the plan with which we started at the Labour Commission, and that was, to regard the working-class evidence as the dominant evidence. We heard one working man after another for a long time before we heard anybody on the other side. The evidence of employers, and still more official evidence, was kept in the background. It was very important when it came; but it was kept in the background. And then the methods of cross-examination which one naturally applies to an experienced witness should be rather suspended. One can generally get to know whether a man is speaking *bonâ fide* or not. If he is not, of course he should be cross-examined sharply; but if he is speaking only what he believes, he should be allowed a very great margin. The ordinary laws of sticking rigidly to the point should not be insisted upon; he should be encouraged to say what he chooses. The members of the Commission should be men of a strongly sympathetic nature, who would abstain from asking any question of a kind that would unnecessarily annoy working-men witnesses. They should be much more careful with regard to the working men's evidence than with regard to the evidence of educated people. It would seem to me that, in so far as the inquiry was made by a Commission, as distinguished from Assistant Commissioners, that would have to be the mode of starting. In fact, I should myself like that the witness, on the supposition that he was acting *bonâ fide*, should not be cross-examined in the ordinary way at all. I would like him to be examined by the Chairman, and by people who would look at the problem of poverty from the same point of view as he did. The questions of cross-examination I would prefer, if possible, to be put through the Chairman.

10,203. I understand, quite; your view is, as I understand, that there is considerable dissatisfaction, then, amongst the

P

working classes with regard to the present mode of the administration of the Poor Law ?—That is my opinion.

10,204. Then you were making a suggestion that the Charity Organisation Society should work with the Poor Law guardians, with regard to the administration of outdoor relief ; do you desire that the Charity Organisation Society should be changed from a purely voluntary association ; that it would be set up by legal enactment, to act with the guardians ?—I should desire that ; although where the Charity Organisation Society is strong in men and women, and money, as it is in certain places, for instance, in Oxford, and to a less extent in Cambridge, there, I take it, no change can make any considerable improvement. The only change that needs to be made in such cases is one that would enable working men to take a direct part in the administration of relief. I am convinced—for I have made inquiries on this subject from representative working men—I am convinced that the leaders of the working men would be as firm as anyone in insisting that scamps and lazy people should be put to a severe discipline ; that they would be in many ways sharper than people not in the same rank of life in seeing through a fallacious story, and would have no sympathy at all with the tramp ; in fact I believe that probably the professional tramp is even more odious to large classes of the working men than he is to the rest of society.

10,205. Would you tell us exactly what is in your mind as to the relations which should exist between the public body and the Charity Organisation Society, or the voluntary committee that you speak of ?—Where suitable Charity Organisation Societies exist, they should be semi-established, have certain public authority, and responsibility. I do not myself wish that they should handle public money themselves ; I may say that a suggestion has been made, I think by Professor Sidgwick, that in certain cases the Charity Organisation Society might distribute public money. That is one method of attaining very much the same result as that which I rather prefer to get by another method. I wish that no relief should be given at all, except interim relief, until the case has been examined by the Charity Organisation Society. The guardians, acting with the advice of the Charity

Organisation Society, to have much greater freedom of classification in workhouses, and outside workhouses according to thrift and past conduct than they have at present.

10,206. May I ask upon that point what you exactly mean about much greater freedom of classification in workhouses and outside than they have at present?—I would propose that the Charity Organisation Society should report that the case belongs to one of three classes, which I will call A, B, C. The A class could contain those cases that the Charity Organisation Societies deal with in those districts in which they have an abundance of money and do not take an extremely austere view of what human nature may be expected to do; the A class would consist of some of those cases which such Charity Organisation Societies would relieve as things are.

10,207. I understood you to say that the Class A the Charity Organisation Society were going to recommend to the guardians?—Yes.

10,208. Then I understood you to say in the last sentence you used, that the Charity Organisation Society were to relieve them?—That it was to recommend to the guardians for good treatment those whom Charity Organisation Societies who are at once liberal, and wise and prudent in their conduct, would now relieve; provided only those cases were such as were not likely to establish a harmful precedent.

10,209. May I ask who was to be the judge?—The Charity Organisation Committee.

10,210. Then do you contemplate that the guardians would practically act upon the instructions of the Charity Organisation Society?—I propose to give them leave to do as they like. But I should perhaps continue that my proposal is that a certain number of members should be added to the Charity Organisation Committee by external authority. You see the one fundamental flaw of the Charity Organisation Society, that which keeps them in my opinion from ever quite being in harmony with the spirit of this age, is that they are necessarily oligarchic. They have taken upon themselves one of the most important functions that the State can have; and yet they belong to the old world, in this way, that their basis consists exclusively of those people who used to be the governing classes but who are not the governing classes now.

10,211. Without going into the composition of the Charity Organisation Society, what I rather want to get at is this : You have stated that the Charity Organisation Society should recommend to the guardians for special treatment certain persons whom they feel able to recommend from their own inquiries ?—Yes.

10,212. Then, what I want to know is, what is to be the guardians' action then ; are they to be at liberty to disregard the recommendation of the Charity Organisation Society, or are they to be bound to follow the recommendation of the Charity Organisation Society ?—I think they should be at liberty to decide for themselves. But I will just say briefly, that I want the two bodies to have a great number of members in common. I want the Charity Organisation Society, when re-adjusted as an adequate Charity Organisation Society, to have the power of appointing a certain number of guardians, and either the guardians or some other public authority to have the power of appointing some working men, with Friendly Society experience, as members of the Charity Organisation Society.

10,213. Then you would entirely alter the present constitution of these charitable organisations ?—No ; I would like to add, say one-fifth ; I would have four-fifths elected by the subscribers to the Charity Organisation Society, and one-fifth appointed from outside.

10,214. But I mean that would altogether alter their constitution ?—It would so far alter their constitution.

10,215. And do you think that the public support would as readily flow to a semi-official association, such as that would then be, as it does now ?—I think it would flow much more readily, because it would then be possible for the so-called Charity Organisation Societies to begin to be true Charity Organisation Societies.   Up to the present time they have called themselves Charity Organisation Societies, but they have gone only a very little way, and can possibly go only a very little way, towards earning that title ; for they have no control over the greater part of the charities in the place. They being mere self-electing limited corporations for carrying out certain private gifts, it would be perfectly impossible to give them the authority, which I think some body ought to have, of requiring that every person who gives charity not out of his own pocket, but as a middleman, should send to a central office an exact statement of what reliol he gives. That central office should be the office of the Charity Organisation Society. Such statements should not be published in any sense, but should be accessible to anybody who wants to know whether the story that a man gives that he is not receiving aid from elsewhere is true.

10,216. I want to understand what effect you think the organisation such as you contemplate would have in carrying out this suggestion which you have made, namely, that the Board of Guardians should have much greater freedom of classification in workhouses and outside according to thrift and past conduct than they have at present. Have the guardians got not only full freedom—I am now speaking, of course, with regard to the aged poor—have they not got full freedom with regard to the treatment of the aged poor, and is it not a part of their duty that they should classify in their workhouses?—The term classification is rather a misleading one. The sense in which it is used in Poor Law discussions is, of course, quite different from that in which I am now using it. There are three well-recognised divisions, three classes of males, three classes of females, and one for imbeciles; and in large workhouses that classification is no doubt carried out. But that is not the classification which I am aiming at.

10,217. What is the classification that you refer to?—The classification that I refer to is that if a man is reported by the Charity Organisation Committee to the guardians as belonging to Class A, and if the guardians accept that report and act on it, they should then be able to offer him other outdoor relief as they chose and as was suitable to the case.

10,218. That they can do at present, of course?—Yes, but that the out-relief, if given, should be adequate, which all people, I think, desire.

10,219. But they have perfect freedom at present?—Yes.

10,220. The guardians have perfect freedom at present?— They have perfect freedom. But at present they are compelled by law, though, as I repeat here what I got into hot water for saying elsewhere : thank God ! they break the law. They are compelled by law to take no account of merit whatever; and if a man has a pension, or an annuity from a Friendly Society, they are bound by law, though they break the law, to make up his total income to exactly what it would be if he were a scamp.

10,221. What suggestion have you to make with regard to that class of applicant, the man who is in receipt of a pension from some Friendly Society, and to which he himself has contributed ?—I think they should do very much what they do now—only instead of doing it in opposition to the law, the law should be altered so that their action should be in conformity with the law. I think it is most objectionable that the guardians should systematically break the law. If the law is such that right-minded men cannot obey it, the right thing to do is to alter the law.

10,222. Then, your suggestion there is not with regard to a matter of actual practice, but simply that you would like the law brought into accord with the practice of the guardians ?—Yes, with regard to people who are receiving relief from Friendly Societies. But of course there are some guardians who, for some reason or other, do obey that law; and, again, there are many cases in which they practically take account of funds and support of other kinds that a man has to its full extent. The phrase that it is the principle of the Poor Law that no account is to be taken of merit has been repeated over and over again in this very controversy with regard to the treatment of the aged poor, and I would have that changed.

10,223. Yes; but how would you define that ?—The merit, or worth, I define, for the present purpose, as thrift combined with the absence of notorious ill-conduct.

10,224. But how would you define thrift ? I mean to say, do I understand that you would give a person of that kind an absolute right to outdoor relief ?—No.

10,225. You would give no right ?—He has no right at all to be put into Class A.

10,226. Then, allow me to ask you, how would you define thrift ?—My object is to break down the notion that any arithmetical definition of merit can be applied, I want to make the definition of merit more elastic than it has been. I hold that if a man on 12s. a week has secured for himself an annuity of 1s. his thrift is a much more real thing than if a man on 50s. has got an annuity of 3s.; but the law, as at present worded, puts equal savings by the two on exactly the same footing, so far as it takes any account of saving at all.

10,227. Still they are all thrifty, although not equally thrifty? —Well, what I want is that the definition of thrift should not be a mere numerical proposition, but that it should be one left to the judgment of sensible people, guiding lines being laid down. I quite agree with the doctrines that were insisted on from the time of Chalmers down to the present, as to its being essential that all public money should be granted by rigid rule to a very much greater extent than money subscribed from voluntary sources : and it is on that account that I do not think we can get on at all well without a Class B. I do not think you can get on well by dividing the applicants for relief into Class A, those I have been now talking of, and Class C.

10,228. I want to exhaust Class A, before we pass on to Class B. It really amounts to this with regard to Class A, that you leave it entirely to the guardians to form their own conclusions as to the merits of an applicant?—No; they would be guided by, and in almost all cases, I imagine, would follow closely the advice of the Charity Organisation Committee on which they were themselves represented.

10,229. Yes, but I understood you that they could either adopt or reject?—Yes, they could; but as sensible men they would not as a rule.

10,230. Then it does amount to this, that you are going to leave the Boards of Guardians entire freedom in the matter; they are going to consult some body which you desire to set up?—Yes.

10,231. But with regard to their action they are going to be untrammelled?—Yes, until the next election of guardians. But if guardians showed themselves so foolish as to set aside the recommendations of the Charity Organisation Committee, without due cause and in a frivolous way, I think there can be no doubt that they would not long continue to be guardians.

10,232. Is not that answer of yours destructive of a proposition that you put before the Commission at the outset, that the working classes are dissatisfied with the mode of the administration of the Poor Law relief ?   Is not that the mode in which they can show their satisfaction or dissatisfaction with the way in which the guardians administer relief, namely, an election ?—Yes, I hold there would be a large majority among the working classes in support of a stern administration of the Poor Law in cases of all people who do not deserve well.

10,233. Then you would take it, that where a Board of Guardians was very rigid in its administration of the Poor Law, and was repeatedly returned, that that was an evidence of the satisfaction of the working classes with their mode of administration ?—No, certainly not; because you may not be satisfied with your Board of Guardians, but yet you may find it very difficult to get a Board of Guardians you would like better.   That to begin with, and to go on with, I do not gather that the total number of people who have gone to the polls in the cases to which you referred just now, is any very large part of the whole population. So far as I can make out, what the working classes do is to grumble and not vote at present.

10,234. I do not want to push the thing further than this : at present you say that if a Board of Guardians do not act properly on the report of the Charity Organisation Committee, they would be upset, and they would be upset at the next election ; therefore you place value upon the expression of opinion, I believe in that particular case ; in the other case I referred you to, you did not place so much value upon it ?—No.   I think the original question was : " Was the decision to be made by the guardians ? "   My answer is : Not in the first instance.   There are all sorts of difficulties in the way of the guardians getting hold of the true facts of the case.   The sympathetic imagination of the volunteer, which is the mainspring by which we hope to remove poverty— that is not at present available in the administration of the guardians.   I want to make that my starting-point, the fundamental lever with which I would move everything.   Having got that, there would be a report to the Charity Organisation Committee, a decision by the Charity Organisation Committee.   Well, then, it would be possible, of course, for the guardians to set aside the opinion of the Charity Organisation Committee; and I think they should have the right, because the Charity Organisation Committee itself is rather an unstable body. But if they did set aside all this product of volunteer investigation in a frivolous and vexatious way, then they would be doing a thing that would be clearly offensive to the opinions of sensible people of all ranks of society, and their chance of election would be very small. I do not think it is at all likely that they would do it.

10,235. But you contemplate that they may set it aside, either from one point of view or from another; they may think that the report has not been sufficiently favourable or lenient to the applicant, and may disregard it, and still treat the person as a thrifty person, although the Charity Organisation Society says he is not?—Yes.

10,236. And, on the other hand, they may disregard the report which says that he is a thrifty person?—Yes; they would have the legal power of doing it.

10,237. We were speaking about thrift, and you said you would leave the definition of thrift entirely to the guardians on the recommendation of the society?—No, not entirely; and I could really hardly complete my account of Class A without saying something about Class B. You asked me just now whether I had had any experience in the administration of the Poor Law. I have not, but I have had a good deal of indirect experience of the working of Charity Organisation Societies. I have been a member of them for a great many years, and at Oxford and Cambridge my wife has been an active member of the committee. We make it an invariable rule to discuss the questions in detail, if they have any difficulty, at the next meal after she comes back. We always do that, and we always take up the question of whether the case is rightly treated, of what it would be best to do; and at the next meeting of the committee, if from the conversation anything arises which she thinks it would be worth while to bring before the committee, it is so brought. Therefore, although I have had no direct personal experience in the administration, I think I might say I am, to a certain extent, a supernumerary member of the Cambridge Committee, and have been of the Oxford Committee. And I have also made a point of studying the lists

of cases which are given by the London and various other Charity
Organisation Societies, and the way in which they have dealt
with them, and also the lists of appeals that they publish from
branch committees; if, for instance, the Hammersmith Committee
want 4*l*. 5*s*. for a certain case. These studies have convinced me
that it would be impossible to administer public money freely
without making cases that appeared to be precedents for other
cases in which the relief should not be given. The difficulty that
you must, more or less, follow rule when you are acting in a
public capacity is one which, I think, has prevented the guardians
from doing what is best in the interests of society; and yet the
rule is a necessary one. I would propose, therefore, that if a
person is not bad in character, is not a person to whom discipline
is the right thing, not a person to be put down in Class C, I would
then propose that he should be put in Class B. That class consists
of people whom it would be expedient to have relieved otherwise
than in the workhouse, and whom yet one could not relieve with
public money without making rather a dangerous precedent.
Following that plan, I think it would be possible to formulate laws
for admission to Class A, which should be tolerably definite, but
which would not be merely arithmetical, the rules should take
account of what a man's opportunities had been.

10,238. I do not gather yet the exact class of people that would
go into Class B?—Class B would be all those people whom a
Charity Organisation Society (supplemented by a few people
who look at poverty not very much from above) thought it not
undesirable in the public interest, and consistent with charity,
to relieve without disgrace, but whom yet they could not put into
Class A without establishing a dangerous precedent. Those I
would have relieved out of Charity Organisation money, and not
out of public money.

10,239. (*Lord Lingen.*) Charity Organisation money only?—
Yes.

10,240. (*Chairman.*) Out of the funds of this society?—Out
of the funds at the disposal of the society.

10,241. This is the same body, I understand, which is going to
recommend for the A classification?—Yes. In my opinion the
whole of the classification should be done by the Charity Organisa-

tion Society. It should hear the cases, and mark them all: A, to be referred to the public guardians for the best treatment; C, to be referred to the guardians for disciplinary treatment. Then there remain the difficult cases which we have put in Class B, and will treat ourselves.

10,242. B, in point of fact, takes it out of relief from public funds altogether?—Yes; practically it does. A are the simple good cases, C are the bad cases, and B are the doubtful or difficult cases.

10,243. The A and the C classes are to be relieved out of the public funds?—Yes.

10,244. Class B you would not relieve from public funds, but from the funds of the Charity Organisation Society?—Yes.

10,245. But on your committee the guardians would be represented, I understand?—Yes; and to that extent the guardians would vote with regard to whether a person applying should be put upon the public funds or on the funds of the Charity Organisation Society. Then I want to lay stress on the fact that there would not only be guardians members of the Charity Organisation Society committee, but also other members of the Charity Organisation Society committee appointed to be guardians, so that perhaps two-fifths of the bodies might consist of the same people.

10,246. I take it that there is no qualification for appointment upon this committee. So far as the members of the Board of Guardians are concerned the only qualification is that they be members of Boards of Guardians?—Yes. You see it is proposed that the Charity Organisation Society should have great public authority enabling it to do the work which it wants to do now, but is incapable of doing. It wants to know how various private charities in its district are being administered, and it has no means of finding that out unless the people choose to tell them, and very often they do not. I would give it that authority. I would also give it a certain controlling authority over all suitable charitable foundations, and I would give it a voice in the management of public hospitals.

10,247. Yes; but I want clearly to understand the position of Class B, the persons who would be classified under the head of B.

Do I understand that, a decision having been arrived at by this committee, the applicant ought not to be relieved from public funds, but that he must be relieved from Charity Organisation funds; does a duty then devolve upon the Charity Organisation Society to relieve the person?—Yes, the Charity Organisation Society would then do in a systematic way what we have seen in a good deal of the evidence before you, and it is known elsewhere in other ways, is done on many Boards of Guardians now. For instance, it is done in Cambridge to a great extent. A guardian who is also a member of the Charity Organisation Society will say, " Oh, this is a case for the Charity Organisation Society; adjourn it " ; and then the Charity Organisation Society takes it off. Well, that would be the Class B.

10,248. Oh, no?—I mean, it might belong to either of the Classes A and B.

10,249. And there is this difference, is there not, that the Charity Organisation Society inquire into the application themselves, and they decide either to relieve it or not to relieve it as they choose; but I understand you are now going to impose an obligation upon the Charity Organisation Society to relieve certain persons who are put into their hands by a committee composed in the one part of members of the Charity Organisation Society, and the other members of the Boards of Guardians?—That is to say, that unless a Charity Organisation Society was willing to co-operate with public authorities, then it would be in the position of a private school that refuses to have anything to do with the Education Department.

10,250. You would allow the Charity Organisation Society to co-operate or not to co-operate with the Poor Law as they chose?—Yes, only if in any particular case there were a body of people who preferred what I call the oligarchic basis exclusively, that is, preferred to keep themselves aloof from any hope of directly interesting the working men in the task of raising the residuum, then I should hope that another society would be founded, and that the old society would dwindle. I think the tendency of public sentiment would certainly bring that result about very quickly.

10,251. Then I understand, suppose the Charity Organisation

Society were to refuse to become what they practically would be under your proposal, a part of the Poor Law administration, if they were to refuse to do that, and the guardians could not get up any other voluntary society having funds to co-operate with them, your scheme would fall to the ground?—No, I think not quite. But may I first say that I do not quite like the phrase that the Charity Organisation Society would become part of a public department. The voluntary schools are not part of the Education Department. The financial and other relations of the voluntary schools and the board schools would be in some respects similar to those under a Charity Organisation Society as I would have it, and the Board of Guardians. It is quite open now for a voluntary school to say, We will have nothing to do with the Education Department, and I would have the same freedom given to the Charity Organisation Society.

10,252. (*Lord Brassey.*) They would get no grant?—They would get no grant.

10,253. (*Chairman.*) But if they said that they would be very hostile pecuniarily even?—The school would get no grant; and the Charity Organisation Society, that kept aloof, would have no powers. It would remain a private corporation, a self-electing corporation.

10,254. Did I understand that you do propose that the fundamental part of your scheme is that the Boards of Guardians should go for information and instruction to the Charity Organisation Society?—Information and advice, I would rather say.

10,255. That is a fundamental part of your scheme?—Yes.

10,256. Then another fundamental part of your scheme is that a certain class of applicant shall be thrown entirely upon the hands of the Charity Organisation Society for relief?—No, I think that would hardly be the right way of putting it. The Charity Organisation Society would say, this Class A we recommend the guardians to relieve in a way as little painful to the applicant as possible; Class B we undertake ourselves, and do not recommend to the guardians.

10,257. (*Mr. Pell.*) Who is that?—The Charity Organisation Committee.

10,258. (*Chairman.*) Plus the members of the Boards of

Guardians?—Well, they would be integral members of it appointed just as legitimately as the other members. They would be appointed to represent the public interests, as the other members would be appointed to represent the private interests.

10,259. But the one represents the subscriber of the fund; the other represents the body whose interest is to get the applicant off their own shoulders?—They, you see, would only be one-fifth of the whole.

10,260. But I mean so far as it goes?—So far as it goes.

10,261. The proposition I was putting before you, to which I ask your assent, was that the very existence of this voluntary association, whether Charity Organisation Society or some other voluntary association, having funds of their own, is necessary to the carrying out of your scheme?—No. I propose that where suitable Charity Organisation Societies do not exist, and cannot be formed, the guardians be charged to call together volunteer visiting committees.

10,262. I have had that in my mind when I was asking you? —In such a case, the guardians should have some freedom of discrimination; but relief would necessarily be more by fixed rule than if the guardians were aided by independent Charity Organisation Societies. For the Class B would then necessarily fall out, excepting in so far as it were possible for the guardains to do what they do in some places, to make themselves to a certain extent Charity Organisation Societies. There are some guardians who, when they see a case which they could not themselves treat without some hardship, go round, either in their individual or corporate capacity, to private persons and those in charge of private charities in their neighbourhood, and endeavour to ascertain whether relief cannot be given to those cases. I understand that there are some districts in the North in which it would not be possible to get the material for a thoroughly effective Charity Organisation Society; but I think that those districts would probably be able to supply fairly good visiting committees subsidiary to the guardians, and under the control of the guardians. After a time, in the course of development, those committees might be separated from the guardians and become independent Charity Organisation Societies.

10,263. Now we will pass on to C?—Well, with regard to C, I have nothing to say, except that I would like to make the treatment of some of them more deterrent and much more educational than it now is. I am referring now to the distinctly bad class. I think it is a very great trouble at present that there are many persons who prefer to go to prison to going into the workhouse, and yet those are the very people for whom I want more discipline. The difficulty is a great one, and I cannot see that there is any way out of it except to start with the prisons. I think the discipline in the prisons ought to be made, generally speaking, the severer. If you do not want to give a man a harder punishment you may reduce the time, but I think it is unendurable that a person should feel that the best way of getting lodged as he likes is to go to a prison. The workhouse at present has for many people all the deterrence of a prison, and for some more, and yet they are the very people whom I want to deter more still. I want the workhouse discipline to be made rather more severe for them, and I think that account must be taken, therefore, of the over-gentle treatment in many of our prisons.

10,264. Then do I understand that this composite committee would take any action with regard to C?—No.

10,265. It would be outside their province?—It would refer the case to the guardians as undeserving.

10,266. And the guardians would then be at liberty to treat those coming under that in a more rigid way even than they do now?—Yes, but I do not think the change should cease there. I do not think that any sort of treatment of the poor is satisfactory in which the element of personal care does not go a good deal further than it does now. I think that all guardians ought to be compelled by law to take that amount of care about the individual inmates of the workhouse which the best guardians do.

10,267. Are these mainly the suggestions which you have to make for an improvement in the administration of the Poor Law, as far as the aged poor are concerned?—I have worded what I have said as much as possible with reference to the aged poor, and I think that the aged poor are in many ways so much easier to deal with. The complications in their case are so much less than in the case of other classes of the poor, and especially of the able-bodied poor, that I think it might be very well to begin with the aged poor, though my principles do not necessarily confine me at all to the aged poor.

10,268. When you spoke of the system you spoke of a system that may be applied to all outdoor relief, but you believe it is more applicable to the aged poor than it is to the others ?—I think one might very well begin with the aged poor; although, if this Commission were a Commission on the reform of the Poor Law in general, I should not lay so much stress upon the distinction between the aged poor and the other classes of the impotent poor.

10,269. Then I understand that you would contemplate the establishment of this system in the first place only for the aged poor ?—Still I rather supposed that any recommendation going beyond that would be beyond the powers of the Commission. That was all. My detailed plan is suggested for the purpose of illustration of a principle applicable to the relief of the aged poor at once, and perhaps to be extended to other classes of impotent poor.

10,270. These suggestions you have made are in the main the propositions you have to put before us with regard to any alteration in administration; I mean so far as suggestions are concerned. We have had some evidence to the effect that outdoor relief tends to lower wages; is that your opinion ?—I think it certainly does tend almost invariably to lower wages, but I think it is possible to spend taxes for the benefit of the poor in such a way as not to lower wages.

10,271. Aged poor ?—Yes, but only on condition that you say to the people of this generation, " The State will not tax itself for your benefit out-and-out; what we give to you, we require you to return to the coming generation." I think money taken from the well-to-do and given to the present generation, the adult generation, for their own greater comfort, while pleasant to the working classes for the time being, is likely to dry up the sources of future wages, unless it is combined with conditions which will increase the earning power of the coming generation.

10,272. Let us confine ourselves to the question of outdoor relief to the aged poor. Do you believe that the giving of outdoor relief to the aged poor, without, of course, hedging it round with proper precautions, would have the effect of reducing wages; do not let us go into the future generation, but the present existing state of things?—I am afraid I cannot answer that without reference to the future generation. You see all these statements about wages are repetitions of doctrines that were universal among the economists of the beginning of the century; you have the same phrases, the same tone of thought; you can trace the economic dogmas of present Poor Law literature direct from those times; and the doctrines which they laid down I think were fairly true in their time. The doctrine is that if you tax the rich, and give money to the working classes, the result will be that the working classes will increase in number, and the result will be you will have lowered wages in the next generation; and the grant will not have improved the position of the working classes on the whole. As regards this a change has come, which separates the economics of this generation from the economics of the past; but it seems to me not to have penetrated the Poor Law literature yet; and this is the main thing that I desire to urge. That change insists upon the fact that if the money is so spent as to increase the earning power of the next generation, it may not lower wages. For while on the one hand the tax on capital would tend continually to cause a shrinking of capital, possibly some emigration of capital, and also some possible emigration of business men—while there would be that force continually at work tending to lower wages—there would be brought into action another force tending to raise wages; and it is reasonable to hope that instead of a mere reckless increase of population, which would have been the inevitable consequence early in the century, there would be a rise in the standard of living, and wages would rise. That is the one thing that I most care to say here. It is more interesting to me than the details of my scheme for reform. It seems to me that whenever I read Poor Law literature of to-day I am taken back to the beginning of the century; everything that is said about economics has the flavour of that old time. Statements which were true then, taking account of the conditions of the working classes and of the state of wealth, are reproduced and made the basis of arguments which seem to me to be not valid now. I once ventured to say that, as regards the relief of distress,

Q

the conditions of 1834 were not substantially the same as at this time; and I was at once told that it was a national calamity that anybody who wrote on economic matters should be so ignorant as not to know that they were substantially the same. That has been repeated more or less emphatically by people of high authority, and I do not think it is true. The particular purpose that made me accept your invitation to come here was that I might submit to cross-examination the statement of my opinion that it is not true.

10,273. After you have had an opportunity of explaining that, may I take it, that for all practical purposes what you say is this : that a tax levied from the well-to-do, for the benefit of those who are not so well-to-do, does not lower wages, if it is spent in some educational form which will raise the condition of the people ?— Raise the earning power of the people.

10,274. That is not the point here just now. That may be true with regard to the abstract proposition of raising taxes from one class and giving it to another; I do not express an opinion upon that, but we are dealing now with Poor Law administration, and the proposition put before us by some witnesses is that if you give outdoor relief in the shape of money grants, or if you would give it in the shape of pensions to people when they come to a certain age, the result will be to lower the wages of persons below that age; is that your opinion ?—I understand that I am now asked to confine myself to the immediate effects ?

10,275. Yes ?—And going away then entirely from those ultimate effects, from what I have now been discussing ?

10,276. Yes. We understand that that is closed; you have expressed an opinion generally, not with regard to Poor Law administration or Poor Law relief just now. You have told us your views generally with regard to the operation of a tax raised from one class for the benefit of another class, and you say that if the money was spent in a manner such as you describe it would not have the effect of lowering wages ?—Yes. All I meant is that that is only part of my statement, that the statement is not complete, that is all.

10,277. But that is it broadly ?—It is a considerable part of what I had wished to say.

10,278. Then I would ask you to confine your attention for a moment to the question of the relief of the poor; what effect in your mind would be caused on wages by the granting of money relief to persons coming to a certain age, whether out of the Poor Law or any other State fund ?—I do not believe that there is any general statement capable of being made about it. An entirely different relic of old economics has been imported into Poor Law discussions with regard to this point. It is that fallacy which we economists are so busy in fighting in some, though not all, of the arguments for an eight-hours day. Many of the working men believe that they can raise the aggregate of wages by merely diminishing the supply of work; they believe that there is a certain fixed amount, a sort of work fund, and that if one man is allowed to work overtime he takes away from one of his neighbours a certain amount of work that that person might have done. Of course that is true under certain conditions and limitations, but it is not true in the sweeping way in which the Socialists urge it. They desire, as they have told us before, that if eight hours does not raise wages they would lower the hours of work to six; and if that does not do they would lower them still further to four. Many of the writings as to the necessity of giving relief, if any is given at all, in such ways as shall prevent the old men from doing work and from competing with others seem to me to involve that fallacy. They really imply that there is a certain work fund, and that if you allow an old man to go on who would not be able to support himself completely, but who could half-way support himself, by his work, and has the other half of his support given from other sources, you then take off some of this work fund and lower wages. In my opinion it is the policy which at the present moment is one of the most dangerous in the programme of the Socialists.

10,279. Then you do not agree ?—I do not agree with it as an unconditional statement. I think that the rate of wages temporarily, and in any place, depends upon the supply of labour relatively to the demand; and if by any local or temporary action you put an increased supply of labour in, you lower the wages, whatever be the method by which you increase the supply, whether that is working overtime, or whether it is inducing an old man to work who otherwise would have folded his hands and found time slow. I quite admit that any cause that increases disproportionately the amount of labour competing for a particular kind of employment in a particular place may lower wages there for the time. Many of those changes which are most beneficial for society may lower wages just for the particular time and in the particular place. But if we are able to keep old men and old women out of the workhouses, doing a great deal of work in the homes, looking after children, and so on, or even if we are able to let them go on working at their trade at lower wages than men in full strength, I think we are not lowering wages generally.

10,280. You are not?—No, because we are increasing the sum-total of things produced, and we are not increasing relatively the number of people among whom they will be divided. Perhaps things may be put in this way : Supposing that there is a market for cattle, and 100 extra cattle come into the market, the prices will go down; but supposing that you have got the supply fixed, and the demand fixed, and then a certain person says : " I will sell that lot of cattle for half price "; he would not lower the price of the rest. The persons who got those cattle for less than their price would be so much better off, just as would be any employer who happened to get old men to work for less than their labour was worth to him; but the price of the rest would not be altered. What alters the price is altering the supply relatively to the demand.

10,281. You do not think there would be a natural desire on the part of those who had got the cattle at the higher price to get rid of their cattle too, and that the competition between the two would necessarily lower the price of the whole?—Not unless the competition of sellers is increased; as it would be if there were more cattle brought into the market.

10,282. (*Mr. Henley.*) I did not quite understand your suggestion with regard to greater freedom of classification in workhouses, with regard to the age. You say greater freedom of classification, what do you mean by that?—Well, of course one knows that even that limited classification that is allowed by the law, and is practised in certain workhouses, cannot be, or is not, as a matter of fact, carried out in all. There are many who think that the increase in the size of the workhouses, leading to an increased distance of the residents in the workhouses from their own friends, is so great an evil that it is better to submit to a less classification than that which the law even now allows than to increase the size of the workhouses so as to carry it out. I think that means should be found for getting over that difficulty. I think there are several ways in which that could be done; and I think that, further, there should be workhouses in which, among other things, the liberty of going in and out is of a different character from that which it is necessary to have for paupers of Class C.

10,283. That is hardly classification, is it?—Oh, yes, in my sense.

10,284. Perhaps you might not be aware that under Article 99 of the Consolidated Order "the guardians shall, so far as circumstances will permit, further subdivide any of the classes enumerated in Article 98 with reference to the moral character, or behaviour, or the previous habits of the inmates, or to such other grounds as may seem to them expedient." Therefore the guardians are not only compelled by this order, if they have room, to so classify, but they have absolutely a free hand with regard to classification?—Yes.

10,285. Were you aware of that?—Yes. I knew its general substance, except as regards its last clause. The only words that struck me at all as unfamiliar were "such other grounds." I do not know whether "such other grounds" would include merit. If they do, then the ordinary doctrines on the subject in Poor Law publications are invalid. If the guardians have the power of classifying with regard to merit, if the meaning of that clause is that, then it is a power which I believe is not known; and the contrary has been expressly declared by the highest authorities.

10,286. That is the order?—I know, but I do not know what the meaning of these words is. If the meaning of these words goes so far as to allow them to classify with regard to merit, then it is all I want; only I think it is a fact not generally known.

10,287. Now I understand that all people applying for relief to a recognised Charity Organisation Society would have to pass through the hands of the Charity Organisation Society, and that the guardians would have in the first instance to accept their recommendations?—No, they would act with the recommendations of the Charity Organisation Society before them ; and being sensible men, would probably follow those recommendations in most instances.

10,288. Then suppose there was a case of misadventure ; suppose a person had died ; now the relieving officer, or whoever administered the law, would be liable to be indicted for manslaughter. Who would be responsible under such circumstances ; would the guardians be responsible, or the Charity Organisation Society ?—I started by saying that interim relief could be, of course, given before the case had time to go before the Charity Organisation Society.

10,289. It was rather a case of this sort, where the guardians, upon the advice of the Charity Organisation Society, refused relief to a person, and that person died in consequence ; who would be responsible ?—But they would never do that ; they could not do that. The Charity Organisation Society would have three courses : one, to recommend public relief, under Class A, another, to recommend public relief under Class C——

10,290. Which they would pay themselves ?—Public relief under Class C which they would not pay themselves ; and a third course to undertake the case themselves, that is to put it under Class B. They would not have the power of recommending no relief if a man were in need of it.

10,291. If they undertook relief in Class B, and a person starved, would they be responsible for it ?—They would be in just the same position as they are now.

10,292. Who would incur the legal responsibility ; they take that particular class out of the hands of the guardians ?—A man can always get Class C, you see, the workhouse still remains ; no privilege, which he has now, would be taken away from the poor man ; he would still be able to say, " What you are giving me under Class B is not sufficient ; I shall fall back upon the provision in Class C under the existing law."

10,293. Suppose a man is ill in bed, and he cannot be removed, the guardians now are entirely reponsible for that man : I am speaking now of Class B ; would the Charity Organisation Society be legally responsible for him ?—Are they responsible if he has not applied for relief ?

10,294. No, he must have applied for relief in the first instance ? —Very well. Take the case of a person who, as things are to-day, comes before the Charity Organisation Society, and he is told, " Your case is one they will undertake "; the case is mismanaged, and he dies; the position of the Poor Law authorities would be the same as in your case under my proposal.

10,295. Then you do not intend a person to make an application and then it be referred to the Charity Organisation Society, but in the first instance the application is to be made to the Charity Organisation Society ?—Interim relief is to be given independently; but for anything beyond that interim relief an application is to be made to the Charity Organisation Society, who say, either, " Do not go to the public authorities at all," or " You had better go to the public authorities. We will recommend you to be put in Class A; or we can recommend you only to be put in Class C."

10,296. Then do you not deprive the applicant of the protection which the law now throws over him in receiving relief ?—No.

10,297. What is his protection against the Charity Organisation Society ?—The Charity Organisation Society, which puts him into Class B, confers a favour on him. If he does not choose to take the favour, he need not.

10,298. Did the working people that you spoke of complain of the Poor Law, or the administration of the Poor Law ?—I do not suppose they know themselves which, the greater part of them. I mean this, that the letter of the law I think they are very seldom acquainted with.

10,299. I merely wanted that question answered, whether they complain of the Poor Law or of the administration of the law, because they are two very different things ?—What I think they complain of is that although the Charity Organisation Society believe that they, the Charity Organisation Society, do practically cover all the ground which the Poor Law, as at present administered, does not cover without hardship, they, the Charity Organisation Society, are mistaken; or at all events that the notion of the working classes is that a great number of cases escape the observation, and the help, of the Charity Organisation Society which ought properly to be referred to them.

10,300. In the great bulk of England there are no Charity Organisation Societies at work, and what I want to know is, do the working men whom you have spoken to complain of the Poor Law, as it stands, or do they complain of the administration of the Poor Law by Boards of Guardians ? Well, I will put it in another way. Are there any points in the Poor Law that the working men have complained to you about, that they think ought to be amended ?—I think that they believe that the work-house test is, as I myself consider it, a barbarous test adapted to the urgent necessities of the time in which it was invented, and inappropriate as a universal test to the present.

10,301-2. That is not the Poor Law, that is the administration by orders. Do they complain of anything in the Poor Law ?— I think they do complain that the letter of the law says that the relief should be administered without merit. That clause which you read to me just now I should be very glad to have interpreted. If it does mean that there is an error in the repeated statements made in the publications of the Charity Organisation Society and elsewhere, that the principle of the Poor Law is that relief should be given without reference to merit; then that would alter the situation very much——

10,303. That is the administration, but what I wanted to get at from you is—you are perfectly conversant with the Poor Law statutes—is there anything in the statutes that they complain of ? —Well, I do not think I can recollect having had any discussion with working men on the letter of the Poor Law as distinguished from its practical administration.

10,304. We have had several suggestions made to us here which I need not tell you now, but one was about the old Act of Elizabeth, as to the ability of the younger men to contribute towards the support of their parents. Have you had those questions brought before you ?—I have ; but I have nothing to say that would be of any value.

10,305. Now we come to the administration of the Poor Law. Have you had any complaints as to the administration of the Poor Law from the working men, or any practical suggestions ?—I think the best way in which I can answer that is by saying that some time ago I tried to formulate what I understood to be the opinion of the working classes on the subject. I wrote the questions out and showed them to some. I showed them to two men who I thought were the best representatives that I knew of the older and the younger school of trades unionism. The questions were as follows. I add the answer given by that one of the two who was least dissatisfied with things as they are : " (Q.) Will the working classes endure the total abolition of outdoor relief ?—(A.) No. (Q.) Will their leaders advise them to do so ?—(A.) No, certainly not at once, out and out. (Q.) So long as the main question about out-relief relates to its total abolition, will the leaders at large exert themselves to make the people at large understand the dangers of lax and lavish out-relief ? And will any efforts they may make in this direction have much chance of success ?—(A.) The leaders would not in my opinion so exert themselves, and if they did they would not succeed. (Q.) If out-relief were given (even before the age of sixty-five) to persons who are not able-bodied, who have lived sober industrious lives, and have made such provision for the future as was within their means, but have been borne down by continued misfortunes, would not many of the leaders of the working classes exert themselves to prevent out-relief from being given recklessly and to apply all needful discipline to those who were habitually idle and profligate ?—(A.) I feel confident that if there were more discrimination in administering relief, the leaders of the workmen would do all in their power to check reckless giving, and they would support the application of all needful discipline to the undeserving, the reckless and the profligate." That has been the outcome of the whole of my experience with the working classes on the subject ; and, as I said before, what has brought me to take an interest in Poor Law is the problem of poverty rather than that of pauperism. I have continually said to the leaders of the working classes, " Why do you not exert yourselves to help to squeeze out this residuum ? " and they say, so long as the sentiment among the working classes exists—and to a very great extent we believe it is a just sentiment—that the Poor Law is, on the whole, hard, it is impossible to get the working classes to co-operate in that treatment of the poor which we recognise to be necessary, and by which alone the residuum can be improved away.

10,306. Those are rather answers to suggestions of questions of yours; but have you ever had any direct complaints from the working men as to the administration of the Poor Law ?—Only in that way, that I have heard them complain very bitterly about the breaking-up of the home. They say that the opinion of the Charity Organisation Society that no home is ever broken up that ought not to be broken up is not true; it does not coincide with their opinion.

10,307. They have not complained of the action of the guardians except with regard to the breaking-up of the homes ?—I do not think that I have heard much personal attack of the guardians.

10,308. Have you ever made any effort to ascertain whether that statement is true or false ?—No, my complaint is that the public has never made any such attempt—that no Commission has either by Sub-Commissioners or by themselves ever made such an attempt—that the only information on the subject that is practically available is such as has been collected by Mr. Charles Booth.

10,309. With regard to this Charity Organisation Society, do I understand you that, if they were in some way legally constituted, their views could be enforced on the Boards of Guardians, that the guardians would be compelled to accept their recommendations ?—The guardians under my proposal would be free to do what they chose; but as sensible men they would, I presume, follow the recommendations of the Charity Organisation Society in most cases.

10,310. Would the guardians be compelled to act with them; would the guardians in a large town where a Charity Organisation Society exists be able to say, " We do not want your assistance at all " ?—Under my proposal a Charity Organisation committee, in return for its having certain public representatives appointed to aid in its work, would have the power of appointing an equal number of members of the guardians, and the guardians would have to accept those members.

10,311. Could the guardians prevent the Charity Organisation Society being affiliated with them ?—I do not like to use the word affiliated, but I am proposing that this law should be a compulsory law; that the Committee of the Charity Organisation Society, when duly approved, should have the power of nominating certain guardians.

10,312. I have not quite got an answer; I am afraid I do not sufficiently explain myself. You have now a Board of Guardians elected by the ratepayers ?—Yes.

10,313. You propose to set up a body which is a perfectly independent body, without any legal responsibility at all; would the guardians, as representing the ratepayers in the town, be compelled, I use the word again, to be affiliated, or in any shape legally united to the Charity Organisation Society ?—My statement seems to be a perfectly definite and precise statement of the proposed law; they would have to obey the law; the law would be that they would be compelled to admit to their body certain people appointed by the committee of the Charity Organisation Society.

10,314. (*Mr. Pell.*) Who are they, pray ?—That the guardians would have to admit among themselves a certain number of people appointed by the members of the Charity Organisation Society, that they would be compelled to do it; they would be also called upon, either they or some other authority, to nominate certain members on the committee of the Charity Organisation Society. Those would be parts of the law; they could not disobey that law; beyond that the law would not go.

10,315. (*Mr. Henley.*) That is how the two bodies are to be constituted. But what would be the power to compel the guardians to refer any cases to the Charity Organisation Society ? —The law would be that the Charity Organisation Society should hold itself open to receive all applicants; there would be no law to prevent the Boards of Guardians from receiving people directly, but as a matter of fact the Boards of Guardians would probably not do that.

10,316. I cannot quite get an answer to my question. Would the guardians be able to keep the Charity Organisation Society at arm's length; to have nothing to do with it at all ?—They would have to obey the law, a perfectly definite law, which I have just formulated, and nothing beyond that.

10,317. What I want to know is, what your proposal is ?

Would the guardians have power to keep the Charity Organisation Society at arm's length, and say, "We will have nothing to do with you whatever"?—I cannot translate "keep at arm's length" into legal language. I do not know what it means. They would have the power of refusing to pay any attention to the recommendation of the Charity Organisation Society if they liked.

10,318. Not only that; but to refuse to have any communication with them whatever?—They would not have the power to disobey the law by which a certain number of guardians might be elected members of the Charity Organisation Committee.

10,319. That is not my point. I mean the Board of Guardians sitting as a body, would they have the power absolutely to ignore them, and say, "We shall have nothing whatever to do with you"?—I have said they could refuse to act on these recommendations if they liked; that would include a power of declining even to read the recommendations.

10,320. Even to receive them?—Yes.

10,321. Supposing they receive these recommendations, would there not be a very great risk in a large town, where the guardians are elected by the ratepayers, and are generally a very independent body, that the men of independent minds would decline to serve under such conditions?—I should have thought that, on the contrary, the result would have been that, whereas up to this time the guardians have been rather a class looked down upon, because they were the mechanical administrators of a law that was out of harmony with the general social movement of the age, they would attract to themselves a great number of people of a higher class.

10,322. You think so?—That is my opinion; particularly, I think, that those persons who were both guardians and members of the Charity Organisation Committee would be like those people who now hold that double office; generally exceptionally fine people.

10,323. Have you ever attended a meeting of a Board of Guardians for a large town like Liverpool, Birmingham, or Manchester?—No.

10,324. I am afraid you are unable to tell us what class of people they are?—I think they are the same class of people that serve upon juries to a large extent.

10,325. (*Mr. Roundell.*) Your experience of the Charity Organisation Society is based upon Oxford and Cambridge ?—How far do you think it would be practicable for Charity Organisation Societies to be established generally ?—I think that there is a very great tendency on the part of the rising generation to care about these things. Oxford and Cambridge represent, as it has been often said, what cultured England is going to be twenty years hence; and the difference in the tone and sentiment of the undergraduates now from what it was twenty years ago is something astonishing. The number of movements that there are by both Universities for working with the poor is very remarkable; and one of the best developments of the higher education of women has been the very great interest which many of the students at the women's colleges have taken in social problems. I believe that a considerable number of the best workers for the London Charity Organisation Society are young people from those colleges, who have taken the question of poverty seriously to heart, in a way in which people of that age did not often do twenty years ago.

10,326. Then should you think, taking the ordinary English towns, that through the agency of the clergy and the intelligent classes there is good hope of these Charity Organisation Societies being formed as a rule ?—I would speak with great diffidence, but it is my impression that the movement of the age is strongly in that direction.

10,327. Would you answer this : How far do you think that private charitable people will be likely to bring themselves into relation with these organised agencies ?—I think that the tendency of the age is in that direction also. Of course, everybody likes to be an autocrat with regard to the administration of the funds over which he has control; and no doubt there are places in which such people refuse to be interfered with in any way. I have in my mind a town, not Oxford or Cambridge, in which I once lived, and in which there was a Charity Organisation Society which had not established a claim to public confidence : it was in the hands of some very well-meaning but not very clear-headed people at that time. And I gather that there are other towns in which the fortuitous combination of people, who come together to form a Charity Organisation Society, does not always earn general confidence. I think if the Charity Organisation Societies were semi-established, one would always get a somewhat stronger class of people, such as we now get on the best societies; and that then the people who subscribe to other independent movements, for I should be sorry to see the independent movements die out, would require those in charge of these private funds to enter into communication with the Charity Organisation Society. Besides which, you know, I would propose that the law should be that they should be compelled to state to the Charity Organisation Society what relief they were giving, and to whom. I would not at present go so far as to propose that the law should compel them to discuss matters of policy with the Charity Organisation Society, or go by the advice of the Charity Organisation Society, but I would propose that the law should compel them to state to the Charity Organisation Society what support they were giving to any person and in what form.

10,328. This Class B was to be relieved, if at all, out of charity funds, not out of public funds?—Yes.

10,329. How would you propose that these charity funds should be found?—It would, I am afraid, sometimes happen that the necessities of the case would cut down Class B to a very small class, because the funds available would be too small. I would, however, start by laying hands on all doles and everything of the sort that was already public property, and handing them over to the Charity Organisation Societies, not the guardians, the Charity Organisation Societies then established, as their "nest egg." If they found that their total funds were small, they would have to recommend for Class A a few cases which it would have been better not to relieve from public funds, as they might make rather dangerous precedents. That is, they would cut off some people from Class B at the upper end. And they would have to send a few hard cases to the workhouse, thus cutting off a few from Class B at the lower end, and putting them to Class C.

10,330. You spoke about the need of more individual care of the cases in the workhouses, and in another part you spoke about the need of what you called sympathetic imagination in dealing with the cases of the poor. In saying all these things do you contemplate a higher type of officer for the administration of the Poor Law, and also for the office of guardian ?—I think that the class of guardians is improving. I think that it will continue to improve. But I think there ought to be more subdivision. Some Boards of Guardians have a great many too many cases coming before them, and they ought to divide themselves up into several committees. I think that the number of relieving officers ought to be increased. I think their quality has improved. I think the account of the condition of the relieving officers which one reads of in 1834 no longer applies to the present time. But the main thing I rely upon is not the improvement of the official element in the administration of the Poor Law. The main thing I rely upon is volunteer aid. I do not think that the details of the Elberfeld principle are applicable to England. But I think the Elberfeld principle is fundamentally right. I think the State ought not to shovel money, so to speak, upon anybody.

10,331. (*Mr. Pell.*) You are aware that the Poor Law only deals with destitution ?—I am aware that it does.

10,332. Your scheme contemplated dealing with distress as well as destitution, I think ?—Yes ; but I should say that the term destitution has never been defined.

10,333. Upon whom do you propose to put the expense of this additional apparatus for the relief of distress, upon imperial funds or upon local funds ? If it has never occurred to you, I would not press it ?—It has occurred to me to think it over. I am considering how I can answer your question shortly.

10,334. You know the various schemes for pensions that are before the public. Mr. Charles Booth has the merit of being logical, he puts it entirely upon the Exchequer ; other schemes put it partly upon private resources and partly upon the rates ?—Well, the only short answer I can give is—partly upon imperial funds and partly upon local. I think the question is most complicated, and that there are a great number of different considerations of which account has to be taken.

10,335. (*Mr. Broadhurst.*) Do you admit that one of the virtues of relief is that it should be immediate and simple in its form ?—I am not sure about its being simple. No ; I want relief to be very often very complex ; the centre of relief, I think, should be the aim of raising a man out of the position of being a pauper; and that means, I think, a great variety of methods of treatment of individual cases. I would like it to be as quick as it can be, but I do not think I want to make it simple.

10,336. Well, but would it not frequently occur that, if it is not simple and expeditious, fatal results might ensue before relief came?—I would have interim relief given at once; but I would not have a difficult case decided in a hurry—not until a great many inquiries had been made, and all sorts of ways had been thought of. Indeed, I think that is the practice already in the best Charity Organisation Societies. Just as an experienced doctor does not give a Holloway's pill, the same medicine, for every complaint, and to every patient, but a special treatment for every single patient, so I think our prescriptions should not be simple but complex.

10,337. What is the object of instituting a supplementary Board of Guardians in the form of charity organisation; what is your object?—Because, while I think that the assumption on the part of the well-to-do, that they alone have any rights and any particular duties with regard to the residuum—while I think that is extreme, I think it is true that they have much greater rights, and much greater duties, because they have much greater opportunities than any other class; and a Charity Organisation Society which was mainly in their hands would, I think, be likely to call into action a good number of forces that would be lost if we had only the Boards of Guardians. Where a Charity Organisation Society cannot be found, then I would have the Board of Guardians, with a visiting committee of their own under them; but I think the better course is one in which the special opportunities and resources of the well-to-do classes have full play, while yet there is added at the background the authority of a semi-public body: moreover, this would give an opportunity for some of the best of the working classes to take a direct share in the burden of the work. Because we are learning every day, more and more, that it is not the money that is given in charity so much as the work, by which real good is done; and there is no reason at all why many of the best of the working classes, particularly experienced members of Friendly Societies, should not do a great part of this work, if, as I believe, they are willing to do it. Now there is no place for them to work in, and I want to make a place.

10,338. But could not work be found for them in the existing system, with any necessary improvements that might be found? —Well, I think that if we were legislating—proposing, as some of my friends have been asked to do, to provide a constitution for some Oriental country—if we were proposing a Poor Law constitution for a new country, I think it is a question whether we should have Charity Organisation Societies in their present form at all. I think it is quite likely that the more natural development would be on the Elberfeld plan. The Elberfeld plan, which, you know, is very much like the Elizabethan plan; the spirit of Elberfeld and the spirit of the sixteenth century Poor Law are much the same; I think that that plan is, perhaps, more the natural one. But, then, you see, the Charity Organisation Societies are in possession. They have arisen out of an abnormal condition of things, which itself arose out of the abnormal condition of England during the first part of this century.

10,339. But do you not think that your scheme of Charity Organisation Societies in conjunction partly with the Boards of Guardians would have a tendency to racing poor people from pillar to post?—No.

10,340. Partly to a properly constituted authority and partly to a body not so well constituted?—No. On the contrary, one of the great defects that I find in the working even of the Cambridge Charity Organisation Society is its want of publicity. So that chance often decides whether a deserving person is relieved in a manner agreeable to himself, and with pleasant surroundings, by the Charity Organisation Society, or whether that person goes to the guardians in the first instance, and would not come into contact with the Charity Organisation Society at all; if there were not at Cambridge an understanding between the guardians and Charity Organisation Committee, such as I wish to see made universal. It is notorious that the number of people who know how to get access to the Charity Organisation Societies in England is really very small. On my plan the Charity Organisation Society would be a semi-public body, and it would be in various ways

R

directly made known—I will not use the word advertised, but made known—and then a person who wanted relief would know where to go. There would be one place, the office of the Charity Organisation Society; who if they found his case a good one, but yet requiring funds that they had not the control over, would pass him on to the guardians under Class A. Perhaps I should like to add that one thing that has strengthened my conviction that some such change as this is required is that I have noticed with regard to the Cambridge society that there have been cases which the society has desired to relieve but could not. There has been no ethical or other ground against giving the applicant the aid desired, except this, that on going into the figures it is found that it would involve the society in a permanent outlay for many years. Not because the case is a bad one, but simply because the society cannot afford it; though it is relatively a rich society, it has to pass them over to the guardians. Now under my plan the money would be found by passing those people over to the guardians marked Class A.

10,341. Have you any knowledge of rural life, of the administrations in rural unions?—I have never been on any Board of Guardians myself.

10,342. So that you can give no opinion as to the probable working of your scheme in rural districts?—I think that the first part of my scheme would not work to any very great extent in rural districts. I think that in rural districts one would have, for a very long time at least, to fall back upon the second alternative mainly; but then the cases in which I am most interested for my own purposes are in the towns.

10,343. Do you think it would be possible to have one system for rural unions and another for urban unions?—I propose one system to be worked wherever there is a suitable Charity Organisation Society, whether in town or country, and another system where there is not a suitable society, whether in town or country. May I just mention that the aggregate population of towns with more than 50,000 inhabitants each is now about five times as much as it was in 1830? It was two-and-a-half millions in 1831, and it is twelve millions now.

10,344. Your desire appears to be that some of the men

experienced in giving relief from voluntary societies should be incorporated in the system of Poor Law relief ?—Yes.

10,345. That under your plan would be only possible in towns ?—That plan would be only possible where there could be found an adequate Charity Organisation Society; but I believe there are a great number of rural districts in which, when the initiative was once given, the Charity Organisation Society would grow.

10,346. But is it not desirable everywhere in all Poor Law systems, both rural and urban ?—Yes; most desirable.

10,347. Have you ever thought out how it could be realised in the rural localities, where the hardships of the Poor Law system are presumably more severe than in towns ?—Yes; I have made my suggestion. It is that where a Charity Organisation Society does not already exist, an endeavour should be made to form one, where the endeavour fails, the guardians should be required by law—and this law should be worded quite unmistakably— to invite volunteers to assist them, and to inquire into particular cases—the hope being that the volunteer committee so formed would after a while become a Charity Organisation Society.

10,348. Have you taken the opinion of your trades union friends on your duplicate or double-barrelled system of relief; of Charity Organisation Societies and Poor Law; have you discussed it ?—With one or two.

10,349. Do you find it to go at all ?—I have not heard any objection to it.

10,350. Did you hear any approval of it ?—I came away from the discussion fairly well satisfied with myself; I do not know that I could go any farther.

10,351. You are speaking about severer discipline in the workhouses to some particular kind of people ?—Yes.

10,352. What sort of severer discipline do you want, and who for ?—The resolute tramp; the man who can work and will not.

10,353. The tramp is of a different class already. He is administered and provided for specially; the casual ?—More or less; but not in all unions, I think; and I think there are some people who want to abolish the tramp ward in all unions—the casual relief ward in all workhouses.

10,354. What do they propose to do with the casual ?—I could not answer the question well. I have not full information upon that matter.

10,355. What is the severer discipline to the others than the casuals ?—Well, I do not think that a man who has a pension should be allowed to discharge himself and drink it all up; and then come back scarcely like a man, and go on living in the workhouse. That is one case. I think that generally speaking we have got to recognise, that partly through the suppression of the gipsy encampments, there has got into the large towns a quantity of unstable excitable blood, for whom the privileges of absolute freedom are not well adapted. And that, of course, applies to the aged as well as to others.

10,356. I was leaving all that to ask you a final question, I think. Have you given any consideration or formed any opinions as to the possibility of a universal scheme of pensions ?—Yes; there are two especially that I think have a great deal to be said for them, Mr. Charles Booth's and Mr. Moore Ede's modification of Mr. Charles Booth's. My objections to them are that their educational effect, though a true one, would be indirect; that they would be expensive; and that they do not contain, in themselves, the seeds of their own disappearance. I am afraid that, if started, they would tend to become perpetual. I regard all this problem of poverty as a mere passing evil in the progress of man upwards; and I should not like any institution started which did not contain in itself the causes which would make it shrivel up, as the causes of poverty itself shrivelled up. But I would far rather have either Mr. Booth's scheme or Mr. Moore Ede's scheme than things as they are.

10,357. Lesser evils than the present ?—I will not say they are lesser evils, but they are not the things that I like best. If there is so much public money accessible for the diminution of poverty as those schemes would require, I would like to do some other things with some part of it.

10,358. What other things ?—Well, that comes back upon the fundamental position, which I desire to make the basis of all my evidence. It is, that while the problem of 1834 was the problem of pauperism, the problem of 1893 is the problem of poverty; that a man ought not to be allowed to live in a bad home, that extreme poverty ought to be regarded, not indeed as a crime, but as a thing so detrimental to the State that it should not be endured, and that everybody who, whether through his own fault or not, was in effect incapable of keeping together a home that contributed to the well-being of the State, that person should, under the authority of the State, pass into a new form of life. We cannot do it now. It is impossible to do it. The ethical force does not exist. We cannot get the ethical force until we have convinced the working classes that there is no real hardship in the present state of things, and it seems to me, therefore, that to have Commission after Commission to hear the evidence from one side, which is perfectly well as far as it goes, and not to hear the evidence from the other side, is not satisfactory.

10,359. (*Mr. Booth.*) I understand that your general position, the basis upon which the proposals you have made are in the first instance justified, is that poverty, having changed its character, needs changed treatment ?—That is so.

10,360. And that that is true, whether the form be that of pauperism or other forms ?—That is so.

10,361. That you consider the dangers are less than they were; the dangers of what you call sympathetic treatment are less than they were fifty years ago ?—Yes.

10,362. And that the necessity of making the system more sympathetic is greater ?—Yes.

10,363. And that by sympathetic treatment you partly also mean democratic treatment, bringing in the working classes into the administration ?—Yes; partly. My reason for that is partly, I think, that in 1834 there was not the trained working-class intelligence which could have been utilised for the purpose. The working-class intelligence that we want to utilise is almost entirely a creation of the last sixty years, and in a great measure of the last twenty years.

10,364. So that all the conditions of the problem are very much changed ?—They are all different; almost separated as the poles.

10,365. And therefore justify an entire reconsideration of

the principles, whether applied to the old or all round ?—Entirely. I think this age has got to settle its own problems guided by reasoned experience, but not applying experience crudely. I think many references to the experiences of the beginning of the century are crude; are based simply upon an indifference to an analysis of the conditions.

10,366. But with regard to the old, many of these points are specially applicable ?—Some of them.

10,367. And you go on to say, I gather, that as to the old, while the general conditions have improved, from certain causes the old have not altogether shared in the improvement ?—Just so. I think that there have been very special causes tending to make the case of the old harder than it used to be, in spite of the fact that a growing feeling of duty is making the working classes willing to sacrifice themselves in some respects, though not in all, more for the old than they used to.

10,368. That is to say, privately, for their own old people ?— Yes.

10,369. So that you would, perhaps, go so far as to say that the condition of the old has not improved; not only that it has not improved relatively ?—I do not know that I would go quite so far as that.

10,370. But recognising, as I believe you do, a very great improvement all round, you would say that the improvement with regard to the old is very much less ?—Is less, decidedly.

10,371. And then, I think, you think also, that the problem is complicated by the fact that the rich are in some ways more separated from the poor by modern conditions ?—I think that is so. One of the best of the many good works of the Charity Organisation Society has been, when a person has applied for help, to try to find out his old employer, and to get his old employer to take an interest in him as a human being. It is a splendid thing to do. But the problem itself which they deal with is, to a very great extent, a problem of modern times; the continual migration of the people, the separation of the employer from the employed during the daytime, when they are in the workshop, and still more the separation at night, when they go home to their separate suburbs, is a cause of a difficulty which did not exist to anything like the same extent in 1834.

10,372. So that the very existence, the rapid growth of special organisations to bridge the interval proves partly or indicates partly the rapid growth of the interval ?—Yes. What I may call the charitable middleman could have been done without in 1834; now he is a necessity of the situation.

10,373. So that your proposals go forward to make use of that, and strengthen it, give it a more important position ?—That is so.

10,374. And all that you say is chiefly, in fact mostly or entirely, true of towns; it is far more true of towns than of country ?—Nearly all of what I have said.

10,375. But side by side of that we have the fact that the great growth is in the town population ?—That is so.

10,376. Instead of being a mere fraction of the population, it is now about half ?—Yes.

10,377. And that the proportion is continually increasing ?—Rapidly increasing, not only in this country but in all others.

10,378. With regard to the point about relief being given only to destitution which has been raised, you understand that the law as acted upon is of that character that relief is limited to cases of destitution ?—Yes.

10,379. Without regard to merit ?—My opinion is that the term destitution had a historical origin, and that it is used now with entire neglect of its historical origin, and in a sense and for purposes different from those for which it was originally used. The centre of the doctrine about destitution originally was that the independent labourer ought not to be in a worse position than the dependent; and the people of 1834 argued with perfect truth that the independent labourer often had not nearly enough food. So they could not allow even the most deserving of the dependent poor to have more than the bare food which they were compelled to allow to all. But that is no longer the case. Practically the food-buying power of the labourer is from three to five times what it was; and the destitution that the framers of the 1834 Report had in their minds does not exist now among the same class of people. The fundamental reason of their conclusion was that one must not make he dependent labourer better off than the independent. Now you can do a great deal which could not be done then, without breaking that canon, because the position of the independent labourer is so very much better.

10,380. But if the wording of the law leaves it open to the guardians to recognise merit, if the clause which Mr. Henley read does give them that power, you would feel that the law did what was necessary?—Yes; only, though I am not a lawyer, I believe it is very dangerous to interpret a clause without being quite sure that there is not some other clause that limits its operation. Now, the people who have written on the subject of Poor Law relief have been so able, and have had so much official experience, and they have so often said that it is a fundamental principle of the Poor Law that the guardians cannot take account of merit in determining the amount of the relief, that I should be very interested to know on good authority whether that clause does empower them to take account of merit or no in determining the amount of the relief.

10,381. With regard to the effect of public relief on wages, would you say that it may be looked at in two ways, as to the direct competition of those workmen who are partly supported by the rates, and in a general way as expressed in what you have said to-day? What you have said to-day I take to have been entirely with regard to the general effect of money provided by the rich for the poor; and what I want to ask you is whether there is not a special possible effect on wages due to the actual competition of subsidised individuals?—I think that anything that increases the supply of labour in any particular market tends to force down real wages in the market, but tends also to raise the real wages of the people who produce the things consumed in the market; therefore, I think that if a certain number of old men who are now considered past work could be added to the ranks of effective labourers all over the country, that would have the effect of increasing the general well-being of the working classes. While I admit that if they are added disproportionately in any particular trade they would tend to cause a glut of the things produced in that trade and injure that trade, though possibly to the greater benefit often of other trades.

10,382. But do you think that the granting of pensions

would increase the supply of old labour?—No. The remark with regard to the influence of pensions on wages had to do with the effects that a tax might have in diminishing the supplies of capital.

10,383. That is as I understood it; that is to say, it is a general consideration, not of the specific character of bringing more labour into competition?—Just so. It is the taxation side of the pensions that I had in view, not the bringing of labour into competition in that particular case.

10,384. You do not think that more old people would come into competition for work if they had an allowance of public money?—Not necessarily. May I put the case in this way: suppose you could conceive a mad Emperor of China to give to every English working man half-a-crown for nothing: according to the current notions, so far as I have been able to ascertain them, that would lower wages, because it would enable people to work for less. I think that nine economists out of ten at the beginning of the century would have said that that would lower wages. Well, of course, it might increase population, and that might bring down wages; but unless it did increase population, the effect according to the modern school would be to raise wages because the increased wealth of the working classes would lead to better living, more vigorous and better educated people, with greater earning power, and so wages would rise. That is the centre of the difference.

10,385. Unless the allowances to old people increased their numbers, or increased the number of them who took work, it would not have a direct effect—a competitive effect upon wages? —No.

10,386. Then with regard to Poor Law expenditure you would see no objection to increasing expenditure by increasing the number of relieving officers, by increasing the efficiency of the service?—I think we are wrong in allowing the amount spent in poor relief to become a continually and rapidly diminishing portion of the total income of the country, while yet in answer to a great number of suggestions of reform, the answer is : " Oh, the relieving officers are already overworked." The remedy is to take some of that money which is now going into the pockets of the rich, and which by tradition was the property of the poor, and to apply it for this purpose—the increase of the number of relieving officers.

10,387. Then with regard to the point which has been raised —not to-day—but which has been raised with regard to this subject, that those who have paid their rates regularly have to some extent an ethical claim on the rates for relief, what is your view on that subject?—My view on that subject is that there is a great deal to be said for it, and I have never heard anything said against it. I have challenged a great number of people to give any argument against it, on general grounds, and many of them have given me in writing or in print an answer, but it has always come to this, "That is the law." Of course it is the law; the only question is whether the law is a good one. The law is, that taxes are not levied on what is *primâ facie* the equitable principle that everybody should contribute to the necessities of the State in proportion to his means. Analyse that, and it means that a person whose income leaves no surplus above the necessaries of life should not be taxed at all. We cannot afford to act on that maxim, because it would introduce political dangers, and therefore we do tax the poor; but if the poor say, "I have paid that money in poor rates, for the relief of people in distress. I am in distress, there is no reason why I should have it given back to me with unnecessary disagreeableness"; then I think there is no answer; and I repeat here what I have said elsewhere, that I have looked over a considerable number of Blue Books, and in every other place where I could expect an answer, and I have found none. The only attempt at an answer has been "That is the law." Of course it is; that is the starting-point.

10,388. Now to come to your actual proposals, I have not exactly gathered which body comes first in the combination, the Charity Organisation Society or the guardians, or may either come first? May the person seeking relief seek it from either and be referred by either to the other?—I do not think it would be necessary to prohibit a working man from going to the guardians in the first instance; but I should myself wish to prohibit the guardians from giving more than interim relief until they had referred the case to the Charity Organisation Society and received a report from the Charity Organisation Society. When they have received the report, if they chose to put it into the fire without reading it, I think the only thing to do would be to wait until the next election of guardians.

10,389. Whichever body is first referred to has the responsibility of giving the immediate relief ?—The Poor Law authorities would retain their responsibility for giving *ad interim* relief if it were demanded of them, but there would be nothing in the law to prevent the Charity Organisation Society from doing as they do now, granting interim relief if they thought that best; they would not be compelled to do so, but they would be at liberty to do so, of course; Poor Law authorities would be compelled to give it.

10,390. That is to say, that if a poor man applies first to the Poor Law authorities, they are bound to take the immediate responsibility of relief if it is necessary ?—Yes.

10,391. On the other hand, if he applies first to the Charity Organisation Society, that Society has the option either to relieve him at once, or to send him at once with a note instructing him to apply to the guardians ?—If they choose, they may say, " We do not give interim relief, or we do not give it in this case; you must apply to the guardians for interim relief; as regards permanent relief, we will investigate your case, and make a report."

10,392. Then I understand the guardians are obliged to accept as their partner in this matter any Charity Organisation Society that exists that applies to them ?—No; any " suitable society." A society would have to be accepted by the Local Government Board as suitable for the purpose. There might be started almost a bogus Charity Organisation Society, a society not representative of the population either as regards its numbers or its funds. The question whether a Charity Organisation Society was suitable for the purpose would be decided by the Local Government Board, and it would generally be that any of the chief existing societies would be regarded as suitable. There would have to be some rule as to the amount of funds that they got from private sources.

10,393. It is not until they have been accepted as suitable by the Local Government Board that the guardians are forced to receive their representatives as guardians ?—Yes.

10,394. Then I understand that your proposal is, that there should be two perfectly distinct classes of public relief, divided by a middle body which was dealt with entirely by voluntary action ?—Yes.

10,395. And that the extent of the middle body would be measured largely by the energy and depth of the purse of the particular Charity Organisation Society ?—Particularly by the depth of the purse at the command of the Charity Organisation Society, including such doles as might be handed over to their administration by the public authorities.

10,396. They would deal with as many cases as they could or would deal with, and those would be of the middle class, those who were not strictly suitable for honourable public relief, and not bad enough for deterrent public relief ?—Yes, and especially such cases as would be likely to form bad precedents. For instance, there are many things that the Charity Organisation Societies do which the guardians do not do, and perhaps could not safely do; taking tools out of pawn, sending a person to the seaside, paying rent, and all sorts of exceptional things of that kind.

10,397. Of a character that you would not like to give any rights with regard to ?—Of a character that might be likely to form bad precedents.

10,398. At any rate they are those cases for which charitable funds are more applicable than the rates ?—Quite so.

10,399. I want to ask you what methods you would wish to adopt to make relief as you say as little painful as possible to the best class ?—I would like, perhaps, to add one thing : the English people, perhaps, like all other people, are very much the servants of words, and the discussion as to the relations between public pensions and public relief is to a great extent a question of words. I think it is rather open to consideration whether those who were put into Class A might not be said to receive a public " subsidy " instead of public relief; and similarly as to those who went to the workhouses that were specialised for them with a greater outlay per head, more being given in kind, not in money; it is the same principle whether this increased amount is given in money or in kind; but I want to reverse the present presumption that this amount of public relief may not depend on merit or worth. Those houses specially devoted to Class A might have a different name; they might be called hospitals. I believe there is historical tradition for the use of that word for such purposes.

10,400. (*Mr. Arch.*) Do I understand that this Charity Organisation Society takes under its administration charities which have been left by donors in days gone by?—I think that there might be some charitable gifts which it would be better on the whole to leave in the hands of the guardians, but I think that with this double giving on the one side and taking on the other, it would be fair and best to put a good number of public foundations under the control of the Charity Organisation Committees.

10,401. (*Chairman.*) What do you mean by "leave in the hands of the Boards of Guardians"?—The word "leave" was not well chosen; I meant, to hand over to the guardians.

10,402. (*Mr. Arch.*) Are you aware, I suppose you are, that in the rural villages there are no Charity Organisation Societies? —Yes.

10,403. How would you establish them?—I hope that the growing spirit of the age will establish them; not an independent society for each village (that is going rather too far), but an independent society for each union, with, perhaps, local branches in the villages.

10,404. And in the interim between now and the time when the intelligence of people will be able to do that, you would leave the destitute poor to make their first appeal to the guardians, there being no Charity Organisation Society?—Well, I would do something at once; I would compel the guardians to exert themselves to call into existence a body of voluntary visitors. Of course, the Board of Guardians might say that they tried and failed, and it would be for the electors, aided by the Local Government Board, to decide whether they had tried *bonâ fide*.

10,405. Do you think you could compel, or that any body

of men could compel, the present trustees, who, generally speaking, in the rural villages are the clergymen, do you think you would be able to compel these gentlemen to hand over these charities placed in their hands to the Boards of Guardians ?—I think so; I think that is just what the law can do.

10,406. But do you think that the parishioners, who in their various parishes receive a portion of these charities at Christmas and other times, would be willing for the trustee to hand over their charities to assist the poor rates ?—I think it would be clearly for the good of the State; and it would be decided by a law passed by the State, passed in Westminster.

10,407. You said something about the Charity Organisation Society electing the Board of Guardians ?—Electing a certain number.

10,408. Of the Board of Guardians ?—A distinct minority; I proposed one-fifth.

10,409. Do you think that the ratepayers of our rural villages would ever submit to that ?—Yes, if they get a *quid pro quo*, and a good deal more than a *quid pro quo*, by having a voice in the control of the Charity Organisation Society.

10,410. You think so ?—I think so.

10,411. And do you think there would be any difficulty in getting a proportion of the working men upon these Boards of Guardians; or, I will put it in another way, do you think that the Charity Organisation Societies which will be composed, I suppose, mainly of the well-to-do, would very largely sanction putting a lot of these working men upon these Boards of Guardians to have some control over their charities ?—According to my proposal they would not be recognised by the Government unless they did consent to that; and, of course, you must be aware that a great number of Charity Organisation Societies are exerting themselves very much to get working men to co-operate with them, and they find it very difficult, partly because their hours of meeting are not convenient to the working men, and partly because the working men have a reasonable dislike to going into a close corporation by any but a public door.

10,412. (*Mr. Loch.*) I think by way of criticism of workhouses you mentioned that people preferred the prison to the workhouse ?—I am referring to a great number of statements of that kind I have seen in reports of police-courts and elsewhere.

10,413. Is that your sole evidence ?—Yes.

10,414. You have never seen figures to show that the able-bodied paupers in receipt of indoor relief have increased, while the prisoners in England and Wales in local prisons have gone down ?—Of course.

10,415. And does that not rather go against that statement ? —Not in the least, so far as I understand it.

10,416. Why not ?—Because the number of people who would elect the prison in preference to the workhouse is very small, and the causes that are diminishing the number of people in our prisons and increasing those in our workhouses are very big, and cover a very wide area. I did not mean to imply that in all workhouses the rule was so hard that a person who has had experience of both houses preferred the prison.

10,417. You made a general statement, and that general statement you qualify now very largely; you would seem to say that practically there were large causes at work, which would make it apply only to one or two instances here and there, very few in which the workhouse would be preferred to the prison ?—My own memory is different from yours; I do not recollect that I made a general statement; if I did, it was by mistake.

10,418. You also think that the workhouse at the present time is so managed as to put any persons of respectability who enter in, into unfair converse with those of unclean and unsuitable habits ?—I think it depends very much upon the workhouse. In some workhouses there is very little of that; in others there is a great deal, I believe.

10,419. Can you mention the workhouses in which it is bad ? —I was talking to a member of the working classes only yesterday, who said that the great terror of the workhouse is the compulsory intercourse with people of bad habits. She, of course, referred to a small union.

10,420. Can you mention yourself any workhouse ?—No; that is not what I have come here to do.

10,421. Did this person to whom you have referred know of the conditions of any such workhouse ?—Yes.

10,422. Could you name the workhouse ?—I will endeavour to ascertain. I should also say that I am under the impression that there is a good deal of evidence in the Report of the Select Committee of the House of Lords in 1888, and I had thought here, that there are small workhouses in which it is not possible to separate the residents of cleanly habits of mind from those who have not those habits, as much as would be desirable.

10,423. Then your reply is to the effect that all that you have to say refers to certain particular workhouses, and that it is not a general statement ?—I think I said from the first, that that part of the evil of life in the workhouse which consisted of the compulsory association with persons of bad character was not very great in those houses in which the sevenfold classification could be carried out.

10,424. And, therefore, if the workhouses are carried out in accordance with what we accept as a fairly good method of classification, your objection so far drops to the ground ?—I do not say that it drops to the ground.

10,425. So far ?—No ; because I think an objection cannot drop to the ground which was not raised.

10,426. Did you not object to it on the ground of workhouses being too small ?—I objected to it in regard to those workhouses in which it exists.

10,427. Have you any notion in what proportion these workhouses are ?—No ; no definite notion.

10,428. You have never gone into any question of that sort ? —I have not collected the statistics on the subject.

10,429. Are there statistics ?—I should like to say that I have confined my evidence to facts within my knowledge. I have carefully stated the limitation of my knowledge, and you are asking me questions on matters of which I have already stated I have no special knowledge.

10,430. I thought the statements of the witness were much more general than those he is now making, and that is my reason for putting those questions. With regard to the working classes, I understood you had put certain questions to two leading members of the working classes; the first of these questions was, "Would you consent to the abolition of outdoor relief?" Do you think that that is a question to which, unless they had been into the matter in some detail, they could very well have an immediate reply?—I think it was a matter that they had considered carefully.

10,431. May I take it that you can make no clear suggestion on that point to the Commission; the point how a Commission can obtain a fair idea of the actual knowledge and experience of the working classes on the matter of poor relief?—I do not know whether my opinions are really worth anything, but I have opinions.

10,432. Would you say what your opinion is?—I would like a Commission appointed to inquire into the general conditions of poor relief.

10,433. Suppose we take our own question here, the question of the aged?—I was rather wishing to avoid appearing to criticise the action of this Commission. I would like that Commission to contain a representative of a place like Wigan, in which outdoor relief has been given carefully, but readily, and as some people think without bad results. I would like the official element to be comparatively small, because recent Commissions on this class of question have consisted to a very large extent of people with official experience whose ways of looking at the problem of poverty are very much the same; and it has sometimes happened that when the majority of a Board of Guardians are of one opinion the witnesses that have been selected have been from the minority, no witnesses having been called from the majority. I would like to redress that one-sidedness by having rather a preponderance of people who think that the present tendencies are going rather too far. I do not say I think so myself, but I want to get their view, and I cannot get their view. And I would also like a great number of working men to be on the new Commission.

10,434. Have the working men at the present moment the kind of knowledge that you think is desirable with the view of coming to a conclusion on this point?—I think they have the knowledge that we want, and which I find I do not get from

s

reading Blue Books, and the publications of the Charity Organisation Society. I find we always get the problem looked at from one point of view; it is a most important point of view, perhaps the most important; but the other point of view is scarcely represented at all. I have heard one side over and over again; I want to hear that side which I do not know so well.

10,435. But I have understood you to say that the working classes have very little knowledge at present of this matter ?— They know where the shoe pinches; I want to find out where the shoe pinches.

10,436. You want, not a change in the administration of the law, but their view of the administration of the law ?— What I want is that more evidence should be got from persons most concerned as to how far, even in places where charity is well organised, it covers all the area of distress, except that which may be suitably relieved in ordinary workhouses. I have spent some time in trying to get information of that kind. I cannot get it, and I can find very little in the publications of the Charity Organisation Society, and very little in the Blue Books of modern times. There is more in the earlier Blue Books that helps me to form an opinion on similar questions in earlier times.

10,437. I will not proceed further in any questions. The points which have a bearing on the policy and work of the Charity Organisation Society are numerous, and it would lead us to a long discussion, for which at this late hour there is no time.

10,438. (*Mr. Humphreys-Owen.*) Your guiding principle, I suppose, is that work of this kind must be carried on with the hearty co-operation of the poorer classes, and not merely against their indifference or absolute opposition ?—That is my view.

10,439. And you also believe that if the working classes are persuaded that the administration is fair and humane they will co-operate with it, and will not oppose it ?—Quite so.

10,440. Could you suggest to us any means by which the working classes could take such a share, beyond those which you have already indicated in the administration of the existing Poor Law, as would give them that sympathy with it ?—I think that if we could stop the quotations of some so-called principles of the Poor Law that seem to me so needlessly irritating, as well as scientifically unsound; and if we could make a clear declaration of our resolve to stop unnecessary hardship at all costs, I think then we should get a much larger response to the invitations to the working classes to take a share in the voluntary work of the Charity Organisation Societies; or, where Charity Organisation Societies were not in existence, of the committees of volunteers attached to the guardians.

10,441. Do you think that the objection that is made to old age pensions is well founded, that they relieve the capitalist and the landowner of the performance of a duty which primarily falls on them at the expense of other sections of the community ? To put it in another way, that an industry does not justify its existence unless it pays such wages as enables its employés to provide for old age ?—Yes, I partly agree with that; but the causes which have made the agricultural labourer unable to make adequate provision for old age without a sacrifice of very many pleasures, and in some cases many duties, are so firmly rooted in the country that I should not be very hopeful of changing those conditions rapidly. I think that the wages of agricultural labour, the real wages, are rising, and will go on rising, but I cannot see any reason to believe that they will reach a healthy level for some time to come.

10,442. May I ask whether you have inquired into the actual circumstances of either of the two famous agricultural unions, Brixworth and Bradfield ?—I have read the evidence about them with very great interest. I think that the administrators in a case of this kind are far more important than the method of administration. I think almost the worst law administered by Mr. Garland would have worked better than the best law administered by an ordinary person. I noticed a story in the *Charity Organisation Review*. It was Mr. Willink, I think, who said he had a coachman who, after he had been in his service only a very few months, was attacked by a complaint which the doctor said would render him never able to work any more. Mr. Willink told Mr. Garland, and added, " I am a little puzzled to know what to do." " Puzzled ! " Mr. Garland said; " why, of course you won't drop him," in a way that made Mr. Willink feel it would be impossible to do so. I quite understand that where a union is under the strong moral influence of a man of that sort, there is scarcely any law that will work very badly under the administration which he will bring about.

10,443. Now, your proposal, I think, is, to put it broadly, to substitute positive law for that moral influence; do you think you can do it?—No; I do not think I do want to substitute law for moral influence; but I think that law can be so adapted as to evoke moral influence, or it can be so adapted as to make moral influence rather hard to develop. That is all I think you can do by a change of the law.

10,444. I think that you and the supporters of the rigid administration of outdoor relief seem to be at one, because what they say is that they propose to strengthen the springs of moral action, not to impose duties by positive law. They wish to strengthen the springs of moral action by making thrift and duty to parents and other virtues of that class more easy to the poor?—I agree with that to a certain extent. I agree that patience in bearing other people's sufferings is as clear a duty as patience in bearing our own; but I think there is some little danger that it may be carried too far. There are some who think that the present methods of poor relief and charity will very soon leave little suffering which is not needed to educate people of braver and stronger heads; and those who think thus are quite right in calling for patient adhesion to the present methods. But so much patience with the sufferings of others appears excessive to myself and to those who think that there are still many hardships, which cause more pain than they are worth for the purposes of education.

10,445. If, therefore, on a close inquiry into the circumstances of unions where this policy is pursued you found that the hardships did not cause more pain than they were worth you would modify your opinion as to the practical duties before us?—Quite so. All I desire is that evidence should be got; all I complain of is that we have not the evidence.

10,446. As to whether the giving of outdoor relief enabled labourers to compete with others and so to lower the rate of

wages, I did not quite follow your argument upon that point ?—
My argument is that if outdoor relief or any other cause has the
result of enabling people to work who would otherwise be idle,
the result will not be a lowering of the general level of wages;
although if the people who are so brought into work are more
numerous in any one trade than in others it will lower the rate
of wages in that particular trade by glutting that particular
trade.

10,447. Then you would not quarrel with the idea if it means
this : that persons by receiving outdoor relief are enabled to
compete with others in the same market in a way which they
otherwise would not do ?—I think that it may lower wages just
in the same way as the making of brushes in prisons may lower
wages, or just in the same way as a shower of brushes from
heaven would lower wages in the brush trade. But I do not
think that the making of brushes in prisons lowers wages throughout the country; I think it raises the real purchasing power of
wages throughout the country.

10,448. As to your machinery, has it struck you that the
essence of your idea is what you expressed yourself when you
pleaded for a larger number and a higher class of relieving officers ?
Is not that the real function of your Charity Organisation Committee, to inquire very fully and place the results of the inquiry
before the Boards of Guardians ?—Yes. Only you see I am
constantly fighting against those tendencies of Socialism that are
towards increased bureaucracy; and one of the reasons of my
interest in this problem of Poor Law administration is that I
find that the present tendencies of poor relief are used rather
to strengthen the hands of those Socialists who say that bureau-
cratic organisation is needed to relieve the poor from unnecessary
hardship. I am therefore quite consistent in preferring the
independent work of the Charity Organisation Society, when
that can be carried out without excluding the working classes
from their fair share in the work and responsibility.

10,449. (*Chairman.*) I think, although you have advocated
here some representation of guardians upon the Charity Organisation Society, that is not because you are dissatisfied in any
way with the work of the Charity Organisation Society ?—No.

Charity Organisation Societies are, of course, of many different kinds. I think it would be difficult to conceive a body of people to whom the country is under greater obligations than the leaders of the chief societies, and of the London society in particular. I think that the self-devotion with which they have pursued the higher interests of the people, without fear and without caring for favour, doing what they thought to be right, with steady persistence and resolve, showing great versatility and an immense deal of the higher wisdom of kindliness, will make them a landmark in English history. I think that the things of which England may be proud are not her wealth, but her trades unions, her Friendly Societies, her co-operative societies, and her Charity Organisation Societies.

The witness withdrew.

THE COMMITTEE

APPOINTED TO INQUIRE INTO THE

INDIAN CURRENCY, 1898

MINUTES OF EVIDENCE OFFERED TO THE COMMITTEE BY
PROFESSOR ALFRED MARSHALL

[C. 9222 of 1899.]

ANALYSIS OF EVIDENCE GIVEN BY PROFESSOR ALFRED MARSHALL, JANUARY 11 AND FEBRUARY 16, 1899 [1]

Is Professor of Political Economy in the University of Cambridge, and gives evidence on questions of economic principle, 11,757-8.

Relation between volume of currency and level of prices, 11,759-60, 11,799.

Other causes affecting prices, 11,760-2.

Relation between currency, bank money, and real capital, 11,763-4, 11,794-8, 11,800.

Causes governing the rate of interest and the rate of discount, 11,765-9, 11,794, 11,802-13, 11,852.

Alleged influence of custom in steadying prices in India, 11,770-2.

Dependence of India on foreign capital, 11,773, 11,814.

Want of elasticity in Indian currency; not to be avoided by a mere increase in the currency; the methods of the German Reichsbank might be followed, 11,773-9, 11,852.

Classes affected by a rise or fall in prices; relation between movements in wages and movements in prices, 11,780-5.

Interest of the Government of India in the rate of exchange; growth of Indian expenditure due to moral and material progress; importance of raising revenue in the least irritating manner possible, 11,786.

Reasons for approving of the rate of 1s. 4d. for the rupee, 11,787, 11,834-6.

Rate of Indian exchange indicates proportion between rupee prices and sterling prices, certain allowances being made; causes acting on rate of exchange, 11,788-91, 11,824-7.

Alleged effect of depreciation of currency in stimulating foreign trade, 11,792, 11,815-22, 11,834-44, 11,850-1.

[1] Published in 1899, C. 9222.

Possibility of establishing and maintaining a gold standard and gold currency in India, 11,793, 11,829, 11,845–6.

Alleged effect of import duties in enabling a debtor country to retain gold, 11,828–9.

Need for more thorough economic training of Indian administrators, 11,852.

COMMITTEE ON INDIAN CURRENCY

Professor ALFRED MARSHALL called and examined (January 11, 1899)

11,757. (*Chairman.*) You are Professor of Political Economy in the University of Cambridge ?—Yes.

11,758. What is the general nature of the evidence you are willing to give to this Committee ?—In trying to make up my mind as to what currency arrangements are best for India, I have been specially hindered by my ignorance as to the nature and extent of the business relations between the country at large and the centres of European commerce in Calcutta and other large towns. But, on being informed that the scope of the Committee's inquiry extended beyond questions of practical administration, and raised some broad issues of economic principle, and that I might be excused from expressing opinions on questions that required much knowledge of India, and might confine my evidence to the general relations of currency and trade, I have ventured to accept the invitation with which the Committee have honoured me.

11,759. Then, in questioning you, we will confine ourselves to the limits which you yourself have laid down. I will ask you first, what do you consider to be the relation between the volume of currency and the general level of prices in a country ?—I hold that prices vary directly with the volume of currency, if other things are equal; but other things are constantly changing. This so-called " quantity theory of the value of money " is true in just the same way as it is true that the day's temperature varies with the length of the day, other things being equal; but other things are seldom equal. This theory has been the cause of much controversy; but it has never been seriously denied by anyone who has taken it as a whole, and has not stopped short, omitting the words " other things being equal." The fact is that in every

267

state of society there is some fraction of their income which people find it worth while to keep in the form of currency; it may be a fifth, or a tenth, or a twentieth.   A large command of resources in the form of currency renders their business easy and smooth, and puts them at an advantage in bargaining; but, on the other hand, it locks up in a barren form resources that might yield an income of gratification if invested, say, in extra furniture; or a money income, if invested in extra machinery or cattle.   In a primitive state of society, even in one as far advanced as that of India, only the rich care to have much of their resources in the form of currency.   In England, all but the very poor keep a good deal;   the lower middle classes keep a relatively very large quantity;   while the very rich who pay all their tradesmen by cheques use relatively little.   But, whatever the state of society, there is a certain volume of their resources which people of different classes taken one with another care to keep in the form of currency;   and, if everything else remains the same, then there is this direct relation between the volume of currency and the level of prices, that, if one is increased by 10 per cent., the other also will be increased by 10 per cent.   Of course, the less the proportion of their resources which people care to keep in the form of currency, the lower will be the aggregate value of the currency, that is, the higher will prices be with a given volume of currency.

11,760. How may this relation between the volume of the currency and the general level of prices be permanently changed? —It may be changed permanently, first, by changes in population and wealth, which change the aggregate income; secondly, by the growth of credit agencies, which substitute other means of payment for currency; thirdly, by changes in the methods of transport, production, and business generally, which affect the number of hands through which commodities pass in the processes of making and dealing. These causes are specially difficult to trace in India. In some parts of India the local informal petty cash seems to have fallen much out of use, and in other ways the work of the recognised currency has been increased. On the other hand, the rapidity of circulation of currency has also been much increased, and there has been a somewhat extended use of notes.

11,761. How may the relation be temporarily modified?—

Passing by the effects of fluctuations and commercial credit on prices, it seems specially important, with reference to the Indian currency problem, to note that the level of prices which a given volume of currency will sustain, is liable to be affected by any lack of trust and confidence in the currency itself.

11,762. Temporarily affected or permanently?—Both, I think. The lower is the credit of the currency, the lower will be the share of their resources which people care to keep in the form of currency; the more, therefore, the currency will be depreciated, and the higher prices will rise. Here I would like to separate what appears to be agreed amongst students from what is controversial matter. I think it is agreed that, if the credit of a currency falls, its value falls relatively to commodities, even when there is no change in its volume. I think it is agreed that the history of the assignats and the American currency during the time of the forced paper currency shows that. I think it is also agreed that there is something fiduciary in the value of gold and silver; that is, that part of their value depends upon the confidence with which people generally look forward to the maintenance and extension of the monetary demand for them. Of course, their value is, in the long run, controlled by cost of production; but that influence is remote, and new supplies are always small relatively to the existing stock. And so fluctuations of their value are mainly governed at any time by currency legislation, actual and prospective. No one thinks of gold as likely to be demonetised; but, if there did appear to be any real prospect of that, everyone would agree that its value would fall, since the sole demand for it then would come from the industrial arts; and everyone would admit the same to be true as regards silver. But whether, in fact, silver is at the present time in that condition is a controversial matter. My own opinion is that silver just at present, at the particular time at which we are, is not as good a metal to be used as currency as it was in earlier times; nor as good a metal as it may become again in later times, when the East—or, since we must include Africa and South America— when the non-Western world has got into the habit of using currency for the ordinary transactions of life, and has not got to the stage at which gold would be likely to be used very frequently.

11,763. What do you consider to be the true relations between currency, bank money, and real capital?—Currency and bank money are both forms of command over real capital. They are commonly called capital; but they are really command over capital, in my opinion.

11,764. You mean the power to obtain capital?—Yes. Currency, especially legal tender, is a direct command; other forms of credit paper and bank money are command one stage further removed. Bank money can go by telegraph, but real capital must pass through the hands of the Custom House Officers.

11,765. Is the interest on permanent investments governed mainly by the relation in which the stock of real capital stands to the demand for its service?—That is my opinion. Assuming for the moment that there is no question of any change in the volume of the currency, the interest on investments is governed by the relation between the supply of capital and the need for services of capital by borrowers—whether thriftless borrowers who desire to anticipate future incomes, or thrifty borrowers who desire to use it as a means of creating future income, and who purpose to turn it into implements, irrigation works, railways, etc. If real capital is scarce, those who need it must pay a high price for it, and, if that high price does not call forth an increased supply of real capital either from home resources, or by borrowing from abroad, the industries of the country must be capital-starved; and she will not be able to keep her place in the march of progress. But now, assuming the arts of production to remain stationary and that there is no change in the pressure of population on the means of subsistence, a rise in prices will enable the borrower to pay interest at less outlay and to pay back capital at less outlay than would otherwise be the case. It is important to lay stress upon there being no change in the efficiency of production, because this goes to the root of the controversy between those who think it would be right to keep the purchasing power of money constant relatively to commodities, and those who do not. The pith of the matter may be put by an illustration. A person who borrows a peck of green peas in April, and returns two pecks in June, has paid no interest at all, he has not even returned the corpus of the loan. This is, I think, beyond question; but the application of the principle contained in it to the equity and expediency of currency legislation is a matter of controversy. It seems to be clear arithmetically that, if a man borrows 100 rupees under contract to pay back 105 rupees at the end of the year, and if meanwhile the purchasing power of money has risen 10 per cent., he cannot get the 105 rupees which he has to pay back without selling one-tenth more commodities than would be sufficient for the purpose at the beginning of the year. Assuming, that is, that the things which he handles have not changed in value relatively to things in general, he must sell at the end of the year commodities which would have cost him 115 rupees 8 annas at the beginning, in order to pay back, with interest, his loan of 100 rupees, and, therefore, he has lost ground unless the commodities have increased under his hands 15½ per cent. While nominally paying 5 per cent. for the use of his money, he has really been paying 15½ per cent. On the other hand, if prices had risen so much that the purchasing power of money had fallen 10 per cent. during the year, and he could get 100 rupees for things which cost him 90 rupees at the beginning of the year, then, instead of paying 5 per cent. for the loan, he would really be paid 5½ per cent. for taking charge of the money. This illustrates the principle that the general rate of interest will be raised by a gradual and anticipated fall in the value of currency relatively to commodities, and that it will be lowered by a rise in that value, even where there is no change in the conditions of general demand and supply. The high rate of interest on permanent investments in India seems to be attributable partly to a relative scarcity of real capital, and partly to the continuous fall in the value of the rupee relatively to the currencies of the West. This matter has been long discussed, but latterly, within the last ten years, it has obtained increasing attention from economists. In particular, one of the ablest of the younger school of American economists, Mr. Fisher of Yale, has written a book on *Appreciation and Interest*, which bears very closely upon this matter. If a diagram be made out, showing the average rate of market discount in London, it will be found, as a matter of fact, that the high rates do go with high prices. That is contrary to a good deal of what is assumed *a priori*, but I think it is really quite consistent with the theory when properly developed. I am not sure that it might not be worth while for the Committee to reproduce some of Mr. Fisher's tables which bear upon this subject. He takes the question of rupee paper only incidentally; but the table which he has worked out seems to show that the interest on rupee paper, reckoned at purchase price, is very little higher than that on the Indian gold loan before 1874; then it fell to about ·1 per cent., then it rose rapidly, with the distrust in silver, to ·7 per cent., and it has remained about that level to 1895, the end of Mr. Fisher's table, except during the years 1888 and 1889, when it was 1 per cent.

11,766. The rise of value, do you mean, or the interest?— The difference in the annual return to a person who invested 1,000*l.* in rupee paper, and a person who invested 1,000*l.* in the Indian gold loan, was ·1 per cent. in 1874, then it rose to ·7 per cent. and it has remained about that for the greater part of the time.

11,767. Any tables that you think would be desirable and would illustrate your own evidence, put them in at your pleasure in your evidence?—Here is Mr. Fisher's table. (See p. 273.) It is carefully obtained by averages from many entries, and with due allowance, in the case of repayable bonds, for the time they have to run to maturity.

11,768. Now, what do you wish to say to us as to discount?— Other things being equal, interest for short loans will, of course, oscillate about the rate of interest to be obtained for permanent investments, allowance being made for the convenience, in some cases, to the lender of being able to recover quickly command over the capital which he has lent. But the rate of discount is specially sensitive to a casual stringency, and, in spite of the internationality of a certain class of bills, discount varies more locally than interest on permanent investments. Mr. Beckenridge, in the *Political Science Quarterly*, for March 1898, has compared the rates of discount in different parts of America, which, like India, is a continent; and he has shown that there is a steady rise in passing from the Eastern States to the Middle, thence to the Southern, thence to the Pacific, and thence to the Western.

RATES OF INTEREST REALISED FROM DATES NAMED TO
MATURITY OR IN PERPETUITY

	Silver.	Gold.	Difference.	Exchange on India. Pence per Rupee.
1865	4·3	4·1	·2	23·2
1868	4·3	4·0	·3	23·0
1870	4·3	4·0	·3	23·6
1871	4·1	3·8	·3	23·2
1872	3·9	3·7	·2	22·6
1873	3·9	3·7	·2	22·4
1874	3·9	3·8	·1	22·2
1875	4·0	3·6	·4	21·9
1876	4·1	3·7	·4	20·5
1877	4·1	3·7	·4	20·9
1878	4·2	3·9	·3	20·2
1879	4·4	3·7	·7	19·7
1880	4·3	3·6	·7	20·0
1881	4·0	3·4	·6	19·9
1882	3·9	3·5	·4	19·5
1883	4·1	3·4	·7	19·5
1884	4·1	3·3	·8	19·5
1885	4·1	3·5	·6	18·5
1886	4·1	3·5	·6	17·5
1887	4·1	3·4	·7	17·2
1888	4·1	3·1	1·0	16·5
1889	4·1	3·0	1·1	16·5
1890, 1st half.	4·0	3·0	1·0	17·6
1890, 2nd half.	3·9	3·1	·8	19·3
1891	3·8	3·1	·7	17·1
1892	3·9	3·1	·8	15·3
1893	3·9	3·0	·9	15·0
1894	3·9	3·0	·9	13·5
1895	3·4	2·8	·6	13·4

11,769. Does a change in the volume of currency in a Western country alter the rate of discount temporarily or permanently ?— The whole theory of discount is full of paradoxes, because the increase of prosperity sometimes raises discount, and sometimes lowers it. No interpretation can be given of a rise in discount, unless it is known to what cause the change is due. Speaking generally, discount will rise in consequence of a greater willingness of borrowers to borrow, or of a greater unwillingness of lenders to lend : the first generally indicates increased confidence, and perhaps increased prosperity; the latter generally indicates the

T

opposite. Looking at the special case of the effect of an increase
in currency on the rate of discount, the cycle in the West seems
to be this. The new currency or the increase of currency goes,
not to private persons, but to the banking centres; and, therefore,
it increases the willingness of lenders to lend in the first instance,
and lowers discount; but it afterwards raises prices, and, therefore, tends to increase discount. This latter movement is cumu-
lative. The loans to one man make him a good customer for
others at good prices, and make them therefore eager to borrow,
and that makes them good customers; and so the movement
grows. Thus, a fall in the purchasing power of money tends,
after a while, to raise the rate of discount as well as the rate of
interest on long investments. And, though the matter may be
regarded by some as open to question, I myself go with those
who hold that statistics bear out the *a priori* probability that,
first, the rates of discount would generally be higher when prices
are rising than when they are falling, because the borrowers
would be eager for loans; and secondly, that they would generally
be higher during periods of high prices, than in periods of low
prices; not because one is the cause of the other, but because both
are the results from the same cause—the prevalence of a confident
spirit in the business world. Those periods are liable to be
broken in upon by cyclones of distrust, and those cyclones raise
discount for a time to the very highest levels of all. They are
accompanied by falling prices, and a little later are followed by
falling discounts. There does not seem to me to be any single
and uniform relation statistically or *a priori* between the rate
of discount and the rate of exchange.

11,770. How far do you consider that Western experience in
this matter is applicable to India?—I am afraid that my answer
to this question must necessarily be rather long. The fact is that
India, being governed by England, has necessarily had its affairs
discussed largely by Englishmen, who are apt to take their
opinions of what goes on in India very much at second hand.
Sir Henry Maine gave countenance to the opinion that custom
ruled the economic arrangements of India; and, in a certain
sense, that is no doubt true, but I think that the doctrine requires
to be analysed. There is no doubt that custom does rule the

general tenor of life in India, but it does not, in my opinion, rule prices. The matter is one of greater importance than it looks. The common opinion of the world on Indian matters is formed largely on the basis of statements made by a few prominent English writers on currency, who have claimed to speak with special knowledge of India, and have been received as authoritative by foreign economists. I will quote from one writer. He is an able man, much travelled, and with great knowledge of affairs; and he has attained a position sufficient to cause him to be selected as one of three examiners for an important international prize relating to bimetallism a few years ago. He says : " Prices have not fallen for the reason that gold is scarce——"

11,771. (*Sir F. Mowatt.*) Are you speaking of Indian prices for the moment ?—No, he is referring to prices in England. He says :—" Prices have not fallen for the reason that gold is ' scarce,' nor will they rise because of an increased production of gold, if meanwhile the exchanges with silver-using Asia continue to fall. The exchange value of any bushel of wheat in Mark Lane has for fifteen years past approximated, and will approximate, an ounce of silver bullion; because with open mints an ounce of silver bullion is $2\frac{1}{4}$ rupees, and $2\frac{1}{4}$ rupees per bushel represents cost of production and exportation from the Punjab wheat fields. If the United States were to melt and sell her silver currency, and if the Indian mints were reopened, then, even if the production of gold sextupled, the price of wheat would still fall with each fresh fall in the gold price of the ounce of silver." I quote from a letter printed in the *Economist* of September 15, 1894. That doctrine, in a somewhat less extreme form, is the basis of many of the ablest and best known arguments in favour of the adoption of bimetallism at such a ratio as would lead to a general rise of prices. When I was at Oxford fifteen years ago, I had to study Indian prices; and I began a set of inquiries which have included the making of a very large number of diagrams, based chiefly upon Mr. O'Conor's figures. I have many of them here, but they would probably be too extensive to be printed. I would like to state, broadly, the results that I have deduced from them. I should say I have confirmed those results by many conversations with natives of India and with Englishmen who have been engaged in administering India. The results are, first, the chief purchases and sales in India are of grains, and the variations from year to year in the local prices of these in any one place are many times as great as in England. They are commonly 200 or 300 per cent., sometimes 400 per cent., in the course of one or two years. Secondly : They are greatest in those grains which are not affected by European trade. Here is one example.[1] That represents the movements of the annual price of jawar, which Mr. O'Conor tells me is the most important of all those food grains which are not exported to Europe, and on the prices of which, therefore, the so-called disturbing influence of gold does not operate.

(*Sir J. Muir.*) There seem to be enormous fluctuations there.

11,772. (*Chairman.*) The greatest variations, as I understand, are in grains which are unaffected by European trade?—Yes. I have a number of diagrams here which would support these propositions, if necessary. Thirdly : For any one grain they are generally the largest in those districts which are most remote from European influences. Fourthly : They are much diminishing under the influence of European trade. I have here a diagram which was published in the statement exhibiting the " Moral and Material Progress of India," for the years 1882–83. It is interesting in two ways. It shows that the variations in the prices of grains were very much greater earlier in the century than now ; and that the average level of prices of grains has very much risen. I believe there is some doubt as to whether the details of measurement are all perfectly correct, but I think there can be no doubt as to the general truth of the picture which they present. Fifthly : As that figure shows, the purchasing power of silver in terms of grain has fallen throughout the centuries. Sir William Hunter says, that it was " two or three times greater " at the time of Akbar's land settlement than it is now ; and it has fallen fast during the present century, the fall being broken only by periods of bad harvests. Sixthly : In consequence of a rapid change in the conditions of production of cotton and iron, combined with a lessened cost of transport, the rupee price of the chief imports into Calcutta after 1873 fell faster than the average gold price of commodities in England. The assertion of some advocates of

[1] For the diagram, not reproduced here, see C. 9376.

bimetallism that the fall in the gold price of commodities in England was largely caused by the forcing down of prices by the Indian customers fits most ill with that fact.[1]   There has been a controversy as to whether Mr. Sauerbeck's index-number does not exaggerate the fall in prices since 1873.   Certainly there is no other important index-number which shows so great a range. Neither that of the *Economist*, nor the one which is generally followed abroad, Dr. Soetbeer's, shows so great a fall.   But, to give the argument to which I am opposed every advantage, I have taken Mr. Sauerbeck's index-number for average gold prices in England.   That shows the fall in the rupee prices of the chief Indian imports at Calcutta down to 1886 to have been considerably greater than the fall of average English gold prices. After 1886 there is a rise in these rupee prices.   Seventhly : The average prices of all goods in India since 1873 have been so disturbed by bad harvests, especially in 1877 to 1879, that their variations from year to year bear no resemblance to English prices. For this purpose, as Mr. O'Conor has not supplied us with a general index-number, I have fallen back on that which was compiled by Mr. Atkinson from Mr. O'Conor's figures, and published in the *Statistical Society's Journal* for March 1897.   That shows no relation to the English curves of yearly variations; but, on the whole, it is a curve of greater disquiet.   If we look, on the other hand, at the broad movements of prices, it seems to be true that about 1885 a rise in normal rupee prices set in, by which I mean a rise not especially attributable to bad harvests. This is what the old-fashioned economic theory would have led us to suppose, because, when we watch the movements of the gold prices of silver and the gold prices of commodities in England, we find that the average level of gold prices of commodities was falling very fast until 1885, and the gold price of silver was not falling specially fast during that time—not so fast as afterwards. After that time the gold price of silver did fall somewhat faster, and the English gold prices did not fall fast; that is to say, the English silver prices rose fast.   By English silver prices I mean the prices which would have to be paid in London for commodities in general if prices were reckoned in bar silver.   Eighthly : The

[1] For the diagram, not reproduced here, see C. 9376.

average price of Indian exports has kept fairly close to the general movements of English prices expressed in silver. If you draw two curves representing, (a) rupee prices of Indian exports in Calcutta, as given by Mr. O'Conor, and (b) Mr. Sauerbeck's gold prices for England, divided by the gold price of silver, so as to represent the silver prices of commodities in general; you will see that, speaking broadly, the two curves do move together; the general relation between them is that which would have been anticipated by economists generally. Ninthly : The London prices of wheat and silver have seldom moved closely together; that is specially important with regard to the statement I recently quoted about an ounce of silver and a bushel of wheat. When they have done so, separate causes for these movements can generally be found. For instance, a spell of bad weather in July 1890 came about the same time as a change in the United States currency policy; these causes raised the prices of wheat and silver; and the subsequent fine weather lowered the prices a little while before the speculation in silver collapsed. And, indeed, when they have moved more or less together, it is as often as not the case that the movement in the price of wheat has gone before that of silver; and Mr. O'Conor has told you that the Calcutta price of wheat follows the London price. In evidence of this I will show diagrams representing the average prices of wheat and silver in London for each year of this century, and the prices for each week during the last twelve years. As to the interpretation of these facts, any suggestion that I make must be highly speculative. I fancy I see a different character in the curve prices for England and for India. I think that this difference corresponds to the fact that the production in England is chiefly— I will not say capitalistic, because that is a matter of secondary importance—but chiefly commercial, chiefly the production by people of things to sell to others. I should expect that, in contrasting a country of that kind with a country in which production is largely for domestic consumption, variations in prices would show themselves chiefly by sudden jumps up, in consequence of bad harvests, from a normal level; and I should expect that those variations in production which come, as they do in England, through the influence of changes in credit and the confidence of farmers that wheat was a paying crop, would be gradual and that you would get more rounded shapes in diagrams showing variations of annual prices. That is, I should suppose that you would get, in the case of a primitive country, a tolerably flat base with sharp peaks; and that in an advanced country you would get more nearly uniform waves. Jevons, in page xiv of the Introduction to his *Investigations in Currency*, still held something of the old doctrine which, as a young man, I used to hear in England, that you can never get prosperity in general business until you have a succession of good harvests. Jevons laid stress upon the fact that the stock of grain was so much the most important part of movable capital even in England, that it was to be expected that harvests should control the rate of discount and the activity of business generally. But wheat supply is less important now, and the Registrar-General has laid stress on the fact that the variations in the marriage rate no longer pay any attention to the price of corn. One would expect that curves representing movements of the price of corn in England early in the century would have shapes more corresponding to those for India now than those for England at the present time; and that appears to have been the case. I would venture also to throw out a suggestion of a very hazardous character. I have seen a great deal of evidence before various Commissions, this included, to the effect that the ryot knows nothing of what happens in Calcutta, that he knows nothing of exchange, and that prices inland cannot be directly affected by anything that happens at tidal waters. It seems to me that it is possible that, though the ryot knows little or nothing of any disturbing causes coming across the sea; and although almost every important movement in price in any district in India is due to local causes; yet, the power of friction being great, when the influence of European trade comes upon the side on which the friction is working, then that influence may tell. And, seeing that the broad movements in upland prices (as distinguished from their annual oscillations) appear to conform more closely to the general relations of gold, silver, and commodities in world markets than I should have supposed beforehand; I am inclined to think that the cause may be this, that, when local circumstances have raised very much the price of any particular grains,

then European influences may help friction and prevent them
falling back as low as they otherwise would, and *vice versâ*.

11,773. Do you wish to say anything as to India being dependent on foreign capital?—I think the dependence of India upon
foreign capital is a matter which must be taken into account in any
practical legislation; and that one has to recollect that what
governs the flow of capital from one country to another is not
merely the relative strength of different economic forces, but the
opinion that is held with regard to those economic forces by the
people who have capital to invest. Now, those who are able to
lend capital to India live exclusively in countries with a gold
standard; and those people are apt to regard gold value as a
fixed point, and to treat variations in the gold value of the rupee
as equivalent to variations in its real value. In my opinion, this
old common fallacy is not nearly so far away from the truth now
as it was some time ago. The popular reasons for it, I think, are
quite invalid; but, in fact, I believe that gold has been within
the last twenty years, say, a good measure of value; though this
is due solely to accidental causes—to the balancing of strong
forces acting in opposite directions; and I see no reason for
believing that that will continue. But this habit of thinking of
gold value as a fixed point, whether right or wrong, does affect
the willingness of investing nations to send their capital to India;
and it makes them grasp, as recent events have shown, at an
opportunity of getting back their capital on good terms in gold.
This fact was one at least of the main arguments for the closure
of the mints, and it is an even stronger argument against any
vacillation in carrying through a steadfast policy. On the other
hand, the very fact that the Government is bound under penalty
of permanent injury to India to fulfil any implicit pledges it may
give, is a strong reason against the Government's giving even
indirectly any pledges without having fully counted the cost and
being thoroughly resolved to meet it. It would seem to me in
the present emergency specially unwise to let the late exceptional
stringency of discount in Calcutta hurry the Government into an
increase of rupees. That would certainly impair the credit of
the rupee.

11,774. You mean an increase in the issue of rupees?—Yes.

That would impair the credit of the rupee, increase the export of capital, and would raise, and not lower, the mean level of discount. On the other hand, the introduction of some elasticity into the circulation would raise the credit of the rupee, and would restrain any tendency of discount to rise to an injuriously high level.

11,775. How do you say that seasonal fluctuations can best be mitigated?—Stringencies and crises which arise from unexpected deficiencies of currency relatively to the demand for it are not to be avoided by a mere increase in the volume of the currency. They are just as likely to occur with a large stock of currency as with a small; indeed they may be caused by an inflation of currency leading to distrust, not only of currency, but of all other agents and instruments of credit. For instance, in 1893 it was not a scarcity of currency, but a belief that the currency had been unduly increased, and might be increased even more, which led to a crisis in the United States; 50 per cent. was the common rate of discount for a considerable time. We have heard much about the agony of 18 per cent. at Calcutta, but 50 per cent. was the common rate of discount in America for a considerable time; and, whilst currency was thus generally in discredit, other means of payment were disorganised, and in Chicago a large business was done in buying currency at a premium, the average rate being $100\frac{1}{2}$. It is remarkable also, incidentally I may say, that the stringency of 1893 was almost entirely Western; while that of 1890 was almost entirely Eastern. That illustrates the fact that with all her 200,000 miles of railway America is not a country but a continent; and we must allow for the same difficulty in India, even though she has 20,000 miles of railway. But, although seasonal fluctuations are not amenable to control by a mere increase of currency, I believe they are amenable to control by arrangements which shall provide that there shall be a stock of currency which shall be used only in case of emergency. That currency may be, and I think should be, largely of paper; but the extent to which it may be of paper and the extent to which it must have a bullion backbone is, I think, not to be settled save for one country at a time; it must vary with changing conditions of time and place.

11,776. How far would the English practice be a good guide

for India in this matter ?—England is, in my opinion, but I speak with great diffidence, a specially bad example for India to follow in matters of currency. For, first, currency is but a small part of the means of payment used in England ; and under most, though not all, conditions, bank money is the main means of payment ; and that is elastic. Secondly, an imperative demand for increased currency is rare in England ; and, when it does occur, it is on a very small scale relatively to England's total business and resources. The importation of the amount of ten millions of sovereigns makes an enormous difference in Lombard Street, but it is a mere nothing relatively to England's total business. Whereas, if the same difficulty arises in a country in which the main payments have to be made with currency itself, you want an importation of currency, or an increase of currency, standing in some moderately high relation to the total business of the country ; or, at all events, to that part of the total business of the country which is carried on on Western methods. Thirdly, England is near to other great gold markets. Fourthly, her financial houses are numerous and able. There are a vast number of able minds at work on her financial problems. Mr. Bagehot, than whom there is no higher authority on such a matter, says that there never was, since the world began, so high and massive a brain-power applied to any one question as is applied to these questions in England : and, so far as the mass of the ability goes, of course, India is not on a level with England. England's banking system is very highly organised, especially by the aid of the branch banks : it would take too long to develop that, but, I believe, the influence of the branch banks upon moderating stringency in England is greater than it appears, relatively to that of the rest of the banking system. Partly for this reason, currency drawn from London in the spring or autumn completes its circuit quickly ; more quickly than in Germany ; and, of course, much more quickly than in India. All these considerations seem to me to point to the necessity of working rather on the lines of the German Reichsbank than on the lines of the English Bank with regard to the regulation of the currency. I believe it is not generally known that the plan of the German Reichsbank of providing for increased issue in time of difficulty is not inconsistent with the principles of Sir Robert Peel himself. It came out in the evidence before the House of Commons Committee of 1848 (it did not come out at the time) that Sir Robert Peel had not supposed that his Act could be maintained under all circumstances; and had told Mr. Cotton, Governor of the Bank at the time, that it might be necessary for the Government to assume the responsibility of suspending it (Q. 4057); and Mr. Cotton, while holding that the Act should not be relaxed, says (Q. 4344–5) that the Act would be unnecessary " if the Bank acted always on sound and well-defined principles "; and that these principles were already " better understood than they were in the year 1839," the events of which had, I think, much to do with Sir Robert Peel's decision not to leave the ultimate responsibility with the Bank. The Committee of 1857 had before it Lord Overstone's evidence that the principles of the 1844 Act had been much misunderstood, and that its framers realised that, though a contraction of the currency will check an external drain, " it will not check or correct the demand for internal purposes " (Vol. I., Q. 4239); and the Committee (Report, §§ 71–74), referring to Mr. Cotton's evidence in 1848, " advert to the question whether provision should be made in advance for such contingencies [as those of 1847 and 1857], and the conditions expressly laid down on which the issue of an increased number of Bank notes may in time of pressure be allowed "; and they " think that such a provision could not be regarded as any violation of the principle of the Act of 1844." The scheme at which they hint is conservative, and may be taken to have foreshadowed the German plan of enabling the Reichsbank to increase its issues to meet any emergency, whether due to the variations from one part of the year to another, or to a variation in one particular year of the general course of business. The elastic plan of allowing the Reichsbank to increase its own issues under certain conditions, the chief of which is that it should pay a tax to the Government, does seem to me to have worked well. I have read criticisms of writers on banking in other countries, who talk of England as being too conservative because she keeps to an old rigid rule, which was adopted to meet a difficulty which has passed away, and which probably will never return quite in the same way. It would seem to me that, if the Government is to prevent difficulty arising in India, not from a real weakness of India, but from the mere absence of the flux—the currency needed to make business move,—it must go on the lines of the 1844 Act, somewhat modified as in the Reichsbank Act. I do not mean that it should follow the letter of the Act, but the principle of it.

11,777. The Reichsbank has the power of contracting its issue when the need for additional currency passes away ?—It has the interest to do so.

11,778. It has the power as well as the interest, has it not ?—Certainly. I may say that it is generally understood that the Reichsbank Act may require to be altered, because the business of Germany has grown so much since that Act was passed; but the principle is, I think, good.

11,779. (*Mr. Hambro.*) Has the Reichsbank to get any Chancellor's letter, as in England ?—No, its action is automatic.

11,780. (*Chairman.*) What do you take to be the immediate effect of a change in prices ?—A fall in the value of currency lowers all dues enforced by contract or custom. Creditors and lessors can often defend themselves against injury in this matter; for creditors are often quite as able to foresee changes in the purchasing power of money as borrowers are ; and they can accommodate the interest which they charge to coming events. Also they can often put pressure on their debtors indirectly. This last power is even greater in the case of lessors. That is shown in the history of inquiries into agricultural depression. It is always found that, when the rent which the farmer has contracted to pay is higher than the land is really worth, the landlord sees his way to making improvements that he would otherwise have left the farmer to make or to go without; but employés cannot, as a rule, foresee ; and they have less power of acting on their knowledge. The consequence is that a rise of wages is seldom or never as fast as that of prices when the cause of the rise is an increase of the currency, that is not accompanied by an increased command over nature.

11,781. Do you hold that the ultimate effects of such a change depend partly on the rate of general economic progress ?—Yes. A sudden fall in the purchasing power of currency, that is to say, a sudden rise of prices, may be due to a very bad harvest at home, and then it is clearly an evil; or it may be due to a bad harvest elsewhere, as the rise in Indian prices in 1891 was caused mainly by the Russian famine, and that was good for India. But, especially in the West, a sudden rise of prices is generally the result of either currency inflation or improvement in credit. In so far as the rise of credit is a revival after the industrial system has been purged from its impurities by the preceding period of low credit, it is a welcome sign of recovered health. But the movement would be as beneficial for the time if it were accompanied by a more cautious use of credit and more uniform prices; and in the long run it would be more beneficial. As it is, the inflation causes lenders to be careless; all business men seem to be having a large margin of profits; speculative buyers can borrow and become rich by selling for many counters what they have bought for few counters, and their gains, which add nothing to the common stock, are merely the result of successful raids on the common stock; and these gains give to business a fictitious appearance of prosperity. In such times, as is shown by the evidence before the last Commission on Depression of Trade, there is relatively little improvement in machinery and general plant. The seeds of progress are not sown in those times of apparent prosperity. No doubt employment is then generally full, especially if England is exporting fast; and she is likely to be exporting fast in consequence of her lending fast to other countries, South America above all others. When she has been exporting fast to South America, there has been plenty of employment in making goods to be exported, but, as a rule, little has come back afterwards. During that time money wages have been rising very fast, but not real wages. I admit that, on the other hand, a sudden rise in the purchasing power of currency, that is, a sudden fall of prices, presses hardly on business enterprise of all kinds. It is likely to make many employers fail, and generally to interrupt industry. Credit shrinks, and disorganisation is apt to spread from one part of the industrial world to another. Such a fall of prices is an almost unmixed injury to the employé, as it is to the employer; but a fall of prices of this kind is seldom or never the product of natural causes. It is nearly always, if not always, the result of a previous inflation of prices and the launching of frail enterprises by fraudulent or incompetent people who have floated into prosperity at the cost of others on the top of the wave of rising prices. To attribute this social *malaise* to the fall of prices, instead of to the previous morbid inflation which caused it, is as reasonable as to attribute the headaches which follow a night of feasting and rioting to want of a sufficiently nourishing breakfast, instead of to the bad condition of the digestive organs that took away the appetite for breakfast. This is, perhaps, the chief centre of difference between those bi-metallists who, like myself, wish for bimetallism only as a means of diminishing fluctuations; and those who wish for it also, and perhaps, mainly, as a means of raising prices. It is agreed on all sides that violent fluctuations of prices are an evil in the long run; but the difference of opinion is as to whether it is the sudden rise of prices, or the subsequent fall, which is mainly responsible for the evil. England passed through great crises and violent fluctuations of prices early in the century; and you will find an important body of opinion on the part of not only professional economists, but of business men, at that time that a rise of prices was not really beneficial to industry. But the memory of that passed away, and I will confess that, for ten or fifteen years after I began to study political economy, I held the common doctrine, that a rise of prices was generally beneficial to business men directly, and indirectly to the working classes. But, after that time, I changed my views, and I have been confirmed in my new opinions by finding that they are largely held in America, which has recently passed through experiences somewhat similar to those of England early in the century. The reasons for the change in my opinion are rather long, and I gave them at some length before the Gold and Silver Commission. I think, perhaps, I had better content myself now with calling your attention to the fact that the statistical aspect of the matter is in a different position now. The assertions that a rise of prices increased the real wages of the worker were so consonant with the common opinion of people who had not specially studied the matter, that it was accepted almost as an axiom; but, within the last ten years, the statistics of wages have been carried so far in certain countries, and especially in England and America, that we are able to bring it to the test. I have accumulated a great number of facts, but nearly everything I have accumulated is implied in this table. It is copied from the article by Mr. Bowley in the *Economic Journal* for last December. It is the result of work that has been going on for a number of years, and seems to me to be practically decisive. It collects the average wages in England from the year 1844 to the year 1891, and then calculates what purchasing power the wages would give at the different times, and it shows that the rise of real wages after 1873 when prices were falling was greater than before 1873 when prices were rising.

AVERAGE REAL AND NOMINAL WAGES IN THE UNITED KINGDOM, FRANCE AND THE UNITED STATES AS PERCENTAGES OF THOSE IN 1891

Country.		1844– 1853.	1854– 1863.	1864– 1873.	1874– 1883.	1884– 1893.	1891.
United Kingdom	Nominal	61	73	82	93	95	100
	Real .	53	51	59	82	97	100
France	Nominal . .	52	65	73	86	95	100
	Real . .	55	61	67	78	94	100
United States	Nominal .	53	58	72	86	95	100
	Real . .	54	53	57	76	95	100

11,782. (*Sir J. Muir.*) Might I ask what is the difference between " nominal " and " real," in connection with this table ?— The real wages are the amount of commodities which the labourer can buy with his money wages. Supposing wages were 30*s.* in one place and 32*s.* in another, the real wages in the first case would be the commodities which 30*s.* would buy at the price of that time, and in the other, commodities which 32*s.* would buy. I may say that all the figures, and especially those for France, are liable to certain errors, which are most conscientiously explained by Mr. Bowley in his article. They are not sufficient to detract much from the force of broad inferences based upon the figures.

11,783. (*Sir F. Mowatt.*) I do not quite understand how you get the full value of the hundred to-day ?—He puts everything up to 100 for 1891, and then works back.

11,784. But does he take the real and nominal as identical now ? Where he takes the 100, does it represent the real and the

nominal ?—He makes the standard for real wages 100 in 1891,
and he makes also a separate standard for the nominal wages in
1891 of 100, and then he works it out upon those.   I now produce
a diagram representing the facts for America.   It has been very
largely used in America, and has had a great deal to do, probably
more than any other single statement of facts, in diminishing the
belief among the people that they could improve their position
by inflating the currency.[1]   I should say that that diagram is
compiled by a mere arithmetical process, from a report made at
the instance of the United States Senate Committee.   It is,
of course, always difficult to be certain that there was no ulterior
motive in the appointment of any committee to make a statistical
inquiry :   but it is quite certain that, if any such motive was at the
back of the appointment of this Senate Committee, it had nothing
whatever to do with this particular subject;   and therefore, so
far as this particular subject is concerned, it may be taken
without question as an impartial investigation.   The work was
practically done entirely by Professor Falkner, who approached
the subject from a purely statistical and scientific point of view.

11,785.   Do you draw any distinction between the cases of
England and India in the respect you have just alluded to ?—
Yes, I do.   It seems to me that Nature, who often plays unkind
tricks as to the supply of gold and silver, has been benevolent in
putting a liking for gold into the West, and for silver into the East.
For improvements in transport and production have made the
labour of the Western worker, and especially of the English
worker, very much more effective in producing commodities than
it was not long ago.   For the Englishman, I should say, it had
been nearly doubled, and it is therefore well, in my opinion, that a
sovereign should command nearly twice as many commodities as
before.   Taking the course of events as it has been, I do not think
it would have been good to have had a gold currency in India
during this time.   That would no doubt have caused a real
stringency.   Prices would have fallen, not only as measured in
terms of commodities, but as measured in terms of labour; because India has not been able to keep pace with the Western
world in the command over capital, in the command of those

---

[1] For the diagram, not reproduced here, see C. 9376.

resources which make labour effective. Her unfortunate liking
to invest in barren stocks of gold and silver, together with other
causes, has made her unable to keep pace with the West, or even
with Japan; though, when one complains of the slow progress of
India, one must recollect that there is scarcely any other old
civilisation in the same latitude, and with the same difficulties,
that has made progress to be compared with that of India.

11,786. On what principle should you estimate the amount
of interest that the Government of India has in the value of the
rupee?—One frequently hears estimates of the interest that the
Government has in a rise or a fall of the rate of the exchange on
London. Now, I do not think that it is possible to state what that
interest is without inquiring whether the origin of the change is in
circumstances affecting the rupee or the sovereign. It seems to me
that there are these two distinct elements : the Government of
India has direct interest in the value of the rupee, and it has
interest in the value of the sovereign; but its real interest in the
rate of exchange is chiefly indirect. For the effect of a fall in the
exchange which was caused by a rise in the value of the sovereign,
the rupee being stationary, would be, in my opinion, quite different,
as regards the interest of India, from the effects of a similar fall
caused by a fall in the purchasing power of the rupee, the sovereign
remaining stationary. Therefore, I would like to take the two
parts separately. The permanent interest of the Indian Government in the value of the rupee is limited to its fixed land dues.
In respect of the importance of those dues, it is unique among
great Governments conducted on Western principles. Its permanent interest in the value of the sovereign is limited to its debts
in gold. But, next, as to interests which are not perpetually
fixed, but yet are very firmly rooted; it has a very heavy interest
in the value of the rupee extending over perhaps fifteen years or
a little more, the average remaining life of the non-permanent
leases. It has also a sub-permanent interest in taxes; because,
though equitably it can raise those so as to take its share of the
growing wealth of the country, its freedom of action is practically
limited by the necessity for going rather more slowly and in a
rather less aggressive manner in the East than is possible in the
West. Lastly, it has an interest as an employer of European

U

labour, in the ratio between the rupee and the sovereign, independent of their absolute values; that is in the rate of exchange. If they both rose equally, or both fell equally, these difficulties would be small. As regards railways, I think those difficulties are, perhaps, less than appears. For I do not think it is possible for a railway ever to have fixed upon the ideally right tariff, and I think that the number of cases in which any railway would lose much by deliberately lowering its tariff is small; and, therefore, I think that the indirect lowering which arises from a fall in the value of the rupee, is not so great an evil to the railways as is commonly supposed. As regards the prices of stores and railway plant, the Indian Government has no interest in the value either of the rupee or of the sovereign, in addition to the considerations already mentioned; because it buys them as a trader, and gives commodities for commodities. These difficulties are in themselves considerable, but the main importance of most of them arises from their bearing on the central difficulty of the position of the Indian Government, which is not directly connected with either the rupee or the sovereign, and would remain if the whole world had the same currency. This difficulty is that the immense increase in the wealth and prosperity of the Western world, which began in the second third of the present century, and has gone on at an ever-increasing pace since the close of the period of the great wars, has made the resources at the command of the Western Governments beyond all comparison greater than any known before. These resources are spent on civil government and on military preparations. The administration of law, education, and sanitation are more thorough and more costly in terms of labour, and far more costly in terms of commodities, than they were. Military expenditure has grown perhaps even faster. If the supplies of gold had been sufficient to maintain uniform prices of commodities, then the apparent expenditure of all Western Governments outside the service of their debt would have been nearly doubled. The present direct expenditure of the English Government would be perhaps 150 millions, and that of local authorities about as much again, after deducting for post office, waterworks, and other remunerative outlays; and the people would have probably protested effectively against the increase. As it is, they have submitted more or less willingly. In the East there has been no such surplus to dispose of, and yet moral considerations have required the Indian Government to follow at no very long distance behind the Western Governments in their civil undertakings. As regards their military undertakings, I do not wish to express any opinion as to their necessity. I am no judge of that. But, as to the civil administration, the English officials have to be brought away from a country where real salaries are high. And, while I fully recognise the duty of the Government to substitute cheaper services wherever they would do the work; and while I hold very strong views as to the wrongfulness of any unneedful expenditure of Indian funds—while I hold that that is short-sighted and foolish, as well as wrong—I yet think that the purchase of services that are inadequate for their work is wasteful; and I do not think that India could obtain the services she requires, taken one with another, at a much cheaper rate. I wish to say that, because, having a good deal to do with the teaching of students who are natives of India, I find that they often do not hold what I consider sound views upon the conditions of true economy in public administration; and I think I ought to bear my share, as one of my generation, in insisting that, on the whole, taking one thing with another, the Civil Government of India is not an expensive Government. Were it an expensive Government I think our presence in India would not be justifiable. In view of this central difficulty arising from the fact that the standards of civil and military efficiency which are set by the West must needs put some strain on the less progressive resources of the East, I think the financial policy of India may be justified in departing a little from those maxims of perfection as to the preference for direct taxation to which the English Government should adhere; and, I think, it must take more account of popular sentiment than it would be right for the English Government to take. I think it must ease its way by not accentuating needlessly the burdens which it is compelled to impose on the people. If the people could appreciate both sides of the question fully, that would be the best of all; but, as they cannot be expected to appreciate fully the necessity for the growth of costly civil and military operations by the Government, it is, therefore, best not to make them think that the Government's revenue and expenditure are increasing faster than they really are. In short, I conclude that moral and material progress are imposing new and costly duties on the Government of India, and armaments are increasing everywhere; and therefore, although the net amount of its fixed sterling payments is, perhaps, somewhat less than at first sight appears, its expenditure measured in terms of commodities must constantly increase, and should be raised in the least irritating manner possible.

11,787. Before leaving that branch of the subject, will you say whether you regard the maintenance of the rupee at 1s. 4d. as equitable, and, at the same time, do you regard it specially as a tax upon trade ?—The function of a legislator as regards currency is to do as little as possible. Almost any currency of which the position is certain will do its work fairly well. Frequent changes in its basis disturb expectations, upset reasonable calculations, and infuse a spirit of unrest into business. They may all aim at increased certainty, but their effect must on the balance be increased uncertainty. They resemble the frequent wakings of a patient in order to administer sleeping draughts. It was, therefore, with much doubt and difficulty that I brought myself to think that it was right to close the mints in 1893. But some of the strongest arguments against closing them then are now arguments against reopening them, and against acquiescing in any other arrangement than a 1s. 4d. rupee. I base myself partly upon the consideration that the original revenues were fixed in rupees—not gold rupees or silver rupees, but rupees —and that gold coins were legal tender well into the present century. I think, therefore, that the descendants of the original holders would have had no technical grievance if England had adhered to the gold standard throughout. Of course, the position of the Indian Government is weakened by the fact that, when gold was showing a sign of falling in value, it refused to take gold as legal tender. But still, taking history as a whole, I cannot see any technical breach of contract in moving the rupee somewhat in the gold direction. Looking at the thing broadly, and without reference to recent events, I should think that it would not have been an unjust arrangement to say that two-thirds of the rents should be paid in terms of silver, and the remaining one-third in terms of gold. Now, if you take one-third of a rupee at its old gold value, and two-thirds of the silver in a rupee, you do get just about 1*s*. 4*d*. It seems to me, therefore, that, if the fixed rents were allowed to be paid in rupees, with open mints, this very great fall in the value of silver would throw the whole burden, or more than the whole burden, of the necessarily increasing expenditure of the Government upon taxpayers other than the permanent and sub-permanent holders; and in that there would be an inequity. I think it would relieve them of some part of their proper share of the public burdens, and would thereby impose an unjustly large share of those burdens on other taxpayers. A slight injustice of this kind is sometimes a less evil than its remedy; but a rupee at 1*s*. 4*d*. seems to me a workable compromise, and substantially just for public and private business contracts. While the evil arising from a change in the currency was an argument, for what it was worth, against the closing of the mints, it is no argument at all in favour of reopening them. On the whole it seems to me, as I have said, that a rupee at 1*s*. 4*d*. is a workable compromise; and, although I have seen it stated that it is a tax upon trade, I have not been able to see that it is any tax upon trade at all. It is a tax upon those who have a specific quantity of rupees to pay under contracts made or implied during the very short time that the rupee was of lower real value than now; but, so far as future trade is concerned, it seems to me to be a change exactly like the adoption of the decimal system, and using the kilogram instead of the pound.

11,788. What do you take to be the general relation between the Indian exchange and prices in India and England?—India is so large that prices at her ports differ widely from up-country prices; and, partly for this reason, much of the produce of India is very little connected either as cause or effect with the course of trade. But, broadly speaking, the Indian exchange, both before and after the closing of the mints, has indicated the proportion between rupee prices at Indian ports and sterling prices at English ports; and, subject to allowance for freights, etc. between India and England, the rule holds that the exchange, or the gold price of the rupee, is the ratio of sterling prices to rupee prices.

Before passing to the way in which that works out, I would like to say a little on the interpretation of the phrase " general prices in India." I have seen in current literature a good many arguments as to the general policy of the Government with regard to currency in India, which seemed to me to be incorrect, because they are based upon a comparison of London prices and Calcutta prices, and the tendency of progress is, of course, to raise up-country prices of exports relatively to Calcutta prices. The papers written fifty years ago by Colonel Sykes, who, I think, was the first person who paid very serious attention to the higher statistical problems of India, showed very great differences between the up-country values and the tidal-water values. It is especially interesting to study these differences in the case of America, because America is on a gold basis and there is no break of gauge in passing from America to her chief customers. A number of people have made inquiries showing the relative movements in different parts of America, and I think it may be said to be established, broadly speaking, that there has not been any great fall in gold prices of agricultural staples up country. I have here one of a series of papers issued by the Sound Currency Committee of New York; and, though it is avowedly written for a purpose, I think we can trust the diagrams, which show that the prices of agricultural produce at Dubuque, Iowa, fell much less than at tidal water. And here I have an elaborate set of diagrams, showing similar results for up-country markets throughout the United States, by Mr. Powers, Commissioner of Labour for Minnesota. His figures have been criticised; but their general effect has not been shaken. No one can look at these general results of Indian and American statistics without concluding that the statement that the prices in India have not risen lately is not a justifiable statement, if it is based upon Calcutta prices, and without allowing for the differences between up-country and tidal-water prices.

I have now to enter very much upon controversial matter, and perhaps it would be well that I should first state what is, I think, a matter of common agreement as to the causes that govern Indian exchange. It is common ground that Indian exchange is raised—that is, made more favourable to India in the old technical sense of the word, which means more favourable to importers, and more unfavourable to exporters—by an increased foreign sale of Indian products. This may arise from increased foreign eagerness to buy these products, resulting in an improved rate of value for them in terms of the goods offered in foreign markets, or from increased Indian supplies of them at the old value. Or it may arise from diminished Indian purchases of foreign products, including gold and silver; and this may be caused by a diminished eagerness on the part of India for them, or by diminished offer of foreign stocks of them at a rate which India will pay. Further, the Indian exchange may be raised by increased borrowings by India. It seems to me it is worth while to have these general considerations before us; because they seem to show that, as regards discount, so with regard to exchange, no general proposition is possible. One cannot say that a fall of the exchange is good for a country or bad.

11,789. You say, " Speaking generally, the Indian exchange is the ratio of sterling prices to rupee prices at the ports." Will you kindly amplify that ?—The Indian exchange is quoted as the sterling price of the rupee, that is, as the price in London of the command of a rupee's worth of goods in Calcutta or Bombay. If the exchange is not by telegraph, something must, of course, be allowed for interest. It is worth the while of an English importer of, say, jute, to pay this price for a rupee, if the jute that he can get with a rupee will sell *net* in London for this price. By *net* is meant, after paying all the expenses; *i.e.* including insurance, interest for the time the capital is locked up in transit, and remuneration for himself. Thus Indian exchange is the ratio which the sterling price of jute, after allowing for freight, etc., bears to the Indian price. In the same way, the exchange is the ratio that the sterling price of calico bears to the Calcutta price after allowance is made for freight, etc. The details of this had, perhaps, better be taken separately for the case in which the imports of silver directly affect the currency of India, and the case in which they do not. The latter case is really the simpler.

11,790. Now, will you say how this works out ?—Since the mints were closed, the currency of India has consisted of Government notes based on silver. Their value is governed in the main by their amount relatively to the work which they have to do; account being taken of the fact that apprehensions as to the stability of the value of such a currency will affect the amount of purchasing power which people care to keep directly or indirectly in the form of currency. The Indian exchange is then governed by the relation between gold prices and rupee prices, being, in fact, an expression of the ratio between them. I will work this out in detail with reference to the trade of the all-round merchant. There is not, really, a very great difference between his case and that of the man who exports without importing in return; because by aid of the exchange banks, the mere exporter is now almost in the position of the all-round merchant. The all-round merchant's case is the typical case. I mean the man who exports and imports back again. If an all-round Calcutta merchant exports jute and imports calico, he makes a good business, provided, first, jute is in great demand in England and calico plentiful there, so that he can get much calico in London for the price of each bale of jute; and, secondly, calico is in great demand in Calcutta, and jute plentiful there, so that he can get much jute in return for each bale of calico which he imports. These are the things that really affect his prosperity. The currency does not affect it directly. If he knows that he can get 100 bales of calico in London for the price of 300 bales of jute, he does not really want to know what the price is, it might be given to him in a sealed bag. If the contents of the bag were guaranteed to purchase him his 100 bales of calico, that is all that he would want to know. If the 100 bales of calico would sell in Calcutta for the price of 450 bales of jute, and the price of 150 bales would enable him to pay all expenses of the double traffic with profits to himself, then the business would be profitable, otherwise not. If there were to be a suddenly increased issues of rupees, and Calcutta prices rose, so that Rs.120 were needed to do the work of 100; then the exchange would instantly follow suit, if there were no other disturbing cause at the time. But, of course, there might be a disturbance. The credit of the country would, perhaps, be lowered, and this might make foreigners withdraw capital from it. That withdrawal would injure the country as a whole, and the exporters themselves in the long run; but for the time it would be a powerful bounty on

exports : and a real bounty due to that cause exporters sometimes get, and attribute it to a different cause, viz. the direct action
of the fall in the exchange. Again, the change under discussion—
the increase of the currency—might lead people to avoid rupees
and seek gold and silver bars for their hoards. This is a special
case of an increased desire on the part of India for a commodity
(silver is now one) such as silver, petroleum, and diamonds, from
whatever cause arising. Let us, then, leave this illustration with
regard to an increase of the currency, and take what has been,
in fact, the chief cause of increased purchases of these commodities by India—the increased output of American and African
mines. Well, the increased desire for petroleum, diamonds, and
silver, any or all, would make India bid more eagerly for foreign
produce, and give more jute, etc., in return for it. The way in
which this would work out in the exchanges would be as follows :
The importers of diamonds, petroleum, and silver, would need
bills on London, and pay an increased number of rupees for a bill
for 1,000*l*., that is to say, in technical terms, the exchange would
fall. Its first effect would be to give a real bounty to exporters
of jute, and impose a real burden on importers of calico. After
a while, the price of jute would have fallen a little in London, and
the price of calico would have risen a little in Calcutta. The
rupee would count for less relatively to calico, the sovereign for
more relatively to jute. The all-round merchant might have to
sell 320 bales of jute instead of 300 in London, in order to get 100
bales of calico, but he would get his own again because he would
sell his calico at home for the price of more jute than before. And,
if, in this state of the trade, he stopped off from importing, he
would require to obtain a larger number of rupees than before for
a bill of 1,000*l*. Thus the increased demand of India for foreign
goods would lower the exchanges, and it would keep them low so
long as there was no other change in the situation except this
increased demand; that is, especially, so long as there was no
change in the supply of rupees or gold relatively to the work they
had to do, and this supposition implies that the mints are not open
to silver. A permanent alteration in the rate of exchange due to
such causes as these is the outward expression of a change in the
real terms of trade between India and other countries. But

an alteration in the exchange due to changes in the currency of
India or other countries has no such deep signification. It may
disturb the business relations of individuals, it does not as a rule
modify the substantial trade relations of countries. Even if the
Indian mints were never reopened to silver, an increased production of silver in the West might lead to a permanent increase in
India's eagerness for foreign imports, and a permanent alteration
in the terms on which she obtained them, just as was done on a
smaller scale by the African diamonds and the American petroleum. The case of silver resembles that of diamonds more nearly
than that of petroleum. For, if the price of petroleum falls,
people buy more of it to use at once; they do not wait to see if
the prices will fall even more next year. But with diamonds and
silver it is different. A fall in their price sometimes make buyers
more eager, sometimes it makes them hold off in expectation of a
further fall. The want of correspondence between changes in the
real price at which silver could be bought, and the amount of it
which India will take, may, perhaps, be explained by those who
know the history of Bazaar rumours. I have been told by natives
that there is a good deal to be learnt in that direction. Of course,
I never got below the surface at all, but to me it is inexplicable.
The common saying that the course of the rupee cannot be predicted as that of any Western coin can, seems to me to derive its
chief justification from this fact. It seems to me that nearly
everything is explicable about the rupee with a little patience;
but on this point I confess the action of the rupee is quite inexplicable to me. What I cannot understand is the relation between the
price of silver and the imports. For instance, if one takes a
diagram showing the net imports of silver into India, and the net
imports of gold into India, and the rate of exchange, one has a
paradox that one cannot solve.[1] I thought that such a diagram
must yield something to study; but, though the causes of some
of the most striking movements of these net imports are well
known, I can get nothing out of it that suggests a general law
connecting movements of these imports and movements of the
exchange. As one instance, I may mention that the Super-
intendent of the Post Office for the North-Western Provinces in

[1] For the diagram, not reproduced here, see C. 9376.

1886—I am quoting second-hand—states that the import of gold
was increased considerably, because of the rise in its rupee value.
People thought that the rise in its rupee value was going on fast,
and for that reason they imported on a very large scale. But in
1892–93 gold was on the balance exported, because speculators and
hoarders took their profits on the purchases of earlier years,
preferring not to wait longer.

11,791. Do you wish to say anything as to the different relations which affected the question when the mints were open ?—
When the mints were open, importers of silver into India were
secure of a better market, and therefore a fall in the Western price
of silver was liable to disturb trade more. There were some
re-adjustments of price levels, rupee prices at the ports being
specially plastic, as Mr. O'Conor has told you. Sterling prices
might yield temporarily a little in some cases, but ere long
equilibrium was reached with more silver and higher prices in
Indian ports than there otherwise would have been. To go over
this difficult question again somewhat in detail : the gold price
of silver having fallen, either the relation between gold and silver
prices of the chief commodities in trade would quickly re-accom-
modate itself to the new gold value of silver or it would not. If
it did, as in my belief it would, the rupee prices at the ports would
rise nearly in proportion to the increased value of gold in terms of
silver. It is however true that, if there happened to be a growing
scarcity of gold, or growing facilities for the production and
transport of cotton, iron, etc., the gold prices of these things might
fall to meet the rupee prices (and this did, in fact, often happen
between 1873 and 1885). In whatever way the re-adjustment was
made, provided only it was made quickly, the premium on the
exportation of Indian goods in return for silver would be small
and would quickly pass away. If on the other hand there were
no rapid re-adjustment of relative prices, the premium on the
importation of silver would lead to a bottomless demand for it.
Silver would be exported by 20,000,000l. or 30,000,000l. worth a
year, if there were no re-accommodation of the relations between
gold prices and silver prices. For it would then be profitable for
anybody whatever to buy silver and take it to India and buy
commodities, and the flow of silver to India must reach enormous

figures. As a matter of fact, there has never been any large and persistent import of silver into India which can be attributed to this cause, and therefore we are compelled to admit that prices at the ports accommodate themselves very quickly to the new conditions. I do not say that inland prices accommodate themselves rapidly.

11,792. Would you wish to add anything on the question whether a depreciating currency gives a bonus to any of those engaged in producing for export ?—The influence of a relatively depreciating currency upon the position of the exporter has been the subject of a very long controversy in which I have taken a somewhat lengthy part, as a good deal of my evidence before the Gold and Silver Commission bore upon that subject. I find that those who think that a relatively depreciating currency gives a bounty to the export trade, generally quote in support of their conclusions facts which I should not dream of calling in question, and I think it may be well to state what seem to me to be matters common to both sides, matters which are not in dispute. The dispute is whether from these facts it follows that a depreciating currency gives a bounty to the export trade. It is common ground that, if the price at which an exporter sells his goods in foreign markets be taken as fixed, than a fall in the value of his own currency, relatively to foreign currency, of one per cent. increases his gross currency receipts by one per cent., and is likely to increase his profits in a much larger proportion, or to turn a loss into a profit. Expert witnesses have been called, and numerous expert writings have been written by people making a point of the fact that they are actually engaged in trade, and in a position to prove that this is the experience of practical life. But really no experience is needed : the result follows from an elementary application of the first rules of arithmetic : and it has never, as far as I am aware, been doubted by any person in the world. It is common ground also that, if the currency in India is rising in value, while that in, say, China, is falling in value, then the employers in India, having to pay relatively increased fixed charges, salaries, wages, etc., may be complaining of hard times, while the employers in China are making good profits. This will perhaps, be expressed by saying that currency changes are giving an advantage, or a premium, or a bounty to the Chinese employers as compared with the Indian. If these employers in India are producing for export to foreign countries, they may be described as exporters; and it may be said then that the Chinese exporters have a bounty in comparison with the Indian exporters. But this appears to me to be an incorrect way of expressing an undoubted fact; for, first, the gain of the Chinese employer is independent of the accident that his goods are exported; and, secondly, it is at the expense partly of the creditors who are financing his export industry, but mainly of the employés in it. Now, if one says that the export trade of a country is conterminous with the undertakers of business enterprise, who are generally employers, and that anything that benefits the employers is a bounty on the export industry, then the proposition may be conceded. But, as I hold that the creditors who finance an industry that produces for export have some share in the export trade, and that the employés who make the thing for export have a very large share—quite as large a share as the undertaker,—holding that, I do not admit the proposition. If the statement is that a depreciating currency gives a bounty to the employer who is producing for export, I admit it; only, I add, the bounty is just the same, and at the expense of just the same people, as that which he would get from a depreciating currency if he were producing for his home market, and not for export. Again, it is common ground also that, when a country lends capital or returns any of its borrowings, or increases its payment of foreign dues (for example, increased sales of Council bills), or has increased its imports above their wont, then there is an increased demand for exporters' bills; that this is necessarily accompanied by a fall in the value of that country's currency relatively to foreign countries, causes a stimulus to exports, and increases, for the time, the profits of exporters. But all this does not go to show that a depreciated currency is a bounty to exporters in the way of causing an increase of exports relatively to imports. On the contrary, any stimulus to exports relatively to imports which is not accompanied by lending to foreign countries, or returning loans, must necessarily be followed and compensated by an exactly equal falling off of exports relatively to imports. For it causes an excess of exporters' bills, and that gives at once a bounty to imports. If the bounty is not sufficient, the discount on exporters' bills rises, and, therefore, the bounty on imports rises, until precious metals or other goods come in. In other words, a bale of jute has to be sold in London for a price that will bring back enough yards of calico to fetch, in Calcutta, a price that will pay for the jute and the expenses of the traffic. Here I am getting back on old ground. Whether this can be done or not depends, so far as London goes, on the needs of England for jute, in comparison with their power of producing calico; (sovereigns are mere counters in the transaction); and, so far as Calcutta goes, it depends on the needs of India for calico, on comparison with her power of producing jute. Rupees are mere counters in the dealings between the two nations, though not in the dealings between individual members of the nations. Nor is the case altered if we interpose a third country, and look at the competition in neutral markets between countries with a depreciating currency and countries with a currency that is not depreciating. Let us suppose, for instance, that China tea and Indian tea of equal quality are sold in London, presumably at the same price, and therefore in return for the same amount of English goods. If the Chinese currency is depreciated, a smaller part of the value of these return goods will have gone to the employés and to the creditors in China with whom the capitalist tea grower has relations, but that is a distribution within the country. It is a gain of one class at the expense of another. The change in the currency does not affect the amount of calico which can be brought back for a chest of tea of a given quality, and therefore it does not affect the advantages of the trade as between the nations. Of course, both countries have dues in Europe, and cannot bring back European goods in return for all their exports, China and India being both borrowers; but, so far as these are concerned, local currency counts for nothing at all. The question that is of importance to them both, as regards paying dues in London, is, whether they must give more tea to buy the means of paying 100*l.* in London than before; and, if the Chinese tea and the Indian tea are of equal qualities, the same number of pounds of Indian and Chinese tea will go for the purpose of paying a given due.

It is, however, quite natural that capitalist employers in a country in which currency is not depreciating should look with envy on the position of those who can pay wages and other dues in a depreciating currency, and therefore retain for themselves a larger share of the price which they get for their goods, whether sold in the home or foreign markets. But this envy has little effect on the course of trade. If gold prices have remained stationary, while the rupee has depreciated 10 per cent. in terms of commodities, then the employer in India is better off than English employers. He gets 10 per cent. more rupees for his produce, whether he sells at home or abroad : he has to pay but few more rupees in wages, since wages have not risen fast; and so he gets higher profits whether he sells at home or abroad. Most of his sales are, in fact, to gold countries; so he regards as a benefit arising from the exchange and accruing to the trade what is really a benefit arising through the depreciation of the currency and going to the employer chiefly, but being taken from the employé.

11,793. Do you think India especially hindered from obtaining a gold standard, or a gold currency, by reason of her poverty, and the fact that she has to make gold payments ?—I think she is hindered, but I think the difficulty, on examination, appears much less than at first sight. The difficulty of keeping gold in a country seems to arise from its having been required to make large payments abroad, especially on short notice. When foreign capitalists withdraw their capital, which they commonly do when credit is bad, something or other must be sent to meet the country's obligations, under pain of bankruptcy; and those things which have the most elastic market, and are most easy of transport, naturally go first. Diamonds are as easy of transport as gold, but they have not as good or as quick a market as gold; therefore, gold goes first, and silver second, if a country is outside of the Western world. But in the Western world the first line of defence is not now in gold or in silver; the first line of defence is in International Stock Exchange securities. Poor countries, unfortunately, seldom have such; they hold very few securities, except their own, and those are specially unmarketable at such a time. The developments of modern business have caused a country to be liable, under severer penalties than before, to pay up many millions' worth of capital at short notice; and this first line of defence, International Stock Exchange securities, is not largely available for poor countries, including, I believe, India. I admit that to be a very great difficulty, but that seems to me to be the only point in which India is in a specially bad position. As regards the second line of defence, the precious metals, she is perhaps in a particularly strong position. She normally imports 11 crores' worth, and, therefore, she could pay 11 crores abroad by merely suspending her normal imports. The third line consists of goods which are portable, valuable, of elastic demand, having well-organised world markets, and having also a well-organised local machinery for collecting them from up-country, and putting them on world markets. In this third line, India is stronger than almost any other country that is not rich. Her exports of cotton in various forms equal about 20 crores, and imports of cotton nearly 30 crores. Now, cotton is a portable commodity, and elastic in the world's demand; and, therefore, by importing less and exporting more, she could meet a portion of her debt. Again, she exports hides, rice, and tea for about 30 crores. The world markets for hides and rice are large and elastic; and, so long as Chinese competition remains strong, it may be said that the market for tea is elastic, because Indian tea could push out Chinese. If Indian tea had completely pushed out Chinese tea, then tea would be for this purpose rather a bad defence, just as coffee is in the case of Brazil. Jute, I should think, is also elastic, since there are other fibres in some competition with it, though perhaps not so elastic. Moreover, there are some (although not many) of India's imports, other than cotton goods, which are not indispensable.

The witness withdrew.

Adjourned.

Professor ALFRED MARSHALL, recalled and further examined
(February 16, 1899).

11,794 (*Mr. Le Marchant.*) In your evidence at Question 11,765
you say that the " high rate of interest on permanent investments
in India seems to be attributable partly to a relative scarcity of
real capital." Would you from that regard the addition to the
currency under open mints as not having increased the real capital
of India ?—In my opinion it does not. It is very difficult to say
what position the metallic currency of a country holds in its real
wealth or real capital. It is a matter on which there has been a
great deal of academic discussion; I think, to a great extent, the
discussion has been with regard to the meaning of words. If a
country has an unsound currency, say a paper currency, liable to
large fluctuations; and imports bullion to put that currency
on a sound foundation; then it does get a return for the expense
to which it has been put in getting a sound currency. But when
once it has got a good currency; then if, through an unfortunate
increase in the production from the mines, it has to import a
good number of millions of ounces of precious metals in order to
make a more diluted currency do the work that the old currency
did well before, that seems to me to be no increase of wealth;
the country is giving its real capital in return for a thing that
merely causes people to carry about larger purses, and—so to
speak—use more cumbrous weighing machines, without any
increase in their real wealth.

11,795. If the additional currency is sent there because it is
cheap in terms of the money or of the commodities of foreign
countries, if it is sent in preference to other commodities because
it is the cheaper thing to send, there is a strong probability, is
there not, that it will not be a gain to the country receiving it ?—
So far I should say there will not be a gain.

11,796. And the degree to which it would add to the real capital
would depend on the circumstances of actual want for it and the
uses of it ?—Yes. It would depend very much, I think, on the
question whether the currency without that increased supply of
precious metals was in a wholesome condition, or in one in which
it was liable to be unduly disturbed by shocks to general credit.

x

11,797. It has sometimes been suggested that, with open mints, the additional currency that arose from silver imports was a natural increase of Indian capital as distinguished from foreign capital, and formed a fund available for promoting local enterprises which would otherwise have depended on foreign capital?— It does not seem to me that that statement, as it is commonly made, and as it is commonly understood, is at all true. At the same time I should be unwilling to give it a direct negative, because there does seem to me to lie concealed behind it a certain element of truth. It seems to me that, as India is passing from what we may call a mediæval condition to a modern Western condition, it is using a great deal more currency as a specific medium of exchange on modern methods in lieu of the old-fashioned barter and payment of dues in kind. That is giving India a commercial power, which she can only obtain by this means, that is, by having an increased number of what I may call weighing machines. So that, had the general level of precious metals not been disturbed by the increased production of the mines at all, I think it would have been necessary for India (unless she had developed a banking system, which could not be expected in the circumstances) to import extra bullion in order to put her machinery of exchange on the efficient but expensive Western system. And, so far, I should not say that the bargain was a bad one for her. I imagine that part of the importation of silver was caused by this need for increased Western appliances and was not to be regretted, and so far did give her an increased power of meeting her own needs and supplying those things which meet the needs of the rest of the world, and thereby caused them to contribute to her needs.

11,798. So far, in fact, as it supplied the necessary mechanism of circulation, which in this country would be provided by expansion of credit money or by banking devices, to that extent it would be an advantage?—Yes, by expanding credit money or, of course, expanding coin.

11,799. Would you regard the importation of silver as having contributed directly to a higher level of prices in India?—Yes, I think the level of prices is higher than it would have been had there not been so much importation of silver for currency purposes.

Had silver not been imported for those purposes, then I think prices could not have risen and would probably have fallen, because there was an increased demand for currency owing to the adoption of Western methods of business.

11,800. So far as the additional silver caused labour to be brought into operation and production, to that extent it would have contributed to the increase of wealth ?—Yes, or so far as it enabled people to do their business by the Western methods, which are more quick, precise, and elastic, and, generally speaking, efficient than the primitive methods.

11,801. How far would the same facilities exist under a gold standard ? Would the same essential conditions exist ?—Broadly, yes. The term " essential " is a little difficult to understand. The existence of a gold standard without a gold currency would, of course, act in certain important respects differently from a silver currency.

11,802. With regard to discount and the volume of currency as affecting it, would you regard the rate of discount as affected not so much by the total volume as by the distribution of the currency—the hands in which it stands ?—I should think that that was largely true.

11,803. I think you refer more especially to capital rather than currency in that relation; I gather that you viewed capital as being the command of currency ?—My own way of looking at things is this : I prefer to talk of currency as giving a command over real capital, and bank money as giving a command over currency, and therefore giving a command over real capital in a secondary degree.

11,804. Assuming that there was a scarcity of currency in banking circles that would involve a high rate of discount ?—Certainly.

11,805. It would also depend, would it not, on the facility for introducing fresh currency from abroad ?—Certainly—the facility and the time required.

11,806. At the moment of demand ?—Yes.

11,807. There might be different conditions bearing on the introduction of fresh currency, according as the standard was silver or gold ?—I should think so, probably. Perhaps I should say that

I have been a good deal surprised at seeing it stated frequently before this Committee that high exchange and high rate of discount habitually go together. I understand that that is the prevalent opinion in the business world in Calcutta. It does not fit in with what I should have supposed *a priori*, and, on looking at the chart, I find that, so far as yearly fluctuations go, the opposite seems to be rather the rule. Indian banking is a matter on which I feel myself beyond my depth, but I feel that I could not talk with any satisfaction about the relation between discount and prices until this doubt of mine has been laid before the Committee. I am not able to see *a priori* why there should be that correlation, nor am I able to see that there has been. The charts, on the contrary, seem to me to indicate not only that that law does not hold, but that the opposite law holds as a rule from year to year. And that has led me to guess at the cause of this general opinion; and I think it may be possible that the movements under discussion are mainly those from week to week, and month to month, rather than from year to year; and, secondly, that there may be a great difference between the effects of a scarcity or of bad crops of food grains, and of those products which are chiefly used for export. In this diagram the red curve is the rate of discount, and the green curve is the rate of exchange.[1] I cannot see any general tendency for their movements up and down to coincide; rather it seems to me that often one goes down and the other goes up.

11,808. Might the relative movements of the two differ in the case of countries such as India and England, which are not on a common basis, whereas, if you take capitals like London, New York, and Paris, where gold is the basis of currency, and passes most easily from one to the other owing to their extensive banking relations, the rate of discount might more quickly affect the rate of exchange ?—I said in my first day's evidence that I could not trace any general connection between high rates of discount and high exchanges statistically with regard to the world in general, or with regard to India in particular, and that I could not see why there should be any such coincidence. India seems to me to stand on a different footing from England. First, so long

---

[1] For the diagram, not reproduced here, see C. 9376.

as it had silver, because the rate of exchange was liable to be
violently disturbed by causes that had nothing to do with India's
special circumstances or trade—to be disturbed much more
violently than the gold exchange could possibly be disturbed
between two neighbouring countries such as England and France.
Secondly, because the business of Calcutta appears to me in many
respects to follow lines more different from those of the rest of
India than the business of London does from the lines followed
by the rest of the business of England.   And, thirdly, because the
difference between the effects on Indian business of a check to the
supply of the things that India consumes herself, and the effect
of a check to the supply of the things that she exports has nothing
exactly corresponding to it in a Western country.   My own guess
is that a famine or generally a scanty supply of food grains tends to
raise discount, partly because it draws currency from the banks,
and generally from Calcutta and Bombay, to the uplands.   That
guess receives some support from a comparison of the black, blue,
and red lines in this diagram.[1] But I think that a very active
export season, which itself is generally a consequence of very
fine crops of things suitable for export, also raises discount.   So
that I should rather suppose that, when it is said a high rate of
exchange goes with high discount, what is meant is that, given the
amount of currency available for general trade purposes, and the
amount of bank money available in Calcutta, if the export trade
is active, you will have a high exchange and a high rate of discount.
That is the only solution I have been able to guess at of this
paradox, that, speaking broadly, a high rate of exchange seems
to go, not, as has so often been said before this Committee, with
a high rate of discount, but rather the other way.

11,809. (*Chairman.*) I do not think that has been the uniform
tendency of the evidence given before the Committee.   For
instance, when Lord Rothschild was before us, he was asked by
Mr. Le Marchant, "There would be no necessary connection
between a rate of exchange and a high rate of discount ? " and
Lord Rothschild said, " I do not think so." The Committee, of
course, have come to no conclusion upon the point; but I simply
wanted to draw your attention to the fact that, on this particular

---

[1] For the diagram, not reproduced here, see C. 9376.

point, you have the high authority of Lord Rothschild in agreement with your views?—Yes. The distinction which I wanted to bring out was this. It may be true that the minor movements in the busy season of exchange and discount go together. That is indeed what I should expect as regards the slight variations from week to week and month to month, especially from week to week; but it does not seem to me that, comparing one year with another, these statistics, which are among the few that are beyond the possibility of doubt, support the notion that high yearly rates of discount and of exchange go together.

11,810. (*Mr. Le Marchant.*) In fact, would you say that, if the high rate of discount is owing to adverse causes, such as exceptional expenditure on famine relief, which have altered the usual channels in which currency flows, a high rate of discount would be likely to concur with a lower exchange—from insufficiency of exports?—It might. At present I feel great difficulty in putting forward any general proposition with regard to them except that when business slackens they would both be lower, both being affected by the same cause. It seems to me to be something like the question whether a greenhouse is likely to be hotter when there is a good fire in the stove. The bigger the fire in the stove the hotter the greenhouse, of course; on the other hand, the colder the weather is, the colder the greenhouse will be, and therefore the bigger the fire must be. Just in the same way the rate of discount is continually raised because exchange is low, and with the effect of raising exchange. You get two sets of causes, one of which tends to make a high rate of discount go with a low rate of exchange; and the other set of causes tends to make the two rates be high together, and low together; and I have not been able to see either *a priori* or statistically that one of these sets of causes prevails over the other. Speaking generally, with regard to England, I suppose that the high rate of discount does force exchange up, and bring in bullion quickly; and that, if the high rate of discount is for any reason maintained after the country has attracted the gold that it needs from abroad, then you may have for a certain time high rates of discount with a falling exchange. But the supplies of the material of currency in India being so very far off, the time and cost of transport of bullion being so much greater than in the case of England, I should not be able at all to guess *a priori* the extent of the power that the discount would have over the influx of bullion, and through that over the exchanges.

11,811. (*Mr. Campbell.*) Has it occurred to you that the rate of exchange with open mints depends very much on the price of silver ?—Most certainly. I discussed that.

11,812. And that, if the cost of silver were tending downwards over a course of years, you might have a declining exchange, even although you had periods of stringency in the money market ?— Certainly.

11,813. That is a very important factor in the question, is it not ?—Certainly.

11,814. (*Mr. Le Marchant.*) You were referring, in your answer to Question 11,773, to the dependence of India on foreign capital. The opinion has been advanced that foreign capital is not so beneficial to India—that it entails a yearly drain for remittances. How do you regard that ?—I cannot see a reasonable foundation for that opinion at all. I hold in the most clear, and, if I may say so, confident manner the opinion that there never was a country which needed foreign capital more than India does. It needs foreign capital partly to enable India to throw aside those mediæval methods of production which still prevail in many branches of industry—to develop means of inter-communication in all directions, and partly to educate the natives themselves to store up capital. When the natives have once got to see that the function of a surplus of income over expenditure is to be devoted to making the future happier, then, I think, their own capital will grow, and India may be able to move fast ahead, somewhat as Japan has been doing lately, with less dependence on foreign aid. But a check to the use of Western capital in India at the present stage would seem to me to be the greatest calamity that could happen to her.

11,815. At Question 11,790 you say, "An alteration in exchange, due to changes in the currency of India or other countries, has no such deep signification." Would you regard a change from a silver to a gold basis as in any way calculated to disturb the permanent trade relations of India ?—No, I should regard it as like a movement towards bringing the railway gauge on the side branches of the world's railways into unison with the main lines.

11,816. And promoting a facility of interchange?—Yes.

11,817. You are aware of the opinion often expressed, that it would disturb the balance of exports and imports, and thereby render the payment of obligations more difficult?—Yes, I have heard that opinion.

11,818. What importance do you think should be attached to the apprehension as to the imports becoming excessive and exports deficient?—To myself personally the matter has unfortunately been one of considerable importance. There is no other question on which circumstances have caused me to spend so much time in controversy against my will. I am quite clear that it is impossible for a country's exports to increase relatively to its imports, except when it is sending away capital, provided no part of her dealings with other countries is omitted from the reckoning. It may not be easy to see how the adjustment is being made. But this statement that whatever a country buys it must pay for unless it is borrowing, unless some other country is making it a present, seems to me to be as true with regard to the trade between countries as it is with regard to the budget of a private person. If a person says he is getting a great number of things and is not paying for them, I should then say, " Then you must be borrowing." If he says, " No, I am not borrowing," then I should say, "Somebody must be giving you things." Or, as a last resort, he must be stealing. These last two explanations, of course, would not apply between nations. Nations do not make presents to one another. They do borrow and they do lend, and the dislocations between the exports and imports, which are continually attracting attention, seem to me to be all due either to a change in the relations of borrowing or lending or to a change in the character of the services and goods rendered. For instance, we export to India every year a great number of prime young men. If their value were capitalised, as it would be if they were slaves, it would be several thousands of pounds apiece. We bring them back afterwards, if they come back at all, more or less shrivelled and worn out. Those are vast unreckoned exports. India complains that she sends us a tribute of goods for which we have given no return. We have given a return for many of them in the shape of men in the prime of life, who, on the whole, I think are very cheap for the purpose.

11,819. You have spoken in your evidence of the premium on bills, owing to a low exchange or a depreciating currency, as being paid by importers. Do you regard the Government of India as being an importer of services, and so having to pay the premium for remittances in common with other importers?—I am not quite sure whether I follow the first part of your question, but, taking the last part first, I regard the Indian Government as, in effect, the largest trader in the world; I think that its exports consist largely of services, and its imports consist of jute and hides, and so on, which it does not import directly, but takes when imported through the ordinary course of trade.

11,820. Would you say that it "imports" or "exports" jute, and so on?—I was then looking at the Indian Government as having its seat in England. It would be better, no doubt, to regard it as located in India, and exporting jute.

11,821. To that extent there is a competition between the Government and merchants who equally require to export those articles?—Yes.

11,822. Do you think that any difference would be introduced into that competition by a gold standard?—Yes, I think a great number of minor differences would be introduced. I do not think there would be any fundamental change. I think the greater fluidity of movements between India and the West in general, and England in particular, that would arise, would cause the fluctuations and disturbances to be more numerous, but less intense. A great number of causes which tend to produce certain effects do not produce those effects at all, if there is too great resistance. For instance, a certain thing may become cheaper in one place than in another, and that causes a tendency for it to go from the first place to the second; but, if the difference in the level of prices is not likely to last long, it does not move. Gold being more portable than silver—I understand that the charges are not much more than a quarter as much for a pound's worth of gold as they are for a pound's worth of silver, as between England and India—and the market that gold has, both for buying and selling

in England, being so much freer and truer, and so much less liable
to be worked against the individual dealer by powerful combinations of capital, it would seem to me that a great number of minor
adjustments would go on with a gold currency in India, or even
with a thoroughly well-established gold standard, which do not
take place without such gold currency or standard.

11,823. Would you regard the power of meeting those temporary
disturbances—in other words, the demand for gold exports—as
depending on banking facilities which would distribute the pressure
over a longer period of time?—Speaking generally, yes.

11,824. I think you have spoken of exchange as being determined by the relative level of prices in India and abroad?—Yes.
That is to say, that in my opinion the international distribution
of the precious metals with open mints must be such that the gold
and silver values of the different commodities bear the same
relations to one another all over the world, allowance being made
for transport; and that, if at any time any external change, such,
for instance, as new American currency legislation, upsets that
arrangement, then there will be a general shifting which will show
itself through the exchanges; the exchanges not being the real
active force, but the channel through which the real force acts;
and after a time there will be a new settlement, and a new rate of
exchange, and a new international level of prices.

11,825. With a gold standard, do you think the degree of
pressure for gold would be partly determined by the rapidity with
which Indian prices adjusted themselves to prices abroad?—Yes;
very much so.

11,826. And what would be the immediate influence bearing
on prices? Would it be a rise in the rate of discount? The
export of gold would compete with other exports?—Yes.

11,827. And, so far as it went, it would tend to cause other
exporters to lower their prices?—Yes.

11,828. An opinion has been expressed that a debtor country
has a difficulty in retaining a precious metal in the absence of a
protective tariff. The idea, I think, is that a protective tariff
turns the balance of payments in its favour, and assists it in
acquiring and retaining a precious metal. What importance do
you attach to that theory?—It seems to me that the theory has

some portion of a foundation in fact : that is, that there are two facts nearly corresponding to the statement, but not quite : but for the particular purposes for which it is used the statement is not, in my opinion, correct. There is no doubt, I think, that the immediate effect of the imposition by any country of protective duties, or rather high duties—I do not lay stress on their being protective—is to raise prices there—to make gold for a time a more eligible means of making payments than those goods which would have to pay this differential tariff, gold coming in free from such a tariff. If gold when it arrives is put away, as to a great extent it has been by Russia, that process may go on for a very long while. If Russia chose to prohibit all imports, except gold, and to put gold in store when it arrived, of course she could go on draining the rest of the world of gold. But, if the gold is allowed to go into the currency and act upon prices, that process can last only a very little while. When the gold has raised prices in the country, then, in spite of the heavy duty that is imposed upon other goods, other goods become as good cargoes to send to the country as gold would be. When the high level of prices that corresponds to a high import tariff has once been reached, then I am not able to see that that tariff is any protection to the stock of gold at all. It may seem as though it ought to be ; one might expect it to be ; but, when one comes to look at the reasons, I cannot see why it should be at all. The protective tariff has brought gold by making the country require more gold to do its business than before : the country has got the gold ; there is again equilibrium, and I cannot see that without the tariff it would be more willing to give up the gold required to do its business at a normal level than with the tariff. While, on the other hand, it is, I believe, common ground to all parties, protectionists and free traders alike, that a high tariff, whether it is in the ultimate interests of the country or not, does diminish the volume of her foreign trade for the time. The consequence is that the feelers which that country throws out into all other countries are less numerous, and less elastic, and less widely diffused than under free trade. If, then, something or other, say, for instance, a discredit of that country's commerce arising in foreign markets, compels that country to pay unexpectedly part of its obligations, then gold would be likely to leave that country, as it would leave any other country under the same conditions. I think it would be even more likely, because there is always an easy market for gold. But an easy market for goods requires to be made before-hand; it is the product of years of trade; and, since the feelers that a protective country would have thrown out would be less than those which a free country would throw out, therefore it would be more difficult for that country to throw, say, twenty millions of pounds extra upon the world's markets without making a glut, and possibly even getting smaller returns in return for larger imports of goods. It would be more difficult, I think, then in the case of a protective country than in the case of a free trade country to meet unexpected foreign demands without exporting gold. On the whole, I conclude that once equilibrium has been reached, a protective tariff operates rather against the retention of gold than in favour of it.

11,829. You would, therefore, consider the fact of principal importance with regard to the command of gold to be that India produces a variety of exports for which the demand is world-wide ? —Yes, and with organised feelers running out into various markets.

11,830. (*Mr. Campbell.*) On the question of exports and imports, did I understand you to say that a country could not export more than it imported unless it was sending away capital ? —Except when it was sending away capital; allowance being of course made for the payment of its interest upon borrowed capital; and the trade being taken broadly, so as to include, for instance, the services which an English man of business resident in Calcutta renders to the country. His profits are, of course, the payments for his services, and they enter into the trade in that way.

11,831. But do you not think it possible that a surplus of exports might be invested in securities which would operate exactly in the same way as any other imports ?—When one country invests in another country's securities, I call that lending to the other country.

11,832. So that a country might be exporting in excess of its imports without being unprosperous; in fact, it might be an evidence of prosperity ?—I think one can never say that the excess of imports over exports is an evidence of prosperity or adversity until one knows the causes.

11,833. It might be ?—It might happen to be caused by increased prosperity; but I do not think by itself it could be taken to be an evidence of either prosperity or adversity.

11,834. At Question 11,787 you say that you consider 1s. 4d. " an equitable adjustment and one which does not operate as a tax on trade." If the intrinsic value of the rupee in silver is 11d., will not the lowering of rupee prices involved in its artificial enhancement to 1s. 4d. place the trade of India at a disadvantage with other countries whose currency is on an intrinsic silver basis ?—It would put the trader, that is, the undertaker or entrepreneur, at a disadvantage : because, while he would sell his goods for the equivalent of the same amount of foreign goods as if there had been no currency disturbance, and while, therefore, he would be able to bring back a substantial real return for his exports, he would by the currency change be forced to keep a less quantity of that for himself and give more of it to his fellow-men than he would have been able to do if the currency had not been appreciated. This is a most important social question; but I do not see that it has any connection with foreign trade. To take the converse case, what happens when a currency is depreciated, is that a person who is under obligations to make certain currency payments (those obligations being in some cases fixed by definite contracts, in particular when he has already borrowed money at a definite rate of interest, but in other cases governed by custom), he is allowed through the change in the value of the currency to discharge those obligations at less cost to himself and less benefit to those who are engaged with him in trade. It seems to me, therefore, that the common opinion that a depreciating exchange is for the benefit of an export trade rests upon the natural habit of regarding the interests of the entrepreneur, the undertaker, as co-extensive with those of the trade. It has never been denied that a rise of prices or a fall in the value of currency is for the benefit of those who are undertaking the risks of speculation; but I conceive that it has never been shown that an entrepreneur gets a benefit from a fall in the value of the currency of his country, in consequence of his being engaged in foreign trade, which he would not get if he were not engaged in foreign trade.

11,835. He might get it in both cases?—He would get it in both cases, I think. Conversely, if the gold value of the currency were raised and prices lowered, as indicated in your last question, the employer would have to make heavier real disbursements out of the gross returns of his business.

11,836. Then would you not describe it as a tax on Indian trade from which other countries on a silver basis are relieved?— No, that is my point. I object to the use of the word " trade " there. In my view, the Indian export trade consists of three classes, speaking broadly. First, the undertaker of the risks, who is the person who figures most largely in the eye of the public; secondly, the people who supply that undertaker with such capital as he may want beyond his own, and, thirdly (and in my opinion by far the most important of all) his employés. I believe that the greatest harm is done, and the seeds of social discord are sown, if the interests of the export trade of a country are spoken of, when people have in mind only the interests of the entrepreneur, the undertaker.

11,837. (*Chairman.*) The interests of the capitalists?—Well, I would rather say the entrepreneur, because he may be borrowing capital.

11,838. It includes capital arising from two sources, his own capital or his borrowed capital. What you really are at, I take it, is capital and labour?—I wished to present the three classes of people.

11,839. The employé represents labour?—The employé represents labour; then there is the capitalist who is himself not engaged in the trade, but lends his capital.

11,840. That is capital?—That is part of capital. Then there is the third interest, that of the undertaker, the man of business, the employer who takes the whole risk, and supplies nearly always some part of the capital.

11,841. I only want it to be clear that, where you say that there are three classes, and that the most important is the employé, you are thinking of what has been called throughout this inquiry " labour " ?—Yes, provided that skilled labour be counted too; for instance, salaried managers and so forth.

11,842. (*Mr. Campbell.*) At Question 11,792 you say, " If the statement is that a depreciating currency gives a bounty to the employer who is producing for export, I admit it." But you add, " the bounty is just the same, and at the expense of just the same people, as that which he would get from a depreciating currency if he were producing for his home market, and not for export." And I think you go on to say that the bounty to the exporter is at the expense of the employés ?—Of the employés, and possibly, to some extent, of the person who has lent capital to them.

11,843. But the fact that there is a bounty is not altered or done away with by the fact that the advantage is gained at the expense of the classes that you name; the fact of the bounty remains ?—There is no doubt that it is a bounty, but the question is whether it is a bounty to the export trade. I say there is no bounty to the export trade, but there is a bounty to one class in the export trade at the expense of other classes in the export trade.

11,844. (*Chairman.*) That is, what one gains another loses ?—That is my opinion; and the question whether these shiftings from one class to another are substantially equitable and in the interest of the country as a whole, or not, depends, in my opinion, as indicated in my first day's evidence, on the question whether the currency retains a constant value in terms of man's efforts. An increased purchasing power of the currency in terms of commodities seems to me a good thing if it corresponds to an increasing command over nature which man has obtained by improvements in production and transport.

11,845. In Sir Robert Giffen's letter to *The Times* of the 19th May last, it is stated that " by the necessity of the case the exchange is chronically against India." What do you say to that ?—I should have thought that, as India is on the balance an importer of precious metals, the tendency would have been the other way. It is commonly said that the exchange is against Australia, because she is naturally an exporter of gold. Of course, when you have two different currencies—gold and silver

—it becomes a rather difficult question to say what you will take as your par of exchange; but still I cannot myself take the sentence in any sense in which I should agree with it. I think it is possible that Sir Robert Giffen meant something rather different from what I have taken him as meaning.

11,846. (*Mr. Le Marchant.*) I think the intention of the writer may have been to say that there was a large amount of fixed payments that India has to make—the home charges and so on—and, in addition, interest and dividends on railways and all the profits on foreign capital; and that, taking those requirements in the aggregate, it meant a pressure of payments against India?—That the balance of payments was against India. I think he may have meant that.

11,847. (*Chairman.*) I do not think that that exactly governs the case. For instance, take the remitting of money in respect of investments of capital in India. You pointed out this morning the enormous advantage to India of the importation of Western capital to develop its resources. Now, if India gets its capital, India must export something to provide for the interest on that capital, and that is what some gentlemen are good enough to call a drain on the resources of India; in other words, if India gets 100,000,000*l.* which she has invested in railways, and she has to pay in London 5,000,000*l.* sterling, and that 100,000,000*l.* invested in railways in India produces, say, an income of 7,000,000*l.*, they call the remittance to London a drain on the resources of India?—Well, it is part of a stream—the stream on balance being one of benefit which India receives.

11,848. But you can hardly say that in that case the exchange would be chronically against India?—No, I think not. But I am always unwilling to express an opinion upon a sentence without seeing its context.

11,849. Now one other question. Who in India benefits, and who loses, temporarily or permanently, by a fall of exchange? Who is the gainer and who is the loser?—I presume you are referring to a fall of exchange other than that which arises by the ordinary intercourse between any two countries from the deficiencies of exporters' bills.

11,850. No, I do not confine it to that?—Then I think one

would want to take the cases separately. First, with regard to
these variations in exchange between India and other countries
which are of the same order as variations in exchange between
England and France. With regard to these, a fall of exchange
is generally an indication that a country has been importing over-
much; it is an indication that, to reduce the trade to a position
of equilibrium, exporters are to push on and importers to hold
back; it is for the time being a bounty on exporters and a penalty
on importers. These fluctuations are not in themselves, I think,
matters of any importance, nor do they in any way depend upon
monetary arrangements. They depend on the movements of
trade themselves. The movements of exchange are partly a
method of clearly stating the temporary absence of adjustment
between exports and imports (all reckoned in); and partly a
method of indicating to those concerned a clear and definite
channel by which they can help to re-adjust the mutual obligations between that country and other countries, and derive
benefit to themselves in so doing. Then, secondly, we come to
those fluctuations in exchange between silver-standard countries
and gold-standard countries, which arise from a purely external
cause, such, for instance, as the repeal of the Sherman Act. A
fall in the Indian exchange, if it results from a fall in the purchasing power of the rupee, seems to me to give at once a bounty to
every undertaker of risks, every person engaged in speculation
in India; that is, every person who stands to gain by a rise in
commodities relatively to currency. In so far as Indian prices
up-country respond to the repeal of the Sherman Act, anybody
engaged in manufacturing up-country for up-country demands
would, I think, get that bounty, but the people with whom he
was in contact would lose. He had borrowed, say, 1,000 rupees,
and had to pay back say, 1,100 rupees; those rupees would be
worth less to the person who got them than they would have
been had it not been for the repeal of the Sherman Act, and that
person would suffer. Indian employés, particularly as they would
not be likely to possess an energetic trades union leader who could
prompt them as to the right time to strike, would receive wages
at the old rate in a currency which was worth less; and they
would suffer. I do not think that a fall in the purchasing power

Y

of the rupee caused by external events, such as the repeal of the Sherman Act, would quickly spread up-country very far : but, so far as it does go, I think the results are as I have explained. In Calcutta I imagine that the undertakers of business risks concerned with the export trade are of several kinds, bankers, merchants, etc.; and that a great deal of the bounty would go to them, and that not nearly the whole of it would get to the grower of tea or jute, or whatever might be the product for exportation. Some, I think, would go to the merchant, some, perhaps, to other intermediary dealers, and some to the capitalist producer. Those who had lent money to all these would lose a little, in so far as they were not able to anticipate what was going to happen. The employés would, I think, lose a great deal. I wish again to lay stress on the fact that those who lend capital are not in so bad a position as those who supply labour; I have argued that history seems to show that they are able to anticipate changes in the purchasing power of money very much, and to accommodate the rate of interest which they charge to those changes, and so to prevent their bearing nearly as large a proportionate share of the burden as that which the unfortunate employés have to bear.

11,851. I suppose the greater portion of that reasoning would apply to a depreciated currency ?—The whole of it in my opinion applies to a depreciated currency from whatever source the depreciation comes.

11,852. Is there anything further which you wish to state for the information of the Committee ?—I should like to say a little more as to the fluctuations of the rate of discount; and as to the need that they should be softened and controlled by the maintenance of an adequate reserve of coin and notes in normal times, ready to be drawn upon in times of exceptional pressure. I am aware that these matters do not fall fully within the terms of this Committee. But as one side of the problem of Indian currency is being thoroughly investigated, the present seems to be a suitable occasion for inquiring whether violent fluctuations of discount are not an evil of the same order as those of exchange; and whether there is not a partial remedy for them, which would cost much less than it is worth to the community, but which is not easily to be attained by private effort without some aid and

direction from Government. It seems to be established that the
very high rates which prevailed early in 1898 were mainly due to
exceptional causes, and not to the closing of the mints: that
similar stringencies occurred before 1873 with a 2*s.* rupee, and
afterwards with open mints and a fallen rupee. The fall in the
gold value of the rupee is itself, I have already argued, one cause
of the maintenance of a high *average* rate of discount. But, when
we consider that this average rate has remained almost stationary
in Calcutta during half a century, while it has fallen fast in almost
every other great trading country, and in some countries has
enabled enterprise to obtain the use of the necessary capital at
little more than half the rates that prevailed fifty years ago, I
think we must throw some part of the blame on the want of
adequate provision for the fluctuating needs of Indian business.
It is, of course, real capital alone that can provide the substantial
force needed to make business prosperous. A supply of currency
is but the flux that makes real capital fluid, and enables it to get
at its work. And a mere permanent increase of currency does not
make capital more fluid; it simply depreciates the currency.
What is wanted is a currency which expands when business
expands, and thus enables real capital to become fluid when it is
wanted to be fluid; and which shrinks when business shrinks,
and thus preserves itself from becoming superfluous and falling
in value. By this means only can the currency retain its full
power; and be ready by expanding again to supply the needful
flux for business, when it again becomes exceptionally active.
Foreign drains of bullion arising when there is no good stock available to meet them, give shocks to credit, which ought to be avoided.
And any shock to credit, whether arising from within the country
or from without, makes solvent traders as well as others need
an unusual stock of currency to enable them to meet exceptional
demands. The discussion of these matters in England, about
eight years ago, in which Mr. Goschen took the leading part,
resulted in the general adoption of the belief that a great commercial country was guilty of false economy, if it allowed the
reserve of bullion and currency, which it keeps against such
needs, to run too low. And the Directors of the Bank of England,
aided by Lombard Street generally, have earned the gratitude of

the country by increasing that ultimate reserve. The combined strength and elasticity which the currency of a country requires as provision against external and internal drains is most efficiently provided by a large reserve stock of bullion and coin. But this is expensive. And when, as appears to be the case in India, the drains to be guarded against are, in a large measure, internal, and dependent on the season of year, and therefore capable of being foreseen, it seems better to adopt the more economic provision of a moderate reserve stock of bullion and coin, combined with a limited and automatic elasticity of fiduciary paper currency. India's relative poverty makes it expedient that she should use the most economical of those devices which modern banking experience and science have shown to be at once effective and free from risk. But for this purpose the co-operation of Government is needed. And I wish respectfully to urge that the Government is not morally free to give the go-by to this question. By the terms of its existence, it is ever extending Western methods of public finance, and aiding the extension of Western methods of private business over the great continent of India. These powerful methods work for good; but because of their very power, they are apt to do much harm when they get out of gear. And therefore the Government, which promotes their extension, seems to me bound also to take thought how far India may require a parallel introduction of those powerful devices which the Western world finds necessary for grappling with occasional disorders of modern business and credit. I do not venture to urge any particular plan for the discharge of what seems to me the bounden duty of the Government in this matter. It must lie with those who know more of India, and more of the practical side of banking than I do, to decide whether there is the material in India for the formation of a bank corresponding to the Bank of England, or—which would probably be better for the special purpose—to one of the great continental banks; or whether a more direct route will be necessary for the present.

But this question leads me to wish to make a remark on one other subject, which lies perhaps rather far from the special business of the Committee; but which has been brought home to me by contact with candidates for the Indian Civil Service. The nineteenth century is handing down to the twentieth a vast number of complex economic problems, which are occupying much, perhaps the greatest part, of the attention of the most thoughtful statesmen of the West. Western Governments are aided by the advice and criticism of a large number of able business men, not a few of whom have had time to consider the broader problems of economics, as well as the details of their special trades. There is every sign that the difficulty and urgency of these practical economic problems will grow during the twentieth century as fast in India as in any other country. And the Government of India cannot expect as great a volume of assistance from business men trained in high thought, as a great Western Government can. For active life in India is short; it is interrupted by visits to Europe; the climate is hostile to severe mental toil after the day's work is done; and the number of able English business men in India who have an aptitude for high and hard thought in matters ranging beyond their own affairs can never be very large. If India is to prosper, the difficult economic problems of her government must be solved mainly by the Government. But English officials in India have plenty of occupation for their strength in doing the day's work. And, if they have not learnt to separate the apparent from the real in the action of economic forces before they go to India, they can hardly learn to do so in India. It seems therefore urgently needed that some half-dozen of the young men who go out to India every year, should take with them a good grounding in economics, and have already got to understand the main bearings of those modern economic forces which are revolutionising the West, and are making great changes in the East. But under the present Regulations it is impossible for every candidate to make more than a rapid and superficial study of economics without gravely impairing his chance of being selected for service. I would like, even though it be not quite in proper season, to plead most earnestly for a change in this respect. If, for instance, those who acquitted themselves with distinction in the paper on economics and economic history in the first part of the examination, were encouraged to present themselves for an advanced paper in economics in the second examination, they would be

helped much on the way to becoming efficient administrators of
Indian finance, and in later years wise counsellors.

Note.

PROFESSOR MARSHALL submitted to the Committee a number
of Diagrams and Statistical Tables, not here reproduced. The
originals are deposited in the Marshall Library in the University
of Cambridge. The following were reproduced by the Committee
in Appendix II to their Report, published as C. 9376 in 1899, and
are there available. The numbers given below refer to their
numbers in this Appendix.

64. Diagram of Prices in India and England : General Commodities in England (gold and silver prices) from 1846 to 1897 ;
Silver in London from 1846 to 1897 ; General Commodities and
Wages in India from 1861 to 1896 ; Indian Imports from 1873
to 1898 ; Indian Exports from 1873 to 1894.

65. Diagram showing Food Prices in India from 1861 to
1895 ; Rainfall in India from 1861 to 1896 ; Rate of Discount in
Calcutta (Bank of Bengal) from 1860 to 1897 ; and Rate of Indian
Exchange on England from 1861 to 1898.

66. Diagram showing Net Imports of Gold and Silver into
India, Rate of Indian Exchange on England, and London Price
of Silver, from 1860 to 1897.

67. Diagram showing Rate of Indian Exchange on England
from 1870 to 1897 ; Imports of Cotton Piece Goods into India
from 1870 to 1896 ; and Exports of Wheat from India from 1873
to 1897.

68. Diagram showing the Price of Jawar from 1861 to 1896.

69. Diagram showing course of Wages and Prices in United
States from 1860 to 1891.

ROYAL COMMISSION

ON

LOCAL TAXATION

(1897)

MEMORANDUM BY PROFESSOR ALFRED MARSHALL ON THE
CLASSIFICATION AND INCIDENCE OF
IMPERIAL AND LOCAL TAXES

[C. 9528 of 1899.]

QUESTIONS

The following questions were sent by the Royal Commission on Local Taxation, in the autumn of 1897, to certain financial and economic experts. A copy of a Memorandum by Sir Edward Hamilton [1] was sent to them subsequently. Professor Marshall's reply is reprinted below.[2]

1. Is the classification of Imperial Taxation indicated in the accompanying Table a correct classification; if not, what alterations can you suggest? (See Table on pp. 332, 333.)
2. Assuming the classification, is it complete, and are the several items correctly distributed?
3. In particular should such an item as the net revenue of the Post Office be treated as a tax, and if so, under which of the heads specified in the Table?
4. In considering the equity of any tax or system of taxation what tests should be applied?
5. Can you offer any suggestions which would assist the Commission in determining the question of the real incidence of taxation as distinguished from its primary or apparent incidence?
6. Could you, for example, state your view as to the real incidence of—
   (a) The Inhabited House Duty;
   (b) Rates levied on houses and trade premises;
   (c) Rates levied on agricultural land;
   (d) Taxes on the transfer of property;
   (e) Taxes on trade profits;
   (f) Death duties?
7. Is it possible to frame any criterion whereby the purposes

---

[1] Printed by the Commission, C. 9528.

[2] It was originally published by the Commission together with the other replies in 1899—C. 9528.

for which taxation should be raised locally can be distinguished from those for which taxation should be raised by the central Government?

8. Should the two kinds of purposes and the expenditure on them be kept distinct or should the expenditure for local purposes be partly borne by the central Government?

9. Should local rates be divided between owners and occupiers of real property, and if so, in what proportions?

10. Should ground values be separately rated for local purposes, and if so, on what principles?

11. Under what conditions and in what manner would the rent which could be obtained by an owner of land or rateable hereditaments be affected, if at all, by—

    (a) The increase of an old rate;

    (b) The imposition of a new rate;

    (c) The reduction or abolition of a rate?

12. Under what conditions and in what manner would the rent which could be obtained by an owner of land or rateable hereditaments be affected, if at all, if an occupier by whom a rate had hitherto been paid were empowered to deduct the whole or a portion thereof from the rent in the same manner as he is now entitled to do in the case of Income Tax (Schedule A)?

13. What is the effect, if any, upon rent of rating property—

    (a) On different scales of duty according to the value of the property;

    (b) On different scales of duty according to the character of the property or the purposes for which it is used?

14. Can you make suggestions to the Commission as to any methods of raising revenue for local purposes, otherwise than by means of rates?

15. Does any point not included under any of the foregoing questions occur to you on which, having regard to the terms of reference to the Commission, you wish to express an opinion?

Terms of Reference to the Commission

" To inquire into the present system under which taxation is raised for local purposes, and report whether all kinds of real and personal property contribute equitably to such taxation; and if not, what alterations in the law are desirable in order to secure that result."

TABLE CLASSIFYING TAXES RAISED BY PARLIAMENT IN 1895–6[1]

NOTE.—The Classification includes the Taxes assigned to the Local Taxation Accounts as well as the Taxes payable to the Exchequer. The figures represent the Net Receipts under the principal heads of Tax Revenue as given in the Finance Accounts for 1895–6, pp. 19–22.

DESCRIPTION OF TAX.	Taxes incidental to the Ownership, Occupation, or Transfer of Property.			Taxes not incidental to Property.				GRAND TOTAL.
	Rateable Property. (1.)	Non-Rateable Property. (2.)	Total. (3.)	Taxes levied in respect of Commodities. (1.)	Taxes levied in respect of Incomes derived from Personal Exertion. (2.)	Miscellaneous Taxes. (3.)	Total. (4.)	
	£	£	£	£	£	£	£	£
1. CUSTOMS DUTIES	—	—	—	20,965,000	—	—	20,965,000	20,965,000
2. EXCISE DUTIES :								
Duties on Consumable Articles (including Licences falling on Consumable Articles).	—	—	—	29,704,000	—	—	29,704,000	29,704,000
Licences (other than those falling on Consumable Articles).	—	—	—	—	—	1,632,000	1,632,000	1,632,000
Railway Passenger Duty	—	—	—	—	—	259,000	259,000	259,000
TOTAL EXCISE DUTIES	—	—	—	29,704,000	—	1,891,000	31,595,000	31,595,000
3. DEATH DUTIES :								
Probate and Account Duty	48,000	133,000	181,000	—	—	—	—	181,000
Temporary Estate Duty	150,000	13,000	163,000	—	—	—	—	163,000
Estate Duty	3,540,000	6,383,000	9,923,000	—	—	—	—	9,923,000
Legacy Duty	724,000	2,007,000	2,731,000	—	—	—	—	2,731,000
Succession Duty	897,000	154,000	1,051,000	—	—	—	—	1,051,000
Corporation Duty	34,000	6,000	40,000	—	—	—	—	40,000
TOTAL DEATH DUTIES	5,393,000	8,696,000	14,089,000	—	—	—	—	14,089,000

	(16·5)	(20·5)	(37·0)	(53·4)	(4·3)	(5·3)	(63·0)	Total
4. STAMP DUTIES:								
Deeds and other Instruments	1,946,000	2,059,000	4,005,000	—	—	—	—	4,005,000
Securities to Bearer	—	207,000	207,000	—	—	—	—	207,000
Joint Stock Companies' Capital	—	260,000	260,000	—	—	—	—	260,000
Contract Notes above 1d.	61,000	110,000	171,000	—	—	—	—	171,000
Bills of Exchange and Promissory Notes	—	673,000	673,000	—	—	—	—	673,000
Bankers' Notes and Composition for Duty on Bankers' Bills and Notes.	—	124,000	124,000	—	—	—	—	124,000
Playing Cards	—	—	—	20,000	—	—	20,000	20,000
Licences and Certificates	—	—	—	—	—	167,000	167,000	167,000
Life Insurances	—	67,000	67,000	—	—	—	—	67,000
Marine Insurances	—	145,000	145,000	—	—	—	—	145,000
Patent Medicines	—	—	—	239,000	—	—	239,000	239,000
Receipts, Drafts, etc.	—	1,261,000	1,261,000	—	—	—	—	1,261,000
TOTAL STAMP DUTIES	2,007,000	4,906,000	6,913,000	259,000	—	167,000	426,000	7,339,000
5. LAND TAX (unredeemed)	1,021,000	—	1,021,000	—	—	—	—	1,021,000
6. INHABITED HOUSE DUTY	1,487,000	—	1,487,000	—	—	—	—	1,487,000
7. INCOME TAX:								
Schedule A	4,766,000	28,000	4,794,000	—	—	—	—	4,794,000
Schedule B (including Farmers' profits assessed Schedule D).	—	59,000	59,000	—	119,000	—	119,000	178,000
Schedule C	—	1,300,000	1,300,000	—	—	—	—	1,300,000
Schedule D:								
Fishings and Shootings	22,000	—	22,000	—	—	—	—	22,000
Railways in the United Kingdom	645,000	388,000	1,033,000	—	—	—	—	1,033,000
Quarries, Mines, etc.	447,000	404,000	851,000	—	—	—	—	851,000
Railways out of the United Kingdom	—	390,000	390,000	—	—	—	—	390,000
Foreign and Colonial Securities and Coupons	—	495,000	495,000	—	—	—	—	495,000
Municipal Interest, other Interest, and other Profits	—	239,000	239,000	—	—	—	—	239,000
Public Companies	—	1,929,000	1,929,000	—	—	—	—	1,929,000
Trades and Professions	—	726,000	726,000	—	2,902,000	—	2,902,000	3,628,000
Schedule E	—	—	—	—	1,124,000	—	1,124,000	1,124,000
TOTAL INCOME TAX (at 8d. in the £)	5,880,000	5,958,000	11,838,000	—	4,145,000	—	4,145,000	15,983,000
8. POST OFFICE (excess of Revenue over Expenditure)	—	—	—	—	—	2,994,000	2,994,000	2,994,000
GRAND TOTAL	15,788,000	19,560,000	35,348,000	50,928,000	4,145,000	5,052,000	60,125,000	95,473,000
PERCENTAGES OF GRAND TOTAL	16·5	20·5	37·0	53·4	4·3	5·3	63·0	100·0

333

---

[1] For Memorandum explaining the basis of this Table, see C. 9528, p. 63. *Cf.* also pp. 33–37 of Sir Edward Hamilton's Memorandum, printed in the same volume.

ANSWERS BY PROFESSOR ALFRED MARSHALL

I have found it difficult to answer satisfactorily within a moderate compass the questions proposed by the Commission, so I have thought it best to answer a few somewhat fully, and merely to indicate my opinion as to the rest.

I., II.—1. I hold that taxes are paid by persons, not things. Things are the channels through which many taxes strike persons; and in considering the incidence of taxes on persons and the equity of that incidence, we have to take account of all the circumstances of those persons as owners, users, sellers, purchasers, etc., of those things. I submit that the present inquiry must be taken to relate not to the distribution of the burden of taxation between different kinds of property, but to the distribution of the burden between different classes of persons with special reference to their interests in different kinds of property.

2. Further, when we say that a thing is the channel through which a tax strikes persons, we must be sure that the thing is self-contained. If it is only one part of a group of things which cannot be easily separated—this particular thing being taken by the tax-gatherer as representative of that group for convenience— then we get into hopeless confusion if we treat the tax as impinging on that representative thing alone and not the group. For instance, in old times the windows of a house were taken as representative of the house, and were taxed heavily. But the tax did not strike, and was not intended to strike, persons as owners and users of windows only; it was intended to strike them, and did strike them, as owners and users of houses. Now, just as the window is a more or less good representative of the house; so the house is a representative, perhaps a better representative, of a certain scale and style of household expenditure in general; and when houses are taxed, the tax is, and is intended to be, a

tax upon the ownership and use of the means of living in certain general conditions of comfort and social position. If part of the tax assessed on houses were removed, and the deficit made up by taxes assessed on furniture and indoor servants, the true incidence of the taxes would be nearly the same as now, but the indications of the table would be much changed.

3. I am aware that tables similar to this table have been approved by high authorities, academic as well as practical, and it is therefore with great diffidence that I express the opinion that, when taken as a basis for a scheme of finance, they suggest wrong inferences. For instance, it corresponds in some respects to Sir Alfred Milner's Table I. on p. 582 of Vol. IV. of the Report of the recent Royal Commission on Agriculture, and suggests a second table corresponding to Table II. on p. 583 of that volume; which shows £m.3,000 of rateable property bearing about £m.10 of taxation, i.e. at the rate of ·79d. in the £ on capital value; and £m.6,000 of non-rateable property bearing about £m.14 of taxation, i.e. at the rate of ·54d. in the £. But this result implies that furniture, etc. estimated at £m.1,000 escape taxation altogether. That, I submit, is as wrong in principle as it would have been if, when windows were taken by the tax-gatherer as representative of houses, a table had been made out in which the capital value of the windows had been estimated separately, and entered as the basis of the whole window tax; while the capital value of the whole of the rest of the house had been entered in another column as escaping taxation altogether. If the furniture, etc. were reckoned with the houses, this change alone would materially alter the general effect of Sir A. Milner's results. Where he now gets ·79d. he would get ·6d., where he now gets ·54d. he would get ·64d. And when corresponding changes had been made for the equipments of factories, shops, mines, railways, etc., the general purport of his conclusions would be inverted. I do not, however, suggest that a table so modified would be of good service. It would, for instance, still fail to take account of the fact that a considerable part of the tax assessed on large houses is really a tax on the habit of employing many indoor servants. Again, it would not indicate how taxes levied through the channel of immovable and other tangible property bear on creditors and the

owners of the machinery of credit (see VI–e, 3).   Another weakness of the method is shown in its treatment of railways under classes 2 and 7.

4. The old window tax was bad; because, though intended to be a tax upon houses and not upon windows, its pressure was so intense on the point on which it impinged, that many people diminished their windows to the injury of happiness and health. And in like manner it may be argued that, though taxes which impinge on houses do really rest on general expenditure, yet their pressure at their point of impact is so intense as to cause people to seek by preference modes of expenditure which require but little house-room.   The question whether this is so is important, but the figures in the table throw little light upon it.

5. Similarly, it may be contended that when heavy new taxes are imposed upon buildings used for trade purposes, the pressure at their point of impact on those trades which happen to require large buildings in proportion to their net returns is unjust or impolitic; but in such matters also the table affords no guidance.

III.—So long as the net revenue of the Post Office is reaped, not solely by rendering services to the public, but in part by prohibiting other people from rendering similar services, it must, I think, be entered in a general list of taxes, but in a separate class.

IV.—1. Equity assumes definite rights; it is equitable that every shareholder in a company should pay calls in proportion to his holdings.   But, save in such exceptional cases, there is no definite basis for equity.   For while one function of the State is to create, maintain, and regulate rights; its second, and scarcely less important, function is to give expression and effect to the public conscience.   Accordingly, I think that the so-called canons of equity in taxation are not in general canons of equity pure and simple : they are canons of equity combined with and modified by obligations of duty.   It is in this broader use of the term that I propose to discuss the " equity " of taxation.   I use here the term " tax " to include licences, rates, etc.

2. When a special tax is levied for a particular purpose and the case is not one for any interference by public authority with

existing rights of ownership—as, for instance, where an arterial system of land drainage is created—the owners of the properties to be benefited may fitly be assessed on the " joint stock principle," according to which calls are made from shareholders in proportion to their stake in the common venture. Such taxes are strictly "remunerative" and stand in contrast to those "onerous" taxes which supply the means of discharging public duties, of paying interest on the national debt, of supporting the general expenses of government, etc.

3. Onerous taxes, Imperial and local, must be treated as a whole. Almost every onerous tax taken by itself presses with undue weight on some class or other; but this is of no moment if the inequalities of each are compensated by those of others, and variations in the several parts synchronise. If that difficult condition is satisfied, the system may be equitable, though any one part of it regarded alone would be inequitable.

4. A non-remunerative tax assessed on anything is *primâ facie* onerous to its owner unless and until he can shift the burden elsewhere; but it does not follow that, in considering the equity of a system of taxation, the continuation of this same tax should be regarded as onerous to a new holder into whose hands the thing has come either by purchase or inheritance. The new holder has, no doubt, acquired a property of less value than if there had been no such charge upon it. But the question whether this charge is one to be henceforth counted as entitling him to some exemption from other taxation cannot be solved without inquiry as to the conditions, implicit and explicit, under which the original title to the thing was obtained. Such inquiries are of importance chiefly in relation to rights in land and to durable monopolies, whether complete or partial.

5. It used to be held that all persons should contribute to the system of onerous taxes in proportion to their net incomes. But now the opinion seems to be gaining ground that the poorer classes should contribute a smaller percentage of their revenues than the middle classes; and these, again, a smaller than the richer classes. This arrangement seems to me to be "equitable" in the broader sense of the word.

6. It is true that so long as a person retains the right of voting

z

on the levying and expenditure of taxes, it is not safe that he should wholly escape onerous taxes. But it may be safe and reasonable to return to him or his children the equivalent of his payments in such benefits as will increase physical and mental health and vigour, and will not tend towards political corruption.

7. I take net income to be gross income after deducting for wear and tear, and for replacement of capital. These deductions are large in the case of incomes derived from perishable property, and incomes derived from personal exertion.

8. Income, so defined, seems, on the whole, the best basis of a system of taxation; but it has many deficiencies. It presses unduly on those who do not spend the whole of their income, but save some of it : they are taxed on their savings, and they are taxed again on the revenue derived from their savings.

9. Taxes on expenditure evade this difficulty, but have others of their own. Expenditure in general cannot be defined, still less can it be assessed. Nearly all taxes on particular forms of expenditure have technical faults, which make them productive of great harm to the community in proportion to the funds which they yield. The chief exceptions are taxes (and rates) on houses and stimulants : for they can be kept at a high level without much economic waste; but at present they press with disproportionate weight on the poorer classes. Assessed taxes on male servants, horses, carriages, and dogs were once " progressive " in England; perhaps they should be so now.

10. Perhaps also it may be possible to partially exempt savings from taxation for a limited number of years, so as to avoid the injustice of charging twice the income from which they are saved. Any such plan must necessarily proceed on broad lines, and ignore the lighter considerations of equity when seeking to adjust the weightier; and it would need to be introduced gradually and tentatively. I am inclined to think it might with advantage be at once tried experimentally on a small scale as regards investments at home in immovable property, with special reference to local taxation.

11. But even if the total burden of a system of taxation could be adjusted progressively to expenditure, there would still remain a fundamental inequity. For such taxes would not strike at

indulgence in easy-going habits of life. If, of two persons with equal capacity, one works twice as hard as the other, taxes adjusted to expenditure will strike him more heavily than the other, though he has deserved better of the State. Some account might conceivably be taken of this consideration in adjusting taxation between different parts of the same country where different habits of activity prevail; as, *e.g.*, between the north and south of Italy, or of France, or, again, between England and Ireland. But even that is doubtful; and, as between individuals, no account at all can be taken of it. On the whole I conclude that no near approach to equity in taxation is attainable.

12. In recent discussions on taxation, and especially local taxation, there has, perhaps, been some tendency on the part of reformers to assume that if an existing arrangement can be shown to be at all inequitable it should be changed : while those who would retain things as they are have, perhaps, been too ready to assume that a new scheme has been put out of court as soon as it has been shown to work inequitably in some respects. In opposition to such tendencies, I venture to suggest that, even in the interests of equity, canons based on mere considerations of equity are often of but secondary importance in practice. Speaking generally, those systems of finance have caused the least injustice and hardship which have most favoured the development of the energies and inventiveness of the people; which have hindered them the least in the selection of those routes for the satisfaction of their wants; which, partly in pursuance of this end, have given a preference to taxes which were productive and elastic, in proportion to the army of officials needed to levy them; which have avoided vexatious meddlings, and which have been most definite and certain, and free from surprises and from opportunities of corruption. The body politic has a great power of so adjusting itself to the pressure of taxation as gradually to diminish the inequities which are inherent in every imposition or remission of taxation when new. In the interest of equity itself, these and other more or less technical considerations should, I submit, be allowed a large and often a predominating influence.

V.—1. The greater part of economic science is occupied with
the diffusion throughout the community of economic changes
which primarily affect some particular branch of production or
consumption; and there is scarcely any economic principle
which cannot be aptly illustrated by a discussion of the shifting
of the effects of some tax " forwards," *i.e.* towards the ultimate
consumer, and away from the producer of raw material and
implements of production; or else in the opposite direction,
" backwards."

2. It is a general principle that if a tax impinges on anything
used by one set of persons in the production of goods or services
to be disposed of to other persons, the tax tends to check production. This tends to shift a large part of the burden of the
tax " forwards " on to consumers and a small part " backwards "
on to those who supply the requirements of this set of producers.
Similarly, a tax on the consumption of anything is shifted in
greater or less degree " backwards " on to its producer. Thus
nearly all taxes are shifted in some degree.

3. A tax upon a pure monopoly cannot be shifted; provided
it is assessed either upon the monopoly as a unit, or on the net
profits of the monopoly. In neither of these cases does it affect
the calculations of the monopolist as to the price which will give
him the greatest aggregate excess of receipts over outgoings.
But it will be shifted, more or less, if it is assessed on his gross
receipts; or according to any other plan which causes it to increase
with the amount of services he renders to the public, for then
the tax will make it worth his while to diminish the amount of
his services, and thus raise their price.

4. In whatever way the tax is assessed, the monopolist may
raise his price if he thinks that, by making the consumers believe
that the tax is paid by them, he can induce them to agitate for
its repeal. Action of this kind has done much to confuse the
public mind as to the true incidence of taxes.

5. The ownership of land is not a monopoly. But much that
is true of a tax on monopolies is true also, though for different
reasons, of a tax on that part of the value of land which is not
due to recent investments of labour or capital in it by its owner.
Any tax which is so levied as to discourage the cultivation of

land or the erection of buildings on it, tends to be shifted forward on to the consumers of the produce of land or the users of buildings; and, if the buildings are used for the purposes of any trade, then further forward still on to the consumers of the products of that trade. But a tax on that part of the (annual) value of land, which arises from its position, its extension, its yearly income of sunlight and heat and rain and air, cannot settle anywhere except on the landlord; a lessee being, of course, landlord for the time. This (annual) value of the land is sometimes called its "inherent value"; but much of that value is the result of the action of men, though not of its individual holders; and therefore it is perhaps more correct to call this part of the annual value of land its "public value"; while that part of its value which can be traced to the work and outlay of its individual holders may be called its "private value." Speaking generally, a tax on the "public value" of land does not diminish the inducements of cultivators to cultivate it highly, nor of builders to erect expensive buildings on it. Such a tax therefore does not, in general, diminish the supply of agricultural produce or of houses offered on the market, any more than a tax on the net profits of a monopoly does. It therefore is not shifted away from the owners of land.

6. Taxes on buildings and on that part of the value of land, urban or rural, which results directly from investments of capital by its owners, have peculiarities of their own which will be discussed under Question VI. a–c. In general they tend to be shifted in the same way as, though more slowly and irregularly than, taxes on movable goods. We may, then, illustrate the general process of shifting by the typical case of a tax upon the product of a staple trade.

7. An unexpected and heavy tax upon (say) printing would strike hard upon those engaged in the trade, for if they attempted to raise prices much, demand would fall off quickly; but the blow would bear unevenly on various classes engaged in the trade. As printing machines and compositors cannot easily find employment out of the trade, the prices of printing machines and wages of compositors would be kept low for some time. On the other hand, the buildings and steam engines, the porters, engineers,

and clerks would not wait for their numbers to be adjusted by the slow process of natural decay to the diminished demand; some of them would be quickly at work in other trades, and very little of the burden would stay long on those of them who remained in the trade. Part of the burden, again, would fall on subsidiary industries, such as those engaged in making paper and type, and a part of it would be borne by authors, publishers, booksellers, etc.

8. This case illustrates well the contrast between the incidence of Imperial and of local taxation, for if the tax were only local, the compositors would migrate beyond its reach; and the owners of printing houses might bear a larger and not a smaller proportionate share of the burden than those whose resources were more specialised but more mobile. If the local tax were uncompensated by any effect which tended to attract population, part of the burden would be thrown on local bakers, grocers, etc., who would meet with diminished custom.

9. So far I have avoided technical phrases. But the kernel of the problem can, perhaps, be brought out better by a free use of them. The income derived from " land " in the narrower use of the term—that is, from the " public value " of land—is a " Rent " in this strict sense that its amount is governed by the general market relations of demand for, and supply of, the commodities which it produces, and not by the exertion or sacrifice of its owner. A tax upon this rent does not therefore alter the action of the owner; for he takes none in order to earn this rent : it does not " enter into the cost of production " of the commodities raised on the land. A tax on it does not alter that cost; does not restrict the supply of the commodities; does not raise their value; is not shifted forwards; and, of course, cannot be shifted backwards.

10. Income derived from durable improvements in land is popularly called rent. A tax upon it would diminish the inducement to make similar improvements and prevent some old improvements from being renewed, and thus, in the very " long run," it would increase that " cost of production " which has to be covered to make production profitable, and would ultimately stint production. Most of it would, therefore, ultimately be

shifted forwards on to consumers, though, perhaps, a small part might be shifted backwards on to those who supplied the appliances needed for making the improvements. In the very long run, therefore, the income derived from these improvements has to be regarded as profits on investment.

11. But yet popular usage is right in treating this income as a rent rather than as profits for most purposes. For the tax could not for a long time produce an appreciable effect on the amount of such improvements, nor therefore on the supply of the commodity, nor therefore on the price which the consumers paid for it. Meanwhile, the income derived from the improvements would be governed practically in the same way as the rent of land; that is, by the general market relations of demand for, and supply of, the commodities, and not by the slackening or increasing exertions or sacrifices of the owner of the improved land. In short, the income would be a " Quasi-rent," partaking partly of the nature of rent, and partly of the nature of profits; but being more akin to a rent than to profits for the purpose of discussions as to the incidence of taxes for a long time, perhaps a whole generation. But it would be more akin to profits than to rent for discussions as to their ultimate incidence.

12. In the case of less durable improvements, we should have similar results but for shorter periods. For the tax would quickly affect the supply of such improvements, and, therefore, of the commodities raised from the land; and would, therefore, raise their price.

13. More generally, the shorter the time required for altering the stock of appliances for production, the shorter is the time during which the income derived from them is to be regarded as a quasi-rent—that is, as an income, a tax on which must be borne by the owner of the appliances, and cannot be shifted by them appreciably, either forwards or backwards; or, in other words, the shorter is the time required for the tax to act on the income as though the income were profits from fluid applications of capital.

14. All skilled workers, whether employers, employed, or professional men, are in the possession of specialised appliances for production, the stock of which cannot be very quickly altered.

Part of their income is the earnings of effort, and a tax on this part would immediately stint effort, and would, therefore, be immediately shifted more or less from the workers on to the community. But part of their income is of the nature of returns on investments in specialised appliances of such a nature that their stock cannot be increased or diminished quickly, and this part of their income is for the time a quasi-rent; a tax upon it will, for a considerable time, remain on the workers and not be shifted.

15. If any land, whether improved or not, or any machinery or industrial skill, or any other thing, can be easily and immediately applied to more than one branch of production, then the income derived from it is always to be regarded as profits or earnings, rather than as rent or quasi-rent, in any question that exclusively concerns any one of those branches. A special tax on the thing in that use alone would cause it to be turned quickly to other uses, and the tax would be shifted at once on to the consumers of the things produced by it in that use.

VI–a.—1. It will be convenient first to discuss an Imperial tax on buildings in general.

2. In English urban tenures there are commonly three distinct interests. First are those of the " ultimate " owner, popularly but incorrectly called the " ground owner "; he has an annuity secured on both building and land for the present, and will be owner of both when the building lease falls in. Secondly are those of the " interim owner," sometimes called " the building owner "; he owns both building and land to the end of his lease, unless he has himself leased them out. In that case he has a secured annuity on them during the lease granted by himself, with a reversion of both building and land from the end of that lease to the end of the first lease; there may thus be a series of interim owners. Lastly, there is the tenant, who may hold on lease.

3. The building has practically no value apart from the land, but that value which the land would have if cleared of buildings has been called the " site value " of the property. It is convertible with the " public value " of the land (see V–5), provided

it be so reckoned as to exclude the value of improvements made below the surface by the owner or his predecessors.

4. If a uniform Imperial tax be levied on the annual value of all land and buildings, the building part of it tends to settle on the occupier; or on his customers, if he uses the building for trade purposes; but the site part of it tends to settle on the owner for the time being, that is, on the interim owner, in so far as it is imposed during his lease; and on the ultimate owner when he comes into possession. If, however, agricultural land is exempt from the tax, then the tenant escapes only that part of the site tax which is assessed on the excess of the value of the land for building uses over its value for agriculture. This is of little importance practically, except when a large garden attached to a house is taxed at the value of urban land.

5. Passing to the Inhabited House Duty, we find trade premises and very small houses exempted from that. In consequence, tenants of large houses cannot make the owners bear the whole tax on the site value. For the owners will not erect large houses till there is already such a scarcity of them that they give to the owners as good a return as could be obtained by an equal outlay in building trade premises, etc. Houses of a medium size and premises used for trade and dwelling combined are partially exempted from the Inhabited House Duty, and their case is probably about the same as it would be if there were no exemptions at all.

6. These are tendencies, not actual results. But the differences between the two are not very great now, so far as the Inhabited House Duty is concerned, for that has altered its form but little of late years. The various causes by which such tendencies are retarded will be discussed in relation to rates, which change rapidly.

7. The tax has been assumed to be " onerous." But if it be so expended as to confer direct benefit on owners or tenants, the results will be different. This consideration, also, may be neglected in considering the Inhabited House Duty; it is of first-rate importance in regard to rates.

VI–*b* (also XI., XII. and XIII.).—1. The Inhabited House

Duty, being onerous, tends to check building. But many rates are so expended as to provide the householder with necessaries, comforts, and luxuries on cheaper terms than he could provide them for himself. An increase of such expenditure may attract tenants instead of driving them away, may increase local building instead of checking it, and may raise the ground rents at which land can be let on building leases. The ultimate effects of such rates can be ascertained fairly well by discovering the effects of onerous rates, and then reversing those. Other rates, *e.g.* school rates, are onerous to some classes of society, and beneficial to others. Rates devoted to improved school buildings tend to attract artisans, but slightly to repel well-to-do residents for the time being; though in the course of a generation they may so much improve the character of the neighbourhood as to raise the value of the land for building expensive houses, as well as for other purposes.

2. Such considerations show that any general statement as to the incidence of rates must be incorrect. But fairly definite conclusions may be reached as to the incidence, immediate and ultimate, of onerous rates, that is, of rates, the burden of which is not compensated by any equivalent local gain. And thence the incidence of other rates can be inferred more or less, when account has been taken of their special circumstances.

3. If onerous rates are approximately uniform all over the country, then their incidence resembles that of similar Imperial taxes; the fact that they are levied and spent by local authorities does not materially affect the distribution of the burden imposed by them between ultimate owner, immediate owner, and tenant.

4. Next, as to the distinction between rates on site and on building values. It is true that the tenant does not distinguish between them. But anyone, whether ultimate owner or not, who is thinking of erecting buildings on the land, will reflect that expensive buildings would be subject to heavy rates. If in doubt between putting expensive and inexpensive buildings on any site he has chosen, he will be turned towards the inexpensive by the expectation of a rise in the rates, in so far as they are assessed on building values. But his decision will not be affected by that part of the rates which is assessed on site values; though,

of course, before deciding whether to erect any buildings at all, he will have had to consider whether the site value would escape rates if kept vacant. Thus the site value and the building value parts of exceptionally heavy onerous rates press temporarily with almost equal weight on the owners; but ultimately the building value part alone presses upon the tenant : it alone tends to drive away population and trade.

5. These are general tendencies; the causes which prevent them from being applied in prediction resemble those which prevent the mathematical reasonings from being applied to the course of a ball on the deck of a ship that is rolling and pitching in cross seas. If the ship would but stay at one inclination, the movement of the ball could be calculated. But before any one tendency has had time to produce much result it will have ceased to exist, and its successor cannot be predicted. Just so, though economists settled once for all, nearly a century ago, the general tendencies of the shifting of taxation; yet the relative weight of onerous rates in different places often changes so rapidly that a tendency may make but little headway before it is stopped off, or even reversed, by changes which cannot be predicted. We here need a study of the past and present distribution of onerous rates, with an inquiry as to its causes : its general drift is to some extent indicated in Mr. Cannan's article in Vol. V. of the *Economic Journal*.

6. Partly in accordance with his suggestions it may, perhaps, be surmised that : (i) Those rates which are truly onerous are less in amount and vary less from place to place than is commonly supposed. (ii) A place which has incurred a large debt for enterprises that have been unfortunate or wastefully managed may expect a large share of onerous taxes for a long while, but such cases are not numerous. (iii) A place which has a large pauper population and offers no great attractions for industry or residence has a prospect of long-continued high poor relief rates; and such cases are considerable, even when allowance has been made for future widening of rating areas so as to make rich districts bear a larger share of the burden of the neighbouring poor. Inequalities of school rates come partly under this head. (iv) Subject to the two last exceptions, exceptionally onerous

rates are chiefly due to transitional causes.   One possible cause
is present bad management, but that is likely to work its own
cure. A more frequent cause is a recent wakening of the district
to a sense of responsibility in sanitation and other matters : such
of the consequent expenditure as is necessitated by natural
defects of the situation may be permanent; but even this, if
wisely conducted, diminishes the relative disadvantages of the
district and increases its attractions to builders.

7. In short, it seems probable that the cases are somewhat
rare, in which the truly onerous rates of a district are fairly
certain to last for a considerable part of the life of a house or the
duration of a building lease.   That is, it may be surmised, that
there are not very many cases in which a builder, after taking
account of the direct and indirect local benefits which are obtained
at the expense of high rates, will be repelled by the fear of rates
from building in a place which he would otherwise have selected
without hesitation.

8. [Mr. Cannan has observed that there is no obvious connection between the numbers of the population of the different
towns of England and Wales and their rates.   To this may be
added that there is no very palpable connection between their
pace of growth and their rates.   Nearly all those large towns
which increased fast (more than 20 per cent.) between the census
years 1881 and 1891 had, in 1891–2, medium rates (between
3s. 6d. and 4s.); and all those which in 1891–2 had very high
rates (above 5s.) increased at a medium pace in the preceding
ten years, the lowest percentage of increase of population among
them being that of London (10·6) and the highest that of Leeds
(18·9).]

9. If these surmises be correct, it follows that the total
pressure of onerous rates on the enterprise of building speculators
and other interim owners is not very great; and that many rates
which have appeared to be onerous have really enriched them.
But vicissitudes of the rates increase slightly the great risks of
the building trade, and inevitably the community pays for such
risks more than their actuarial equivalent.   And, since uncertainty causes speculators to fortify themselves against onerous
rates even in places where, in fact, rates have not been specially

onerous, tenants and ultimate owners in these favoured districts gain less by that good fortune than appeared from the broad reasonings with which we started (VI–*b*, 4).

10. Here, perhaps, is the right place for discussing a suggestion that has been made, that an equalisation of rates would relieve owners, and especially ultimate owners, at the expense of tenants. It is argued that the building owner deducts from the ground rent, which he offers for a particular site, any onerous rates on building value (as well as on site value) which he anticipates as exceptional, and which he believes he could avoid by building elsewhere; and that he does so because the future tenant from whom the rates are deducted will make a similar deduction from the rent he offers. It is argued that the tenant will perforce pay those rates which he cannot escape by moving elsewhere; and that the builder, knowing he will be recouped, will not deduct them from the ground rent which he offers. This is plausible, but apparently invalid.

11. It is true that an equalisation of rates would raise the aggregate of site values, if it removed rates from the best sites and increased rates on the inferior sites. But the equalisation is at least as likely to transfer part of the burden of rates from the inferior sites to the better sites, and, if it did that, it would lessen the aggregate of site rents. This is, indeed, a new version of an old paradox. Improvements in agriculture, specially applicable to rich and well-situated land, would raise aggregate farm rents very much. But improvements which brought up the least favoured land, account being taken of situation as well as fertility, to the same level with the most favoured would destroy agricultural rents altogether in a country that had more land than it needed. Similarly, if we could conceive rates so adjusted as to make all building sites equally advantageous, no site would have more than mere agricultural value.

12. A tax on one site has thus the effect of a betterment on a rival site which escapes the tax. It has been observed that if two similar premises are adjacent, but the boundary between high and low rates comes between them, so that they share equally the benefits of rates to which they contribute unequally; then their rents vary inversely as the rates. Such facts have been

quoted as inconsistent with the general principle that the greater part of rates are borne by the occupier, but they appear to be quite consistent with it.

13. Here may come the answer to Question XIII. Differential rates, which favour any special use of land, will raise or lower aggregate rents, according as the places which they specially favour are, or are not, those which already have special advantages for that use. If applied over the whole country, or in places chosen at random, they will slightly lower aggregate rents.

14. Similarly, the under-assessment of the older and more highly-rented parts of a town, which is said still to be not very uncommon, tends to raise rents. If carried very far it might lead people to prefer small sites in the central area to large sites outside, and in the result aggregate rents might conceivably be higher than if there had been no rates at all. This, again, is akin to an old paradox, viz. that a tax of so much per acre, or any other tax which differentiated against poor soils, might conceivably raise aggregate rents.

15. The migration of tenants, in order to escape high rates, is hindered less, perhaps, than is commonly supposed by ignorance and indifference. But it is much hindered by the special requirements of each individual. Low rates in Devonshire will not draw there people who prefer London life, and manufacturers who must live in or near a district where they can obtain the special things and services needed in their trade. The tenant is further hindered by the expense and trouble of moving; that may be the equivalent of two years' rent; and, if so, he will lose by moving unless the differential advantage which he secures in rates amounts to 2s. in the £ sustained for thirty years.

16. The mobility of the working classes is, in some respects, greater than that of the well-to-do; but, when rates are compounded, friction sometimes acts on the side of the tenant. The manufacturer is often affected as much by the rates on his workmen's dwellings as by those on his own premises; and though high rates may be among the causes which have driven some manufacturers out of large towns, it is doubtful whether a curtailment of expenditure from the rates would have much lessened this centrifugal force. For most new expenditure from

the rates materially increases local comforts or lessens local discomforts from the point of view either of the manufacturer or
his workpeople.

17. The case of the shopkeeper is the most urgent. His
rates are large relatively to his income, and many of them are
distinctly onerous from this point of view. His work belongs to
that group in which economic progress is raising supply relatively
to demand; a little while ago its remuneration was artificially
high, at the expense of society. Now, his remuneration is falling
to a lower and perhaps more equitable level, and he is slow to
recognise the new conditions. His mind fastens on the injustice
which he suffers when rates are suddenly raised much, and he
attributes to that some of the pressure on him which is really
due to deeper causes. His sense of injustice is sharpened by the
fact that he does not always bargain on quite even terms with
his landlord; for, to say nothing of the cost of fixtures and the
general expense of moving, he might lose a great part of his
custom by moving to equally good premises even a little way off.

18. But shopkeepers are constantly rising and falling, coming
and going. Their minds are alert, and they take full account
of the rates; and thus, after a few years, they shift the burden
of onerous rates on to the owners and customers more fully than
almost any other class does. Hotel and lodging-house keepers
may rank here with shopkeepers.

19. To sum up: rates, the current expenditure of which
gives full value to the occupier, remain with him, as they should.
Other rates are borne by the occupier to a rather greater extent,
and for a rather longer time, than they would be if he were allowed
to deduct them from his rent as he does Income Tax, Schedule A.
He, however, transfers most of them rather quickly to his
immediate landlord; unless he is known to be unwilling to
move, and his landlord takes advantage of that. Interim
owners, as a class, have a great power of self-defence; they are
in a position to check the supply of buildings, and they do it
until nearly the same net return as before can be got from new
building. By that time much capital expenditure from the rates,
which was at first of small benefit to the tenants, bears fruit;
and those rates, so far as building value goes, are put back again

upon the tenants, but are not a net burden to them. Meanwhile, that part of the rates on building values which is exceptionally onerous will have driven away population and trade and will have inflicted a small burden on those who, for personal and other reasons, must continue to live, or work, or trade or hold property there. Among these will be the ultimate owner; and that is why the occupier will not pay quite the whole of the exceptionally onerous rates, even in so far as they are assessed on building values. The ultimate owner will bear a little even of this part of the onerous rates, and he will pay the whole of all onerous rates, whether exceptional or not, which are assessed on site rents.

20. Heavy onerous rates in one place act as a betterment to rival places which escape similar rates. It is, therefore, not true that an equalisation of onerous rates would enrich site owners at the expense of occupiers. An equalisation of remunerative rates, while their expenditure was unequal, would be, generally speaking, unjustifiable.

21. A small increase in rates is apt to escape the attention of well-to-do residents, but it presses perceptibly on shopkeepers, lodging-house keepers, etc., and it influences their action; but, though thus a disproportionately great evil to them at first, an increase ceases to be any burden at all to them ere many years are past: unfortunately, they do not always recognise that this is so.

22. The incidence of a long-established rate is little affected by its being collected from the tenants, and not from the owners, but it is vitally affected by the proportions in which the rate is assessed on site and building values respectively; the main part of the former settles on the owners, and of the latter on the tenants. On the other hand, the incidence for the first few years of an increase in onerous rates is much affected by the mode of collection. The occupier bears more of the burden than he would if part of the rates were collected from the owner, or he were allowed to deduct a part of them from his rent.

23. The removal of onerous rates yields a passing benefit to the tenants, but the greater part of the gain goes to the interim and afterwards to the ultimate owners. If these owners have

acquired the property since the rate was imposed, the remission
of the rate is a present to them of so much public property.
As regards those rates which fall on trade premises, and especially
shops, the case is still stronger.   When a new rate is imposed,
they bear for a time a burden out of proportion to their resources;
and so, when the rate has well settled in, and they have thrown
on their customers that part which cannot be shifted on to the
owners and which the tenant of a dwelling-house would, therefore,
continue to bear for himself, then the sudden remission of the
rate enables them to retain themselves for some time a double
share of public property.

24. The above remarks apply only to neighbourhoods that are
making progress.   Where the population is receding, and building
has ceased, onerous rates tend to press upon owners.   But in
such places economic friction is generally strong.

VI–c.—1. My opinion as to the incidence of rates on agricultural land has already been indicated.   In so far as the rates
are remunerative in the immediate present they stay with the
farmer, but are no net burden to him.   Rural populations
probably bear less onerous rates than is commonly supposed.
They have gained by improved police service and the abolition
of turnpikes, and they have increasing access to advantages
purchased by high rates in the neighbouring towns, to which
they do not contribute.

2. A considerable part of those rural rates which are really
onerous is fairly uniform all over the country, and its incidence
is like that of an Imperial tax on rent.   A tax on that part of
rent which results from the " original and indestructible powers
of the soil " must settle on the owner of the soil.   But the farmer
" always has a lease, even when he has none," and a new tax
collected from the farmer would be likely to remain for some
time on him, unless there were other causes at the time tending
to readjust his relations with his landlord.

3. A tax on that part of a landlord's income, which, though
called rent, is really the return to capital applied to the land by
him or his immediate predecessors in title, stands on a different
footing.   If a tax be levied on that, and not on the income derived

AA

from capital applied to other uses, then the tax discourages
cultivation and tends to raise the price of produce. If the
country cannot import food, the consequent rise of price may be
such as nearly to recoup the farmer soon, and therefore the
landlord ultimately. [If the tax had been on all agricultural
produce, and the whole of that produce had been strictly necessary, then, according to a third old paradox, it would have raised
the value of produce in the same ratio as it lowered produce-
rents; it would, therefore, have left real rents unaltered.] As
it is, such a tax would press at first on farmers in their capacity
of implicit lessees, and afterwards on landlords; and it would
diminish a little the employment of farmers and labourers in
making improvements for the landlord. But the tax would not
bear on the returns to the farmer's own capital, and it would
therefore afford a slight stimulus to modes of cultivation that
did not require additional landlord's capital.

4. If the onerous tax were local only, its incidence on consumers through prices would be still smaller. But local production would be checked more rapidly, and meanwhile the local
farmer would be in a rather better position for transferring to
the landlord that part of the tax which fell on the returns to
(the quasi-rent of) landlord's capital sunk in the soil.

5. Such taxes on agricultural land as have been imposed for
a long time are no direct burden on present landowners, farmers,
or labourers; though they may give to present owners in certain
cases some indirect claim to consideration. Speaking generally,
any remission of such taxes would be a present of public property
to the owners, a small part being caught by the farmers on the
way. Any relief as regards old rates should therefore apply
only to new buildings and other fresh investments of capital.
That would stimulate agricultural activity, give new employment to farmers and labourers, help to keep the profit on the
land, and diminish our dependence on foreign imports of food.

6. It must be remembered that land may be for a time
yielding very little net rent, that is, very little money income
in excess of what is needed to remunerate landlord's capital,
and yet be a valuable property. It may have possibilities as
urban land, or it may contain minerals; and, in any case, its

ownership is likely to yield an income of satisfaction outside of the money rent received for it. In so far as this is the case, land is apt to be under-assessed even when rated at its full rental value. Properly, it should be assessed at a percentage on its capital value.

7. For reasons which are partly economic, partly traditional, the owner of a farm has something more of partnership with his tenant than has the urban landlord; there are traces of *métayage* even in tenures which are thoroughly " English." When seasons and markets are favourable to the farmer, he pays his full rent and avoids making demands on the landlord that might set him thinking whether the rent ought not to be raised. When things go badly, the landlord, partly from sympathy and partly as a matter of business, makes temporary remissions of rent, and bears the expense of repairs, etc. which he would otherwise have left for the farmer. There may thus be much give and take between landlord and tenant without any change of nominal rent. Such adjustments obscure the incidence of agricultural rates, as the eddies of wind rushing past a house will often carry snowflakes upwards, overbearing, but not destroying, the tendency of gravitation. The tendencies of the incidence of rates may even become wholly obscured for a time if the rating question happens to have been made a political issue. For all men are apt to believe and to prove temporarily that changes, which they are advocating, will benefit others more than themselves. (See V. 4.)

VI–*d.*—1. If A has a thing which has a less money value to him than it has to B, they will probably trade, unless there is a tax on the transfer. If there is, they will not trade until A's need for it, measured in money, has diminished relatively to B's by the amount of the tax. But no one can say whether this will be effected chiefly by a rise in the net price which B will give for the thing, or by a fall in the net price which A will take. On the average, however, A will be the weaker party, and the delay will throw more of the burden on him than on B.

2. The tax is bad, even when it impinges only on commodities for immediate use. But in fact it impinges chiefly upon

instruments of production, and thus it is very bad.   For it hinders
their adjustment to the needs of the community.   A heavy tax
on the transfer of land and buildings assists the laws of entail
in keeping property in the hands of landlords who cannot do
their duty by their tenants.   These taxes resemble taxes on
underfed labourers; they are collected barely once, but they are
paid several times.

3. Taxes on the transfer of any kind of property slightly
lower its value even to a willing purchaser; for the same reason
that, of two stock exchange securities on the same basis, that
one will sell for the higher proportionate value which belongs
to the larger issue.

VI–e.—1. Profits, in my opinion, are not an economic entity.
They include some interest on capital, some earnings of ability
and work, and, often, some insurance against risk.   But there is
no uniformity of practice in the business world, and no common
agreement among economists as to how much of the earnings of
work and ability shall be reckoned as profits in any particular case.

2. If this difficulty could be overcome, there would remain
a more serious one, which would by itself prevent the adaptation
of the old broad doctrines about taxes on profits to the more
refined results of modern analysis.   The elements of which
profits are composed obey different laws, and they enter in
different proportions (whatever definition of " profits " be taken)
in different industries, in the same industry in different places,
and in large and small businesses even in the same industry and
in the same place.   It would, for instance, be necessary to discuss
on different plans the profits of a large joint stock company,
where salaries of a thousand a year are not reckoned with profits;
and those of a small tradesman whose profits include the earnings
of much manual labour.   Some taxes on profits would increase
the influx into the learned professions, and tend to lower the
earnings of medical men.   Others would increase the pressure of
candidates for apprenticeship to the bricklaying trade.   All taxes
on profits would tend to check the growth of capital and to
increase its emigration; some of them would tend perceptibly
to increase the emigration of persons and so on.

3. Generally speaking, the incidence of taxes on profits is widely and evenly diffused; they run over rapidly from one part of a trade to another and from one trade to other trades. And this is one reason why there are very few incomes from movable or personal property in England which have not helped to bear the burden of rates. The case of income derived from property abroad is different.

VI-*f*.—1. The old objection to taxes on inheritance that they are paid out of capital, and that the heir is apt to live up to the full income which he has inherited, seems to me to have great force still. No doubt this question, as well as the allied question whether much war expenditure may safely be defrayed by loans, has changed its position during the century with the growth of wealth and the development of international markets for capital. But the very fact that death duties seem less inequitable, and to press less hardly on anyone, than other taxes of equal intensity, suggests that they may still affect savings much as our forefathers thought they did. On the whole I think no one generation should very much increase them; experience alone can show whether we have outgrown the stage in which the incidence of such taxes lies heavily on the springs of prosperity.

2. Special death duties on any one kind of property are duties on its compulsory transfer and lower its value. Such duties, if assessed on the " public " value of land, would not affect production; if assessed also on farm buildings, etc. they would be a discriminating duty against a special form of investment of capital, and would diminish production and be partly incident on the community.

VII., VIII.—1. It is with the utmost diffidence that I hazard opinions on these large questions.

2. The scope of local government has changed, is changing, and is likely to change faster than ever. Our duty at present is to experiment freely, but to move cautiously; to abstain equally from any formal recognition of existing customs which might tend to stereotype them, and from any organic alteration which might claim to govern future development. We should aim

rather at handing down to the coming generation some serviceable experience, together with freedom in dealing with the problems which have just risen above the horizon, and others that have not yet risen.

3. For, indeed, it is possible that the recent changes in the general relations of " central " and " local " government will be carried much further. The government of a Swiss canton or an American State seems to belong to an intermediate class which may be called " provincial," standing between the central authority and the local authorities properly so called. It seems possible that the London and other County Councils may grow in importance and responsibility; and that the term " local " will be generally applied to minor authorities, subordinate to these provincial authorities. I therefore deprecate any attempt to delimit the functions of local government just now.

4. If much freedom is allowed to first-class local authorities, some are sure to pioneer new paths, which the whole country is not yet ready to tread. They will have more initiative, more invention, more willingness to take trouble for the public good than is always found in the officials of a large central department. But other local authorities will lag behind. The chief work of the central authority should perhaps be, on the one hand, to help the most enlightened local authorities in comparing, criticising, and profiting by the experiences of one another; and, on the other hand, to put pressure on the more backward to work up to a high level.

5. This requires some approach to uniformity in local work, partly for statistical purposes. But all power of variation, that is consistent with order and economy of administration, is an almost unmixed good. The prospects of progress are increased by the multiplicity of parallel experiments, and the inter-communion of ideas between many people, each of whom has some opportunity of testing practically the value of his own suggestions.

6. The constructive work of government, and especially of local government, is life itself in one of its highest forms. Taxation is but a means; and in a country which has rid herself, as England has now, of all taxes which are in themselves

mischievous, the reform of taxation should be subordinated to the development of the constructive work of government.

7. I am opposed to the allocation of central taxes to local purposes. I prefer frank contributions from the Exchequer, given in aid of local services, and on the condition of their being efficiently performed. Of course, they should not be given in aid of remunerative rates; but onerous rates are generally devoted to purposes of national as well as local importance, *e.g.* poor relief, asylums, police, education. When the appropriate department at Westminster had satisfied itself that local authorities were performing any of these duties with vigour and intelligence, it should abstain from interference except for urgent cause. But when they are laggard, or behind the general progress of the country, the department should threaten the withdrawal or diminution of the grant, should specify the faults which had to be removed, and should revert temporarily to methods of detailed supervision.

8. Each first-class local authority should have considerable freedom of experiment as to methods of raising revenue. It should, however, be prohibited from taxing persons on account of property which they own, or income which they earn, outside of its area. And since new taxes, and especially new local taxes, are apt to be much more vexatious, burdensome, and unjust than the same taxes would be if they had time to diffuse themselves and settle, every proposed change in the scheme of taxation should be submitted to the central government. Great and sudden changes should be discouraged, and especially such as might press with exceptional weight on any one class.

9. The central government should remain the guardian of the ratepayer of the future against debts incurred for extravagant expenditure in the present; especially because the growth of migratory habits among the people increases the chance that those who have voted for new ventures, partly because they will give additional employment to labour, will not stay in the locality to bear their share of the rates involved. It should prohibit wasteful tolls, octroi duties, etc.; but it should recognise as *primâ facie* reasonable a claim of a local authority to assess outlying districts to special rates, the expenditure of which will

benefit those districts; and it should adjudicate on such claims : or perhaps it should set up gradually more and more powerful and extensive provincial authorities for dealing with them.

10. As regards the supply of water, local interests cannot be isolated. The chief sources of water supply should therefore be declared national property; and, after compensation to private owners, they should be leased, subject to conditions, to local authorities.

11. The same is true of fresh air. The central government should see to it that towns and industrial districts do not continue to increase without ample provision for that fresh air and wholesome play which are required to maintain the vigour of the people and their place among nations; this is, perhaps, the most important public financial responsibility which has not yet been faced. We need not only to widen our streets and increase the playgrounds in the midst of our towns. We need also to prevent one town from growing into another, or into a neighbouring village; we need to keep intermediate stretches of country in dairy farms, etc., as well as public pleasure grounds.

IX., X., XI., XIV., XV.—1. I have even greater diffidence in offering suggestions as to the practical results to which these principles point than in submitting the principles themselves. My knowledge and experience in these matters are small; and I have not even been able to consider the particular questions proposed by the Commission with the care they require. But by answering them as best I can, I may, perhaps, clear up ambiguities in my earlier answers.

2. As regards rural land, the change most needed in the interest of the community is to diminish the burden of those rates which press differentially against the application of capital to agriculture (see VI c. 5). Some wish that this should be effected chiefly by a large subvention, in some form or other, from the Imperial Exchequer, laying stress on the repeal of the corn laws and the recent increase in the death duties on land.

3. Others regard these as the withdrawal of special privileges rather than the imposition of special burdens; they dwell on

the facts that the English law knows nothing of "landowners," and that " landholding " has never been divorced from special obligations to the poor, with the consent of those immediately concerned, and the approval of economists generally. Resting on these broad facts, more than on details in the history of the Poor Law and the Land Tax, they wish the burden of the rates to be transferred from man's action in improving and developing the land to his privileges in holding for private use a part of Nature's free gifts : they do not wish much of it transferred to the public exchequer, where it would be borne, in a more or less disguised form, chiefly by industry.

4. I do not wish to urge either of these views, though I incline to the latter. But I assume (see VII., VIII., 7) that there be contributions from the national exchequer towards the poor rate and some other rates, which may be large or small; I myself wish them to be rather small. And I propose that a preliminary rate for the purpose of poor relief be made on the public value of agricultural land, that is, on its value as it stands after deducting for any buildings on it, and any distinct improvements made in it at private expense during, say, the preceding twenty years. This rate might be large or small. I should prefer it to be considerable, say a penny in the pound on the capital value of the land, *per se.* I regard this as practically public income reserved to the State rather than as a tax.

5. As regards land which has a special site value, of which the test might generally be that its capital value is more than (say) 300*l.* per acre, my opinions are more decided. I think that its site value should be assessed to a rather heavier preliminary poor rate than I have suggested for rural land; and in addition to a " fresh air rate " to be spent by local authority under full central control for the purposes indicated above (VII., VIII., 11). This fresh air rate would not be really a heavy burden on owners, most of it would be returned to them in the form of higher values for those building sites which remained. There may be great difficulty in allocating the betterments due to any particular improvement. But, as it is, the expenditure of such private societies as the Metropolitan Public Gardens Association, and much of the rates raised on building values for public improve-

ments, is really a free gift of wealth to owners who are already fortunate.

6. For rural and urban districts alike, after allowing for this preliminary poor rate and the contributions from the Imperial Exchequer towards those local services which are of national concern, the remainder of the necessary funds should be obtained by rates on immovable property, supplemented by some minor local taxes at the discretion of the local authorities. These main rates should be graduated somewhat after the fashion of the Inhabited House Duty, which should be suppressed; but the graduation should proceed gently at first, and should not cease at 60*l*., as that for the Inhabited House Duty does. Those who live in expensive houses are just those who now pay less than their fair share to the general expenses of the country; and very high rates on their houses would not inflict on them a heavier burden than would be inflicted by any other methods that have been proposed for extracting from them their fair share. [The standard unit of rating might be at houses rented at 40*l*. for urban districts, and 30*l*. for rural. Suppose the rates on those houses in any place were at 4*s*.; then 4*s*. should be the rate for all trade premises of not less than 40*l*. in urban, or 30*l*. in rural districts. There should be lower rates for less valuable houses and trade premises, and the only higher rates should be those levied on larger houses. For them the rate might rise gradually from the standard rate of 4*s*. to, say, 8*s*. for 200*l*. houses, and 10*s*. for the largest houses. Special regulations would be needed for expensive lodgings and hotels. Such parks and grounds attached to large houses as were open to the public under reasonable conditions might be wholly or partially exempted from rates.]

7. The tenant of a farm or any other premises should be at liberty to deduct a portion of the rates from his rent in the same way as he deducts Income Tax, Schedule A. Perhaps this portion should be a half in every case, except that of large houses (see VI*a*. 5). The tenant of a large house should deduct only what would be half his rates if he were rated at the standard level. [That is, where 4*s*. was the standard rate, if a 90*l*. house were rated at 6*s*., the tenant should deduct 9*l*., not 13*l*. 10*s*.]

The immediate landlord should deduct in proportion from his payments to the superior holder next to him, and so on.

8. The plan of dividing the rates between tenant and owner is simple, and is supported by very high authority. It would diminish the injustice which a sudden increase of rates inflicts on farmers, shopkeepers, and other traders; and the modification now proposed would further diminish that injustice. It is true that this division of the rates is to some extent illusory when a rate has been long unchanged. For then nearly the whole of that part which is assessed on public or site value of land will be borne by owners; and nearly all the remainder of it will be borne by tenants or their customers; and this result will not be materially affected by a law allowing the tenant to deduct a half or even the whole of his rates from his rent. I propose to attain equity so far as old rates are concerned, not by this division, but by the special assessment of public or site values.

The alternative plan of allowing the tenant to deduct all the rates assessed on land values, and only (say) a third or a quarter of those assessed on the remaining value of the premises, would have some advantages, but would be more strange.

9. Taxes on immovable property have their faults; but so have all taxes. And theirs are perhaps less than those of any, except the alcohol taxes, the death duties, and the income tax. And these are, perhaps, pressed as far as they ought to be pressed in time of peace. They are all essentially war taxes. On the whole, therefore, I think that the taxes on immovable property ought not to be diminished, and that if the local taxes on it were diminished, Imperial taxes on it ought to be increased. I am, therefore, not anxious to suggest substitutes. I think it better to try to remove such evils as there are in local rating, to aid by contributions from the Exchequer, and perhaps to make a little more room for rates by withdrawing the Inhabited House Duty, or to use that duty as a fund for the assistance of specially poor districts.

10. But I see no objection to local authorities having the whole responsibility, subject only to general control from Westminster, of the beer and spirit licences and some others; nor to their defraying the expenses of the roads by taxes on all vehicles

and horses, with partial exemption for those belonging to farms. Local taxes on servants and on carriages and pleasure horses would be often of least use where they are most wanted; and perhaps the same may be said of taxes on advertisements, etc.

11. With the great increase in the facilities of locomotion which electricity seems to promise in the next few years, the geographical separation of rich and poor may become even more marked; it may become even more true than now that local rates are sometimes least productive where they are most wanted. Possibly we should look for a remedy, not so much to increased aid and control from the Imperial Government, as to the development of three orders of government—Imperial, Provincial, and Local in the narrower sense; each provincial government having large responsibilities and powers over an area wide enough to include rich and poor in fair proportions.

MEMORANDUM ON FISCAL POLICY OF INTERNATIONAL TRADE (1903)

BY ALFRED MARSHALL

Ordered, by The House of Commons, to be Printed,
11 November 1908

[H. of C. No. 321]

PREFATORY NOTE

THIS Memorandum is written from the point of view of a student of economics rather than an advocate of any particular policy. I have not held back my own conclusions on the questions to which my attention was directed. But I have endeavoured to select for prominence those considerations which seem at once important and in some danger of being overlooked, whether they tell for or against my conclusions.

The problem of the incidence of import duties is extremely complex. It is indeed too large and difficult to be handled shortly. But it is passing from the student's closet to the market-place; and it seemed to me, therefore, right to attempt to present its chief outlines in a short compass; and I have done so in Part I. of this Memorandum. I can but hope for a lenient judgment on its grave imperfections.

Part II. is concerned with England's fiscal policy in view of recent changes, and especially with the direct and indirect effects of various *systems* of import duties. The indirect are often much more important than the direct effects; in some of them the economic element predominates, and in others the ethical and the political. It is impossible to discuss fiscal policy without reference to all these elements; and many of my opinions are therefore given in Part II. with the greatest diffidence. But I have endeavoured to distinguish, though not to separate, those suggestions which fall mainly within the province of the economist from those which do not.

August 1903.

P.S.—Some large corrections of, and additions to this Memorandum were lost in the post abroad in August 1903; and when I re-read the uncorrected proofs of it in the autumn, I was so dissatisfied with it, that I did not avail myself of the permission

367

kindly given to me to publish it independently. The haste with which it was written and its brevity are partly responsible for its lack of arrangement, and for its frequent expression almost dogmatically of private opinion, where careful argument would be more in place. It offends against my rule to avoid controversial matters; and, instead of endeavouring to probe to the causes of causes, as a student's work should, it is concerned mainly with proximate causes and their effects. I elected, therefore, to remain silent on the fiscal issue until I could incorporate what I had to say about it in a more careful and fuller discussion; and I am now engaged on that task. But it proceeds slowly; and time flies. When, therefore, I was recently honoured with a suggestion that this Memorandum should be published as a Parliamentary paper, I reconsidered the position, and gratefully accepted the suggestion.

I have revised it slightly, chiefly by the aid of rough notes made in 1903. I have added some explanations especially under heads (A), (K), and (L); and I have re-written the discussion of the relations between England and her Colonies, at the end of the Memorandum. But in other respects it remains substantially as it was written originally.

Ampezzotal, August 1908.   A. M.

CONTENTS

PART I.—THE DIRECT EFFECTS OF IMPORT DUTIES

(A) *The Problem can be partially solved by a simple Study of Price Movements*

1. The first issue to which my attention has been called is the incidence of import duties. It is my opinion that, in nearly all important cases, they are borne almost exclusively by the consumer. But there is no absolute rule in the matter. Cases can be conceived on a large scale, and have actually existed on a small scale, in which a perceptible part of the burden of an import duty is borne by foreigners. And, of course, a part of the pressure of every new tax of whatever kind is apt to rest temporarily on producers, merchants, shippers, and others; until they are able to shift it to its permanent resting-place on the shoulders of consumers.

2. The problem cannot be completely solved by a mere study of price movements. That indeed seems to show that the consumer must necessarily bear the whole burden of every such tax, together with the profits on it of each stratum of traders through whose hands it passes. But the *primâ facie* case thus made out is not valid, at all events in relation to a system of import duties in contrast to a single duty.

The *primâ facie* case is this :—As a general rule the exporters are indifferent as to the market to which they send their goods; and select that which will yield them the best price after paying all the costs. If, therefore, the cost of delivering any commodity in a certain market is increased by the levying of an import tax of 1*l*. upon it, exporters will avoid that market until, by making the commodity scarce in that market, and rather more abundant than before in other markets, they have raised its price (duty paid) in that market by 1*l*. relatively to its price in other markets in which there has been no new tax. The ultimate consumer may, therefore, be expected to have to pay this 1*l*., together with profits on the extra capital required for moving the taxed commodity by all the dealers through whose hands it passes on its way to him. And price statistics show that he has to do so, if he has no alternative source of supply.

3. This *primâ facie* case for the conclusion that the *whole* burden of an import tax is *always* borne by the consumer is invalid, because it neglects the fact that the purchasing power of money in any country may be affected by its tariff policy. For taxes on certain imports into a country raise their value in that country relatively to things which are not taxed; and one of these is gold. Therefore the purchasing power of gold is generally low in a country which levies many high import duties; and when we know that a certain fiscal policy has raised the price of any given commodity to a consumer by, say, a quarter, we have not got an answer to the question how great the burden on him really is.

4. It is, however, important to remember that, if the taxes affect a small portion only of the country's imports, they will not cause an appreciable substitution of gold and other untaxed imports for taxed imports; that is, they will not appreciably alter the general level of prices. The taxed commodities will cost more money to the consumer (near the frontier) by the full amount of the tax; and this increase of price will indicate a nearly corresponding increase of real cost, because the value of money will be but little changed.

5. There are, moreover, other difficulties besides that connected with changes in the purchasing power of money, which resist the endeavour to decide by direct observation what is the incidence of import duties.

For instance, improvements in production and transport are constantly raising money incomes relatively to prices; and if the influence of such improvements is being felt in the same decade in which a tariff is raised, the rise in money incomes relatively to prices may be considerable; and yet it may be much less than it would have been if the tariff had not been raised. No doubt the influence of this disturbing cause can be partly eliminated by comparing the movements of incomes relatively to prices in countries in the same industrial phase, whose tariffs have not moved in the same direction. But, not to mention the difficulties of obtaining such statistics, they cannot be interpreted without taking account of the different influences which are being exerted in different countries by education, by wise and thrifty household management, and by the development of latent natural resources through the spread of railways and otherwise.

The question cannot be handled effectively except by a study of those causes of causes on which this Memorandum touches but slightly. All that can be done here is to indicate that a country cannot expect to throw any considerable share of the burden of her tariff on other countries, unless she is in a position to dispense with a great part of the goods which she imports from them; while she is at the same time in the possession of such large and firmly established partial monopolies, that those countries cannot easily dispense with any considerable part of their imports from her. So far as the latter condition is concerned, England was in a strong position early in last century. But not even America is in a strong position now; while England and Germany are, as it seems to me, in weak positions.

A thorough answer to the question can be found only by going back to the great truth which Committees of the House of Commons at the beginning of last century investigated, and which was stated forcibly by Ricardo. It is that gold is a mere commodity in international trade; and that the levels of international prices do not govern the course of international trade, but are governed by it.   Reasoning on this basis is troublesome; and the difficult argument which follows under head (B) is not essential for the main purpose of this Memorandum. A résumé of it is given in § 55.

(B) *A Partial Theoretical Solution of the Problem of the Incidence of Import Duties*

6. Suppose two countries, A and B, to trade with one another, and only with one another; and to levy no taxes on imports. The price of A's goods in B will differ from their prices at home only by costs of transport (including costs of handling), and *vice versâ*. But now A puts a tax of 50 per cent. on all imports, except of course gold. The prices of A's goods will still be higher

in B than at home merely by the cost of carriage. But the prices
of B's goods to consumers in A are now bound to rise 50 per cent.
relatively to their level in B : for, unless and until that happens,
it will answer to send gold instead of goods from B to A. This
rise in price of B's goods in A relatively to their price in B takes
place whatever be the urgencies of B's demand for A's goods,
and of A's demand for B's goods. But it is mainly on the urgencies of these reciprocal demands that the incidence of the tax
depends; and the observed price movement, *taken by itself*,
proves nothing conclusively.

7. The burden of these taxes will be thrown mainly on B in
the exceptional case in which B's demand for A's goods is very
urgent (and inelastic) while A's demand for B's goods is not. For
then the tax will first raise the price of B's goods in A; secondly,
diminish their sales there a little; thirdly, lessen the supply of
A's goods in B a little; and since B's demand is inelastic, the
small check to their supply will cause each of these goods to be
disposed of for a much greater quantity of the labour and general
commodities of B than before. It might conceivably exchange
for just double as much as before of B's goods in B, or *in bond* in
A; and therefore for just as much as before *duty paid*. In this
case, the whole burden of the tax would be thrown upon B.

Here the solution of this particular case ends, so far as essentials
go. But its secondary consequences in terms of price movements
should be added. Since A's goods can be disposed of in B's
markets on such favourable terms, gold will be sent from B to buy
them. Therefore, gold will become very plentiful in A; prices
generally will rise there, and a rise in money wages will follow in
due course. Therefore, though B's goods in A sell for twice the
price they do at home, yet their prices will not represent much
more effort than before; they may not represent any more effort
at all. In B, on the other hand, gold will have become relatively
scarce, and will command more of B's goods and services than
before. Therefore, although A's goods sell in B for only their
price at home, together with cost of carriage, yet their real cost
to B will be very much increased. The consumers in A will be
nearly as well off as before, and their Government will have got
the taxes mainly at the expense of B.

8. On the other hand, A will have to bear the burden of her own taxes in the far more probable case in which B is in no urgent need for her goods. For then, when the merchants slacken their deliveries of A's goods in B, the market will be unresponsive. Each bale of A's goods will bring back about as much of B's as before. A day's labour in A, or a bale of A's goods, will command about as much as before of B's goods in bond, and the taxes on B's goods will be paid in the main by those who consume them in A. In this case there will not probably be any considerable movement of gold, and the *primâ facie* suggestions of price statistics will correspond pretty closely to the actual facts.

This assumes that A's demand for B's goods is elastic. For the sake of completeness, however, it may be well to take an improbable case corresponding to that in § 7; but with the parts of A and B inverted : and we may even suppose A's Government to spend a great part of the taxes in purchases of imported goods. Then the private consumers in A being in urgent need of their old supplies of B's goods, they may have to force the trade, and to accept less and less of foreign goods in return for each bale of their own : so that A may ultimately have to bear even more than the whole burden of her taxes.

9. The two countries A and B, being taken to be shut off from all trade except with one another, it is *primâ facie* not altogether unreasonable to suppose that B's demands for A's goods are somewhat urgent; and that, therefore, the burden of the taxes will fall in a considerable measure on her. But in the real world B always has access to other markets, and therefore she will not consent to pay any of A's taxes unless A has something like a monopoly as regards nearly all her exports; or else, from geographical or other causes, B is very much at A's mercy. It is only under very rare conditions that a country is practically the sole market for even a single product which another country has exceptional advantages for producing. A tax on such a product might indeed rest permanently on the producers; but taxes on other products would nearly always be borne wholly by the consumers as soon as the producers could make arrangements for selling in other markets, either their old products, or others to which they could gradually divert their energies and

resources. It is theoretically possible that, even in the absence
of such a monopoly, A's taxes might permanently lower the price
of B's goods in world markets ; and therefore in bond in A's ports.
But in fact this never does occur on a considerable scale in the
modern world, for reasons some of which are indicated later on.

(C) *A Broad Treatment of some Representative Cases*

10. The effect of an import duty is felt in the first instance at
the frontier. If the commodity is bulky, it may very well be
imported in spite of a heavy duty, and yet be sold in other parts
of the country at a low price.   To take a strong instance, timber
is sometimes almost without value on the Pacific slope, while in
other parts of the United States its price responds to taxes on
importations from Canada.   But in countries no part of which is
far removed from the frontier suitable for importation, such as
the United Kingdom and Belgium, the full effect of an import
duty is felt by nearly all consumers even of commodities as bulky
as wheat.

11. Again, it is not denied that exceptional geographical causes
may put a country very much at the mercy of a stronger country
which lies between it and the main movement of the world.
Possibly Germany, and even Austria-Hungary, may be able to
throw a small part of the burden of their import duties on countries lying to the east of them.   And yet Germany cannot throw
on England any share of the burden of her own import duties ;
even though there are a few chemical and other German products,
which England cannot easily forego.   England can always take
these as her first choice, and for the rest of her trade Germany
must force her way with goods which England has no special
reason for obtaining from her rather than from other sources.
And what is true of Germany with regard to England is true of
England with regard to the whole Western world.   There may be
some small markets in which her connections by steam-ship or
otherwise give her an advantage tending towards a mitigated
monopoly.   But in the aggregate they count for little.   There is
thus no considerable exception to the rule that England has now
to pay the burden of her own import duties.

12. There has, indeed, never been a country, the whole of

whose exports were in such urgent demand abroad, that she could compel foreigners to pay any large part of any taxes which she imposed on her imports. But England's exports approached to it twice. Once they consisted chiefly of wool, which was indispensable to Flemish weavers. And again, in the first half of the nineteenth century, they consisted chiefly of manufactures made by steam machinery, which was not in general use anywhere else; together with tropical products, which she had special facilities for obtaining. It is possible that the rest of the world would have given twice as much of their own goods as it did give for many of them, rather than go wholly without them. As it was, England did no doubt throw a considerable part of the burden of her taxes (import and export) on the foreign consumer : though it may be true that she made her taxes (or prohibitions of import) heavy just where they ought to have been lightest; that she thus checked that growth of the vitality of the masses of her people which ought to have resulted from her new command over the forces of nature; and hastened the day in which she would cease to hold the unchallenged leadership in industry.

13. But any powers which she may have had of throwing a considerable part of the burden of her import duties on foreign consumers of her products has been destroyed by two inevitable causes. Her arts and resources of production have become the common property of all countries of the Western world, and in some important cases have been developed by others faster than by herself; and the growth of her population has made her demand for many of her imports more urgent than is the demand of any other country for any of her exports. In this respect she is, however, not in a much weaker position than Holland and Belgium and Germany, as will be argued later.

14. I assume that we are concerned with settled trade relations, and not with exceptional or temporary incidents. Almost every trader has opportunities of springing hard bargains upon particular customers, who have made their plans on the expectation that he would deal with them in a regular manner. Such undignified action brings its own nemesis. But practices which would be thought bad business as between individuals have been suggested in the present controversy as appropriate for inter-

national trade policy; and it may be well, therefore, to state clearly that I do not deny that small gains may be snapped by sudden import duties.

15. For instance, if a country is the chief purchaser of an important speciality for which a second has exceptional advantages, then an import tax on it would be borne in the main by the producer for some considerable time. This might occur in the case of a tax levied by England on Greek currants, or on some classes of heavy wines. There is no important commodity the supply of which is in this position. But, as we shall see presently, the collective relations between those countries which are large exporters of wheat, and those which are large importers of it, have some peculiarities.

16. Similarly, if manufacturers in any country have adapted expensive plant to the needs of a particular foreign market, they may pay nearly the whole of an unexpected tax levied on their goods there; for it is better to work with but low returns on their investment than to let their plant lie idle. Conversely, if a tax on the importation of certain goods is suddenly removed, those producers whose plant is specially adapted to those goods may be able to add nearly the whole amount of the tax to their price; and may thus reap very high profits, until new plant is ready to meet the increased demand resulting from the cessation of the tax.

17. When a warm day is being followed by a frosty night, a room with an open window may become colder as the newly-lighted fire in it obtains strength; and again, darkness may begin earlier on a day when the sun sets at 5.30 than on another day when it sets at 5.15. But no one could gain credit by pretending that such facts prove that the fire did not make the room warmer than it would otherwise have been, or that the setting in of darkness is not mainly controlled by the hour of sunset. And yet cases in which the effect of remission of an import duty has been over-ridden by bad harvests, or a great temporary rise in freights, or other causes, have been gravely adduced as affording grounds for the belief that " low prices [of wheat] of recent years . . . are only remotely connected, if at all, with our policy of free importation " (see a letter written with authority to *The Times* of the 25th June, 1903). I propose later on to indicate what is in my

opinion the true interpretation of the history of English wheat prices since 1820.

(D) *Illustrations from Recent German History of the Effects of High Tariffs on the Purchasing Power of Money and Wages*

18. Of course a small change in a country's fiscal policy will not materially affect the purchasing power of money in it. Therefore if the imposition of a tax on any minor import raises the price of it to her consumers by the full amount of the tax, relatively to the price at which it is to be had in other countries that have made no such change; then it may be concluded that the full burden of that tax falls on the consumers, until it is shown that the general purchasing power of money in the first country is lower than in the second. The *onus probandi* lies on those who urge that it is lower.

19. There are, however, reasons why those who advocate a " protective " policy should be unwilling to lay stress on the undoubted fact that the general purchasing power of money is low in countries with a high protective tariff. For this fact cuts two ways. On the one hand, it does mitigate that extra burden that a country seems to take on itself by any new import duty which raises the price of a commodity by a given sum of money. But, on the other hand, it calls for a similar deduction from any *primâ facie* statistical evidence that may be offered of the prosperity of the country with the high tariff. The advocates of the high tariff gain a little by dwelling on the connection between high tariffs and high prices : but they lose a great deal.

20. This may be illustrated by the effects of that movement towards high tariffs which set in twenty-five years ago in Germany. In the preceding, comparatively free trade period, it was reckoned that the purchasing power of money was two-thirds as high again in Germany as in England. (The common way of putting it was : " a thaler equals 5 fr., which equal 5*s*.") I took considerable pains to verify this statement; and I found it to be approximately true, even after allowing for the fact that many comforts and minor luxuries had then to be bought either from England, or from world markets which were largely under English influence. Many of these things are now made with as good appliances in

Germany as in England. Further, German and Alsatian iron ores have been made effective by modern processes applied with consummate technical skill, and Germany is now abreast of England in the mastery of steel, which is the master of the world.

Thirty years ago it used to be said that in active occupations an Englishman could generally do as much in one hour as a German in one and a half. But since then the levelling up has been almost incredible to anyone who has not watched it step by step; and now the difference in effective value between the hour's work in the more progressive parts of Germany and the English hour's work is relatively small. Although by far the greater part of this progress is unquestionably due to education, to improved food, and to improved domestic economy; yet it may perhaps be conceded that a small part of it is due to the defence which the German protective tariffs gave to weak nascent industries against the invasion of the more mature and stronger industries of some other countries, and especially England.

But granting this, it yet remains true that undiscriminating import duties, imposed to gratify powerful interests, and not needed to protect any nascent industry, have (partly, indeed, by strengthening cartels or trade combinations) so raised prices against the consumer, that the real wages of the German workmen have risen less rapidly than those of the English. Money wages in the more progressive parts of Germany have probably risen rather faster than in England; though, save in the heavy iron industry, the condition of which is temporarily exceptional, they still lag behind. But the prices of the necessaries of life have risen, while those in England have fallen; so that six marks—instead of three, as was the case thirty years ago—are required, I believe, to purchase as much of them as 5s. do in England now [1903]. In spite of Germany's vast technical advances, in spite of the growing energy of her people, in spite of the development of German iron ores—while those of England are running short— I believe it to be true that the real wages of the German are increasing less rapidly than those of the Englishman; and that if Germany abandoned protection, which has now no considerable service to render her, the wages of the German would rise a great deal. To hazard a bold guess, I should expect them to rise by about a fifth.

(E) *Wheat Prices in England since* 1820

21. I now take up the point (see § 17) that, though, of course, the effects of a change in taxation on the price of wheat may be lessened, and even overborne, by fluctuations in harvests, by changes in freights, and by other disturbances arising out of a great war, and so on ; yet, when this is done, I believe that nearly every movement in the world's market for wheat, and especially in the relative prices of wheat in English and Continental ports during the nineteenth century, will be found to be such as could have been anticipated from the doctrine that a tax on such a commodity as imported wheat raises the price of that wheat near the frontier by at least the full amount of the tax.

22. The European wheat trade in the first half of the nineteenth century was conducted under very difficult conditions. Wheat is too heavy a crop to be carried long distances, even on good roads, and the roads in Central and Eastern Europe were very bad. Some parts of North-Western Europe had good roads, and some had excellent water communication. But, as most of them bore a relatively dense population, they needed their own crops for themselves ; and, indeed, wheat is not partial to moist lowlands. Further, a large organised production and trade need confidence on the part of producers and exporters that they will find a steady market for any goods which they may offer. But there was no large market for wheat except England, and her perverse mixture of prohibitions and sliding scales rendered it an act of gambling rather than of sober business to grow wheat for the purpose of meeting her uncertain demand. Consequently, her imports were made up of the surplus of wheat crops of districts in most of which rye was the staple food ; and the supply which she got from any one port would often vary tenfold from one year to the next.

As a result, when Jacob, the best authority on the question, was sent to investigate the Baltic and Black Sea sources of supply in 1826–27, he reported that, "if the quantity of corn grown in this country were diminished one-tenth . . . we should have to pay the foreigners double as much as we now pay the English farmer. There is corn enough . . . but it must be drawn from such a distance with land carriage."

In the next twenty years the main roads were improved a little. Railways, indeed, made an appearance in Central Europe before 1846; but, of course, they went first to thickly peopled districts, which had little grain to spare. And it was not till the Crimean War had shown the supreme military importance of railways running to the frontiers, that many of them were driven through the large wheat-fields of Central and Eastern Europe.

These broad facts underlie the main movements of England's wheat trade between 1820 and 1860; and the influence of the abolition of the Corn Laws cannot be understood without taking account of them.

23. It happened that in the few years which followed 1846, European harvests were mostly good. But the Crimean War was accompanied by general bad harvests; freights were for a time very high, and the Russian trade was of course interrupted. To these powerful causes of high prices another was added. For while, before the repeal of the Corn Laws, the world's stock of gold had been shrinking relatively to the work it had to do, and, in consequence, general prices had been falling, the new supplies of gold upset men's cool judgment and forced general prices up to a temporarily inflated level. It was just when all these exceptional causes were working together that that rise of wheat to a little over 70s. occurred, which has been urged as a reason for doubting the influence of the policy of free importation on the price of wheat. And a second rise in 1867 to a price a little above 60s. has been forced to the same service; though it is amply accounted for by simultaneous exceptionally bad harvests in America and Europe in 1867, following after the indifferent harvest of 1866.

24. We now come to the era when ocean telegraphs, and the increasingly cheap construction and efficiency of steam transport by land and sea created a single wheat market for the two hemispheres, with England as its focus. As is well known, wheat has physical peculiarities which make it the best pioneer crop in a deep loose prairie soil; and it is also the best of the very few crops which can be marketed on favourable terms and on a large scale in districts very far removed from any great centre of industry. The

farms of the pioneers of American agriculture were granted to them, freely indeed, but on condition of being brought under cultivation. So the farmers looked to the title-deeds of the land itself, and not to their crops, for the main reward of their labour. If they could feed themselves and sell their surplus for enough to cover their small purchases from the stores, and to pay interest on the capital which they borrowed at starting, they were in a good position. For in a few years their land with its buildings became a valuable property, which yielded them a good return for all that they had undergone.

England was at that time the only large country which could be trusted to take steadily large quantities of American wheat; and if she had imposed a moderate tax upon wheat, it would not have greatly affected those supplies which came to her from farmers who were earning the title-deeds of their land. These supplies were a considerable, though not a large part of the whole; and, therefore, by this little sharp practice, she might perhaps have thrown on them for a short time a small but perceptible part of the burden of her tax, on the supposition that a rise in the price of wheat would diminish its consumption. But this raises a new point.

25. It is, indeed, an almost universal rule that a tax on the importation of a commodity lessens its consumption more or less; and the consequent diminution of demand tends to induce foreign producers to offer it on terms which are lower, though not always perceptibly lower. Wheat has conformed to this rule throughout all history, so far as is known, until about forty years ago. But now nearly the whole of the English people can afford to buy as much bread as they want, and yet have money enough left to buy some more expensive foods : and, as Sir R. Giffen seems to have been the first to observe, a rise in the price of wheat still leaves bread the cheapest food, which they will consent to eat in any quantity; so that, having to curtail their purchases of more expensive foods, they buy, not less bread than they would have done, but more. Consequently, a general tax on the importation of wheat into England now might increase rather than diminish England's total demand for wheat : and, unless it led to a great increase of supplies from England herself, it might raise and

not lower the net price which foreigners obtained for their wheat.

In Germany, on the other hand, in spite of her recent great advance in wealth, a rise in the prices of wheat and rye compels many people to substitute potatoes and other cheap foods for part of their consumption of bread; and therefore an increased tax on imported grain, harvests being normal, is sure to diminish importation.

26. So large a part of the best wheat land in the United States is already taken up, that pioneer wheat farming is diminishing. The growth of wheat as a sole crop is going out, and the supply is becoming increasingly sensitive to changes in the price which can be obtained for it. The fall in price on the distant wheat-fields has indeed been slight : and there has often been a rise, as Mr. Powers has well shown, even when the price in Liverpool was falling rapidly in consequence of the great diminution in transport charges on the west of the Mississippi, as well as between Chicago and Liverpool. But the fall in price on some farms has been enough to check wheat-growing on them; and partly in consequence, there has been a slight check to the downward movement in Liverpool.

27. The practical cessation of the production of wheat as a bye-product, in the business of converting common prairie land into the valuable private property of a fully-equipped farm, has thus had similar effects to those which would have been caused by the lands reaching the stage in which the law of Diminishing Return makes itself felt; and it is frequently asserted that the land in the North-Western States generally has reached this stage. No doubt some land has done so; but there seems no good reason for believing that the law is likely to act at all powerfully over a large area for a long time to come. And, provided the general purchasing power of money is not lowered by the renewed activity of the gold mines, it seems reasonable to think that continued economies in transport will allow the price on North-Western farms to rise a little, without entailing any rise in Liverpool. A letter, written with authority, to *The Times* of the 29th June, 1903, based an urgent appeal for a fundamental change in our fiscal policy, partly on the fact that between 1880 and 1900 the popula-

tion of the United States increased 52 per cent., but its cereal products only 27 per cent.   It was perfectly natural to select for comparison census years, because exact statistics of population are available only for them.   But, unconsciously, some bias has been introduced thereby.   For 1880 was an exceptionally prolific year, and 1900 was not a very good one.   If we invert the bias, and select for comparison the years 1881 and 1893, we find the wheat crop rising from 383,000,000 to 685,000,000 bushels, and the maize crop rising from 1,195,000,000 to 1,924,000,000 bushels.

28. It has already been indicated (§ 10) that other causes besides the prices at the frontiers affect the average of the prices of wheat over a large country, such as Germany or France, which is herself a great producer of wheat.   Consequently it is not to be expected that the differences between the average prices over any two countries should always be equal to the differences between their import duties, loaded with traders' profits.

But comparative statistics of wheat prices in North-Western Europe since 1820 show that the correspondence has been very close :   closer, indeed, than I should have ventured to predict with any confidence before looking at the figures.   The statistics are easily available.   But I would call attention to the following broad results :—From 1820 to 1840 the average price of wheat in England was about double that in the specially wheat-producing districts of Germany, and quite half as much again as in the industrial districts of Westphalia and the Rhine Province; while now the price in Germany is about a third as much again as in England.   In France, with an almost stationary population, protection has compelled the people to pay about as high a price for their wheat now as they did early in the century.   These facts prove, not indeed that the present cheapness of wheat in England could have been produced by England's present fiscal policy alone, but that they could not have been produced without that policy.

29. If in England a tax were imposed only on foreign and not on Colonial wheat it would, under existing circumstances, diminish the English demand for foreign wheat, and thus probably cause it to be offered temporarily on very slightly lower terms : *i.e.* the price here would probably not be raised at once by quite the

full amount of the tax.   But if the fall of the price attainable for
wheat from Argentina, the United States, and other countries
continued, a check would be given to the production of wheat in
those countries.   In Argentina less new land would be broken
up for wheat; and in the United States mixed farming would
spread faster even than it is doing now, and wheat would take a
less prominent place in the rotations.   That is to say, the time
during which even a very small part of the burden of the tax
could be thrown on foreign producers would be short; and during
that time Germany and other wheat-importing countries would
gain the benefit of slightly cheaper supplies of wheat from places
other than British Colonies, as fully as this country would;
though this country alone paid the cost.   We thus pass from the
direct incidence of taxes of imports to the more general results of
various international trade policies.

PART II.—ENGLAND'S FISCAL POLICY CONSIDERED WITH
REFERENCE TO THE ECONOMIC CHANGES OF THE LAST
SIXTY YEARS

(F) *England's Fiscal Policy assumes the Relative Maturity
of her Industries*

30. The second question on which my opinion is invited is,
"How far, and in what directions, the circumstances which
formerly made Free Trade the best policy for this country have
been altered?"

31. The principles on which our present fiscal system was
based sixty years ago seem to me to be not ultimate but derivative.
They were obtained by applying certain truths, which are as
universal as the truths of geometry or mechanics, to certain conditions which were transitional. If these principles are converted
into dogmas, the same error is made as if the rules laid down for
building a bridge, when the only materials available consisted of
pine logs, were regarded as sacred dogmas governing for ever
the construction of bridges for purposes and under conditions of
which the original builders had never dreamed, and when the
materials to be used were steel or granite. The art of engineering
involves an organised study and judgment of the proportions of
diverse considerations, tending in different directions; and no
one can be certain of getting the right proportions even for the
problem which he knows best. It is not by applying without
question the judgments as to proportion, which were made by
the great men who founded our present system, but by forming
our own judgment on the facts of our own generation as they did
of theirs, that we can show ourselves worthy to be their followers.

32. Looking back, it is easy for us to see that they made a
grave error of judgment as to the proportions of one leading
problem of their own age, though not of their own country.
They misjudged both the needs and the potentialities of backward

countries, and especially of new countries. They assumed that every country which has latent resources and faculties for an advanced industry will attract that industry to her from other countries as easily and surely as one county of England would under like circumstances attract it from other counties. But this is not true now, and it was even less true then.

33. If the neighbourhood of coal and other causes concentrate, chiefly in the middle-west of England, those industries in which man's command over nature is rapidly increasing, the benefits arising from this new power are in great measure spread over the whole country. Those born in Devonshire and Sussex who have a turn for the rising industries can generally remove to them without snapping their main ties as human beings. But a new country which is dominantly rural, which lacks the stimulus and culture of a nervous town life, and which has no access to the economies of manufacture on a large scale, derives comparatively little consolation from knowing that there are busy hives of industry and thought in remote places.

34. The difficulties of the pioneers of manufacturing industry in a new or even in an old country were much greater sixty years ago than now. It was rather more difficult then to induce skilled artisans of good character to change their homes. More depended on rules of thumb; and less could be done by the quick intelligence of the worker and the scientific and technical studies of the employer. The leaders of improvements now are often not machine-users but machine-makers; and they are always glad to fit up new works with better appliances than the average of those which are to be found in the chief homes of such machines where some of the plant must be at all events a few years old. But early in last century it was difficult for anyone outside a trade to get the best appliances; and if he imported expensive machinery, and any of it was broken by operatives to whom it was strange, he could not always get the repairs made well except in the place from which he had bought it. For the system of interchangeable parts did not exist; and there were no repairing shops, except in England, and perhaps Belgium and France, which were to be compared with those which are now to be found even in second-rate towns in almost every new country. And to these

inevitable difficulties there were added frequent applications of the force of large English capitals in underselling, even at a loss, pioneer manufacturers.

35. List and Carey, the great German and American founders of modern protective policy, insisted on two fundamental propositions : one was that Free Trade was adapted to the industrial stage which England had reached, and the other that State intervention was required on behalf of pioneer industries in less advanced countries. Had English Free Traders appreciated fairly the force of the second of these positions, their powerful arguments that Protection was an almost unmixed injury to England would perhaps have been accepted by the whole civilised world. As it was, this, their one great error, put many of the most far-seeing and public-spirited statesmen and economists in other countries into an attitude of hostility to their position as a whole. It has caused, and it is causing to-day, able men to deny, directly or indirectly, economic truths as certain as those of geometry; because English predictions, suggested by this one great error, have proved both misleading and mischievous.

(G) *The Bases of England's Fiscal Policy Sixty Years ago*

36. It has been noted that at the very time at which English economists were preparing the way for uncompromising Free Trade, England's exports consisted to so large an extent of things of which she had some partial monopoly, that she might hope then —as she cannot hope now—to throw on foreigners some perceptible share of the burden of her import duties. It is further to be noted that they did not condemn all import duties, but only those which were levied in an inconvenient way, such as duties on raw material; or were unjust, such as those whch pressed heavily on the poor; or, lastly, were *differential*. By differential taxes are, of course, meant taxes levied exclusively or with special weight on commodities which are produced in certain places or by certain methods, or are imported by certain routes or in certain ships; while other commodities, capable of serving more or less well the same needs, are treated differentially, and escaped the tax in whole or in part.

37. They objected to a differential tax that it set consumers and

traders on evasions, either by substituting for the taxed commodity some other which was less serviceable, but not taxed; or by obtaining the commodity in part from some other and more costly source of supply. In so far as either of these substitutions was made, the consumer was prejudiced, and the revenue gained nothing : it was only in so far as the tax was not evaded that the revenue gained all that the consumer lost—subject only to deductions for cost of collection, etc. They found that in a few exceptional cases, such as tea, coffee, tobacco, etc., there was very little evasion (unless by smuggling), and therefore little waste. But they found by a study of detail, and not by any general or *à priori* reasoning, that in the case of all commodities for which the English climate was suitable, or for which inferior substitutes could be obtained, the evasions caused by a tax were very great; the waste was, in fact, so great as to exceed many times the small part of the burden of the tax which could be thrown upon foreigners. They therefore advocated the abolition of all such taxes as contrary to the principle of economy in taxation.

38. A chief corner-stone of our present fiscal policy is the great truth that the importation of goods which can be produced at home does not in general displace labour, but only changes the direction of employment. Of course, any violent change is, to some extent, an evil; but there is a strong *primâ facie* possibility that if the business men of a country, when left to follow their own judgment, decide that it would be more costly to make certain goods at home than to import them in exchange for other home-produced goods for which there is a foreign demand, their judgment is right. Unfortunately, however, when those in the industries, with which the imported goods compete, set themselves to persuade the public and Government that a protective import duty should be levied, their private interests are at a great strategic advantage in competing with those of the public. For it is possible to point to the particular places in which additional employment would be given by the tax. It is easy to find out the particular employers and workmen whose profits and wages would be raised by it; to invite the employers to subscribe to a " campaign fund " on its behalf; and to urge both employers and employed to exert all the political influence, direct and indirect, which they possess,

in putting pressure on the Legislature in their favour. Good strategy prompts that as much as possible of the argument and appeal in the special interests of any one industry should come, not from those who have a direct stake in that particular industry, but from others who have a " log-rolling " understanding with them. In earlier times, as now, unscrupulous politicians would boast that, by going from one constituency to another, and holding before each a protective duty which would give a visible bounty to a considerable portion of the constituency, they could work up an eager cry for a protective policy, and could thus shout down any arguments based on the general interest.

Those who cared more for the well-being of the masses of the people than for class interests or for political power found themselves in a difficult position. For, though they knew that such taxes must lessen employment and lower real wages in the aggregate; and that those industries which gained by the taxes would gain at the expense of a greater aggregate loss to other industries; yet they could not always point out the particular industries which would suffer most : while the far more numerous workers, who had nothing to gain by such taxes, had seldom any organisation and were not vocal. Thus the benefits of such taxes, because easily seen and described by persons who could easily make themselves heard, were apt to count at the polling booth, and even in the counsels of statesmen of upright intentions, for more than the evils. For those evils, though greater in the aggregate, were less easily seen; and they did not directly appeal to vocal classes.

39. Fortunately for the success of Free Trade, many of the protective duties then levied were ill-chosen; they pressed on raw materials, and thus limited employment in a conspicuous way; and the evils of one of them—that which fell upon the food of the people—were palpable enough. But this accidental gain has somewhat diverted attention from the general argument by which economists proved that protective taxes lessened rather than increased the aggregate employment, wages, and profits. It is, therefore, important to lay stress on that argument.

40. The argument starts from the fact that employment in making a thing is not provided by the mere desire to have it, but

by that desire combined with the appliances for making it, and the means of supporting those at work. The older economists expressed themselves badly, and laid too great stress upon the *capital stocks* of machinery, raw material, food, etc.; whereas more recent economists lay greater stress on that *net inflow* of new supplies of food, raw material, machinery, manufactured products, etc., together with personal services which constitutes the national income or dividend. This change of emphasis is very important in some connections, but not in regard to the particular point now in hand. Then, as now, the basis of economic doctrine was that the source of all wages and profits (as well as rents) was in the aggregate efficiency of national production; things obtained from foreigners in exchange for recent exports, or as interest on exports loaned in earlier years, being counted in place of the said exports.

The economists then argued :—

Firstly, whatever increases this total efficiency of production increases that aggregate supply of goods (of past and recent make) which affords employment and income (wages, profits, and rent) to the various classes of the nation.

Secondly, if goods which can be produced at home are yet imported freely from abroad, that shows that they can be got generally at less cost by making other things with which to buy them from abroad than by the direct method of making them at home.

[There may be exceptional cases in which goods are sold with but little attention to cost of production; and there may be other cases when a home industry is temporarily disorganised, and it is reasonable for the public to incur some sacrifice for its relief. But such cases, because exceptional and on a small scale, have little relevance to this broad issue.]

Thirdly, therefore a tax which puts obstacles in the way of the importation of things, which consumers prefer to buy from abroad, does not enlarge employment or raise wages; it is not in the interest of " producers." It is sure to be in the interest of *some* producers (if among producers are counted landlords and other owners of natural sources of production). But it is sure also to injure other producers more than it benefits the favoured group;

because it lessens the aggregate flow of desirable things available as a basis of employment and for distribution among the various classes of the nation.

This fundamental truth is, of course, not inconsistent with the counsel that, as the prudent husbandman puts seed-corn into the earth, so a nation should be ready to sacrifice something of present income in order to develop industries which are immature, and perhaps exposed to the competition of others which are strong. But this counsel had no application to England, because her industries were relatively mature.

41. The founders of our present system had to combat the objection that, though Free Trade might be for the advantage of all nations if adopted by all nations, it was a mistake to open English ports freely unless and until foreigners would reciprocate this generosity. To that two replies were made.

The first was that foreigners would certainly adopt England's policy as soon as they saw how successful it was. The events of the next few years gave some support to this hope. But it was based on a misconception of the position. It ignored the fact that protection to immature industries is a very great national good; and that, though that good may be bought at too great a cost, it would have been foolish for nations with immature industries to adopt England's system pure and simple.

Their second answer was sufficient by itself, and was complete without a flaw. It was that if, in spite of taxes levied by other nations on her goods, she could get them in exchange for her own at less cost than she could make goods like them for herself, it was in her interest to do so. Of course, here again there might be exceptional cases. It might be possible to retaliate by taxes, a part of the burden of which would be borne by foreign consumers of English goods. But, as has already been noted, it was decided not to try for such small gains.

42. A suggestion of more practical importance was that the remission of taxes on goods coming from any country should be made conditional on the lowering of the taxes levied by that country on English goods. This course was adopted in some cases. But it was not in harmony with the large and bold comity, nor with England's leadership in that comity as in industry,

which were the glory of the great and noble, if somewhat too sanguine, men who threw England's ports open as wide and as quickly as they could.

43. This decision of theirs has not the strength of a scientific demonstration. It does not rank with their refutation of the assertion that the importation of goods which can be produced at home tends, as a rule, to lessen employment and to depress real wages. On the contrary, it is based on a judgment of relative quantities; and such judgments are at best fallible, even for the time and place in which they are held.

And, further, relative quantities change rapidly even in an age of apparent stagnation; while the last sixty, and especially the last twenty, years have been full of subversive changes. Each age must judge such matters for itself : and none has as yet been called on to judge for itself so independently as that which is now opening out.

(H) *Transition to Present Conditions*

44. To anyone who approaches with an open mind the fiscal problem adopted by England sixty years ago, there appears a strong presumption that the more perfectly it was adapted to the conditions of that time the more certainly would it fail to meet exactly the widely different conditions of the present time. Even if all the chief forces in operation now had been working then, the great changes in their relative proportions must, it might reasonably be supposed, have called for great changes in the policy designed to meet them.

I for one was so much impressed by those arguments of Carey and his followers, which had found scarcely any echo in English literature, that I went to the United States in 1875 to study the problems of national industry and international trade from the American point of view; and I was quite prepared to learn, not indeed that the American system was applicable to England, but that it might contain ideas capable of adaptation to English conditions.

I came back convinced that a protective policy, in fact, was a very different thing from a protective policy as painted by sanguine economists, such as Carey and his followers, who assumed that all other people would be as upright as they knew themselves to be, and as clear-sighted as they believed themselves to be. I found that, however simple the plan on which a protective policy started, it was drawn on irresistibly to become intricate, and to lend its chief aid to those industries which were already strong enough to do without it. In becoming intricate it became corrupt, and tended to corrupt general politics. On the whole, I thought that this moral harm far outweighed any small net benefit which it might be capable of conferring on American industry in the stage in which it was then.

Subsequent observation of the course of politics in America and elsewhere has strengthened this conviction. It seems to me that the policy adopted in England sixty years ago remains the best, and may probably remain the best, in spite of increasingly rapid economic change, because it is *not* a device, but the absence of any device. A device contrived to deal with any set of conditions must become obsolete when they change. The simplicity and naturalness of Free Trade—that is, the absence of any device —may continue to outweigh the series of different small gains which could be obtained by any manipulation of tariffs, however scientific and astute.

45. I proceed to consider some of the changes which may be urged as affording a *primâ facie* case for reconsidering the fiscal policy adopted by England sixty years ago. They may be roughly classified thus :—

(i) The increase in the strength and purity of Government in its administrative machinery, and the broadening of the functions which it is expected to perform, and does perform, with general approval.

(ii) The advance of the United States, Germany, and other countries.

(iii) The tendency to an increase in the taxes levied both by old and new countries on the importation of manufactured produce.

(iv) Changes affecting England's industrial leadership.

(v) The growth of powerful industrial aggregations and combinations, fostered by tariffs and other Government favours, whose power to manipulate trade gives cause for anxiety.

(vi) The new possibilities of closer relations between England and other English-speaking countries, resulting partly from the development of electrical and steam communication.

(I) *The enlarged Resources and increased Efficiency of Government*

46. It is commonly charged against the English economists and statesmen of sixty years ago that they had an undue distrust of Government. They certainly did distrust Government as they knew it; but it is not certain that they were very wrong in doing so. Government at that time was, indeed, less corrupt and incapable than it had been when it evoked the wrath of Adam Smith, and led him to deny, not as is commonly supposed, that there were many important things which Government might undertake to do, but that it was at all likely to perform efficiently many important duties. Even after the Reform Bill, Government remained largely under the dominion of the less enlightened and impartial members of the well-to-do classes; and it discharged very imperfectly those urgent duties which none but the Government could perform at all. There was, therefore, little to be gained by urging it to take up tasks in which private enterprise and philanthropy could make some headway.

47. Since then shorthand reporting, the electric telegraph, and the improved printing press have given strength to the general movement towards higher ethical standards, which has been steadily cleansing Parliament, and invigorating Governmental departments. And in England this tendency has been further strengthened by the influence of Free Trade in diminishing the money value of political power—an influence which, in my opinion, would have been partially reversed if success had attended the Fair Trade movement of twenty years ago, or should attend the similar present movement for Tariff Reform.

48. The experience of other countries seems to show that even now there is danger to a Parliament which listens to the representations of interested classes when framing its fiscal

policy. Perhaps the case of Germany is the strongest, because German public officials have been always recognised as inferior to none in honesty of purpose; and there are probably few persons who have a higher standard of honour in private life than the " Agrarian " members of the Reichstag. But yet the methods which they and certain powerful manufacturers have used, both in legislation and in controlling the votes of their dependents, has probably done more than anything else to increase the probability that a German working-man, who takes life seriously and has a strong feeling of duty, will be an ardent Socialist. The importance of this consideration seems to have escaped the notice of most Englishmen.

49. England's dangers are not the same, but they are not very different. She excels all other countries in the solid strength of her Trade Unions; and perhaps her greatest danger is that they be tempted to use that strength for the promotion of the interests of particular groups of workers, at the expense of wider interests, as the landowning classes did when they had the power. There is no more urgent duty incumbent on those who care for the higher as well as the material well-being of the country than to resist this temptation; and the worst method of preparing for this task is to bring back again into English politics the notion that there is plenty of money to be got by influencing votes in Parliament, and by controlling the public press.

50. Further, though Government is in some respects better placed for grappling with such difficulties than it was; yet, on the other hand, the amount of constructive work which the modern age is requiring from it is probably growing much faster than its power of getting through its work. This is partly because human life is much larger and more complex than it was; partly because our growing knowledge and wealth and standard of public duty make us ever less willing to acquiesce in grave social ills, and even in discomforts, many of which cannot be adequately handled save by the authority and force of Government; and partly because the increased intelligence and probity of Government officials generally make us willing to take the risks of Government for intervention in many matters, in which Adam Smith and his immediate followers would have truly asserted that such a

remedy would probably be worse than the evil. Connected with these undertakings there must necessarily be openings for certain classes of employés, and also of builders, manufacturers, traders, etc., to reap money gains through Imperial or Municipal politics. We must proceed with, and even enlarge, many of these undertakings. But that is an additional reason against an intricate system of combative finance which would occupy much of the best time and strength of Parliament and Government, and which might tend to lower the tone of public morality.

(J) *The Advance of the United States, Germany, and other Countries*

51. As the United States, Germany, and other countries have advanced in industrial efficiency, their growing wealth has enabled them to consume very largely increased quantities of all those goods which England is specially expert in producing, and also to produce many goods which are serviceable to her either for direct consumption or for use in her industries. Their progress has thus improved her position in many ways, while injuring it in others.

Old countries cannot in any case expect to grow as rapidly as those which are only just beginning to develop some of the best of their resources. Still less can they hope to do so if some of their own best mineral and other resources are running short. By far the larger part of whatever relative retrogression England may be showing, as compared with the United States and Germany, is directly traceable to the recent development of their great resources.

52. The United States present a unique combination of agricultural and mineral riches worked in a temperate climate by a mixture of races of great energy and alertness. The material resources of national prosperity are a good climate and large areas yielding generous returns to labour in the production of staple foods and textile materials, together with coal or water power, and minerals. In all these respects, excepting climate and coal, the United States is incomparably better supplied than England is; and in the earlier stages of nearly every great branch of her production, labour of a given efficiency will go much further

than in England—in some cases more than twice as far. The
best English ideas have nearly always been accessible to Americans.
When early in the last century England took great pains to prevent the exportation of her best machines, the manufacturers
of Europe set themselves to smuggle the machines or drawings of
them out of England piecemeal and under various disguises. But
the prouder Americans inquired exactly what was the operation
which a machine took over from the human hand, and then
devised one for themselves; and it sometimes turned out better
than the English one. Foreign trade, therefore, is not necessary
to the United States. Her domestic trade is larger than that of
the whole Western world was when she achieved her independence.
Protection could not possibly do her much harm; and it is probable that the help given by her to a few industries, which really
needed help, about compensated for the economic loss (but not
for the moral injury) caused in other directions by her protective
policy.

53. As to Germany, it has been suggested in § 20 that the
protective policy to which she has latterly given herself has, on
the whole, hindered rather than helped the use which she has
made of the high industrial energies of a population very much
greater than that of the United Kingdom. If we take coal and
iron together, and remember that the very rich beds of inferior
iron ore in Luxemburg and Lorraine have been rendered available
for making steel by recent inventions, her mineral resources
appear about equal to those of this country; and, of course, her
agricultural resources are much larger. Her position for foreign
commerce is in some respects better than that of England. The
ocean routes from her ports are indeed a little longer than those
from English ports; but even here there is some compensation,
because her ships can make up their cargoes in convenient ports
of Holland, Belgium, France, and England. And, what is of far
greater importance, she has almost exclusive access to large areas
of Eastern Europe which are ready to use Western goods, but
are not yet ready to make such goods themselves; and she is
able to send light goods to them in through railway wagons cheaply
and quickly. In fact, the greater part of the increase in Germany's
foreign trade during recent years, of which much has been written,

is with these countries : it is due to advantages which scarcely any fiscal policy could destroy.

54. Germany, like the United States, owes much of her strength to the large population within her own borders, among whom there is absolute free trade. One of the chief causes which retarded her rise was the fact that Prussia, the largest and most vigorous German State, was not a compact unit, but a number of disjointed fragments divided from one another by artificial frontiers. The Zollverein, following an earlier Swiss, and a still earlier French, precedent, was the most important movement towards free trade that the world has ever seen, except the contemporary reform of the British fiscal system. It abolished in every direction artificial hindrances to the " simple " and " natural " tendency of each man to deal with those persons who are best able to meet his wants in return for his meeting theirs. It stopped the laborious passing of goods in bond from one Prussian island to another; it put an end to vexatious inquiries, and diminished the labour of custom-house officers. In short, its influence was largely in the opposite direction to that which would be exerted by the commercial federation of the British Empire; though in many respects similar to that which would be exerted by a commercial federation of Anglo-Saxondom, if that were possible.

(K) *The Pressure of Foreign Tariffs increases with their Number, and more than in Proportion to it. High Tariffs levied in the New World may ultimately be very burdensome to the Old*

55. In discussing the incidence of a tax on imports in Part I., the keynote of our main argument was that the country B whose goods were taxed would seek other markets for them, until they had risen in value in the taxing country A sufficiently to throw nearly the whole burden of the tax on the consumer. The part which would be borne by the producers in B might indeed be temporarily great if they had made their arrangements specially for sale in A's markets, and in some other exceptional cases. But, as a rule, in the actual world, B would quickly find some other markets for her goods, nearly as good as A's had been before the tax; and she would have a further resource in directing new applications of her capital and labour to other branches of

production for home or foreign markets; and possibly even in diverting some capital and labour, which were already in the taxed industry, to others. There is then a presumption that (save in the exceptional case in which nearly all A's exports have a monopoly value) A's consumers will bear nearly the whole burden of the taxes imposed on B's goods; a burden which could be measured (after allowance for changes in the international distribution of gold, and, therefore, in general prices) by the change in price of B's goods, duty paid, in A's ports, as compared with their price in others where no new tax had been levied. That is to say, it was assumed that A's taxes on B's goods would not exert a very great influence on the value of B's goods in the ports of other countries. For, if A puts a tax on one of B's goods, B can send it to C, D, E, etc., in rather larger quantities, without appreciably glutting their market : or she can send other goods to A or to C, D, E, etc.

56. But the position is greatly changed if A, C, D, E, etc. all put a heavy tax on one of B's goods concurrently. It matters not whether they do it by agreement in a sort of conspiracy, or are merely impelled severally to it by the consideration of their own interests. In either case B must very much diminish her export of it, or else bear a large part of the burden of the tax. And if A, C, D, E, etc. all put heavy taxes on all B's exports, then B is almost sure to bear a large part of the burden. She might, indeed, turn much of her capital and labour chiefly to producing things for her own consumption : but she is almost sure to be in urgent need of some imports, and in order to obtain them she must export. If several of her goods are in urgent demand abroad, she may be able to get most of what she wants to import by exporting rather reduced quantities of these goods, and only of these goods. Their scarcity will give them high purchasing power abroad, and she will then not pay a very great part of the foreign import duties : though she will, of course, be hampered and inconvenienced in many ways. If, however, she has no exports which approach to a monopoly value abroad, she must turn her attention more and more to providing for home consumption; and she must be content to allow a considerable part of the burden of foreign duties on her exports to enter into the

real cost to her of whatever *net* imports she requires. (The foreign raw material which enters into her exports does not count as an import for this purpose. Nor, again, do those which she draws in payment of interest, etc. on capital which she has already exported; such imports are not affected by the taxes levied abroad on her exports.)

57. England is undoubtedly in a worse position than she would be if the commodities for which she has a special aptitude were not generally liable to heavy taxes abroad. But the taxes on her imports levied by a country in the same industrial phase with herself will always be of relatively small importance to her. It is generally to the advantage of both that they should exchange textiles or metal goods whenever merchants see their way to a profitable exchange. But if England made things for home consumption with the capital and labour with which she makes her exports to (say) Germany, and Germany acted in like manner, neither of them would be seriously injured. To put an artificial obstacle in the way of the trade would be unwise; but its total economic consequences would be small after the immediate effect of the disturbance had passed away.

Nor could England be very seriously injured even by a concurrent imposition of taxes on her imports on the part of all countries in the same industrial phase with herself. She might indeed then be unable to market abroad any great quantity of those refined machines and other implements, for which there is little demand except in highly advanced countries; and, therefore, she would be a little restricted in the economies of production on a large scale in this important group of manufactures. But her own markets would afford scope in almost every branch of such work for several establishments of the largest size which can advantageously be controlled by single management; and therefore her loss under this head, though considerable, would not be very great. She would give more attention to products suitable for sparsely peopled countries; and this would help her in obtaining such crude mineral and agricultural products as she needed.

58. Nor is there any very urgent danger to be feared *in the near future* from the concurrent imposition of heavy import duties

DD

on manufactures by sparsely peopled countries. For most of those countries are still in urgent need of capital; and they cannot afford to divert much of it from developing their abundant resources to setting up modern steel and other industries, which may absorb a thousand pounds' worth of capital or more for each person to whom they give employment. Consequently, many manufactured products will long continue to be imported on a large scale even into the more highly developed new countries. And there will also long remain large areas of the world in which there are no organised industries, and where the door must be kept fairly open to the large majority of Western products.

But the world is being peopled up very quickly. It is but a century since Britain accumulated her great Public Debt; and before another century has passed the scene may have changed. There may then remain but a few small areas of fertile soil, and of rich mineral strata, which are not so well supplied with both population and capital as to be able to produce most of the manufactured products which they require, and to be able to turn to a tolerably good account most of their raw products for their own use. When that time comes, those who have surplus raw products to sell will have the upper hand in all international bargains. Acting concurrently, whether by mutual agreement or not, they will be in the possession of an unassailable monopoly; and any taxes, however oppressive, which they may choose to impose on the only products which densely peopled countries can offer to them will be paid mainly by those countries. It is this consideration, rather than the prospect of any immediate danger, which makes me regard the future of England with grave anxiety.

(L) *Changes affecting England's Industrial Leadership*

59. The progress of the arts and resources of manufacture has benefited England more than almost any other country in one important but indirect way. It has so reduced the cost of carriage by land and sea that raw materials and food can come to her, even from the centres of great continents, at a less cost than they could come from the near neighbourhood of the sea-shores and great rivers of the Continent sixty years ago; and the 300,000 miles of railways which have been built during the last sixty

years in America, Asia, Africa, and Australia are rendering greater service to Englishmen than to any other people, except those in whose lands the several railways are placed.

In almost every other respect the progress of the arts and resources of manufacture has benefited England less than any other country. For, even sixty years ago, the excess of the cost of the manufactures needed for her own consumption over that of the raw material by which they were made was small. If it could have been reduced to nothing, she would have gained by the change very much less than she has gained by the lowering of the cost of imported food and raw material for her own use.

On the other hand, countries which used to be dependent on imported manufactures have gained all round : they have gained by lowered cost of transport, and they have gained by the lowered cost of manufacture of commodities for direct use; and that almost equally, whether these goods are manufactured by themselves or imported. For competition compels England, Germany, and other Western countries to give to consumers almost at once the full benefit of any economy in manufacturing processes which they have obtained.

60. In so far as the increasing economy of transport and manufacture enables Western goods to be disposed of in backward countries where before they could not compete with hand-made products, the exporting country gets a great share of the benefit. But people's most urgent needs for some classes of manufactures are now satisfied by manufactures which, with modern processes, absorb very little labour, and therefore sell under competition very cheaply. For instance, further economies in the manufacture of pins might diminish rather than increase the total value of the export of pins, and the number of people to whom that industry gives employment.

Therefore, England's gains from the further progress of manufacture, except in so far as it led to yet further cheapening of long-distance transport, might be less than those of most other countries, even if that progress made a proportionately increasing demand for those industrial faculties by which England obtained her leadership. But it does not.

61. For the very perfection of the textile and other machinery

by which England won her industrial leadership has enabled it to be worked fairly well by backward races. That combination of liberty with order, and of individual responsibility with organised discipline, in which England excelled, was needed for pioneer work in manufactures; while little more than mere order and organised discipline will go a long way towards success, where the same tasks are performed by modern machinery "which does most of the thinking itself." Thus England is at a steadily increasing relative disadvantage in trading not merely with people like the Japanese, who can assimilate every part of the work of an advanced factory; but also with places where there are abundant supplies of low-grade labour, organised by a relatively small number of able and skilled men of a higher race. This is already largely done in America, and it certainly will be done on an ever-increasing scale in other continents.

62. Consequently, England will not be able to hold her own against other nations by the mere sedulous practice of familiar processes. These are being reduced to such mechanical routine by her own, and still more by American, ingenuity that an Englishman's labour in them will not continue long to count for very much more than that of an equally energetic man of a more backward race. Of course, the Englishman has access to relatively larger and cheaper stores of capital than anyone else. But his advantage in this respect has diminished, is diminishing, and must continue to diminish; and it is not to be reckoned on as a very important element in the future. England's place among the nations in the future must depend on the extent to which she retains industrial leadership. She cannot be *the* leader, but she may be *a* leader.

63. The economic significance of industrial leadership generally is most clearly illustrated just now by the leadership which France, or rather Paris, has in many commodities which are on the border line between art and luxury. New Parisian goods are sold at high prices in London and Berlin for a short time, and then good imitations of them are made in large quantities and sold at relatively low prices. But by that time Paris, which had earned high wages and profits by making them to sell at scarcity prices, is already at work on other things which will soon be imitated in a

like way. Sixty years ago England had this leadership in most branches of industry. The finished commodities and, still more, the implements of production, to which her manufacturers were giving their chief attention in any one year, were those which would be occupying the attention of the more progressive of Western nations two or three years later, and of the rest from five to twenty years later. It was inevitable that she should cede much of that leadership to the great land which attracts alert minds of all nations to sharpen their inventive and resourceful faculties by impact on one another. It was inevitable that she should yield a little of it to that land of great industrial traditions which yoked science in the service of man with unrivalled energy. It was not inevitable that she should lose so much of it as she has done.

64. The greatness and rapidity of her loss is partly due to that very prosperity which followed the adoption of Free Trade. She had the full benefit of railways, and no other country at that time had. Her coal and iron, better placed relatively to one another than elsewhere, had not begun to run short, and she could afford to use largely Bessemer's exacting but efficient process. Other Western nations partially followed her movement towards Free Trade, and in distant lands there was a rapidly increasing demand for manufactures, which she alone was able to supply in large quantities. This combination of advantages was sufficient to encourage the belief that an Englishman could expect to obtain a much larger real income and to live much more luxuriously than anybody else, at all events in an old country; and that if he chose to shorten his hours of work and take things easily, he could afford to do it.

65. But two additional causes of self-complacency were added. The American Civil War and the successive wars in which Germany was engaged, partially diverted the attention of these countries from industry: it checked the growth of their productive resources; and it made them eager to buy material of war, including railway plant and the more serviceable textile materials, at almost any cost. And lastly, the influx of gold enriched every English manufacturer who could borrow money with which to buy materials, could apply moderate intelligence in handling them,

and could then sell them at a raised level of prices and discharge his debt with money of less purchasing power than that which he had borrowed.

66. This combination of causes made many of the sons of manufacturers content to follow mechanically the lead given by their fathers. They worked shorter hours, and they exerted themselves less to obtain new practical ideas than their fathers had done; and thus a part of England's leadership was destroyed rapidly. In the 'nineties it became clear that in the future Englishmen must take business as seriously as their grandfathers had done, and as their American and German rivals were doing : that their training for business must be methodical, like that of their new rivals; and not merely practical, on lines that had sufficed for the simpler world of two generations ago; and lastly that the time had passed at which they could afford merely to teach foreigners and not learn from them in return.

67. This estimate of leadership is different from, almost antagonistic to, measurement of a country's leadership by the *volume* of her foreign trade without reference to its *quality*. Measurement by mere quantity is misleading.

Of course, the statistics of foreign trade are specially definite and accessible; and since the fluctuations of business confidence and activity are reflected in foreign trade among other things, the habit has grown up of using export statistics as a *primâ facie* indication of the time and extent of such fluctuations. For instance, vital statisticians have frequently pointed to the parallel movements of exports and the marriage-rate, when the real parallelism to be indicated was between fluctuations of credit and of those of the marriage-rate. Even for this purpose export statistics are not very trustworthy; while for broader purposes they are quite untrustworthy.

Other things being equal, an increase in the efficiency of those industries in which a country is already leading will increase her foreign trade more than in proportion. But an increase in the efficiency of those in which she is behind will diminish her foreign trade.

England has recently [1903] been behind France in motor-car building, and behind Germany and America in some branches of electrical engineering. A great relative advance on her part in those industries would enable her to make for herself things which she had previously imported, and would thus diminish her foreign trade. On the other hand, even a small advance in her power of spinning very high counts of cotton yarn would increase her foreign trade considerably; because that is a thing for which other nations have an elastic demand, and are at present almost wholly dependent on England.

68. England's export trade, though still very much larger in proportion to population than that of Germany and America, is not [in 1903] increasing as fast as theirs. But this fact is not wholly due to causes which indicate relative weakness.

The chief cause of it is that the improvements in manufacture and in transport, aided by Free Trade, enable England to supply her own requirements as regards food, clothing, etc., at the cost of a continually diminishing percentage of her whole exports. Her people spend a constantly diminishing percentage of their income on material commodities; they spend ever more and more on house-room and its attendant expenses, on education, on amusement, holiday travel, etc. Present censuses show a progressive increase in the percentage of Englishmen who earn their living by providing for these growing requirements. That is to say, the number of Englishmen who devote themselves to producing things which might be exported in return for foreign products increases very slowly. Of course, if her foreign trade be measured by the quantity of things exported and imported, it is increasing fast; for a man's daily labour now deals with a much larger volume of goods in almost every industry than formerly. But still it is not increasing [in 1903] as fast as that of Germany and America. How far is this really an evil?

69. American conditions are very dissimilar to ours. But if anyone compares in detail German and English trade statistics, he will find it difficult to point out desirable foreign commodities with which England is not the better supplied. The earnings of England's capital invested in foreign countries and in ships on the ocean enable her to bring home about a hundred and fifty millions' worth of commodities for her own consumption, in addition to those which she buys with her nominal exports. Her

people think that these, taken together, are enough; and prefer expensive summer holidays to increasing still further above the German level their consumption of oranges or silk. Who shall say that they are wrong? It is useless to point out things which England might export and does not : unless it can be shown that the extra things, which she would be able to import by so doing, are more desirable than the things and services which she is providing for herself and which she would need to give up in order to make those things for export.

70. The real test of relative progress which foreign trade offers lies in the opportunity afforded by it for measuring the skill with which each nation applies her industry to producing great results with small manual effort; or, in other words, in making commodities cheap relatively to effort, and effort dear relatively to commodities. In view of her failing stores of iron ore, England rightly exports an ever-increasing proportion of machinery and implements which are of small bulk relatively to their value, and that is an indication of the qualities of leadership; but her imports of electrical plant and aniline dyes show that her hold on leadership is insecure, and can be retained only by renouncing the easy self-complacency engendered by abnormal prosperity in the third quarter of the last century.

(M) *For England, though not for America, Free Trade is Essential to Leadership*

71. The position, then, is this : On the one hand, England is not in a strong position for reprisals against hostile tariffs, because there are no important exports of hers, which other countries need so urgently as to be willing to take them from her at a considerably increased cost; and because none of her rivals would permanently suffer serious injury through the partial exclusion of any products of theirs with which England can afford to dispense.

And, on the other hand, it is not merely expedient—it is absolutely essential—for England's hopes of retaining a high place in the world, that she should neglect no opportunity of increasing the alertness of her industrial population in general, and her manufacturers in particular; and for this purpose there is no device to be compared in efficiency with the plan of keeping her markets open to the new products of other nations, and especially to those of American inventive genius and of German systematic thought and scientific training.

Further, it is more necessary for her manufacturers than for any others that they should be able to buy cheaply, and without friction, any foreign products—whether technically described as " manufactured " or not—which they may want at any stage of their complex and varied work. This could not be arranged by a system of rebates; not even by allowing special privileges to the " Improvement-trade " (*Veredelungs-verkehr*). It would require large classes of factories and workshops to be treated as bonded warehouses. Or rather, it would require the conversion of many manufacturing areas into free-trade zones, each surrounded by a high wall, or a cordon of revenue officers.

In this connection it should be noted that taxes on commodities in general, including those that are free from any differential taint, are likely to press with undue weight on the poorer classes of the community. No doubt there are a few commodities consumed exclusively by the well-to-do on which it would be possible to levy special taxes. But every attempt to obtain any considerable amount of revenue from this source has failed, and must fail : while it causes much more expense and annoyance to those who are affected by it, than would be caused by an equal increase in their contributions to such taxes as are levied now. The main bulk of the burden on consumable commodities falls on the poorer classes, for two reasons. First, the poorer classes spend a much larger percentage of their incomes upon commodities than the richer classes do. And, secondly, the greater part of the taxes on commodities must, for technical reasons, be *specific*, that is, apportioned merely to the quantity of a thing of any given kind; and not *ad valorem*, that is, apportioned also to the fineness or high quality of the thing in its kind. Therefore such taxes amount to more shillings for every pound that the poorer classes spend on the taxed commodities than they do for every pound spent on them by the well-to-do.

The injustice of levying a great portion of the revenue by taxes on commodities is most conspicuous with regard to those which enter directly into consumption. But it extends also to taxes on such things as machinery. For the largest ultimate uses of machinery are in the transport by land and sea of those massive foodstuffs and other things which are chiefly consumed by the working classes, and in making the simpler forms of clothing, etc. Probably about twice as much horse power is used in providing for each pound's worth of expenditure on commodities by the poor as by the rich. The great glory of the fiscal policy of the latter two-thirds of the nineteenth century is, that it found the working classes paying a very much greater percentage of their income in taxes than the rich did, and that it left them paying a less percentage. Sparsely peopled countries, and federated countries, are compelled for technical reasons to obtain a large part of their revenues by taxes on commodities. But England has no excuse for that injustice.

72. Though it be true that the import duties of Western nations inflict greater loss on England than they did sixty years ago, it seems that she stands to gain little and to lose much by any attempt to coerce them into lowering their tariffs. Especially does it seem contrary to England's interests to levy import duties with the object of giving English diplomatists something to bargain with when discussing foreign tariffs. English business would be disturbed by the opinion that such a duty was probable; and again by its actual imposition, and again by the probability that it would be removed, and again by its actual removal. It would disturb business in every way; and it would set particular classes of business men on influencing Government, as it has done in other countries where diplomats are intrusted with a power of this kind. Protective duties are easy to impose, and hard to remove; and the suggested plan would lead to a number of protective taxes based on no scientific system, and conducive neither to the material nor the moral prosperity of the country.

73. But England already grants to every nation with which she deals better terms than that nation gets from any other; and it is not unreasonable that she should demand in return the " most-favoured-nation " treatment. She should regard any refusal to grant it as an act of deliberate commercial hostility, which would justify her in considering whether or not it was worth

while to make reprisals. It is, of course, true that the existence of a most-favoured-nation clause sometimes deters an astute German or other diplomatist from pressing for specially low duties on goods in the production of which England happens to have some advantage over his country, and that in that case England gets no benefit from the efforts of that particular diplomatist. But she is not dependent on any one such diplomatist. Nearly everyone who is trying to get any taxes on imports lowered on behalf of his own country is likely to be working for England's good under this clause, unless he gives himself a great deal of trouble to avoid doing it. The few cases in which he takes the trouble are quoted over and and over again in English controversial literature; while little is heard of the far more numerous cases in which England's masterly policy of quiescence is rewarded by her reaping the fruits of other people's excitements, quarrels, and worries. The clause, in fact, gives England nearly all that she could obtain by interminable tariff wars, and at no cost.

It might, therefore, be well that every foreign nation should know that so unfriendly and unjust an act as the refusal of most-favoured-nation treatment to England would be regarded as an unprovoked injustice; and that in extreme cases it would be met by hostile reprisals. Such reprisals would be like declarations of war : that is, they would be expected beforehand to be very expensive; and, even if successful, to injure the country which made them, nearly as much as the country assailed by them. They would therefore make use of all the weapons of financial combat, concentrated against the offenders. It would not be a conclusive argument against any of them that it was inconsistent with the large-minded, generous, and simple principles which have characterised British fiscal policy for the greater part of a century.

74. One further remark may be made in this connection. It is, that there seems to be no good ground for the opinion that foreign imports compete unfairly with British goods in British markets, because they have not contributed to the expenses of maintaining the British Government. But, as was pointed out long ago, this appears to be a mistake. For by far the greater part of these imports are received in exchange for exports of our goods and services; including the services of those most elaborate

machines known as ships, and of those highly skilled workers known as mariners. All these exports have paid their share of the expenses of the British Government. That share has entered into their cost. That cost has been defrayed by the imports obtained in exchange for them; and therefore it has been paid by those imports.

It is true that a part of British inports are received as interest, or profits, on capital exported in earlier years; but that capital originally consisted of goods which had paid their share of British taxes. The question whether income derived from foreign investments should be liable to special taxation may fairly be discussed on its merits, but not in this connection: though apparently simple, it seems to involve very great difficulties on closer examination.

(N) *Trusts and Cartels*

75. It is, however, urged that special treatment is required for the products of powerful single firms or combinations of firms which, protected by a high tariff, sell at a high price at home, and find additional employment for their workers by producing goods to be sold below cost price abroad. It is further alleged that they can sell such goods more easily in Free Trade England than elsewhere. The economics of industrial aggregation and combination is a vast subject; but I will venture to submit a few fragmentary remarks on it.

76. Speaking generally, American trusts in the proper sense of the word have ceased to exist. What are called " trusts " are single Corporations so vast as to obtain a dominant control approaching to monopoly in some large branch of industry. They aim at constructive economies, and do not always exert themselves much to keep competition out of the trade; they boast that their large scale of buying, producing, and selling enables them to make a profit at prices which leave no margin for smaller producers. Especially in their early days, some of them appear to have acted cruelly and unscrupulously. But, as a rule, they now avoid action which is palpably against the public weal; and it is rather the fear of what they may do in the future when they are more firmly in the saddle, than of what they are doing just now, which

is causing much American thought to be given to the duties of
the State with regard to them. The best opinion seems to be
that as a Joint Stock Company has less right to privacy than an
individual business man, so a Corporation of semi-monopolistic
scope may be fairly compelled to make returns to the Government
for publication of a kind which it would not be well to demand
from an ordinary Company. If those returns tend to show that
it is making a bad use of its power, and, in particular, is selling
below cost price with the set purpose of ruining rivals, it may be
required to level up its prices, or to level them down at its option,
to the same amount for the same thing (cost of carriage being
allowed for) all over the States. Secondly, it is urged that if a
trust sells more cheaply abroad than at home, it thereby proves
that it has no right to be defended by a protective duty; and
though there are several important trusts which are independent
of the tariff, yet the growing power of trusts generally is causing
many able and influential persons, who formerly defended the
policy of Protection, to turn towards Free Trade.

77. The discussion of the combination policy in Germany,
though in advance of that in this country, lags behind that of the
United States; but in the main tends in the same direction. The
cartels are, however, very different from the trusts. They are
federations more or less strongly knit together and not amalga-
mated. Each firm retains much autonomy, except in the matter
of selling, and in some cases of buying. Their constructive
economies are not, as a rule, to be compared to those of the
American trusts, but they effect important economies in the
advertising and distribution of their products; and they are
ruthless in restricting their supplies to the home consumer, in
order to compel him to pay an artificially high price for them.

The strongest cartels are, as might be expected, in trades
which make half-finished goods. They often sell their products
to English and other manufacturers at prices which enable the
finished product made of them to undersell the German product
in foreign markets. This is only one of many instances of the
intricacy and friction which their system introduces, and is tending
to form a strong public opinion against it. [P.S. 1908. The
policy of cartels has become less aggressive towards the foreign

producer and less oppressive to the home producer since 1903. The chief causes of this change appear to be (1) the teachings of experience; (2) the rise of a demand for some reduction of the tariff, to which they owed much of their power of oppression; (3) the tendency towards the fusion of groups of cartels concerned with successive stages of the same industrial process into a single cartel; and (4) the growth of giant (" mixed ") businesses somewhat of the nature of American trusts.   It may even be plausibly argued that just at present the growing strengths of trusts and cartels is hostile to the more extreme developments of dumping. But the near future may differ from the present as much as that differs from the near past.]

78. The statement that a trust or cartel can more easily sell surplus goods in England than in any other market *in which it habitually sells* seems only in part true.   It may be conceded that if the tax remains fixed in amount, then a given fall in the price of the goods in bond will make a less proportionate fall in their price, duty paid, than it would in their price where there was no duty, and, therefore, might not stimulate sales so much.   But this is a relatively small point, and there seems to be no other difference between the two cases. [This argument would of course be inverted if the practice were to lower the tax on dumped goods in proportion to the special reduction of price made for the occasion.   If that practice prevailed, it would render dumping slightly easier into protected markets in which it habitually sells, than into free markets.]

79. Dumping into the English market is annoying to some English manufacturers, while benefiting others in a greater or less degree.   But it is hard to devise a remedy that will not be worse than the disease.   It is not possible to prohibit all selling below the full normal price; it is not easy to say when such a lowering of the price is reprehensible, still less when it is an offence.   English manufacturers, especially in the iron industry, were for more than half a century by far the chief ill-doers in this direction, and the memory of their ill-deeds rankles sorely in American minds.   Even now the accusations levied against some combinations of English shipping companies, not without indirect Government subsidies, are very bitter.   And it might be hard to take formal action

against foreigners, who were selling cheaply in English markets, without laying ourselves open to very sharp retorts, and even retaliations.

(O) *Possibilities of Closer Relations between England and her Colonies*

80. It has already been suggested that the import taxes levied by other countries, whether in the Old World or the New, do not at present press on British industries with nearly as heavy a weight as would appear at first sight; but that heavy import taxes levied in the New World may press with almost unbearable weight on later generations of English people (see under head K). We of the present generation have a high duty to our brethren in the Colonies : we have an even higher duty to our descendants. We are exhausting the coal, without which it will be difficult for Englishmen to offer manufactures to new countries on terms that will enable them to be well marketed, even if no import duty is levied upon them. And we are not steadily diminishing that great National Debt which the forefathers of ourselves and our brethren in the Colonies incurred to secure freedom of the pathways of the seas for British traffic—a freedom without which we and they might have been continentalised by force. A part of the descendants of those who incurred this debt are now powerful nations, owning some of the largest and richest landed properties in the world. But they have contributed nothing to the interest of that debt; and they have contributed scarcely anything to the great naval expenditure that has kept the paths of the seas safe for British traffic during the century in which that debt has remained nearly stationary.

England is still richer than her Colonies. She has, indeed, a larger proportion of very poor people than they have; but she is able, if she wills it, to raise them out of extreme poverty without external help; and her people for the next generation or two will need no aid. A century hence, however, the tale may be different; two centuries hence it almost certainly will. And a century is but a short time in the life of a nation.

Capital is abundant in England; and she has few openings in which it can be made to yield a high return. Her Colonies are thirsty for capital; and they have vast openings in which it can be made to yield a very high return. It is then perhaps reasonable that she should continue to defend their coasts with but little aid from them, while great wealth is flowing into them, earned partly by the expenditure which has created her debt; but she may fairly expect some response to her generosity.

81. It has often been remarked that the memory of the sacrifices which parents have made for their children when young is more nearly certain to impel them to make further sacrifices when the children have grown up, than it is to impel the children when strong to make sacrifices for their parents in the weakness of old age; and that what is true of individuals, is true also of nations. England indeed was at one time harsh to the first-born of her great Colonies; but that was in accordance with principles of Mercantilism; which was then already degenerate, though its faults were unperceived by the Daughter as well as by the Mother; and a better spirit has gradually prevailed.

England has never been harsh to any of her younger Daughters. In recent decades she has been increasingly generous to them; and they in return, under the influence of the same warmer and more generous temper, are showing a livelier gratitude and affection for her. If this gratitude and affection are deep-seated; and if the Colonies recognise the great responsibility to future generations of her people which England has incurred by depleting her coal mines, while not reducing her debt; then it will be open to them to give an assurance that they will requite to her people in later generations those services which she has fully rendered to their peoples in earlier generations; and which she is rendering to them increasingly in the present generation, when the powerful battleships of several restless nations are to be seen in the Pacific and the Atlantic Oceans.

There is more than one form which such an assurance might take; but an Englishman may not attempt to sketch them even in general terms.

If such an assurance were given, or even distinctly adumbrated, Englishmen of the present generation would have a much freer hand than, in my opinion, they have at present when inclined to sacrifice something of material gain for the sake of a high ideal. Imperial unity is a high ideal. A well-to-do Englishman who is not prepared to sacrifice something for it appears to be hardly worthy of his age. And as all classes of Englishmen have a clear responsibility to posterity, it might be reasonable to ask that even the poorer of them should contribute a little towards the attainment of this ideal, if they could be assured that their present sacrifice would redound in a greater national benefit to their descendants. The contribution expected from them must however, in equity, be small relatively to that made by the well-to-do.

Thus England might perhaps contribute to such schemes as that of an " all-red route " round the world, which would promote general intercourse throughout the Empire; if so, she would act avowedly in the interest of ideals, and in spite perhaps of doubts as to their profitableness from a financial point of view. And she might even consider proposals for some departure from that financial policy, which has seemed best suited for her own needs, if she could hope that she could go a little way without being drawn on to go a great way; and that she could do herself no great harm by going a little way. But can she entertain this hope?

82. Among the many changes of the last sixty years, few have been more clearly marked than the advantages which the Revenue officer has obtained in his struggle against the smuggler. He has gained by general improvements in morale and education; by more scientific and thorough departmental organisation; by submarine and other telegraphs; and above all by the compression of nearly all *bonâ fide* international trade within the limits of a few great ports and a few railway stations. It may therefore be expected that Preferential Duties within the Empire could now be worked with less than a quarter of the abuses which would have arisen if an equally large and complex trade had been subject to them, while the Revenue officer had no greater resources at his command than he had early in last century. But the abuses which caused the abandonment of differential duties by England were so great, and infused so much moral poison into many branches of business, that abuses

EE

much less than they might yet count for a good deal in the balance between our present system and one which proposes to cement the Empire by such means. So far as these difficulties are concerned the positions of England and her Colonies seem to be similar.

But in regard to the main issue their positions are far apart. Protective policies come naturally if not necessarily to young countries, which believe that many of their young industries may have a great future, if protected from the competition of powerful rivals in older countries, where capital is abundant and industrial organisation is highly developed. There may be—and in my opinion there are—better methods of bringing public funds to the aid of those who are starting new industrial ventures, the chief fruits of which are likely to be reaped in a later generation and by people who have not borne the main strains and risks of pioneer work. But a protective tariff is the path of least resistance to this end. It is that which is in fact being universally trodden; and a new movement which tempts the Colonies to move a little further on this path, whether wise or not, cannot be a great disaster to them, at all events from the purely economic point of view. But the history of all countries and all ages is repeating itself in the Colonies. Even honourable men there are being drawn into slippery paths. They advocate preferential arrangements effected by raising the tariff against foreign goods without lowering it in favour of British goods; and they put into the forefront their zeal for the high ideal of Imperial unity. They look as little as possible at the private gain which may accrue to them from the particular method of promoting that ideal which they advocate.

England, on the other hand, is the oldest of all industrial countries. She has no industries which need protection on the ground of youth. But she has a few which have needed a stimulus because they have been sleepy. Under the stimulus given to them by the sale of high-class imported products in their own market, the greater part of these few have been markedly aroused during the last few years; and she might indeed have been several hundred million pounds the poorer if that stimulus had been shut out by a tariff. Her industries do not need defence against the cheaper capital of any other country. For good and for evil—in my opinion for good on the balance—she has indeed abstained from as rapid a concentration of this capital into such huge masses as has prevailed in America, and even in Germany; but if she thought such concentration good, she could effect it more quickly than any other country except the United States, and perhaps more solidly than any other. In her case, therefore, import duties, levied otherwise than with a direct view to revenue, seem to me to have no economic justification. They cannot, I have argued, cause foreigners to contribute appreciably to her public burdens. Though they may cause new employment to appear in certain directions, they will necessarily lessen the National Dividend; and therefore they will necessarily lessen the amount of employment at good wages.

I believe that they have this effect in every old country, but that there is none other to which they could do injury at all comparable to that which they would do to England. She still has advantages in competition with other advanced countries due to her cheap capital; to her cheap coal; and to her climate, which is conducive to steady work, and is specially favourable to the finer cotton industries. But her chief remaining advantage lies in that unapproached freedom of movement, that *viability* that gives her much of the strength, without the cumbrousness and want of elasticity, of a single huge firm extending over the whole land. In the phase which the twentieth century seems to be opening out for her, viability for all things great and small, that may be needed directly or indirectly for the production of fine and complex goods, is essential to her. Unless she can produce these with less labour than any other country can, it is in my opinion impossible that she can continue to pay, as she does at present, higher rates of real wages than prevail in any other old country for almost every kind of labour : the real wages of her people must fall to the German level. They might even fall below that; for Germany has advantages of her own. Railways are increasing the economic advantages of her situation in the centre of Europe very fast. Her people had learnt to use their low wages and professional incomes

EE2

thriftily and wisely, before they came under the temptation to imitate English carelessness in domestic economy; and in this matter as well as in the technical economies of business, they have attained a high scientific perfection from which English men and women are yet far.

The suggestion, then, that England should abandon that viability, which is her chief source of strength in comparison with competitors in the Old and the New World, seems to me a radically bad way towards attaining a good end. In particular there is danger in the fact that in these schemes the gain which either side is invited to expect is greater than the loss which she is to incur; and yet, as the scheme includes differential duties which are essentially wasteful, the aggregate material gain must in my belief be less than the aggregate material loss. The schemes would be less dangerous if they started with the frank statement : " Imperial unity is an ideal worth much material loss; let us consider how best to share this loss among us." As it is, the schemes appear to me likely to breed more of disappointment and friction between England and her Colonies than of goodwill and the true spirit of Imperial unity. And, if approached in a spirit of greed, rather than of self-sacrifice, they are likely to rouse animosity in other lands, and to postpone the day at which it may be possible to work towards a federated Anglo-Saxondom, which seems to be an even higher ideal than Imperial unity.

For these reasons it is superfluous to dwell on what appears the well-established fact that from the point of view of mercantile bargaining the best preferences which the Colonies could offer to England would be of but very moderate advantage to her in her present phase. Nor is it necessary to insist that the duty of a trustee to his ward is in some respects more stringent even than his duty to his son; that India is the ward of England; that India is poor, while the Colonies are rich; and that India's commercial policy has been generous.

INDEX

PRINTED IN GREAT BRITAIN BY RICHARD CLAY & SONS, LIMITED,
BUNGAY, SUFFOLK.